The All-New 1987 Holiday Cookbook

BETA SIGMA PHI

Y0-BVN-538

The All-New 1987 Holiday Cookbook

BETA SIGMA PHI

*Over 1,000 Festive Recipes,
Easy Gift Ideas and Menus*

EDITORIAL STAFF

Managing Editor	Mary Jane Blount
Project Manager	Debbie Seigenthaler
Cookbook Editors	Georgia Brazil
	Mary Cummings
	Jane Hinshaw
	Barbara Peeler
	Mary Wilson
Typography	William Maul
	Sharon Whitehurst

PHOTOGRAPHY CREDITS

Hershey Foods Corp; CocoRibe Coconut Rum; Rice Council

© **Favorite Recipes Press, A Division of Heritage House, Inc. MCMLXXXVII**
P. O. Box 1408, Nashville, Tennessee 37202

Library of Congress Cataloging-in-Publication Data
Main entry under title:
The All-New Holiday Cookbook
    Includes index.
      1. Cookery.   I. Beta Sigma Phi.
1987   87-25135
ISBN 0-87197-228-X

Manufactured in the United States of America
First Printing 1987

Recipes for Cover on pages 35, 38, 170, 171.
Recipes for Page 1 on pages 75, 152, 162.
Recipe for Page 2 on page 125.

Contents

Holiday Entertaining

Thanksgiving, Christmas, and New Year's—the three great holidays of the year—come so close together that the celebrations are almost continuous. For those who love good food, Thanksgiving is the high point of the season with its emphasis on family and wonderful things to eat. This is only the beginning of the season, however, and preparations turn to fancier foods and more lavish parties as Christmas approaches. There is a constant flurry of activity and a myriad of activities to be accomplished by New Year's and the final parties of the year.

Even so, in many ways holiday parties are easier than at any other time of year. The house is decorated. Much of the baking—from breads to desserts—is finished, and the guests are in a party mood before they even arrive. The surroundings, the decor, even the menu are not nearly as important as the mood created by bringing together a special group of people. If the group is family and friends and the time is the holiday season, you cannot fail.

The secret of party success is knowing how to have more fun than the guests. A good hostess does this by planning ahead, staying organized, and making everything look spontaneous.

Planning should start immediately after the holidays end and should continue throughout the year. Stock up on decorations, party plates and napkins, and special holiday cooking items at the after-Christmas sales. Dry herbs and flowers and root plants in the spring to use for decorations later. Preserve summer's bounty of vegetables and fruits for holiday dinners and parties. Gather dried plant materials, nuts and cones, bittersweet berries, and vines during the fall to use for natural decorations.

Early in the season, choose the party formats which best suit your personal style so that you will be a confident, comfortable hostess. You will find ideas for informal brunches and lunches, relaxed suppers, and easy dinners as well as Thanksgiving feasts, elegant buffets and unusual chapter parties in the Holiday Menus. Use these ideas to create your own unforgettable occasions. You will find many that are perfect for the holidays when you open your home and heart to your family and friends.

Being well organized is essential to ensure successful parties. Begin by making lists, starting with the guest list. A time schedule is essential. Calls to rental services (for tables, chairs, and serving dishes) and florists should be made a month or more in advance because the holidays are their busiest season.

Select a menu that allows most of the items to be prepared ahead and frozen or refrigerated. This is not the time to serve soufflés or dishes that require last-minute preparation. It is also best not to try a new recipe. Test new recipes first for your family. Then, vote to decide whether it is good enough for the party file.

On the actual day of the party, you should have no more than two or three items to prepare. Do not spend all day in the kitchen. You will feel frazzled and worn out by the time your guests arrive.

Whether you choose a casual or dressy affair, be sure to add those small touches that can make such a big difference in setting the mood: candlelight and Christmas greenery, beautiful table settings, lots of flowers, and exquisitely prepared foods. You'll find suggestions for all these throughout the book. Add guests decked out in their holiday finery and festive music as a background to their lively chatter, and you'll have a perfect holiday party to enjoy—and to remember.

Holiday Recipes from Headquarters

We are very pleased to bring you a selection of recipes from several individuals who work at the Beta Sigma Phi International Headquarters. They have shared a number of their favorite recipes, and we hope you will add them to your collection. Some names you will recognize, while others may be less familiar. All, however, are working toward the common goal of Beta Sigma Phi.

BLUEBERRY-PEACH COBBLER

6 or 7 medium peaches	¾ cup sugar
1 pint blueberries	1 teaspoon baking powder
1 teaspoon grated lemon rind	½ teaspoon salt
1 tablespoon lemon juice	1 egg
⅛ teaspoon almond extract	5 tablespoons melted butter
3 tablespoons sugar	1 teaspoon cinnamon
1 cup all-purpose flour	¼ teaspoon nutmeg
	2 tablespoons sugar

Blanch peaches. Peel and cut into wedges. Spray 9x13-inch baking dish with nonstick cooking spray. Layer peaches and blueberries in prepared dish. Mix lemon rind, lemon juice, almond extract and 3 tablespoons sugar in bowl. Sprinkle over fruit. Set aside. Sift flour, ¾ cup sugar, baking powder and salt into bowl. Blend in egg with fork. Sprinkle over fruit, leaving some areas uncovered. Drizzle with butter. Mix cinnamon, nutmeg and 2 tablespoons sugar in small bowl. Sprinkle over top. Place on top rack of oven preheated to 375 degrees. Bake for 15 minutes. Increase temperature to 400 degrees. Bake for 12 to 15 minutes or until light brown. Let stand for 20 minutes before serving. Serve with Crème Fraîche. Yield: 10 to 12 servings.
Note: May substitute one 20-ounce package frozen unsweetened peaches and one 18-ounce package frozen unsweetened blueberries for fresh fruit.

CRÈME FRAÎCHE

4 cups heavy cream	Confectioners' sugar
1 tablespoon buttermilk	

Combine cream and buttermilk in jar. Let stand, tightly covered, in warm place for 24 to 36 hours or until thick. Sweeten with confectioners' sugar to taste; cover. May store in refrigerator for 2 to 3 weeks.

Walter W. Ross, III

SWEET CHOCOLATE ICEBOX DESSERT

1 pound sweet milk chocolate, broken	4 eggs, well beaten
4 teaspoons (exactly) water	1 teaspoon vanilla extract
	24 almond macaroons

Melt chocolate in double boiler over hot water. Blend in water. Add eggs very gradually, stirring briskly. Cook until thickened, stirring constantly. Stir in vanilla. Arrange 12 macaroons in layer cake pan. Top each with large spoonful chocolate mixture and another macaroon. Cover completely with remaining chocolate mixture. Chill in refrigerator for 24 hours. Cut with warm knife. Serve with whipped cream. Yield: 12 servings.
Note: Do not substitute coconut macaroons for almond.

Walter W. Ross, III

FRENCH SILK PIE

¾ cup butter, softened	3 eggs, at room temperature
1 cup sugar	1 baked pie shell
2 ounces unsweetened chocolate, melted	

Cream butter and sugar in mixer bowl until light and fluffy. Blend in chocolate. Add eggs 1 at a time. Beat for 5 minutes after each addition. Pour into pie shell. Chill until serving time. Garnish with whipped cream and chocolate curls. Yield: 6 to 8 servings.

Walter W. Ross, III

TOMATO COCKTAIL

1 46-ounce can tomato juice	1 teaspoon salt
6 whole cloves	1 tablespoon sugar
1 small bay leaf	1/8 teaspoon white pepper
1/4 cup chopped onion	3 tablespoons mild vinegar

Combine first 7 ingredients in saucepan. Bring to a boil over high heat; reduce heat. Simmer for 15 minutes. Strain into pitcher. Add vinegar. Chill for several hours to overnight. Serve in juice glasses. Yield: 12 appetizers.
Note: May be sealed in sterilized jars for later use.

Walter W. Ross, III

RIVER CLUB MULLIGATAWNEY SOUP

2 large apples	2 cups all-purpose flour
1 medium onion, chopped	3 tablespoons tomato paste
1 carrot, chopped	
1 stalk celery, chopped	2 quarts chicken stock
12 tablespoons butter	1 large onion
5 tablespoons curry powder	2 cups cream

Peel apples, reserving peel. Sauté apple peel, 1 medium onion, carrot and celery in butter in saucepan. Sprinkle with curry powder. Stir in flour and tomato paste. Add chicken stock; mix well. Cook for 45 minutes. Chop apples and 1 large onion. Cook in a small amount of water in saucepan until tender; drain. Strain soup. Combine strained soup with apple mixture and cream in saucepan. Heat to serving temperature. Ladle into soup bowls. Yield: 10 servings.

Walter W. Ross, III

ENGLISH MUFFIN PIZZA

1 15-ounce can tomato sauce	Shredded mozzarella cheese
1/2 cup oil	Favorite pizza toppings such as sausage, anchovies or pepperoni
1/4 to 1/2 teaspoon salt	
1 to 2 teaspoons Italian spice	
1 package English muffins, split	Parmesan cheese

Combine tomato sauce, oil, salt and Italian spice in bowl; mix well. Spread split muffin halves with half the tomato mixture; sprinkle with mozzarella cheese. Add remaining sauce and toppings. Sprinkle with Parmesan cheese. Toast in oven or broil until cheese melts and pizzas are golden brown. Yield: 12 servings.

Walter W. Ross, III

CHEESE ROLL

15 ounces cream cheese, softened	1 tablespoon Worcestershire sauce
1 5-ounce jar Roka blue cheese spread	1 small onion, grated
	Chopped nuts
1 5-ounce jar Old English cheese spread	Chopped parsley

Combine cheeses, Worcestershire sauce and onion in bowl; mix well. Shape into log. Chill in refrigerator. Roll in mixture of nuts and parsley, coating well. Place on serving plate. Serve with assorted crackers. Yield: 1 roll.

Brenda Evans

CHEESE SPREAD

1/3 cup beer	2 cloves of garlic, minced
8 ounces sharp Cheddar cheese	Salt and Tabasco sauce to taste
8 ounces cream cheese	Chili powder

Let beer stand overnight. Combine cheeses in mixer bowl. Let stand until softened. Beat until smooth. Add beer, garlic, salt and Tabasco sauce; mix well. Shape into ball. Refrigerate overnight. Coat with chili powder. Place on serving plate. Yield: 1 cheese ball.

Sarah Nealson

CHEESE WAFERS

8 ounces butter	1/4 teaspoon salt
8 ounces sharp Cheddar cheese, shredded	Red pepper to taste
	7 to 8 dozen pecan halves
2 cups sifted all-purpose flour	

Let butter and cheese stand in bowl at room temperature until softened; mix well. Add flour and seasonings; mix well. Shape into 2 logs; wrap in waxed paper. Refrigerate for 24 hours. Slice as desired; arrange on baking sheet. Top each with pecan half. Bake at 350 degrees for 10 to 12 minutes or until golden. Yield: 7 to 8 dozen.
Note: May use other highly flavored cheeses.

Sarah Nealson

CRAB MEAT-CREAM CHEESE SPREAD

1 1/2 cups catsup	1 7-ounce can crab meat
2 teaspoons horseradish sauce	8 ounces cream cheese

Blend catsup and horseradish in bowl. Mix in crab meat. Place cream cheese on serving plate. Spoon crab meat mixture over top. Serve with assorted crackers.

Donna Westpfahl

HOT CRAB MEAT DIP

1 pound Velveeta cheese, cubed	1/2 cup margarine
1 large white onion, chopped	1 8-ounce package frozen crab meat, thawed, drained

Melt cheese in double boiler. Sauté onion in margarine. Add sautéed onion and shredded crab meat to cheese; mix well. Keep warm until serving time. Spoon into chafing dish. Serve with tortilla chips. Yield: 3 cups.

Brenda Evans

SWEET AND SOUR CHICKEN WINGS

2 large packages chicken wings	½ teaspoon garlic powder
1 12-ounce bottle of chili sauce	1 16-ounce can sweet and sour sauce
1 10-ounce jar grape jelly	1 7½-ounce junior baby food peaches
	¼ teaspoon ginger

Place chicken wings in foil-lined large shallow roasting pan. Combine remaining ingredients in saucepan. Bring to a boil, stirring occasionally. Pour ¾ of the sauce over chicken. Bake at 350 degrees for 1½ to 2 hours or until brown and crisp, turning and basting frequently. Brush with remaining sauce. Bake for 20 to 30 minutes longer. Yield: 24 servings.

Note: Chicken wings may be baked for 2 hours, covered and refrigerated for up to 2 days. Bring to room temperature; finish baking as above. Refrigerate or freeze sauce.

D. J. Murphy

PICKLED WIENERS

1 pound frankfurters	4½ ounces hot pepper sauce
2 large onions, thinly sliced	¼ cup cumin
4 cups white vinegar	2 tablespoons salt
¾ cup sugar	1 teaspoon pepper

Slice frankfurters. Mix with onion in bowl. Simmer remaining ingredients in saucepan for 3 minutes. Pour over frankfurters. Cool slightly; cover tightly. Chill for several days. Yield: 4 dozen.

Brenda Evans

SALMON ROLL

1 16-ounce can pink salmon	8 ounces cream cheese, softened
1 teaspoon liquid smoke	Parsley, minced
2 tablespoons lemon juice	Nuts, crushed
1 teaspoon horseradish	

Drain salmon; discard skin and bones. Combine with next 4 ingredients in bowl; mix well. Shape into roll. Coat with mixture of parsley and nuts. Chill, wrapped in plastic wrap, until serving time. Yield: 1 roll.

Sarah Nealson

SALMON-PECAN LOAF

1 16-ounce can red salmon	1 teaspoon horseradish
8 ounces cream cheese, softened	¼ teaspoon salt
	1 teaspoon liquid smoke
1 tablespoon lemon juice	½ cup chopped pecans
2 teaspoons grated onion	3 tablespoons minced parsley

Drain salmon; discard skin and bones. Combine with cream cheese and remaining ingredients in bowl; mix well. Shape into loaf on serving plate. Chill until serving time. Serve with crackers. Yield: 1 loaf.

Note: May mix half the parsley into salmon mixture and coat loaf with remaining parsley. Loaf may be frozen.

Jane Klinknett

ARIZONA CHAMPAGNE MUSTARD

¼ cup dry mustard	Dash of salt
½ cup cider vinegar	1 teaspoon cornstarch
1 egg, beaten	1 cup mayonnaise
½ cup sugar	

Blend mustard with cider vinegar in bowl. Chill in refrigerator overnight. Let stand until room temperature. Combine with egg, sugar, salt and cornstarch in saucepan; mix well. Cook over low heat for 10 to 15 minutes or until thickened, stirring constantly. Cool. Stir in mayonnaise. Store in airtight container in refrigerator. Yield: 2 cups.

Amy Wykes

CHRISTMAS SNACK MIX

1 9-ounce package pretzels	1 pound mixed nuts
1 7-ounce package Cheerios	1½ cups melted butter
	2 tablespoons Worcestershire sauce
1 15-ounce package wheat Chex	2 teaspoons garlic salt
	1 teaspoon savory salt

Mix pretzels, cereals and nuts in large bowl. Combine remaining ingredients in small bowl. Pour over cereal mixture; mix well. Pour into large roasting pan. Bake at 250 degrees for 2 hours, stirring every 15 minutes. Cool. Store in airtight container. Yield: 3 pounds.

Brenda Evans

OVEN-BAKED CARAMEL CORN

1 cup margarine	1 teaspoon salt
2 cups packed brown sugar	½ teaspoon soda
	1 teaspoon vanilla extract
½ cup corn syrup	6 quarts popped popcorn

Melt margarine in saucepan. Stir in brown sugar, corn syrup and salt. Bring to a boil, stirring constantly. Cook for 5 minutes; do not stir. Remove from heat. Stir in soda and vanilla. Pour over popcorn in bowl, coating well. Spread on 2 baking sheets. Bake at 250 degrees for 1 hour, stirring every 15 minutes. Cool in pans. Break apart. Store in airtight container. Yield: 6 quarts.

Note: May mix peanuts with popcorn before coating.

Robynne Gowan

SPICED PECANS

1½ cups pecan halves	¼ cup sugar
2 teaspoons egg white	1 teaspoon cinnamon

Combine all ingredients in bowl; mix until coated. Spread on baking sheet. Bake at 300 degrees for 30 minutes, stirring occasionally. Cool. Yield: 1½ cups.

Cassandra Clayton

HOT SPICED CIDER

8 cups sweet cider	12 cloves
Grated rind of 2 lemons	4 cinnamon sticks
2 lemons, thinly sliced	¼ teaspoon nutmeg

Combine all ingredients in saucepan; cover. Bring to a boil; reduce heat. Simmer for 15 minutes. Strain into pitcher or serve from dispenser with spigot. Yield: 8 cups.

Amy Wykes

FRUIT PUNCH

2 3-ounce packages apricot gelatin	1½ cups orange juice
1 cup boiling water	1 cup lemon juice
2 cups sugar	7 cups cold water
1 46-ounce can pineapple juice	4 large bottles of ginger ale

Dissolve gelatin in boiling water in punch bowl. Add sugar; mix well. Add remaining ingredients except ginger ale. Chill until serving time. Add ginger ale just before serving. Yield: 40 servings.

Jeanne Rider

MINTED FRUIT PUNCH

3 quarts pineapple juice	4 28-ounce bottles of ginger ale
3 cups orange juice	
1½ cups lemon juice	2 28-ounce bottles of club soda
⅓ cup lime juice	
2½ cups sugar	1 pint strawberries, cut into quarters
1 cup lightly packed fresh mint leaves	

Combine juices in large container. Add sugar; stir until dissolved. Stir in mint leaves. Chill until serving time. Add remaining ingredients just before serving. Pour over ice in punch bowl. Yield: 75 servings.

Jeanne Rider

HOT CRANBERRY PUNCH

1 cup red hot cinnamon candies	3 quarts cranberry juice
1 cup sugar	1 6-ounce can frozen orange juice concentrate
1 quart water	
12 to 15 whole cloves	3 quarts water

Combine candies, sugar, 1 quart water and cloves in large saucepan. Cook until candies and sugar dissolve, stirring frequently. Add remaining ingredients; mix well. Heat to serving temperature. Yield: 30 cups.

Anne Lefler

FROZEN CRANBERRY SALAD

6 ounces cream cheese, softened	1 16-ounce can whole cranberry sauce
2 tablespoons sugar	1 8-ounce can crushed pineapple, drained
3 tablespoons salad dressing	3 cups whipped topping

Combine cream cheese, sugar and salad dressing in bowl; beat until well blended. Stir in cranberry sauce and pineapple. Fold in whipped topping. Pour into 9x13-inch pan. Freeze until firm. Yield: 8 servings.

Naomi Engeman

CHAMPAGNE SALAD

8 ounces cream cheese, softened	1 10-ounce package frozen strawberries, thawed
¾ cup sugar	
2 13-ounce cans pineapple chunks, drained	½ cup chopped pecans
	9 ounces whipped topping
1 banana, sliced	

Beat cream cheese with sugar in bowl. Add fruit and pecans; mix well. Fold in whipped topping. Pour into 9-inch square pan. Chill until firm. Yield: 9 to 10 servings.

Theresa Talley

CHRISTMAS JELL-O SALAD

2 3-ounce packages lime gelatin	1 8-ounce can crushed pineapple, drained
2 cups boiling water	¾ cup chopped drained stuffed olives
8 ounces cottage cheese	
½ cup English walnuts	1 cup salad dressing

Dissolve gelatin in boiling water in bowl. Chill until partially set. Add remaining ingredients; mix well. Spoon into mold. Chill until set. Unmold onto serving plate. Yield: 8 servings.

D. J. Murphy

CINNAMON SWIRL SALAD

2 3-ounce packages lemon gelatin	Dash of salt
	½ cup chopped nuts
½ cup red cinnamon candies	6 ounces cream cheese, softened
3 cups boiling water	¼ cup milk
2 cups applesauce	2 tablespoons mayonnaise
1 tablespoon lemon juice	

Dissolve gelatin and candies in boiling water in bowl. Stir in applesauce, lemon juice and salt. Chill until partially set. Mix in nuts. Pour into 8x8-inch dish. Beat cream cheese, milk and mayonnaise in mixer bowl until smooth. Spoon over applesauce mixture. Swirl through both layers to marbleize. Chill until firm. Cut into squares. Yield: 4 servings.

Gretchen Artman

PISTACHIO SALAD

12 ounces whipped topping	1 8-ounce can crushed pineapple, drained
1 4-ounce package pistachio instant pudding mix	½ cup chopped walnuts
	1 to 2 cups miniature marshmallows

Combine whipped topping and pudding mix in bowl; beat until blended. Fold in pineapple, walnuts and marshmallows. Chill until serving time. Yield: 8 to 10 servings.

Mary Whitney

CUCUMBER SALAD

1 cucumber	½ cup white wine vinegar
Salt	3 tablespoons sugar
½ cup water	2 tablespoons chopped
½ teaspoon salt	parsley or dill
Pinch of white pepper	

Slice cucumber very thinly. Place in deep bowl; sprinkle with salt. Cover with weighted plate. Let stand for 1 to 2 hours. Drain; rinse off salt. Squeeze dry. Place in bowl. Bring water to a boil in saucepan. Add salt and pepper. Cool. Add vinegar and sugar. Pour over cucumbers. Chill for 30 minutes. Sprinkle with chopped parsley or dill just before serving. Serve cucumbers with roast chicken or broiled salmon. Yield: 4 servings.

Note: May substitute juice of 1 lemon for wine vinegar.

Reon Rastad

RUSSIAN POTATO SALAD

4 large new potatoes	½ cup Russian dressing
1 medium onion, grated	½ cup mayonnaise
½ teaspoon celery seed	1 tablespoon vinegar
1 teaspoon salt	1½ cups chopped celery
¼ teaspoon pepper	3 small bunches radishes,
2 teaspoons sugar	chopped

Cook potatoes in boiling water to cover until tender. Drain, peel and cut into cubes. Combine warm potatoes with onion, celery seed, salt, pepper, sugar and Russian dressing; toss to mix. Add mixture of mayonnaise and vinegar; mix well. Chill until serving time. Add celery and radishes; toss to mix. Spoon into romaine-lined salad bowl. Yield: 8 servings.

Paul Drumm

BARBECUED HAMBURGERS

1½ pounds ground beef	1 cup milk
2 teaspoons chopped	1 teaspoon salt
onion	¼ teaspoon pepper
1 egg, beaten	1 teaspoon celery salt
1 cup bread crumbs	

Combine all ingredients in bowl; mix well. Shape into 8 to 10 patties. Brown on both sides in skillet; place in baking pan. Pour Barbecue Sauce over patties. Bake at 350 degrees for 30 minutes. Yield: 8 to 10 servings.

BARBECUE SAUCE

1 12-ounce bottle	2 teaspoons chili powder
of catsup	1 teaspoon butter
½ cup vinegar	½ cup chopped onion
½ cup sugar	Garlic to taste
1 teaspoon celery salt	

Combine all ingredients in saucepan; mix well. Simmer for 15 to 20 minutes.

Beverly Woody

BARBECUED BEEF BRISKET

1 6-pound beef brisket	1 teaspoon onion salt
6 to 8 tablespoons liquid	1 teaspoon garlic salt
smoke	Worcestershire sauce
2 teaspoons celery salt	Favorite barbecue sauce

Place brisket on large foil sheet. Sprinkle with liquid smoke and celery, onion and garlic salts. Seal foil. Refrigerate overnight. Sprinkle brisket with Worcestershire sauce; seal foil. Place in roasting pan. Add a small amount of water to pan. Bake, covered, at 275 degrees for 6 hours. Cool. Refrigerate overnight. Slice brisket thinly. Place slices in foil-lined roaster. Pour barbecue sauce between slices and over top; seal foil. Bake at 275 degrees for 1 hour. Yield: 10 to 12 servings.

Beverly Woody

IMPOSSIBLE MEXICAN PIE

1 pound ground beef	3 eggs
½ cup chopped onion	¾ cup buttermilk baking
1 envelope taco seasoning	mix
mix	1½ cups milk
1 4-ounce can chopped	⅛ teaspoon red pepper
green chilies, drained	
1 cup shredded Monterey	
Jack cheese	

Brown ground beef with onion in skillet, stirring until crumbly; drain. Stir in taco seasoning mix. Spread in greased 10-inch pie plate. Sprinkle with green chilies and cheese. Combine eggs and remaining ingredients in mixer bowl. Beat for 1 minute. Pour over cheese. Bake at 400 degrees for 25 to 30 minutes or until knife inserted near center comes out clean. Let stand for 5 minutes. Yield: 6 to 8 servings.

Theresa Talley

MICROWAVE TACO CASSEROLE

1 pound ground beef	1 16-ounce can refried
1 15-ounce can tomato	beans
sauce	2½ cups corn chips
1 envelope taco seasoning	1½ cups shredded
mix	Cheddar cheese
¼ cup salad olives	

Microwave ground beef in glass bowl on High for 3 to 4 minutes or until cooked through; stir and drain. Add tomato sauce, taco seasoning mix, olives and refried beans; mix well. Crush 2 cups corn chips in 2½-quart glass casserole. Spoon in ground beef mixture. Microwave until heated through. Sprinkle remaining crushed corn chips and cheese over top. Microwave for ½ to 1½ minutes or until cheese is melted. Yield: 6 servings.

Robynne Gowen

HAM ROLLS

1   6-ounce package
    Danish cooked ham
	3 tablespoons melted
	    butter

1 8-ounce package sliced Swiss cheese	3 tablespoons flour 1 cup (about) milk
1 10-ounce package frozen asparagus spears	

Cut ham slices into halves. Cut cheese into 2-inch strips. Cook asparagus using package directions; drain. Wrap 1 ham slice around 1 strip cheese and 1 asparagus spear; place in 9x11-inch baking dish. Repeat with remaining ham, cheese and asparagus. Blend butter and flour in saucepan. Stir in enough milk to make of desired consistency. Cook until thickened, stirring constantly. Pour over ham rolls. Bake at 350 degrees for 30 minutes or until bubbly. Yield: 10 servings.

Linda Potter

SWEDISH HOT DOGS AND POTATOES

1½ pounds potatoes	2 tablespoons tomato
1 small onion, chopped	purée
2 tablespoons butter	⅔ cup cream

8 ounces frankfurters,
    sliced
	Salt, pepper and cayenne
	    pepper to taste

Cook potatoes in boiling water to cover in saucepan until almost tender; drain. Cool. Peel and slice. Sauté onion in butter in skillet over medium heat until golden. Add frankfurters. Cook over low heat for several minutes, stirring occasionally. Add potatoes, tomato purée and cream; mix gently. Cook, covered, until heated through. Add seasonings. Garnish with chopped chives or parsley. Serve immediately. Yield: 4 servings.

Reon Rastad

CHEESE SOUFFLÉ

10 slices wheat bread, crusts trimmed	8 eggs, beaten 4 cups milk
¼ cup melted butter	2 teaspoons dry mustard
4 to 6 cups shredded sharp cheese	Salt and pepper to taste Dash of onion juice

Cut bread into cubes. Pour butter into 9x13-inch baking pan. Alternate layers of bread cubes and cheese in prepared pan until all ingredients are used. Beat eggs with milk and seasonings. Pour over layers. Chill, covered, for several hours to overnight. Bake, uncovered, at 325 degrees for 1 hour. Yield: 18 to 20 servings.

Theresa Talley

EGGS FOR BRUNCH

6 slices bread, crusts trimmed	5 eggs, beaten 2 cups milk
Butter, softened	½ teaspoon dry mustard
½ cup shredded Cheddar cheese	Salt and pepper to taste

Spread bread generously with butter; cut into cubes. Place in buttered 7x9-inch baking dish; sprinkle with cheese. Beat eggs with milk and seasonings. Pour over cheese. Chill, covered, in refrigerator overnight. Bake, uncovered, at 350 degrees for 45 minutes to 1 hour or until puffed and lightly browned. Yield: 6 servings.

Mary Whitney

EGGS NEWPORT

1 10-ounce can cream of mushroom soup	6 hard-boiled eggs, sliced 8 slices crisp-fried bacon,
½ cup mayonnaise	crumbled
½ cup milk	English muffins, toasted
1 teaspoon chopped chives	

Blend soup and mayonnaise in bowl. Stir in milk gradually. Add chives. Alternate layers of egg slices and soup mixture in 1-quart baking dish. Bake at 350 degrees for 20 minutes or until heated through. Sprinkle with bacon. Bake for 5 minutes longer. Serve over toasted English muffins. Yield: 4 servings.

Beverly Woody

GREEN BEAN CASSEROLE

2 tablespoons melted
    butter
	2 tablespoons chopped
	    onion

2 tablespoons all-purpose flour	1 teaspoon sugar Velveeta cheese slices
2 16-ounce cans French- style green beans	8 ounces sour cream Cornflake crumbs

Blend butter and flour in 1-quart baking dish. Drain 1 can beans. Combine drained beans, undrained beans, onion and sugar in bowl; mix well. Spoon into prepared baking dish. Arrange cheese slices over beans. Spread sour cream over cheese. Top with cornflake crumbs. Bake at 400 degrees for 20 minutes. Yield: 6 to 8 servings.

Beverly Woody

CORN AND BROCCOLI CASSEROLE

1 10-ounce package frozen chopped broccoli	1 egg, well beaten ¼ cup melted margarine

1   20-ounce can cream-
    style corn
	1 8-ounce package
	    stuffing mix

1 tablespoon chopped onion	¼ cup melted margarine

Cook broccoli according to package directions; drain. Add corn, onion, egg and ¼ cup margarine; mix well. Spoon into greased baking dish. Mix stuffing mix with ¼ cup margarine in bowl. Sprinkle over vegetable mixture. Bake at 350 degrees for 1 hour. Yield: 8 servings.

D. J. Murphy

CREAMED MUSHROOMS

1 pound mushrooms, sliced	Salt to taste
¼ cup butter	Lemon juice to taste
	1⅓ cups heavy cream

Sauté mushrooms in butter in skillet for several minutes. Add salt and lemon juice. Stir in cream. Cook for 3 to 5 minutes, stirring frequently. Serve in pastry shells, over buttered toast points or as filling for omelets. Yield: 4 servings.

Reon Rastad

MICROWAVE STUFFED PEPPERS

6 medium green peppers	¼ teaspoon pepper
1 pound ground beef	2 8-ounce cans tomato sauce
1½ cups cooked rice	2 cups shredded Cheddar cheese
½ cup chopped onion	
1 clove of garlic, minced	
1½ teaspoons salt	

Cut tops from peppers; scoop out seed and membrane. Fit snugly into 3-quart round glass casserole. Combine ground beef, rice, onion, garlic, salt and pepper and ½ can tomato sauce in bowl. Spoon half the mixture into peppers. Add half the cheese and remaining ground beef mixture. Pour remaining tomato sauce over and around peppers. Microwave, covered, on High for 32½ to 37 minutes or until ground beef is cooked through. Sprinkle with remaining cheese. Let stand, covered, for 5 to 10 minutes. Yield: 6 servings.

Patti Chastain

SCALLOPED SWEET POTATOES

Sliced sweet potatoes	Brown sugar
Crushed pineapple	Margarine
Sliced apples	Marshmallows

Alternate layers of sweet potatoes, pineapple, apples, brown sugar and margarine in baking dish. Bake at 350 degrees until sweet potatoes are almost tender. Top with marshmallows. Bake until light brown.

D. J. Murphy

HOT FRUIT CASSEROLE

1 16-ounce can chunky fruit cocktail	6 tablespoons melted margarine
1 cup drained pineapple chunks	½ teaspoon curry powder
1 cup packed brown sugar	3 bananas, sliced

Combine fruit cocktail and pineapple in bowl. Add brown sugar, margarine and curry powder; mix well. Spoon into baking dish. Bake at 325 degrees for 30 minutes. Mix banana slices gently into hot fruit. Yield: 10 to 12 servings.

D. J. Murphy

NEW YEAR'S DIRTY RICE

2 cups rice	2 tablespoons margarine
1 pound sausage	Salt, pepper and cayenne pepper to taste
2 cloves of garlic, minced	1 cup chopped green onions and tops
2 medium onions, chopped	Snipped parsley to taste
1½ cups chopped celery and tops	½ cup chicken broth

Cook rice according to package directions. Cool. Brown sausage in skillet, stirring until crumbly; drain. Cool. Sauté garlic, onions and celery in margarine in skillet until tender; drain. Combine rice, sausage, sautéed vegetables and seasonings in large bowl; mix well. Add green onions and parsley. Add broth. Spoon into casserole. Bake at 350 degrees for 30 minutes. Yield: 8 servings.

D. J. Murphy

STIR AND ROLL BISCUITS

2 cups all-purpose flour	½ teaspoon salt
1 tablespoon baking powder	⅔ cup milk
	⅓ cup oil

Sift flour, baking powder and salt into bowl. Combine milk and oil in 1-cup measure; do not mix. Pour into dry ingredients; stir with fork until mixture forms ball. Roll to desired thickness on floured surface; cut with biscuit cutter. Place on ungreased baking sheet. Bake at 475 degrees for 10 to 12 minutes or until golden brown. Yield: 10 biscuits.

Annie Mayes

PINEAPPLE-ORANGE-NUT BREAD

1 cup broken walnuts	¼ cup orange juice
2 cups all-purpose flour	Grated orange rind to taste
1 teaspoon baking powder	1 8-ounce can crushed pineapple
1 teaspoon soda	1 cup raisins
¼ teaspoon salt	1 tablespoon orange juice
¾ cup sugar	2 tablespoons sugar
¼ cup margarine, softened	
1 egg	

Process walnuts in blender container until fine. Mix with flour, baking powder, soda and salt. Cream ¾ cup sugar and margarine in bowl until light and fluffy. Beat in egg. Add ¼ cup orange juice and rind; mix well. Add walnut mixture and undrained pineapple alternately, beginning and ending with walnut mixture and mixing well after each addition. Stir in raisins. Pour into lightly greased 5x9-inch loaf pan. Bake at 350 degrees on middle oven rack for 60 to 70 minutes or until loaf tests done. Cool in pan for 10 minutes. Remove to wire rack. Drizzle mixture of 1 tablespoon orange juice and 2 tablespoons sugar over warm loaf. Cool. Wrap tightly in plastic wrap. Keep refrigerated for 2 days before slicing. Yield: 1 loaf.

Barbara Champion

POPPY SEED BREAD

2¼ cups sugar	1½ teaspoons baking
1 cup plus 2 tablespoons	powder
oil	1½ teaspoons salt
3 eggs	1½ cups milk
1 tablespoon poppy seed	¼ cup orange juice
1½ teaspoons vanilla	½ cup sugar
extract	½ teaspoon vanilla extract
1½ teaspoons almond	½ teaspoon almond
extract	extract
1½ teaspoons butter	½ teaspoon butter
flavoring	flavoring
3 cups all-purpose flour	

Combine sugar, oil, eggs, poppy seed and next 3 flavorings in bowl; mix well. Add mixture of flour, baking powder and salt alternately with milk, mixing well after each addition. Pour into 2 greased loaf pans. Bake at 350 degrees for 45 to 60 minutes or until loaves test done. Combine orange juice and remaining ingredients in bowl; mix well. Drizzle over warm loaves. Yield: 2 loaves.

Lisa Brazeal

GREENHOUSE ZUCCHINI-NUT BREAD

2 cups sugar	1 teaspoon cinnamon
1 cup oil	2 cups ¼-inch zucchini
3 eggs	cubes
2½ cups all-purpose flour	½ cup raisins
2 teaspoons soda	½ cup chopped nuts
½ teaspoon baking	2 teaspoons vanilla extract
powder	

Beat sugar, oil and eggs in bowl until thick and lemon-colored. Add sifted dry ingredients; mix well. Stir in zucchini, raisins, nuts and vanilla. Spoon into 2 greased and floured loaf pans. Bake at 325 degrees for 1 hour. Remove to wire rack to cool. Yield: 2 loaves.

Barbara Champion

SIX-WEEK BRAN MUFFINS

2 cups boiling water	2 cups raisins
8 to 10 ounces Bran Buds	2 cups chopped pecans
5 cups all-purpose flour	4 eggs
3 cups sugar	1 cup oil
5 to 6 teaspoons soda	1 quart buttermilk
1 teaspoon cinnamon	

Pour boiling water over 2 cups Bran Buds in bowl. Cool. Mix remaining Bran Buds and next 4 dry ingredients in large bowl. Add raisins and pecans. Add eggs, oil and buttermilk to moistened bran; mix well. Add to dry ingredients; mix well. Store in covered container in refrigerator for 12 hours to 6 weeks. Spoon into lightly greased small muffin cups as needed. Bake at 350 degrees for 20 minutes. Yield: 8 dozen.

Nadalie Poncton

MAYONNAISE MUFFINS

2 cups self-rising flour	1 cup milk
¼ cup mayonnaise	Sugar to taste

Combine all ingredients in bowl; mix well. Spoon into greased muffin cups. Bake at 425 degrees for 18 to 20 minutes or until brown. Yield: 1 dozen.

Note: May use for strawberry shortcake if desired. For less crusty muffins, cover loosely with foil during last half of baking period.

Amy Wykes

DIET ROLLS

3 eggs, separated	3 tablespoons cottage
¼ teaspoon cream of tartar	cheese
1 packet sugar substitute	

Beat egg whites with cream of tartar in mixer bowl until stiff but not dry. Beat egg yolks in bowl. Fold egg yolks, sugar substitute and cottage cheese gently into egg whites, mixing just until blended. Spray baking sheet with nonstick cooking spray. Mound egg white mixture 1 tablespoon at a time into nine 2-inch high mounds on baking sheet. Bake at 300 degrees for 1 hour or until brown. Yield: 9 servings.

Note: May use for strawberry shortcake if desired. For caraway rolls, add 1 tablespoon caraway seed. For onion rolls, add 2 tablespoons minced onion sautéed in 1 tablespoon butter and well drained. May process cooled rolls in blender for use as bread crumbs.

Amy Wykes

CHERRY BONBONS

1 21-ounce can cherry	1 teaspoon vanilla extract
pie filling	1 teaspoon almond extract
1 16-ounce can crushed	12 ounces whipped
pineapple, drained	topping
1 14-ounce can	Finely chopped pecans
sweetened condensed	24 to 30 maraschino
milk	cherries
¼ teaspoon salt	

Combine pie filling, pineapple, sweetened condensed milk, salt, vanilla and almond extract in bowl; mix well. Fold in whipped topping. Spoon into paper-lined muffin cups. Sprinkle with pecans. Top with cherry. Freeze until firm. Remove paper cups; place in dessert dishes. Yield: 2 to 2½ dozen.

D. J. Murphy

FRUIT COBBLER

½ cup butter	½ teaspoon salt
1 cup all-purpose flour	1 cup milk
1 cup sugar	1 21-ounce can fruit
1 tablespoon baking	pie filling
powder	Cinnamon-sugar

Melt butter in 9x13-inch baking dish. Sift flour, sugar and baking powder into bowl. Add salt and milk; mix well. Pour into prepared dish. Spoon pie filling over top. Sprinkle with cinnamon-sugar. Bake at 375 degrees for 45 minutes. Yield: 12 to 15 servings.

Annie Mayes

BEV'S CHERRY CHEESECAKE

1 2-layer package yellow cake mix	2 eggs
⅓ cup margarine, softened	2 teaspoons vanilla extract
1 egg	2 cups sour cream
16 ounces cream cheese, softened	¼ cup sugar
¾ cup sugar	1 tablespoon vanilla extract
	1 21-ounce can cherry pie filling

Combine cake mix, margarine and 1 egg in mixer bowl; mix until crumbly. Press over bottom of ungreased 9x13-inch baking dish. Combine cream cheese, ¾ cup sugar, 2 eggs and 2 teaspoons vanilla in mixer bowl. Beat until smooth and fluffy. Spread over crumb mixture. Bake at 350 degrees for 20 to 25 minutes or until set. Mix sour cream, ¼ cup sugar and 1 tablespoon vanilla in bowl. Spread over cheesecake. Cool. Top with pie filling. Chill, covered, for 8 hours. Yield: 16 servings.

Donna Westpfahl

DATE DESSERT

1 pound dates, chopped	12 ounces whipped topping
Pinch of salt	Coconut
Grated rind of 1 orange	Maraschino cherries
Orange juice	
1 16-ounce package vanilla wafers	

Combine dates with water to just cover in saucepan. Cook until very thick, stirring frequently. Add salt. Cool. Add orange rind and enough orange juice to make of spreading consistency. Spread on vanilla wafers. Stack 4 or 5 vanilla wafers together. Frost stack completely with whipped topping. Sprinkle side and top with coconut. Top with cherry. Repeat with remaining vanilla wafers. Chill until serving time. Yield: 18 servings.

D. J. Murphy

DATE PUDDING

1 cup sugar	1 16-ounce package dates
1 egg	½ to 1 cup nuts
1 tablespoon butter, softened	1 tablespoon baking powder
1 cup milk	
1 cup crumbled bread	

Cream sugar, egg and butter in mixer bowl until light. Add milk, bread, dates, nuts and baking powder; mix well. Spoon into greased 1-quart baking dish. Bake at 350 degrees for 1 hour. Serve with whipped cream if desired. Yield: 8 to 10 servings.

Sarah Nealson

LAZY MAN'S PEACH DESSERT

5 tablespoons margarine	¼ teaspoon salt
1 cup sugar	¾ cup milk
1 cup all-purpose flour	1 29-ounce can sliced peaches
1 tablespoon baking powder	

Melt margarine in 8x12-inch baking pan. Combine sugar, flour, baking powder and salt in bowl. Add milk; mix well. Pour into margarine in pan; do not stir. Pour the peaches and juice over top; do not stir. Bake at 350 degrees for 1 hour. Yield: 8 servings.

Nancy N. Morgan

SUGARLESS PISTACHIO PUDDING

1 small package sugar-free pistachio instant pudding mix	1 package sugarless whipped topping mix
1 16-ounce can crushed pineapple	1 kiwifruit, peeled, sliced

Combine pudding mix and pineapple with juice in bowl; mix well. Prepare topping mix using package directions. Fold into pineapple mixture. Spoon into dessert dishes. Chill until serving time. Garnish with kiwifruit. Yield: 5 servings.

Amy Wykes

ANGEL FOOD SURPRISE

1 bakery angel food cake	½ cup miniature marshmallows
¼ cup chopped maraschino cherries	½ cup chopped walnuts
¼ cup drained crushed pineapple	16 ounces whipped topping

Cut 1-inch slice horizontally from top of cake. Cut 2-inch wide by 2-inch deep ring from cake. Combine cherries, pineapple, marshmallows, walnuts and 2 cups whipped topping in bowl; mix well. Spoon into ring; replace top. Frost top and side with remaining whipped topping. Garnish with pineapple chunks and additional cherries. Yield: 16 servings.

Naomi Engeman

CAT SCRATCH CAKE

1¼ cups all-purpose flour	1 teaspoon vanilla extract
1 cup sugar	1 tablespoon white vinegar
3 tablespoons cocoa	½ cup oil
1 teaspoon soda	1 cup cold water
1 teaspoon salt	

Sift dry ingredients together. Sift again into ungreased 9x9-inch cake pan. Make 3 wells in dry ingredients. Pour vanilla, vinegar and oil into separate wells. Mix with fork. Add water; mix well. Bake at 350 degrees for 30 minutes. Serve warm with vanilla ice cream or hot chocolate sauce. Yield: 9 servings.

Annie Mayes

Enhance freshly baked desserts with unusual containers for perfect gifts. Use pottery, old-fashioned tins, baskets, glass jars, decorative trays or plates, or wooden boards.

CHERRY CHOCOLATE DELIGHT

1 2-layer package red devil's food cake mix	2 21-ounce cans cherry pie filling

Prepare and bake cake mix according to package directions for 9x13-inch cake pan. Cool. Spread with cherry pie filling. Chill, covered, for 1 hour. Serve with whipped topping. Yield: 20 to 24 servings.

Note: May bake in two 8-inch cake pans. Split layers. Spread pie filling and whipped topping between layers and over top. May vary flavors of cake mix and pie filling such as white or yellow cake mix with blueberry pie filling.

Donna Westpfahl

HOT FUDGE CAKE

2 cups all-purpose flour	3 to 4 tablespoons cocoa
2 cups sugar	½ cup buttermilk
½ teaspoon salt	½ teaspoon soda
½ cup margarine	2 eggs
½ cup oil	Vanilla to taste
1 cup water	

Combine flour, sugar and salt in bowl. Bring margarine, oil, water and cocoa to a boil in saucepan. Pour over flour mixture; mix well. Add mixture of buttermilk and soda with eggs and vanilla; mix well. Pour into greased 9x13-inch cake pan. Bake at 350 degrees for 30 minutes. Frost immediately with Hot Fudge Frosting.
Yield: 20 to 24 servings.

HOT FUDGE FROSTING

6 tablespoons buttermilk	1 16-ounce package confectioners' sugar
½ cup margarine	
3 to 4 tablespoons cocoa	1 cup miniature marshmallows
1 cup nuts	

Bring buttermilk, margarine and cocoa to a boil in saucepan. Stir in nuts, confectioners' sugar and miniature marshmallows. Cool for 5 minutes.

Beverly Woody

FRUIT COCKTAIL CAKE

1½ cups sugar	2 eggs
2 cups all-purpose flour	½ cup margarine
2 teaspoons soda	¾ cup cream
½ teaspoon salt	1 cup sugar
1 16-ounce can fruit cocktail	1 teaspoon vanilla extract

Combine 1½ cups sugar, flour, soda and salt in bowl. Add fruit cocktail and eggs; mix well. Spoon into greased and floured 8x8-inch cake pan. Bake at 350 degrees for 45 minutes. Bring margarine, cream and 1 cup sugar to a boil in saucepan. Cook for 2 minutes. Stir in vanilla. Pour over hot cake. Yield: 16 servings.

Anne Lefler

FRUIT COCKTAIL DUMP CAKE

1 20-ounce can fruit cocktail	1 2-layer package cake mix
1 20-ounce can crushed pineapple	2 sticks margarine, sliced
	1 cup coconut

Layer fruit cocktail, pineapple and dry cake mix in 9x13-inch baking pan. Dot with margarine. Sprinkle with coconut. Bake at 325 degrees for 1½ hours.
Yield: 16 servings.

Donna Westpfahl

MINCEMEAT FRUITCAKES

1 16-ounce jar mincemeat	1 pound mixed candied fruit
1 cup chopped nuts	2 cups all-purpose flour
¾ cup raisins	1 teaspoon soda
1 teaspoon vanilla extract	1 tablespoon boiling water
¼ cup melted shortening	
1 cup sugar	2 egg whites, slightly beaten
2 egg yolks	

Combine mincemeat, nuts and raisins in bowl. Mix in vanilla, shortening and sugar. Stir in egg yolks and candied fruit. Add flour and soda dissolved in boiling water; mix well. Add slightly beaten egg whites. Spoon into 2 waxed paper-lined loaf pans. Bake at 325 degrees for 2 hours. Remove to wire rack to cool. Yield: 2 loaves.

Virginia Fawley

HUMMINGBIRD CAKE

3 eggs, beaten	1 teaspoon butter flavoring
1 cup oil	
3 cups all-purpose flour	1½ teaspoons vanilla extract
2 cups sugar	
1½ teaspoons soda	½ cup butter
1 teaspoon salt	8 ounces cream cheese, softened
1 teaspoon cinnamon	
2 cups chopped bananas	1 16-ounce package confectioners' sugar, sifted
1 20-ounce can crushed pineapple	
1 cup chopped nuts	1 teaspoon vanilla extract

Beat eggs and oil in mixer bowl until thick and lemon-colored. Add mixture of flour, sugar, soda, salt and cinnamon; mix well. Stir in bananas, pineapple, nuts and flavorings. Spoon into greased and floured 9x13-inch cake pan. Bake at 350 degrees for 1 hour. Cool on wire rack. Cream butter and cream cheese in bowl until light. Add confectioners' sugar and vanilla. Beat until smooth. Spread on cooled cake. Yield: 24 servings.

Note: May bake in three 8-inch cake pans.

Aletha Taylor

GOOEY BUTTER CAKE

1 18-ounce package pound cake mix	8 ounces cream cheese, softened
½ cup melted butter	1 16-ounce package
3 eggs	confectioners' sugar

Combine cake mix, butter and 1 egg in mixer bowl; mix until smooth. Pour into greased and floured 9x13-inch baking dish. Combine 2 eggs, cream cheese and confectioners' sugar in mixer bowl; mix well. Pour over cake batter. Bake at 350 degrees for 35 minutes or until light brown; center will be soft. Cool. Yield: 16 servings.

Robynne Gowen

LAZY DAISY CAKE

2 eggs	5 tablespoons brown sugar
1 cup sugar	
1 cup all-purpose flour	3 tablespoons butter, softened
1 teaspoon baking powder	
½ teaspoon salt	3 tablespoons cream
½ cup milk	½ cup coconut
1 tablespoon butter	½ cup pecans
1 teaspoon vanilla extract	

Beat eggs in bowl until frothy. Add sugar. Beat until thick and lemon-colored. Sift flour, baking powder and salt together. Bring milk and 1 tablespoon butter to a boil in saucepan. Add flour mixture to egg mixture alternately with milk, mixing well after each addition. Add vanilla. Pour into a greased and floured cake pan. Bake at 350 degrees until toothpick inserted in center comes out clean. Mix remaining ingredients in bowl. Spread on hot cake. Broil until bubbly. Yield: 8 servings.

Barbara J. Sarbacker

MANDARIN ORANGE CAKE

1 2-layer package yellow cake mix	1 4-ounce package vanilla instant pudding mix
4 eggs	
⅓ cup oil	1 20-ounce can crushed pineapple
1 16-ounce can mandarin oranges	
8 ounces whipped topping	

Combine cake mix, eggs, oil and mandarin oranges with juice in mixer bowl. Beat for 5 minutes. Pour into 9x13-inch baking dish. Bake at 350 degrees for 35 minutes. Cool. Blend whipped topping with pudding mix in bowl. Stir in pineapple. Spread over cake. Store in refrigerator. Yield: 16 servings.

Naomi Engeman

Enhance a basic cake with various icings. Use chocolate, caramel or fluffy banana icing, lemon glaze or cherry filling on golden cake; orange cream or mint-flavored icing on chocolate cake; peanut butter frosting and sliced bananas on spice cake.

MARAMOUR CAKE

½ cup butter, softened	Salt to taste
2 cups sugar	1½ cups milk
2 eggs, separated	4 ounces unsweetened chocolate, melted
2 cups cake flour	
2 teaspoons baking powder	1 teaspoon vanilla extract

Cream butter and sugar in mixer bowl until light and fluffy. Blend in egg yolks. Add flour, baking powder and salt alternately with ¾ cup milk, mixing well after each addition. Add remaining milk, chocolate and vanilla; mix well. Beat egg whites in mixer bowl until stiff peaks form. Fold gently into batter. Spoon into tube pan. Place in cold oven. Set oven temperature to 250 degrees. Bake for 1 hour or until cake tests done. Cool in pan. Loosen from side of pan with spatula. Invert onto serving plate. Yield: 16 servings.

Barbara J. Sarbacker

NUTMEG POUND CAKE

2 tablespoons cocoa	2 cups all-purpose flour
½ teaspoon instant coffee powder	2 teaspoons baking powder
⅛ teaspoon soda	¼ teaspoon salt
2 tablespoons hot water	1½ teaspoons nutmeg
¾ cup butter, softened	1 teaspoon cinnamon
1 cup sugar	½ cup milk
3 eggs, at room temperature	

Combine cocoa, coffee powder, soda and hot water in small bowl; mix well. Set aside. Cream butter and sugar in mixer bowl until light and fluffy. Blend in eggs. Mix dry ingredients in bowl. Add to the creamed mixture alternately with milk, beginning and ending with flour mixture and mixing well after each addition. Pour ¾ of the mixture into greased 10-cup tube pan. Smooth top of batter. Mix reserved cocoa mixture into remaining batter. Pour into pan. Bake at 350 degrees for 45 to 50 minutes or until toothpick inserted near center comes out clean. Remove to wire rack to cool. Yield: 16 servings.

Dawn Nash

HAWAIIAN PINEAPPLE POKE CAKE

1 2-layer package yellow cake mix	1 cup cold milk
	1 4-ounce package vanilla instant pudding mix
1 20-ounce can crushed pineapple, drained	
8 ounces cream cheese, softened	2 cups whipped topping
	Coconut

Prepare and bake cake mix according to package directions for 9x13-inch cake pan. Punch large holes in cake. Spread with pineapple. Combine cream cheese, pudding mix and milk in mixer bowl. Beat until smooth and thick. Spread over pineapple. Top with whipped topping and coconut. Chill for 1 hour. Yield: 16 servings.

Naomi Engeman

PINEAPPLE SHEET CAKE

2 cups sugar
2 eggs
1 20-ounce can crushed
   pineapple
1 teaspoon vanilla extract
2 cups all-purpose flour
2 teaspoons soda
½ cup chopped nuts

Combine sugar, eggs, pineapple and vanilla in mixer bowl; mix well. Mix in flour and soda. Stir in nuts. Spoon into greased and floured 10×15-inch baking pan. Bake at 350 degrees for 35 minutes. Frost warm cake with Creamy Frosting. Cool. Store in refrigerator.
Yield: 24 servings.

CREAMY FROSTING

¼ cup butter, softened
8 ounces cream cheese,
   softened
1 teaspoon vanilla extract
2 cups confectioners'
   sugar
½ cup chopped nuts

Cream butter and cream cheese in mixer bowl until light. Blend in vanilla and confectioners' sugar. Mix in nuts.

Nadalie Poncton

AFTER-DINNER CREAM MINTS

8 ounces cream cheese,
   softened
Vanilla, mint or butter
   flavoring to taste
2 16-ounce packages
   confectioners' sugar
Sugar

Beat cream cheese with flavoring in mixer bowl until light. Tint with food coloring if desired. Add confectioners' sugar gradually, mixing well after each addition. Shape into ½ to 1-inch balls. Roll in sugar. Press into molds or flatten with thumb. Store between waxed paper in airtight container. Yield: 16 dozen.
Note: May store in freezer.

Donna Conner

MICROWAVE CASHEW BRITTLE

1 cup sugar
½ cup light corn syrup
⅛ teaspoon salt
1 to 1½ cups roasted salted
   cashews, chopped
1 tablespoon butter
1 teaspoon soda
1 teaspoon vanilla extract

Combine sugar, corn syrup and salt in glass dish. Microwave on High for 5 minutes in 700-wattage oven or for 5½ to 6 minutes in lower-wattage microwave. Stir in cashews. Microwave for 3 to 5 minutes or just until mixture turns very light brown. Stir in butter, soda and vanilla. Spread ¼ inch thick on buttered baking sheet. Cool. Break into pieces. Yield: 1 pound.
Note: May substitute English walnuts, pecans, peanuts or macadamia nuts for cashews. May substitute black walnut or almond extract for vanilla.

Liz White

BOURBON BALLS

6 ounces semisweet
   chocolate chips
½ cup sugar
3 tablespoons light corn
   syrup
½ cup Bourbon
2½ cups vanilla wafer
   crumbs
1 cup finely chopped
   walnuts

Melt chocolate chips in double boiler over hot water; remove from heat. Stir in sugar, corn syrup and Bourbon. Pour over mixture of cookie crumbs and walnuts in bowl; mix well. Shape into 1-inch balls. Roll in additional sugar. Let ripen in airtight container for several days before serving. Yield: 3 dozen.

Virginia Fawley

CHOCOLATE AMARETTO TRUFFLES

2 cups milk chocolate
   chips
¼ cup sour cream
2 tablespoons Amaretto
⅔ cup finely chopped
   toasted almonds

Melt chocolate chips in double boiler over hot water; stir until smooth. Remove from heat. Blend in sour cream and Amaretto. Spoon into small bowl. Chill until firm. Drop by rounded teaspoonfuls onto waxed paper, shaping into balls. Roll in almonds. Chill for 30 minutes or until firm. Yield: 2½ dozen.

Virginia Fawley

CHOCOLATE CRÈME DE MINTS

2 cups milk chocolate
   chips
¼ cup sour cream
2½ tablespoons Crème de
   Menthe

Melt chocolate chips in double boiler over hot water; stir until smooth. Blend in sour cream and Crème de Menthe. Spoon into small bowl. Chill for 30 minutes. Spoon into pastry bag, fitted with decorative tip. Pipe into 1-inch candies on foil. Let stand until firm or chill in refrigerator. Store in refrigerator. Yield: 3½ dozen.

Virginia Fawley

CHOCOLATE-PEANUT BUTTER BALLS

½ cup margarine
2 cups peanut butter
1 16-ounce package
   confectioners' sugar
4 cups crisp rice cereal,
   crushed
2 to 4 tablespoons
   melted paraffin
6 ounces chocolate chips
1 8-ounce milk chocolate
   candy bar

Melt margarine in saucepan; remove from heat. Stir in peanut butter. Combine with confectioners' sugar and cereal in bowl. Mix well by hand. Shape and press into walnut-sized balls. Add chocolate chips and candy bar to melted paraffin in double boiler. Heat until chocolate is melted; mix well. Dip peanut butter balls into chocolate mixture, coating well. Place on waxed paper. Let stand until set. Yield: 8 dozen.

Virginia Fawley

MICROWAVE FUDGY BROWNIES

½ cup margarine	¾ cup all-purpose flour
6 tablespoons cocoa	½ teaspoon baking
¾ cup sugar	powder
1 egg	¼ teaspoon salt
1 teaspoon vanilla extract	½ cup chopped nuts

Microwave margarine in 8x8-inch glass dish on High in 700-watt microwave for 1 to 1½ minutes or until melted. Blend in cocoa. Add remaining ingredients in order listed, mixing well after each addition. Place foil shields over corners of dish. Microwave for 5½ to 6 minutes or until top appears dry, turning dish ½ turn after 2, 4 and 5 minutes. Cool. Yield: 16 servings.

Liz White

DEEP SOUTH BROWNIES

½ cup butter	2 eggs
2 1-ounce squares	½ cup all-purpose flour
unsweetened chocolate	½ teaspoon salt
1 cup packed dark brown	1 teaspoon vanilla extract
sugar	½ cup chopped pecans

Melt butter and chocolate in heavy saucepan over low heat. Remove from heat. Add remaining ingredients; mix well. Pour into buttered 9x9-inch cake pan. Bake at 325 degrees for 20 minutes or until brownies test done. Cool completely. Frost with Mocha Frosting. Cut into squares. Yield: 16 servings.

MOCHA FROSTING

¼ cup margarine,	4 teaspoons strong hot
softened	coffee
2 cups confectioners'	⅔ teaspoon vanilla extract
sugar	

Cream margarine in mixer bowl until light. Add confectioners' sugar alternately with coffee and vanilla, mixing until smooth after each addition.

Paul Drumm

CHINESE CHEWS

¾ cup sifted all-purpose	1 cup chopped dates
flour	1 cup chopped nuts
1 cup sugar	2 eggs, beaten
1 teaspoon baking powder	Confectioners' sugar
¼ teaspoon salt	

Sift flour, sugar, baking powder and salt into bowl. Mix in dates and nuts. Add eggs; mix well. Spread in greased 10x15-inch baking pan. Bake at 375 degrees for 20 minutes. Cut into bars while warm. Sprinkle bars with confectioners' sugar. Yield: 6 dozen.

Brenda Evans

CINNAMON STARS

⅓ cup egg whites,	2 tablespoons flour
at room temperature	2 tablespoons sugar
1¼ cups sugar	1 cup sifted confectioners'
1½ cups ground almonds	sugar
1½ tablespoons cinnamon	

Beat egg whites at medium speed until soft peaks form. Add 1¼ cups sugar 2 tablespoons at a time, beating well after each addition. Beat for 10 minutes or until stiff peaks form. Mix almonds and cinnamon in bowl. Fold gently into egg whites. Chill overnight. Sprinkle pastry cloth with mixture of flour and 2 tablespoons sugar. Roll dough ½ at a time to ¼-inch thickness on prepared cloth. Cut with 3-inch star cutter. Place 1 inch apart on greased cookie sheet. Let stand at room temperature for 2 hours. Bake at 300 degrees for 15 to 20 minutes or until light brown. Mix confectioners' sugar with enough water to make glaze of desired consistency. Brush over hot cookies. Bake for 5 minutes longer. Cool on cookie sheet for several minutes. Remove to wire rack to cool completely. Yield: 2 dozen.

Carolyn Keech

DATE BARS

1 egg	½ cup all-purpose flour
½ cup sugar	½ teaspoon baking
½ cup melted shortening	powder
½ cup chopped nuts	¼ teaspoon salt
1 cup chopped dates	Confectioners' sugar

Beat egg in mixer bowl. Add sugar. Beat until thick. Mix in shortening. Stir in nuts and dates. Add sifted flour, baking powder and salt; mix well. Pour into greased 8x8-inch baking pan. Bake at 325 degrees for 35 minutes or until set but not dry. Cut into bars. Roll in confectioners' sugar. Yield: 2½ dozen.

Sarah Nealson

DATE-NUT ROLL COOKIES

2½ cups chopped dates	2 cups packed brown
1 cup sugar	sugar
1 cup water	3 eggs, well beaten
1 cup chopped nuts	4 cups all-purpose flour
½ cup shortening	½ teaspoon soda
½ cup margarine,	½ teaspoon salt
softened	

Combine dates, sugar and water in saucepan. Cook over low heat for 10 minutes or until thick, stirring occasionally. Stir in nuts. Cool. Cream shortening and margarine in mixer bowl until light. Add brown sugar gradually, beating until fluffy. Blend in eggs. Add dry ingredients; mix well. Chill. Roll ½ at a time to ¼-inch thickness on floured surface. Spread with date mixture. Roll as for jelly roll. Chill in refrigerator. Cut into slices. Arrange slices on ungreased cookie sheet. Bake at 400 degrees for 7 minutes. Cool. Yield: 8 dozen.

Donna Westpfahl

CHEESE-DATE ROLL COOKIES

1 pound mild Daisy cheese, shredded	4 cups all-purpose flour Pitted dates, cut into halves
1 pound butter	

Let cheese and butter stand at room temperature until softened. Cream in mixer bowl until light and fluffy. Add flour gradually, mixing well. Shape a small amount of dough around each date half to enclose completely. Place on baking sheet. Bake at 375 degrees for 30 minutes.

Brenda Evans

FRUITED DREAM BARS

1 cup all-purpose flour	¼ teaspoon salt
1 cup packed brown sugar	½ teaspoon baking powder
½ cup butter	
2 eggs, beaten	1 teaspoon vanilla extract
¾ cup sugar	½ cup candied pineapple
2 tablespoons flour	1 cup shredded coconut

Mix flour and brown sugar in bowl. Cut in butter until crumbly. Pat into 8 x 10-inch baking pan. Bake at 350 degrees for 15 minutes. Combine eggs and remaining ingredients in bowl; mix well. Pour over baked layer. Bake for 20 minutes longer or until brown. Cut into squares while warm. Yield: 2 dozen.

VARIETY 1

Increase sugar to 1 cup.

VARIETY 2

Use 1 cup packed brown sugar for sugar in fruit layer.

VARIETY 3

Add 1 cup chopped nuts to fruit layer.

VARIETY 4

Omit candied pineapple and increase coconut to 1½ cups.

VARIETY 5

Reduce candied pineapple to ¼ cup and coconut to ¾ cup; add ½ cup candied cherries, ½ cup chopped dates, ½ cup chopped pecans and ¼ teaspoon almond extract.

Lee White

OATMEAL COOKIES

1 cup shortening	1½ cups all-purpose flour
1 cup sugar	3 cups oats
1 cup packed brown sugar	½ teaspoon soda
1 teaspoon vanilla extract	1 teaspoon salt
2 eggs	½ teaspoon cinnamon

Cream first 4 ingredients in mixer bowl until light and fluffy. Blend in eggs. Add mixture of remaining ingredients; mix well. Drop by spoonfuls onto greased cookie sheet. Bake at 350 degrees for 8 minutes or until light brown. Cool on wire rack. Yield: 4 dozen.

Brenda Evans

PEANUT BLOSSOMS

½ cup shortening	1 egg
½ cup peanut butter	1 teaspoon vanilla extract
½ cup sugar	1¾ cups all-purpose flour
½ cup packed brown sugar	1 teaspoon soda
	½ teaspoon salt
2 tablespoons milk	48 milk chocolate kisses

Cream shortening, peanut butter, sugar and brown sugar in mixer bowl until light and fluffy. Blend in milk, egg and vanilla. Stir in flour, soda and salt. Shape into small balls; roll in additional sugar. Place on ungreased cookie sheet. Bake at 375 degrees for 10 to 12 minutes or until light brown. Press chocolate kiss onto each cookie while warm. Remove to wire rack to cool. Yield: 4 dozen.

Donna Westpfahl

POTATO CHIP COOKIES

1 cup margarine, softened	1 teaspoon soda
1 cup sugar	2 cups crushed potato chips
1 cup packed brown sugar	
2 eggs	6 ounces butterscotch chips
2½ cups all-purpose flour	

Cream first 4 ingredients in bowl. Add flour and soda; mix well. Stir in potato chips and butterscotch chips. Drop by spoonfuls onto greased cookie sheet. Bake at 375 degrees for 10 minutes or until golden brown. Yield: 3 dozen.

Barbara J. Sarbacker

TREASURE CHEST BARS

½ cup shortening	1 teaspoon baking powder
½ cup sugar	¾ cup milk
½ cup packed brown sugar	1 cup drained maraschino cherry halves
2 eggs	2 cups salted mixed nuts
1 teaspoon vanilla extract	1 4½-ounce milk chocolate bar, chopped
2 cups sifted all-purpose flour	

Cream shortening, sugar and brown sugar in mixer bowl until light and fluffy. Blend in eggs and vanilla. Add sifted flour and baking powder alternately with milk, mixing well after each addition. Stir in cherries, nuts and chocolate. Pour into greased and floured 10 x 15-inch baking pan. Bake at 325 degrees for 25 to 30 minutes or until golden brown. Cool. Frost with Brown Butter Frosting. Cut into bars. Yield: 5 dozen.

BROWN BUTTER FROSTING

¼ cup butter	½ teaspoon vanilla extract
2 cups sifted confectioners' sugar	2 tablespoons milk

Cook butter in saucepan over medium heat until dark brown, stirring frequently. Blend in confectioners' sugar and vanilla. Beat in milk until of spreading consistency.

Cassandra R. Clayton

FRENCH APPLE PIE

2 tablespoons all-purpose flour
½ cup sugar
1 teaspoon cinnamon
3 cups sliced apples
1 unbaked 9-inch pie shell
½ cup butter, softened
½ cup packed brown sugar
1 cup sifted all-purpose flour

Mix 2 tablespoons flour, ½ cup sugar and cinnamon in bowl. Add apples; toss to coat well. Spoon into pie shell. Cream butter and brown sugar in mixer bowl until light and fluffy. Mix in 1 cup flour until crumbly. Sprinkle over apples. Place pie in brown paper bag. Bake at 400 degrees for 15 minutes. Reduce oven temperature to 350 degrees. Bake for 30 minutes or until golden brown. Yield: 6 to 8 servings.
Note: Do not use bag made of recycled paper.

Nancy N. Morgan

DAIQUIRI PIE

1 3-ounce package lemon pudding and pie filling mix
1 3-ounce package lime gelatin
2 eggs, slightly beaten
2½ cups water
½ cup light rum
2 cups whipped topping
1 9-inch graham cracker pie shell

Combine pudding mix and gelatin in saucepan. Blend in eggs and ½ cup water. Add remaining 2 cups water. Bring to a boil over medium heat, stirring constantly. Remove from heat. Stir in rum. Chill for 1½ hours. Fold in whipped topping. Spoon into pie shell. Chill for 2 hours or until firm. Garnish with additional whipped topping, lime slices or graham cracker crumbs. Yield: 6 to 8 servings.
Note: May decrease chilling time of pudding by placing saucepan in bowl of ice cubes and water.

Patti Engle

AMISH SHOOFLY PIES

1 cup molasses
½ cup packed brown sugar
2 eggs
1 cup hot water
1 teaspoon soda
2 unbaked 8-inch pie shells
2 cups all-purpose flour
¾ cup packed brown sugar
⅓ cup lard
1 teaspoon cinnamon
½ teaspoon nutmeg

Combine molasses, ½ cup brown sugar and eggs in bowl. Add mixture of hot water and soda; mix well. Pour into pie shells. Mix remaining ingredients in bowl until crumbly. Sprinkle over pies. Bake at 400 degrees for 10 minutes. Reduce oven temperature to 350 degrees. Bake for 50 minutes longer. Cool before serving. Yield: 2 pies.

Amy Wykes

HAWAIIAN CHESS PIE

3 eggs, beaten
¼ cup milk
1½ cups sugar
2 tablespoons all-purpose flour
¼ cup melted margarine
2 teaspoons lemon juice
1 8-ounce can crushed pineapple
⅔ cup coconut
1 unbaked 9-inch deep-dish pie shell

Combine eggs, milk, sugar, flour, margarine and lemon juice in bowl. Beat until smooth. Stir in pineapple and coconut. Pour into pie shell. Bake at 350 degrees for 50 to 55 minutes or until set. Yield: 6 to 8 servings.

JoAnn Hatfield

OUT-OF-THIS-WORLD PIES

¾ cup sugar
1½ tablespoons cornstarch
1 21-ounce can cherry pie filling
1 16-ounce can crushed pineapple
1 teaspoon red food coloring
1 3-ounce package cherry gelatin
4 bananas, sliced
1 cup chopped pecans
2 baked pie shells

Mix sugar and cornstarch in saucepan. Add pie filling, pineapple and food coloring; mix well. Cook until thickened, stirring constantly. Remove from heat. Stir in gelatin until dissolved. Add bananas and pecans; mix gently. Pour into pie shells. Garnish with whipped topping. Chill overnight. Yield: 2 pies.

Beverly Woody

PEANUT BUTTER PIE

½ cup peanut butter
¾ cup confectioners' sugar
1 baked 9-inch pie shell
1 6-ounce package vanilla instant pudding mix
Whipped topping

Mix peanut butter and confectioners' sugar in mixer bowl until crumbly. Sprinkle ¾ of the mixture into pie shell. Prepare pudding mix according to package directions. Spoon into prepared pie shell. Top with whipped topping and remaining peanut butter crumbs. Chill until serving time. Yield: 6 to 8 servings.

Ann Corrigan

CREAM CHEESE-PEANUT BUTTER PIE

8 ounces cream cheese, softened
½ cup peanut butter
1 cup confectioners' sugar
½ cup milk
9 ounces whipped topping
1 9-inch graham cracker pie shell
Chopped peanuts

Combine first 5 ingredients in mixer bowl. Beat at low speed until fluffy. Pour into pie shell. Chill until firm. Sprinkle peanuts on top. Yield: 6 to 8 servings.

Amy Wykes

Holiday Menus

Brunches

THANKSGIVING BRUNCH

Gladys Simonson, Preceptor Beta Rho

Bloody Marys
Spiced Fruit Cup
*Sausage Quiches**
Hot Caramel Rolls
Irish Coffee

HOLIDAY BRUNCH

Dolores R. Seward, Xi Epsilon Alpha

Fresh Fruit Bowl
*Spinach Quiche**   *Bacon and Sausage*
Homemade Cinnamon Rolls
*Corn Fritters with Butter and Honey**
Cold Fruit Juice   *Coffee*

EASY BRUNCH

D. Jean Colburn, Zeta Nu

*Sausage and Egg Casserole**
Fruit Platter
Muffins

SHARING WITH OUR SISTERS

Maureen Laurence, Alpha Epsilon

*Chili Egg Puff**
Green Salad
Hot Dinner Rolls

NEW YEAR'S
COUNTRY HAM BRUNCH

Sandra Sharp, Gamma Epsilon

Country Ham
Garlic Cheese Grits
Black-Eyed Peas
Red-Eye Gravy and Biscuits
Steamed Carrot Pudding with Hard Sauce

NEW YEAR'S
TV FOOTBALL BRUNCH

Dorothy A. Kramer, Laureate Theta

Bloody Marys
*Fruit Compote**
*Easy Omelet Soufflé**
Hot Cinnamon Rolls
Coffee or Hot Spiced Tea

* See Menu Recipe Index

Lunches

THANKSGIVING WEEKEND LUNCH

Sissy Smith, Epsilon Psi

Fruited Turkey Salad*
Frozen Cranberry Salad
Pea Casserole   Rolls
Fresh Apple Pound Cake   Tea Punch

ITALIAN LUNCH

Anita M. Wilson, Laureate Alpha Mu

Sausage Zucchini Boats*
Tossed Garden Salad with Italian Dressing
Italian Bread
Fresh Fruit Compote   Beverage

GOING AWAY LUNCH

Chapter Members, Iota Phi

Four-Foot Submarine Sandwich*
Eight-Foot Ice Cream Sundae
Lemonade

SEAFOOD LUNCH

Sheri Schlemper, Omicron Phi

Noodles Romanoff with Shrimp*
Toasted Garlic Bread
Tossed Garden Salad

LUNCH FOR TWELVE

Vergie Stockton, Preceptor Beta Omega

Chicken and Spaghetti*
Green Salad
French Bread

HEARTY LUNCH

Jean Kuhn, Xi Iota

Swiss Steak*
Tossed Salad
Mashed Potatoes   Dilled Green Beans

SALAD AND MORE SALAD RUSH LUNCH

Mary Williams, Xi Theta Omicron

Kraut Salad*
Spinach Salad*
Breads and Crackers   Beverage

* See Menu Recipe Index

Suppers

CHRISTMAS EVE SUPPER

Wendy T. Kircher, Zeta Eta

Broccoli-Cheddar Stew with Shrimp*
Herbed Cheese Rolls*
Salad

NEW YEAR'S EVE SUPPER

Susan Foster, Xi Alpha

Baked Potatoes with Stroganoff Topping*
Tossed Salad
A Light Dessert

AFTER-CHRISTMAS SUPPER

Kathy Reid, Xi Gamma Alpha

Ham Balls*
Tossed Salad
Mashed Potatoes   Corn
Hot Rolls

CHINESE NEW YEAR'S SUPPER

Cathy Vins, Xi Alpha

Lumpia*
Sweet and Sour Sauce
Fried Rice*
Rolls

LUCKY NEW YEAR'S SUPPER

Patricia Hudson, Xi Alpha Psi

Sauerkraut and Pork*
Mashed Potatoes
Green Beans

NEW YEAR'S DAY SUPPER

Shirley Jones, Preceptor Iota Theta

Holiday Ham*
Secret Sauce*
Candied Yams*

FAMILY SUPPER

Sally Adams, Xi Xi

Swiss Chicken*
Fruit Salad
Rice Pilaf
Favorite Vegetable

GREEK SUPPER

Annette Lauer, Xi Alpha Epsilon

Greek Chicken*
Greek Salad
Baked Potatoes
Garlic Bread

* See Menu Recipe Index

Thanksgiving Dinners

TRADITIONAL SOUTHERN THANKSGIVING DINNER

Diann Walters, Delta Kappa

Southern Orange Ambrosia

Baked Turkey with Corn Bread Dressing*

Layered Green Salad

Pecan-Asparagus Casserole*

Potato Bread*

Fresh Peach Pie Praline*

THANKSGIVING DINNER

Wilma Hayes, Preceptor Zeta Chi

Ham

Sweet Potatoes

Green Beans

Asparagus

Hot Rolls and Butter

Pumpkin Praline Cake*

GARDEN BOUNTY THANKSGIVING DINNER

Sandra Sharp, Gamma Epsilon

Turkey and Corn Bread Dressing

Fresh Garden Salad   Indian Corn

Garden-Fresh Green Beans

Homemade Potato Rolls

Pumpkin Cake Dessert with Ice Cream*

NEW-FASHIONED THANKSGIVING DINNER

Jackie Vogler, Xi Sigma Phi

Smoked Turkey

Southern Corn Bread Dressing*

Ratatouille   Holiday Yams*

Hot Herb Bread*

Cranberry Swirl Cake*

FEAST FOR THANKSGIVING

Bettie L. Plummer, Laureate Pi

Harvest Fruit Cup*

Roast Cornish Game Hens*

Waldorf Salad*

Mushroom Wild Rice*

Asparagus Spears with Lemon Wedges

Baked Butternut Squash*

Pumpkin Chiffon Tarts   Coffee

THANKSGIVING DINNER

Dorothy M. Durrett, Preceptor Nu

Smoked Turkey*

Oyster Dressing and Gravy

Waldorf Salad

Mashed Potatoes

English Peas and Mushrooms

Peach Pickles   Crescent Rolls

Pumpkin or Cherry Tarts

* See Menu Recipe Index

Christmas Dinners

A FAMILY CHRISTMAS EVE DINNER

Diann Walters, Delta Kappa

Baked Ham
Hot Broccoli and Cheese Casserole
Hot Fruit Curry*
Refrigerator Spoon Rolls
Sweet Potato Custard Pie*

ROCKY MOUNTAIN CHRISTMAS DINNER

Carol Williams, Theta Theta

Baked Ham
Candied Yams
Rainbow Salad*
Black Forest Cake
Holiday Punch*

TENNESSEE CHRISTMAS DINNER

Pam Feldhous, Epsilon Psi

Baked Ham with Pineapple
Five-Cup Salad
Bourboned Sweet Potatoes
Green Beans with Almond Slices
Caramel Chocolate Squares*

CHRISTMAS DAY DINNER

Velda Kloke, Xi Gamma Zeta

Baked Ham in Cider*
Mashed Potatoes   Baked Pineapple
Vegetable Medley Casserole*
Whole Wheat Muffins   Beet Jelly
Simple Cheesecake*

FAVORITE CHRISTMAS DINNER

Wilma Hayes, Preceptor Zeta Chi

Turkey and Dressing
Fruit Salad
Cranberry Sauce
Green Beans
Cauliflower and Cheese Sauce
Hot Rolls and Butter
Strawberry-Nut Pound Cake*

CHRISTMAS GOOSE DINNER

Jackie Vogler, Xi Sigma Phi

Roast Goose
Broccoli Wreath*
Gratin Dauphinois*
Rum-Glazed Fruit
Angel Biscuits
Cranberry Ice*
Christmas Fruit Cookies*

* See Menu Recipe Index

New Year's Dinners

GOOD LUCK DINNER
Wilma Hayes, Preceptor Zeta Chi

Smoked Turkey
Black-Eyed Peas   Cabbage
Cheesy Rice and Broccoli Casserole
Corn Bread
Pecan Pie

STANDING RIB ROAST DINNER
Sandra Sharp, Gamma Epsilon

Shrimp Cocktail
Standing Rib Roast
Frozen Fruit Salad
Twice-Baked Potatoes   Steamed Broccoli
Date-Nut Pudding

NEW YEAR'S
CHICKEN DINNER SPECIAL
Bettie L. Plummer, Laureate Pi

Hot Oyster Stew*
Roast Chicken   Giblet Gravy
Cranberry Ring
Creamed Onions*   Green Peas
Corn Bread
Country Mince Pie
Coffee

A SOUTHERN
NEW YEAR'S DINNER
Dorothy M. Durrett, Preceptor Nu

Center Cut Ham with
Apricots and Brown Sugar*
Seafood Casserole*
Slaw
Squash Casserole   Black-Eyed Peas
Cornmeal Muffins
Apple Pie

Holiday Buffets

EASY HOLIDAY BOWL BUFFET
Deneen Phelps, Eta

Buffet Ham Sandwiches*
Party Mix   Wine Punch*

* See Menu Recipe Index

FAMILY THANKSGIVING BUFFET

Mrs. Robert L. Scofield, Laureate Eta

Cherry-Glazed Roast Loin of Pork*
Marinated Asparagus
Shrimp-Tomato Aspic*
Pear and Sweet Potato Casserole*
Baked Broccoli and Onions Deluxe*
Corn on the Cob
Angel Biscuits*   *Cornmeal Muffins*
Cheese-Crust Apple Pie*

THANKSGIVING DINNER BUFFET

Janice Venrick, Preceptor Beta Psi

Cornish Hens   Corn Bread Stuffing
Marinated Vegetables   Cranberry Salad*
Mashed Potatoes and Gravy
Candied Yams
Green Beans with Almonds
Relish Plate   Hot Rolls
Mystery Pecan Pie*   *Mincemeat Pie*
Date Pudding   Apple Cider

CHRISTMAS DUCKLING BUFFET

Bettie L. Plummer, Laureate Pi

French Onion Soup*
Holiday Duckling with Orange Stuffing*
Mushroom Wild Rice*
Almond Green Beans   Cranberry Sauce
Parker House Rolls with Butter
Assorted Cheese and Crackers
Gala Fruit Wreath*   *Coffee*

THANKSGIVING AT MIMI'S

Dolores R. Seward, Xi Epsilon Alpha

Baked Turkey Breasts
Corn Bread Dressing and Gravy
Green Beans and New Potatoes
Candied Yams
Cranberry Sherbet*   *Relish Tray*
Hot Rolls and Butter
Callie's Pecan Pie*   *Pumpkin Pie*
Iced Tea and Coffee

CHRISTMAS EVE GATHERING

Dolores R. Seward, Xi Epsilon Alpha

Rye Bread Spread with
Salad Dressing, Mustard and Horseradish
Baked Ham   Spinach Salad
Baked Cheese and Green Chili Grits
Brandied Sweet Potatoes
Relish Tray   Cranberry-Apple Relish
Callie's Pecan Pie*   *Cookie Tray*
Mississippi Mud Cake

HOLIDAY BUFFET

Mitzi Smirl, Delta Lambda

Centerpiece and Hors d'oeuvres Ring
Hawaiian, Taco and Cajun Chicken Wings
Baked Tenderloin
Exotic Shrimp Salad*
Assorted Rolls
Sparkling Fruit Bowl*
Fortune Cookies   Vodka Slush

* See Menu Recipe Index

CHRISTMAS OPEN HOUSE BUFFET

Jackie Vogler, Xi Sigma Phi

Brie in Pastry

Shrimp Canapé*   *Party Meatballs*

Vegetable Platter Crudités with Dip

Breadsticks

Meringue Fruit Drops*   *Teatime Tassies*

CHRISTMAS BUFFET

Lou Alexander, Xi Xi Rho

Beef Burgundy

Frozen Cherry Cup Salad*

Fettucini

Muffins

Ice Cream Pie*   *Good Brownies*

NEW YEAR'S EVE BUFFET

Jackie Vogler, Xi Sigma Phi

Beef Filet

Mushroom and Cherry Tomato Salad

Cheesy New Potatoes*

Hopping John

Pea Pods and Water Chestnuts

Cornmeal Crisps*

Jewel Cake*

NEW YEAR'S BUFFET

Barbara Ball, Xi Alpha Kappa

Ham   *Aspic Salad**

Twenty-Four Hour Salad*

Easy Cheesy Potatoes*   *Black-Eyed Peas*

Pickled Beets and Eggs*

Pickles and Olives   *Rolls*

Updated Steamed Pudding with Sauce*

Pineapple Custard

Chapter Parties

THANKSGIVING POTLUCK PARTY

Roberta DeNegre, Preceptor Gamma Upsilon

Fruit Dip*

Cornish Hens or Turkey

Frozen Salads

Relish Trays   *Cranberries*

Hashed Brown Bake*   *Hot Vegetables*

Homemade Breads

Favorite Desserts Spiced Holiday Punch*

CHRISTMAS MEXICAN COOKOUT

Ruth M. Scoggins, Laureate Beta Omicron

Oven-Style Mexican Fajitas*

Brisket of Beef*

Tamales   *Taco Salad*

Hot Cheese Grits

Beans or Rice

Hot Flour Tortillas

Mexican Wedding Cookies

* See Menu Recipe Index

CHRISTMAS HOLIDAY MEETING

Linda Hawkins, Preceptor Delta

Stuffed Mushrooms
Chicken Liver Pâté with Assorted Crackers
Crab Dip Divine*
Coconut Cake   Spiced Pecans
Peppermint Eggnog Punch*

CHRISTMAS GET-TOGETHER WITH SANTA

Nancy Burns, Preceptor Alpha

Crêpes with Curried Crab Meat*
Cranberry Fruit Freeze Salad
French Green Beans with Almonds
Hard Rolls
Minted Angel Cake*   Rosy Punch

CHRISTMAS PROGRESSIVE DINNER

Kimberly L. Birch, Eta Nu

Jezebel Sauce*
Beef Burgundy*
Salad   Dessert

LIGHTING OF THE YULE LOG PARTY

Pam Feldhaus, Epsilon Psi

Mom's Cheese Ball*   Sliced Cold Cuts
Peanut Butter Candy*
Hot Chocolate Mix*

CHRISTMAS SECRET SISTER PARTY

Jane Koehn, Laureate Alpha Zeta

Ham
Relish Tray
Spinach and Artichoke Casserole
Sweet Potatoes Deluxe
Celery Casserole*
Currant Cake*   Lime Sherbet

A NEW BEGINNING

Dolores R. Seward, Xi Epsilon Alpha

Chicken Fried Steak with Gravy
Hopping John
Spinach Supreme   Green Onions
Corn Bread and Butter
Deep-Dish Peach Pie
Coffee and Tea

GETTING BACK IN THE SWING (FIRST PARTY OF THE YEAR)

Brenda Pringle, Xi Alpha Nu

Beaufort Stew*
Tossed Salad with Dressing
Zesty French Bread*

RITUAL OF JEWELS TUREEN DINNER

Andrea Ryan, Zeta Alpha

Lazy Lasagna*
Seven-Layer Lettuce Salad*
Over-Stuffed Baked Potatoes*

* See Menu Recipe Index

BARBECUE PARTY

Diana Bal, Xi Delta Xi

*Barbecued Ribs**
*Crisp Spinach Salad**
Onion Pie
Rice
Ice Cream

FALL DINNER SOCIAL

Sissy Smith, Epsilon Psi

Pork Tenderloin with
*Gingered Fruit Sauce**
Seasoned Rice   *Broccoli Casserole*
Fresh Fruit   *Rolls*
Tea Punch

EPSILON PSI
TASTE AND TELL PARTY*

*All Recipes

Cocktail Meatballs
Hot Cheese Dip
Artichoke Squares
Chutney-Chicken Spread
Crab Meat Delight
Chicken Puffs
Shrimp Cheese Ball
Bambini
Rye Rounds
Instant Mexican Pizza
Party Spread
Potato Skins
Chipped Beef Dip
Spicy Beef Dip
Hot Artichoke Dip
Party Cheese Log
Shrimp Butter
Almond Sheet Dessert

BETA
CHRISTMAS COOKIE EXCHANGE*

*All Recipes

Anise Cookie Cut-Outs
Scotch Fruit Bars
Butter Thumb Cookies
Cherub Puffs
Christmas Cookie Variety
Christmas Rocks
Saucepan Oatmeal Cookies
Date Pinwheels
Fruitcake Cookies
Evelyn's Holiday Horns
Ginger Cookies (Lebkuchen)
Mincemeat Surprise Cookies
Cranberry Chews
Peanut Blossoms
Cinnamon Stars
Noel Wreaths
Pinksters
Two-Tone Walnut Jumbles

* See Menu Recipe Index

Holiday Gifts

FASTNACHTS

3 medium potatoes, peeled, chopped	*3 eggs*
5 cups water	*1½ cups lard*
2 packages dry yeast	*1 package dry yeast*
8 cups all-purpose flour	*2 cups warm milk*
1¾ cups sugar	*8 cups all-purpose flour*
	Oil for deep frying

Cook potatoes in 5 cups water in saucepan until tender. Drain, reserving 3 cups cooking liquid. Mash potatoes with ½ cup reserved liquid in bowl until smooth; set aside. Cool remaining reserved liquid to lukewarm. Dissolve 2 packages yeast in liquid in bowl. Add 2 cups flour; mix well. Let stand, covered, for 3 hours. Add mashed potato mixture, 6 cups flour, sugar, eggs and lard; mix well. Dissolve 1 package yeast in warm milk. Add to potato mixture; mix well. Place on floured surface. Knead in 8 cups flour gradually, dividing dough into 2 portion as mixture becomes stiff. Place in 2 greased bowls, turning to grease surface. Let rise, covered, in warm place overnight. Punch dough down. Divide into small portions. Roll to ½-inch thickness on floured surface. Cut with 3-inch doughnut cutter. Place on floured baking sheets. Let rise, covered, for 4 to 5 hours or until doubled in bulk. Deep-fry in hot oil until golden brown, turning once. Drain on absorbent paper. Cool. Sprinkle with sugar or confectioners' sugar. Yield: 15 dozen.

Patricia Hudson, Xi Alpha Psi
Superior, Wisconsin

SCANDINAVIAN KRINGLER

½ cup margarine, chilled	*1 cup confectioners' sugar*
1 cup all-purpose flour	*1 tablespoon margarine, softened*
2 tablespoons ice water	*½ teaspoon almond extract*
1 cup water	
½ cup margarine	*2 to 3 tablespoons milk*
1 cup all-purpose flour	*Sliced almonds*
3 eggs	
½ teaspoon almond extract	

Cut chilled margarine into 1 cup flour in bowl until crumbly. Add ice water 1 tablespoon at a time, mixing with fork until soft dough forms. Press into two 3x12-inch strips on ungreased baking sheet. Bring 1 cup water and ½ cup margarine to a boil in saucepan; remove from heat. Stir in 1 cup flour until smooth. Add eggs 1 at a time, beating until smooth after each addition. Add almond flavoring. Spread over dough strips to within ¾ inch of edge. Bake at 350 degrees for 50 to 60 minutes or until golden. Cool. Combine confectioners' sugar, 1 tablespoon margarine, almond flavoring and enough milk to make of desired consistency. Spread over cooled kringler. Sprinkle with almonds. Cut each into 10 to 12 slices. Yield: 2 coffee cakes.

Marlyn Brovelli, Xi Gamma Upsilon
DeKalb, Illinois

COFFEE CAN BREAD

1 package dry yeast	¼ cup sugar
1½ cups all-purpose flour	1 teaspoon salt
½ cup water	2 eggs
½ cup milk	2½ cups all-purpose flour
½ cup oil	

Mix yeast and 1½ cups flour in bowl. Combine water, milk, oil, sugar and salt in saucepan. Heat until warm. Add to yeast mixture; beat until smooth. Stir in eggs and 2½ cups flour; mix well. Knead on floured surface until smooth and elastic. Divide into 2 portions. Place in 2 buttered 1-pound coffee cans. Cover with lids. Let rise in warm place for 35 minutes or until dough rises almost to tops of cans. Remove lids. Bake at 375 degrees for 35 minutes or until brown. Cool in cans for several minutes. Remove to wire rack to cool completely. Yield: 2 loaves.
Note: Wrap loaves in plastic wrap. Tie ribbon around loaves just beneath top. Decorate with holly sprigs.

Thelma J. Evans, Xi Kappa
Corvallis, Oregon

CHOCOLATE WALNUT BREAD

¼ cup butter, softened	¾ teaspoon salt
⅔ cup sugar	1 teaspoon cinnamon
1 egg	1 cup buttermilk
2 cups sifted cake flour	1 cup raisins
1 teaspoon soda	¾ cup chopped walnuts
⅓ cup cocoa	

Cream butter and sugar in mixer bowl until light and fluffy. Blend in egg. Sift flour, soda, cocoa, salt and cinnamon together. Add to creamed mixture alternately with buttermilk, mixing well after each addition. Stir in raisins and walnuts. Spoon into greased loaf pan. Bake at 350 degrees for 1 hour. Cool on wire rack. Serve with cream cheese. Yield: 12 servings.

Emma Lee Goodrick, Xi Gamma Alpha
Dubuque, Iowa

Wrap bread with plastic wrap. Place bread loaf on top of inverted bread pan. Tie together with ribbon and bow.

CRANBERRY COFFEE CAKE

½ cup butter, softened	1 cup sour cream
1 cup sugar	1 12-ounce can whole
2 eggs, beaten	cranberry sauce
1 teaspoon almond extract	½ cup chopped walnuts
1 teaspoon vanilla extract	½ cup confectioners' sugar
2 cups all-purpose flour	2 teaspoons hot water
1 teaspoon baking powder	1 teaspoon almond extract
1 teaspoon soda	1 teaspoon butter,
½ teaspoon salt	softened

Cream ½ cup butter and sugar in mixer bowl until light and fluffy. Add eggs, 1 teaspoon almond extract and vanilla; mix well. Sift flour, baking powder, soda and salt together. Add to creamed mixture alternately with sour cream, mixing well after each addition. Layer batter, cranberry sauce and walnuts ½ at a time in greased tube pan. Bake at 375 degrees for 55 minutes. Remove to serving plate. Combine remaining ingredients in bowl; mix well. Drizzle over warm coffee cake. Yield: 16 servings.
Note: Glue preruffled trim to underside of wicker plate holder. Trim with bow. Line with holiday paper plate to hold plastic or cellophane-wrapped Coffee Cakes.

Elaine Rodgers, Preceptor Lambda
Tempe, Arizona

PUMPKIN BREAD

1 cup oil	2 teaspoons soda
4 eggs	1 teaspoon salt
3 cups sugar	1 teaspoon cinnamon
2 cups pumpkin	1½ teaspoons nutmeg
⅔ cup water	1 cup chopped dates
3½ cups all-purpose flour	1 cup chopped pecans

Beat oil, eggs and sugar in mixer bowl until thick. Add pumpkin and water; mix well. Add sifted flour, soda, salt and spices; mix well. Stir in dates and pecans. Fill 8 greased miniature loaf pans ½ full. Bake at 350 degrees for 45 minutes or until loaves test done. Remove to wire rack to cool. Yield: 8 loaves.
Note: Make attractive containers for giving small loaves of bread, cookies or candy from brown paper lunch bags. Stencil holiday design on front. Fold top one inch either toward or away from design. Punch holes through both layers 2 inches apart. Thread fat yarn or ribbon through holes and tie in front. Trim with lace or doily if top edge is toward design. May attach cookie cutter or recipe to tie if desired. Or, fold top of bag accordian-fashion, staple, and decorate with bow to cover staple.

Vivian Turner Howard, Xi Delta Omicron
Savannah, Georgia

For additional bread ideas suitable for gifts, see Holiday Breads, *pages 127 to 136, especially quick loaves, pages 129 to 133, muffins, pages 133 to 134, and yeast loaves, pages 134 to 135.*

ALMOND BALLS

6 ounces semisweet chocolate chips	½ cup sour cream
6 ounces butterscotch chips	¼ teaspoon salt
¾ cup sifted confectioners' sugar	1¾ cups vanilla wafer crumbs
	¾ cup chopped almonds

Melt chocolate chips and butterscotch chips in double boiler. Remove from heat. Stir in confectioners' sugar, sour cream and salt; mix well. Add vanilla wafer crumbs; mix well. Chill for 15 to 20 minutes. Shape into 1-inch balls. Roll in chopped almonds. Store in airtight container in refrigerator. Yield: 3½ dozen.

Sue Bemis, Xi Epsilon Psi
Ypsilanti, Michigan

AUNT BILL'S BROWN CANDY

6 cups sugar	½ cup butter
2 cups evaporated milk	1 teaspoon vanilla extract
½ teaspoon soda	2 pounds pecans

Cook 2 cups sugar in heavy skillet over low heat for 30 minutes or until caramelized, stirring constantly with wooden spoon. Combine 4 cups sugar and evaporated milk in saucepan. Bring to a boil. Add caramelized sugar gradually, stirring constantly. Cook to 250 degrees on candy thermometer, hard-ball stage. Remove from heat. Stir in soda vigorously. Add butter. Let stand for 20 minutes. Add vanilla. Beat until mixture loses its luster. Stir in pecans. Pour onto buttered baking sheet. Cool slightly. Cut into squares. Yield: 6 pounds.

Willie Cook, Preceptor Beta Gamma
Augusta, Kansas

CHERRY MASH CANDY

2 packages cherry frosting mix	1 10-ounce jar maraschino cherries, chopped
2 pounds confectioners' sugar	12 ounces semisweet chocolate chips
1 14-ounce can sweetened condensed milk	12 ounces milk chocolate chips
½ cup melted margarine	2½ ounces paraffin
1 tablespoon vanilla extract	1 pound Spanish peanuts, chopped

Combine frosting mix, confectioners' sugar, condensed milk, margarine, vanilla and cherries in bowl; mix well. Shape into small balls. Freeze until firm. Melt chocolate chips and paraffin in double boiler. Stir in peanuts. Dip cherry balls into chocolate to coat. Place on waxed paper. Let stand until firm. Yield: 10 dozen.

Roberta Smith, Xi Epsilon Phi
Belton, Missouri

CHRISTMAS KISS CANDIES

¾ cup slivered almonds	1 6-ounce package milk chocolate kisses
½ cup confectioners' sugar	1 cup sugar
5 teaspoons light corn syrup	

Process almonds in blender until very finely chopped. Combine with confectioners' sugar in bowl. Add mixture of corn syrup and flavoring gradually, stirring constantly until blended. Divide into 2 portions. Tint 1 portion red and 1 portion green with food coloring. Shape by teaspoonfuls around chocolate kisses, maintaining kiss shape. Roll in sugar. Store in airtight container.

Photograph for this recipe on Cover.

CHRISTMAS BONBONS

2 16-ounce packages confectioners' sugar	½ cup crushed walnuts
½ cup butter, softened	2 drops red or green food coloring
1 cup coconut	2 cups semisweet chocolate chips
1 14-ounce can sweetened condensed milk	1 tablespoon shortening
	2 to 3 tablespoons paraffin

Combine confectioners' sugar, butter, coconut, condensed milk and walnuts in bowl. Mix with hands for 5 minutes. Add food coloring if desired. Mix for 10 minutes longer. Shape into large marble-sized balls. Place in freezer for several minutes. Melt chocolate chips, shortening and paraffin in double boiler; mix well. Dip bonbons into chocolate, coating well. Let stand on waxed paper until firm. Store in airtight container.
Yield: 12 to 16 dozen.

Jane Thiel, Xi Xi
Nampa, Idaho

Place individual candies in decorative bonbon cups. Arrange in holiday tin, box or tray for gifts.

FAILURE-PROOF DIVINITY

2 cups sugar	Dash of salt
½ cup light corn syrup	2 egg whites
½ cup water	1 teaspoon vanilla extract

Combine sugar, corn syrup, water and salt in saucepan. Cook until sugar is dissolved, stirring constantly. Cook to 240 to 248 degrees on candy thermometer, firm-ball stage. Beat egg whites in bowl until stiff peaks form. Pour ⅓ of syrup mixture gradually over egg whites, beating constantly. Cook remaining syrup to 250 to 268 degrees on candy thermometer, hard-ball stage. Pour gradually over egg white mixture, beating constantly. Beat until mixture holds its shape when dropped from spoon. Mix in vanilla. Drop by teaspoonfuls onto buttered baking sheet, swirling top to a peak. Let stand until set. Store in airtight container. Yield: 2½ dozen.
Note: May add 2 drops green food coloring and substitute ½ teaspoon wintergreen flavoring for vanilla. May add 2 drops red food coloring and substitute ½ teaspoon peppermint flavoring for vanilla.

Jane Thiel, Xi Xi
Nampa, Idaho

AUNT MILDRED'S FUDGE

⅔ cup cocoa	4½ teaspoons butter
3 cups sugar	1 teaspoon vanilla extract
⅛ teaspoon salt	½ cup chopped nuts
1½ cups milk	

Combine cocoa, sugar, salt and milk in 2-quart saucepan. Bring to a boil over medium heat, stirring constantly until sugar is dissolved. Cook to 234 to 240 degrees on candy thermometer, soft-ball stage. Remove from heat. Add butter; do not stir. Cool to 110 degrees. Stir in vanilla and nuts. Beat until mixture thickens and loses its luster. Pour into buttered 8x8-inch dish. Let stand until cool. Cut into squares. Yield: 2½ pounds.

Janice Cygan, Xi Delta Zeta
Webster, New York

OLD-FASHIONED FUDGE

4 cups sugar	½ cup butter
2 cups milk	1 tablespoon vanilla
6 tablespoons cocoa	extract
¼ teaspoon salt	

Combine sugar, milk, cocoa and salt in heavy saucepan. Bring to a boil over high heat, stirring constantly until sugar dissolves. Reduce heat to low. Cook for about 1 hour or to 234 to 240 degrees on candy thermometer, soft-ball stage; stir only at 15-minute intervals. Remove from heat. Add butter and vanilla. Cool to 110 degrees. Beat until mixture thickens and loses its luster. Pour into buttered 9x13-inch dish. Let stand until firm. Cut into squares. Yield: 48 squares.
Note: May add nuts and peanut butter with butter and vanilla if desired.

Betty Jo Hunter, Laureate Pi
Huntington, West Virginia

BENEDICTINE MONKS' FUDGE

4½ cups sugar	9 ounces bittersweet
1 13-ounce can	chocolate
evaporated milk	1 7-ounce jar
1 cup butter	marshmallow creme
9 ounces semisweet	1 teaspoon vanilla extract
chocolate chips	2 cups chopped nuts

Combine sugar and evaporated milk in saucepan. Bring to a boil. Cook over medium heat for 8 minutes. Remove from heat. Add butter, semisweet and bittersweet chocolate, marshmallow creme, vanilla extract and nuts. Beat until thickened. Pour into buttered 9x13-inch dish. Chill overnight. Cut into squares. Yield: 5 pounds.

Garlene Knight, Preceptor Beta Epsilon
Cedar Rapids, Iowa

CAN'T FAIL FIVE-MINUTE FUDGE

⅔ cup evaporated milk	1 to 1½ cups chocolate
1⅔ cups sugar	chips
½ teaspoon salt	1 teaspoon vanilla extract
1½ cups miniature	½ cup chopped nuts
marshmallows	

Bring evaporated milk, sugar and salt to a boil in saucepan over low heat. Cook for 5 minutes, stirring constantly. Remove from heat. Add marshmallows, chocolate chips, vanilla and nuts. Stir until marshmallows and chips melt. Pour into buttered 9x9-inch pan. Cool until firm. Cut into squares. Yield: 2 pounds.
Note: May substitute caramel chips for chocolate.

Lucile Davis, Preceptor Nu
Anniston, Alabama

MICROWAVE PEANUT BUTTER FUDGE

3 cups sugar	1 12-ounce jar chunky
¾ cup margarine	peanut butter
⅔ cup evaporated milk	1 7-ounce jar
1 teaspoon vanilla extract	marshmallow creme

Combine sugar, margarine and evaporated milk in 3-quart glass dish. Microwave, uncovered, on High for 5½ to 6 minutes or until mixture comes to a boil, stirring once or twice. Cook for 3 minutes longer, stirring only if necessary to prevent boiling over. Stir in remaining ingredients. Pour into buttered 9x13-inch dish. Chill for 2 hours. Cut into squares. Yield: 5 pounds.

Pat MacMillan, Psi
Little Rock, Arkansas

Buy molded plastic dishes in shapes of bells, candy canes, Santa Clauses and Christmas trees. Pour fudge directly into dishes after beating. Sprinkle crushed peppermints, M and M's, cinnamon candies or Christmas sprinkles on top. Let stand until firm. Wrap with plastic wrap or cellophane. Decorate with bow and candy cane, jingle bells, or recipe card.

NUT GOODIES

12 ounces chocolate chips	*½ cup milk*
12 ounces butterscotch	*¼ cup vanilla pudding*
chips	*and pie filling mix*
1 18-ounce jar peanut	*2 pounds confectioners'*
butter	*sugar*
1 16-ounce jar peanuts	*1 teaspoon maple*
1 cup margarine	*flavoring*

Melt chocolate and butterscotch chips and peanut butter in double boiler. Spread half the chocolate mixture in 10x15-inch pan. Chill until firm. Stir peanuts into remaining chocolate mixture; set aside. Combine margarine, milk and pudding mix in saucepan. Bring to a boil, stirring constantly. Cook for 1 minute. Add confectioners' sugar and flavoring. Beat until very smooth and thick. Spread over chilled chocolate layer. Spread peanut-chocolate mixture over top. Chill until firm. Cut into squares. Store in refrigerator. Yield: 10 dozen.
Note: Do not use instant pudding mix.

Phyllis Mesker, Preceptor Delta Upsilon
Dayton, Ohio

GLAZED GRAPEFRUIT PEEL

4 grapefruit	*4 cups sugar*

Cut peel from grapefruit in strips. Combine with cold water to cover in saucepan. Bring to a boil; drain. Repeat process 4 more times. Rinse with cold water; drain. Combine peel and sugar in saucepan; mix well. Cook over low heat until syrup is absorbed and peel is glazed, stirring frequently. Spread on waxed paper. Let stand until dry. Store in airtight container. Yield: 4 cups.

Lottie M. Stout, Laureate Alpha
Lynchburg, Virginia

For colorful candied grapefruit peel, add enough red or green food coloring to sugar to make of desired color. Line basket with colorful holiday napkin. Arrange candied peel in basket.

MICROWAVE PEANUT BRITTLE

1 cup raw peanuts	*1 tablespoon margarine*
1 cup sugar	*1 teaspoon vanilla extract*
⅛ teaspoon salt	*1 teaspoon soda*
½ cup light corn syrup	

Combine first 4 ingredients in 1½-quart glass bowl. Microwave on High for 2 to 8 minutes, stirring once. Add margarine and vanilla. Microwave for 1 to 2 minutes longer or until peanuts are brown. Stir in soda gently. Pour into buttered baking sheet. Cool for 30 minutes. Break into pieces. Yield: 1 pound.

Sandra Crosby, Xi Epsilon Sigma
Oscoda, Michigan

NEVER-FAIL PEANUT BRITTLE

1 cup sugar	*2 cups raw peanuts*
1 cup light corn syrup	*1 teaspoon soda*
1 tablespoon water	

Combine sugar, corn syrup, water and peanuts in heavy skillet. Bring to a boil. Cook for 6 minutes. Stir in soda. Pour onto buttered 10x15-inch baking sheet. Let stand until cool. Break into pieces. Yield: 2 pounds.

Pat Hall, Xi Delta Omega
Barton, Florida

PEANUT BRITTLE

¾ cup light corn syrup	*2 cups raw peanuts*
1 cup sugar	*1 teaspoon soda*

Combine corn syrup, sugar and peanuts in saucepan. Cook to 300 to 310 degrees on candy thermometer, hard-crack stage. Stir in soda. Pour onto buttered baking sheet. Let stand until cool. Break into pieces. Yield: 1½ pounds.

Wanda Odom, Preceptor Epsilon Upsilon
Denison, Texas

PEANUT BUTTER CUPS

1½ cups peanut butter	*1 pound white almond*
¾ cup butter or	*bark*
margarine, softened	*2 8-ounce milk chocolate*
2½ to 3 cups	*candy bars*
confectioners' sugar	

Cream peanut butter, butter and confectioners' sugar in bowl until light and fluffy. Chill for several hours. Melt almond bark and candy bars in double boiler; mix well. Shape peanut butter mixture into balls; flatten slightly. Spoon 1 tablespoon chocolate mixture into paper-lined miniature muffin cups. Place 1 peanut butter ball in each. Top with 1 tablespoon chocolate. Chill until firm. Yield: 4 dozen.

Jody Lorash, Beta Omicron
Red Lodge, Montana

PEANUT BUTTER CANDY

1 16-ounce package confectioners' sugar	1 cup margarine
2½ cups peanut butter	1 pound Candi Quik chocolate, melted

Blend confectioners' sugar, peanut butter and margarine in mixer bowl. Chill. Shape into 98 small balls. Spoon 1 teaspoonful chocolate into each paper bonbon cup in miniature muffin cups. Place peanut butter ball in each. Cover with 1 teaspoon chocolate. Yield: 98 candies.

Pam Feldhaus, Epsilon Psi
Shelbyville, Tennessee

PEANUT BUTTER BARS

1⅓ cups graham cracker crumbs	1 cup margarine, softened
1 cup chunky peanut butter	2½ cups confectioners' sugar
	12 ounces chocolate chips

Combine first 4 ingredients in bowl; mix well. Spread in 9 x 13-inch baking dish. Sprinkle chocolate chips over top. Bake at 350 degrees for 5 minutes. Spread chocolate over top. Chill until firm. Cut into bars. Yield: 5 dozen.

Margaret Bell, Xi Psi
Oklahoma City, Oklahoma

CHOCOLATE LACE TRAY

10 ounces German's sweet cooking chocolate	Heavy duty aluminum foil

Line a shallow 1-quart *au gratin* dish with heavy-duty aluminum foil. Chill in freezer. Melt chocolate in heavy 1½-quart saucepan over low heat, stirring constantly. Drizzle half the chocolate from small spoon over bottom and side of chilled foil in dish. Chill in freezer for 5 minutes or until firm. Reheat chocolate if necessary to maintain drizzling consistency. Drizzle remaining chocolate over chilled chocolate. Chill in freezer for 15 minutes longer. Lift foil carefully from dish. Peel foil carefully from chocolate. Place chocolate basket on serving platter. Chill in refrigerator for up to 24 hours.

POTATO CANDY

1 small potato, peeled	1 cup peanut butter
16 ounces confectioners' sugar	

Cook potato in boiling water in saucepan until tender. Drain and mash. Cool. Combine potato and confectioners' sugar in bowl. Knead until smooth. Roll into rectangle. Spread with peanut butter. Roll as for jelly roll. Chill for 2 hours. Cut into slices. Yield: 1½ pounds.

Jean P. Spaide, Laureate Upsilon
Allentown, Pennsylvania

CHOCOLATE-ALMOND TRUFFLES

6 ounces semisweet chocolate chips	½ cup almonds, ground
⅓ cup butter	3 tablespoons milk
1¼ cups sifted confectioners' sugar	30 whole almonds
	Cocoa or chocolate sprinkles

Melt chocolate chips and butter in saucepan. Pour over confectioners' sugar and ground almonds in bowl. Stir in milk. Chill for 2 hours. Shape by rounded teaspoonfuls around whole almonds. Roll in cocoa or chocolate sprinkles. Place in bonbon cups. Store in refrigerator. Yield: 2½ dozen.

Mary K. Johnson, Member at Large
Huber Heights, Ohio

ORANGE-CHOCOLATE TRUFFLES

2 Florida oranges, ground	1 12-ounce package vanilla wafers, finely crushed
8 ounces semisweet chocolate	Shredded coconut
¼ cup whipping cream	Confectioners' sugar
¼ cup butter	Chopped nuts
3 tablespoons sugar	

Combine first 5 ingredients in saucepan. Cook over low heat for 10 minutes, stirring constantly. Stir in crumbs. Chill until firm. Shape into 1-inch balls. Roll in coconut, confectioners' sugar or nuts. Yield: 4 dozen.

Photograph for this recipe on Cover.

Fill free-form chocolate lace tray with bonbons, marzipan fruit, petits fours or any pretty candy or cake.

WONDER TRUFFLES

6 ounces chocolate chips	1 16-ounce package
8 ounces cream cheese,	brown sugar
softened	½ cup Brandy
½ cup butter or	Crushed nuts
margarine, softened	

Combine chocolate chips, cream cheese, butter, brown sugar and Brandy in bowl; mix well. Chill for 5 hours. Shape into 1½-inch balls. Coat with crushed nuts. Store in refrigerator. Yield: 2½ pounds.

Dorothy Sewell, Laureate Beta Iota
Bedford, Texas

TURTLES

1 14-ounce package	2 cups milk chocolate
caramels	chips
3 to 4 tablespoons milk	2 to 3 tablespoons paraffin
2 cups chopped pecans	

Melt caramels in milk in saucepan over low heat; mix well. Stir in pecans. Drop by teaspoonfuls onto buttered waxed paper. Chill. Melt chocolate chips and paraffin in double boiler; mix well. Dip caramel patties into chocolate mixture, coating well. Let stand until set. Store in airtight container. Yield: 2¼ pounds.

Carol Jarman, Beta Sigma
New Bern, North Carolina

MOM'S OLD-FASHIONED FRUITCAKES

3 cups all-purpose flour	4 eggs
1⅓ cups sugar	¼ cup dark molasses
2 teaspoons salt	1½ cups golden raisins
1 teaspoon baking powder	1½ cups currants
2½ teaspoons cinnamon	1½ cups chopped dates
1½ teaspoons nutmeg	2 cups chopped candied
1 cup orange juice	fruit
1 cup oil	1⅔ cups broken pecans

Combine first 10 ingredients in large mixer bowl. Beat at low speed for 1 minute, scraping bowl constantly. Beat at high speed for 3 minutes, scraping bowl occasionally. Stir in fruit and pecans. Pour into 2 greased and foil-lined 5x9-inch loaf pans. Bake at 275 degrees for 2½ to 3 hours or until toothpick inserted in center comes out clean. Cover with foil during last hour of baking if necessary to prevent overbrowning. Remove to wire rack. Cool. Store, tightly wrapped, in cool place or in airtight container loosely covered with Brandy-soaked cloth. Serve plain or with whipped cream or ice cream. Yield: 2 loaves.

Debbie Emmans, Sigma Eta
Chesterfield, Missouri

WHITE FRUITCAKES

1 cup butter, softened	1 cup green candied
1 cup sugar	cherries
5 eggs, separated	1 cup candied pineapple
2 cups sifted all-purpose	cubes
flour	½ cup raisins
¼ cup currants	½ cup chopped walnuts
1 cup red candied cherries	½ teaspoon vanilla extract

Cream butter in mixer bowl until very light. Add sugar gradually, beating constantly. Add egg yolks. Beat for 3 minutes. Beat egg whites in mixer bowl until stiff but not dry. Fold gently into egg yolk mixture. Mix a small amount of flour with mixture of fruit in bowl. Add remaining flour to egg mixture; mix well. Stir in fruit. Fold in walnuts and vanilla. Pour into foil-lined 4x10-inch loaf pans. Bake at 300 degrees for 1½ to 2 hours or until toothpick inserted in center comes out clean. Cool. Cake will slice thinly as soon as completely cooled.
Yield: 2 fruitcakes.

Sue Bemis, Xi Epsilon Psi
Ypsilanti, Michigan

TOMATO SOUP FRUITCAKE

1 cup sugar	½ teaspoon soda
½ cup shortening	½ teaspoon cinnamon
2 eggs, well beaten	½ teaspoon cloves
2½ cups mincemeat	½ teaspoon nutmeg
2 cups sifted all-purpose	1 10-ounce can tomato
flour	soup
1 tablespoon baking	1 cup chopped nuts
powder	

Cream sugar and shortening in bowl until light and fluffy. Mix in eggs and mincemeat. Sift dry ingredients together. Add to mincemeat mixture alternately with soup, mixing well after each addition. Stir in nuts. Pour into greased tube pan. Bake at 350 degrees for 1 hour and 20 minutes or until cake tests done. Yield: 16 servings.
Note: May add candied fruitcake mix, chopped dates or raisins if desired.

Nancy Roberson, Xi Theta Omicron
Holden, Missouri

Nestle plastic-wrapped fruitcake in vine wreath decorated with cinnamon sticks for an extra special gift.

KASSIE'S FRUITCAKES

4 cups packed brown sugar	5 pounds candied fruit, chopped
4 cups dark corn syrup	3 pounds raisins
2 cups shortening	2 pounds currants
2 cups milk	2 pounds figs, chopped
4 teaspoons vanilla extract	2 pounds dates, chopped
12 eggs	2 pounds chopped
8 cups all-purpose flour	walnuts
2 tablespoons baking powder	4 cups sifted all-purpose flour
4 teaspoons salt	Wine
4 teaspoons cinnamon	

Grease five 5x9-inch loaf pans and 10 small loaf pans; line bottoms with greased baking parchment. Combine first 5 ingredients in very large bowl. Add eggs 1 at a time, mixing well after each addition. Sift 8 cups flour, baking powder, salt and cinnamon together. Add to egg mixture; mix well. Combine fruit and walnuts in very large bowl. Add 4 cups sifted flour; mix until all fruit is coated. Add batter; mix well with hands. Mixture will be very stiff. Pack into prepared loaf pans. Bake at 275 degrees for 1½ hours for small cakes and 2½ hours for large cakes. Remove to wire racks; remove paper while warm. Wrap each in wine-soaked cloth. Store in airtight tins for about 1 month, adding wine as necessary. Decorate tops with additional fruit and nuts.
Yield: 5 large and 10 small fruitcakes.

Judy Eisenhart, Preceptor Phi
York, Pennsylvania

NO-BAKE FRUITCAKE

1 13½-ounce package graham cracker crumbs	8 ounces chopped dates
	8 ounces mixed candied fruit
2 teaspoons grated orange rind	1 cup golden seedless raisins
1 teaspoon grated lemon rind	1 cup chopped walnuts
½ teaspoon cinnamon	½ cup orange juice
¼ teaspoon cloves	½ cup honey
⅛ teaspoon allspice	2 tablespoons lemon juice
⅛ teaspoon ginger	

Combine first 7 ingredients in bowl; mix well. Add dates, candied fruit, raisins and walnuts; mix well. Beat orange juice, honey and lemon juice together in small bowl. Add to fruit mixture; mix well. Pack firmly into 4x8-inch foil loaf pan. Chill, covered, for 2 days or longer. Let stand at room temperature for 2 hours. Yield: 16 servings.

Arlene Greatwood, Preceptor Beta Eta
Bradenton, Florida

GERMAN FRUITCAKE

¾ cup margarine	1 cup buttermilk
2 cups sugar	1 teaspoon soda
4 eggs	⅔ cup cherry preserves
3 cups all-purpose flour	⅔ cup apricot preserves
½ teaspoon cinnamon	⅔ cup pineapple preserves
½ teaspoon allspice	
½ teaspoon nutmeg	1 cup chopped nuts

Cream softened margarine and sugar in mixer bowl until light and fluffy. Add eggs; mix well. Add mixture of flour and spices alternately with mixture of buttermilk and soda, mixing well after each addition. Fold in preserves and nuts. Pour into greased large tube pan or 3 small loaf pans. Bake at 325 degrees for 1½ hours or until fruitcake tests done. Cool on wire rack.
Yield: 1 large or 3 small fruitcakes.

Estelline Mikeworth, Preceptor Beta Omega
Bellevue, Texas

FRIENDSHIP CAKES

1 2-layer package butter cake mix	⅔ cup oil
	1½ cups drained Friendship Fruit
1 3-ounce package vanilla instant pudding mix	1 cup raisins
	1 cup coconut
4 eggs	1 cup chopped nuts

Combine cake mix, pudding mix, eggs and oil in bowl; mix well. Add Friendship Fruit, raisins, coconut and nuts; mix well. Pour into 2 greased and floured tube pans. Bake at 275 degrees for 1½ hours. Yield: 2 cakes.

FRIENDSHIP FRUIT

1 16-ounce can peaches	1 16-ounce jar maraschino cherries, drained
2 cups sugar	
1 20-ounce can crushed pineapple	2 cups sugar
2 cups sugar	

Drain and chop peaches. Mix with 2 cups sugar in loosely covered ½-gallon jar. Let stand for 10 days, stirring daily. Add pineapple and 2 cups sugar; mix well. Let stand for 10 days, stirring daily. Add cherries and 2 cups sugar; mix well. Let stand for 10 days, stirring daily.

Brenda Pringle, Xi Alpha Nu
Florence, South Carolina

Give decorative jars of Friendship Fruit along with instructions for maintenance, recipes, and Friendship Cake.

BLACK FRUITCAKES

1¾ cups butter, softened	2 pounds golden raisins
2 cups sugar	1 pound candied cherries
6 eggs	1 pound candied
1 teaspoon soda	pineapple
½ cup dark molasses	4 ounces candied citron
3 cups all-purpose flour	Grated rind of 2 lemons
2 teaspoons cinnamon	8 ounces chopped pecans
1 teaspoon nutmeg	8 ounces chopped black
1 teaspoon cloves	walnuts
1 teaspoon mace	1 cup flour
¾ cup peach Brandy	

Cream butter in mixer bowl until light. Add sugar gradually, beating constantly until light and fluffy. Add eggs 1 at a time, beating well after each addition. Add mixture of soda and molasses; mix well. Sift 3 cups flour and spices together several times. Add to molasses mixture alternately with Brandy, mixing well after each addition. Mix fruit and walnuts with 1 cup flour until coated. Stir into batter. Let stand overnight. Mix well. Spoon into 2 greased and paper-lined tube pans. Bake at 275 degrees for 2½ hours. Yield: 2 large fruitcakes.
Note: May substitute grape juice for Brandy.

Barbara Paige, Preceptor Alpha Theta
Ringgold, Georgia

FRUITCAKE

½ cup thinly sliced citron	3 cups sifted all-purpose
½ cup chopped candied	flour
pineapple	1 teaspoon baking powder
1 cup chopped dates	2 teaspoons salt
1 cup whole candied	2 teaspoons cinnamon
cherries	2 teaspoons allspice
1 cup seedless raisins	1 teaspoon cloves
1 tablespoon rum	1 cup orange juice
flavoring	2 cups chopped walnuts
1 tablespoon Brandy	Wine or Brandy
flavoring	2 tablespoons brown
1 cup margarine, softened	sugar
1½ cups packed brown	1 tablespoon corn syrup
sugar	2 tablespoons water
4 eggs	

Combine fruit with rum and Brandy flavorings in bowl. Let stand, covered, overnight. Cream 1 cup margarine and 1½ cups brown sugar in mixer bowl until light. Blend in eggs. Beat for 2 minutes. Sift flour, baking powder, salt and spices together. Add to creamed mixture alternately with orange juice, mixing well after each addition. Fold in walnuts and fruit mixture. Spoon into tube pan lined with greased baking parchment. Place on center rack of oven preheated to 275 degrees. Place shallow pan of water on lower rack. Bake for 2½ to 3 hours or until cake tests done. Remove to wire rack to cool; remove baking parchment. Wrap cake in cloth moistened with wine or Brandy; wrap tightly in foil. Store until ready to serve. Bring remaining ingredients to a boil in saucepan. Simmer for 2 minutes. Place unwrapped cake on serving plate; brush with brown sugar mixture. Decorate as desired. Chill for easier slicing. Yield: 20 servings.

Note: May omit glaze and frost with mixture of 3 cups sifted confectioners' sugar, ⅓ cup softened butter, 3 tablespoons cream and 1½ teaspoons vanilla extract.

Dorothy Sumner, Preceptor Laureate Delta
Ogden, Utah

LIGHT FRUITCAKES

1 pound chopped candied	½ teaspoon baking
pineapple	powder
1 pound mixed red and	¼ teaspoon cream of tartar
green cherries	½ cup butter, softened
1½ cups light raisins	1 cup sugar
1 pound pecan halves	6 eggs, well beaten
2 cups sifted	
all-purpose flour	

Combine fruit and pecans in bowl. Sift in dry ingredients; mix well. Set aside. Cream butter and sugar in bowl until light and fluffy. Add eggs; mix well. Pour over fruit mixture; mix well. Pour into two 5x9-inch loaf pans lined with greased aluminum foil. Place on top oven rack in preheated 250-degree oven. Place pan of water on bottom oven rack. Bake for 2½ hours. Yield: 2 fruitcakes.
Note: May substitute three 1-pound coffee cans for the 2 loaf pans.

Mary Jane Mickelson-Cox, Sigma Lambda
Bridgeview, Illinois

CHRISTMAS FRUITCAKE

2 cups chopped pecans	4 ounces coconut
8 ounces chopped dates	1 14-ounce can
8 ounces candied cherry	sweetened condensed
halves	milk

Grease loaf pan and line with brown paper. Combine all ingredients in bowl; mix well. Pour into prepared pan. Bake at 250 degrees for 1½ hours. Remove to wire rack to cool. Yield: 12 servings.
Note: Do not use brown paper from bag containing recycled materials; these may release toxic chemicals.

Alice White, Xi Eta Epsilon
Sugar Land, Texas

CAJUN PEPPER JELLY

½ cup finely chopped	1½ cups vinegar
green or sweet red	1 bottle of fruit pectin
pepper	Green or red food coloring
6½ cups sugar	

Combine green pepper, sugar and vinegar in saucepan. Bring to a boil. Cook for 4 minutes. Stir in pectin. Bring to a boil. Remove from heat. Stir in food coloring. Pour into hot sterilized 1-cup jars, leaving ½-inch headspace; seal with 2-piece lids. Decorate with bows. Serve with cream cheese and crackers. Yield: 3 cups.

Susan S. Pfaff, Iota Alpha
Hammond, Louisiana

FIG PRESERVES

6 quarts figs	3 lemons, thinly sliced
6 quarts boiling water	1/4 cup sliced preserved
8 cups sugar	ginger
3 quarts water	

Remove stems from figs. Cover with boiling water. Let stand for 15 minutes; drain. Rinse with cold water; drain. Combine sugar and 3 quarts water in saucepan. Bring to a boil. Add lemon slices and ginger. Cook for 10 minutes. Skim; remove lemon slices. Add figs several at a time, maintaining syrup at boiling temperature. Cook over high heat until figs are transparent. Place figs in shallow pan. Boil syrup until reduced to consistency of honey. Pour over figs. Let stand overnight. Return to saucepan. Bring to a boil. Pack into hot sterilized jars, leaving 1/2-inch headspace; seal with 2-piece lids. Process in boiling water bath for 10 minutes. Yield: 5 pints.

Mae Warren, Preceptor Nu
Oxford, Alabama

JALAPEÑO JELLY

1 cup jalapeño peppers	2 3-ounce packages
3/4 cup cider vinegar	liquid Certo
4 cups sugar	Paraffin, melted

Put peppers through food grinder. Combine with vinegar and sugar in saucepan. Bring to a boil. Cook for 2 to 3 minutes. Cool. Stir in Certo. Bring to a boil. Pour into hot sterilized jars, leaving 1/2-inch headspace; seal with paraffin and 2-piece lids. Serve over cream cheese with Wheat Thins. Yield: 3 cups.

Mary Louise Irby, Laureate Beta Omicron
Harlingen, Texas

Top jam jars with doilies and stretch tie bows. Stencil fruit or vegetable denoting flavor on each.

HOT PEPPER JELLY

2 cups chopped red or	1 box Sure-Jel
green sweet peppers	6 cups sugar
1/2 cup minced jalapeño	1 teaspoon margarine
peppers	Green or red food coloring
1 1/4 cups white vinegar	Paraffin, melted

Combine peppers and 1/4 cup vinegar in blender container. Process until liquified. Pour into heavy saucepan. Rinse blender with remaining 1 cup vinegar. Pour into saucepan. Cook for 10 minutes. Add enough water to mixture to measure 3 1/2 cups liquid. Stir in Sure-Jel. Bring to a boil. Add sugar; mix well. Bring to a boil. Cook for 1 minute, stirring constantly. Add margarine and desired food coloring. Pour into hot sterilized jelly jars, leaving 1/2-inch headspace; seal with paraffin and 2-piece lids. Serve with cream cheese and crackers or bagels. Yield: Seven 8-ounce jars.

Cheri Brown, Preceptor Sigma
Fort Washington, Maryland

PINEAPPLE JAM

3 1/4 cups crushed	7 1/2 cups sugar
pineapple	1 bottle of Certo
3/4 cup water	Paraffin, melted

Combine pineapple, water and sugar in saucepan; mix well. Bring to a boil over high heat. Cook for 1 minute, stirring constantly; remove from heat. Stir in Certo. Let stand for 5 minutes. Spoon into hot sterilized jars, leaving 1/2-inch headspace; stir after each spoonful. Cool. Seal with 1/2-inch paraffin and 2-piece lids. Yield: 6 cups.

Marilyn Borras, Xi Epsilon Alpha
Stafford, Virginia

STRAWBERRY BUTTER

2 cups chopped	4 cups sugar
strawberries	2 tablespoons lemon juice
1/2 teaspoon grated lemon	1 envelope liquid fruit
rind	pectin
1/4 teaspoon nutmeg	

Combine strawberries, lemon rind and nutmeg in bowl; mix well. Add sugar; mix well. Let stand for 10 minutes. Combine lemon juice and pectin in small bowl; mix well. Add to strawberries, stirring constantly for 3 minutes. Spoon into four 8-ounce plastic containers, leaving 1/2-inch headspace. Cover with tight-fitting lids. Let stand for 24 hours. Store in refrigerator for 2 to 3 weeks or in freezer. Yield: 4 cups.

Cheri Brown, Preceptor Sigma
Fort Washington, Maryland

SPICED CIDER JELLY

4 cups sweet apple cider	1 box powdered pectin
2 2-inch cinnamon sticks	4½ cups sugar
8 whole cloves	Paraffin, melted

Combine cider, cinnamon and cloves in saucepan. Bring to a boil. Simmer for 2 minutes. Cool to room temperature; strain. Stir in pectin. Bring to a boil, stirring constantly. Add sugar. Bring to a boil. Cook for 1 minute, stirring constantly. Remove from heat; skim. Pour into hot sterilized jelly glasses, leaving ½-inch headspace. Seal with paraffin and 2-piece lids. Yield: 5 to 6 cups.
Note: May package in inexpensive mugs for gifts by filling mugs ¾ full, covering with thin layer of melted paraffin and whipping lukewarm paraffin until frothy for topping mug.

HOT CHOCOLATE MIX

1 16-ounce package instant cocoa mix	3 tablespoons cocoa
1 8-quart package instant nonfat dry milk powder	1 16-ounce package confectioners' sugar
	1 6-ounce jar nondairy coffee creamer

Sift all ingredients together into bowl; mix well. Combine ¼ cup mix with 1 cup boiling water for each serving. Yield: 60 servings.

Pam Feldhaus, Epsilon Psi
Shelbyville, Tennessee

HOT COCOA MIX

1 8-quart package instant nonfat dry milk powder	1 6-ounce jar nondairy coffee creamer
1 16-ounce package instant cocoa mix	½ to 1 cup confectioners' sugar

Combine all ingredients in large bowl; mix well. Spoon into decorated airtight containers. Attach card with instructions to dissolve ¼ to ⅓ cup mix in 1 cup boiling water for each serving. Yield: 64 servings.

Sandi Davison, Preceptor Gamma Upsilon
Kansas City, Missouri

Patricia Hudson, Xi Alpha Psi
Superior, Wisconsin

KAHLUA

3 cups sugar	1 fifth of vodka
4 cups water	1 tablespoon vanilla
¼ cup freeze-dried instant coffee powder	extract

Combine sugar, water and coffee in saucepan. Bring to a boil; reduce heat. Simmer for 1 hour. Cool. Add vodka and vanilla; mix well. Pour into jars or bottles. May be used immediately. Yield: 2 quarts.

Dolores Snyder, Xi Alpha Pi
Hagerstown, Maryland

HOMEMADE VANILLA

8 vanilla beans	4 cups Brandy

Cut vanilla beans into thirds; slit to expose seed. Place in 1-quart jar. Add Brandy; seal jar. Shake well. Let stand at room temperature for 3 to 6 weeks, shaking several times weekly. Divide into small jars for gifts. Use for baking. Yield: 4 cups.

Carolyn Wyckoff, Preceptor Lambda
Arvada, Colorado

NEW YEAR'S DAY BEAN SOUP MIX

2 pounds dried large white butter beans	2 pounds dried split green peas
2 pounds dried large red kidney beans	2 pounds dried lentils
2 pounds dried small white butter beans	2 pounds dried pinto beans
2 pounds dried black-eyed peas	¼ pound dried barley
	¼ pound dried small white navy beans

Layer scant ¼ cup each of first 6 ingredients in order listed in 1-pint jar. Add ¼ cup pinto beans, 1 tablespoon barley and 1 tablespoon navy beans. Repeat with remaining jars. Attach Bean Soup recipe to each jar and give as gifts after Christmas. Yield: 15 jars.

NEW YEAR'S DAY BEAN SOUP

1 pint New Year's Day Bean Soup Mix	1 large onion, chopped
2 tablespoons salt	1 29-ounce can tomatoes
2 quarts water	1 pod red pepper
Ham, chopped	Juice of 1 lemon
	Salt and pepper to taste

Rinse beans; drain. Combine beans with salt in large soup pot. Add water to cover. Let stand overnight. Add 2 quarts water and ham. Simmer, covered, for 2½ to 3 hours. Add remaining ingredients. Simmer for 30 minutes longer. Serve with green salad and croutons. Yield: 6 servings.

Paula Middleton, Xi Mu Eta
Houston, Texas

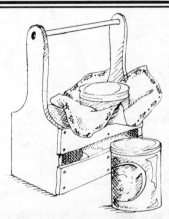

Package jars of mixes in napkin-lined wooden carry-all or tool box.

WILD RICE PILAF MIX

3 cups wild rice	3 tablespoons dried
2 cups dried lentils	parsley
2 cups raisins	2 tablespoons dried
1½ cups dried mushrooms	minced onion
1 cup barley	1 tablespoon basil
½ cup sunflower seed	2 teaspoons garlic powder
3 tablespoons instant	½ teaspoon cinnamon
beef bouillon	¼ teaspoon pepper

Rinse wild rice; drain. Spread in single layer on baking sheet. Bake at 300 degrees for 10 to 15 minutes or until dry. Cool. Combine with lentils, raisins, mushrooms, barley and sunflower seed in bowl. Add bouillon and remaining ingredients; mix well. Divide into gift portions; place in jars. Add recipe for Wild Rice Pilaf and tie with ribbon. Yield: 11 cups mix.

WILD RICE PILAF

⅓ cup Wild Rice Pilaf	1 cup water
Mix	3 carrots, chopped

Combine all ingredients in saucepan. Bring to a boil; reduce heat. Simmer, covered, for 50 minutes. Serve as side dish. Yield: 2 servings.

Mary Ann Madar, Laureate Alpha Delta
Elizabeth Township, Pennsylvania

Layer individual pickled vegetables in pretty glass gift jar. Asparagus is lovely packed like this also (alternate outer spears so that some tips point up and some down).

DILLED ASPARAGUS

Fresh asparagus	Fresh dill
2 cups water	Cloves of garlic
2½ cups white vinegar	Red peppers
¼ cup salt	

Blanch asparagus in boiling water in saucepan for 1½ minutes; drain on paper towels. Bring 2 cups water, vinegar and salt to a boil in saucepan. Place several sprigs of dill, 1 clove of garlic and 1 red pepper in each hot sterilized jar. Pack asparagus, tips down, in prepared jars. Fill to top with boiling brine; seal with 2-piece lids. Invert sealed jars on towel. Let stand until cool.
Note: Spread thin ham slices with cream cheese, add an asparagus spear, roll to enclose asparagus and cut into slices. Serve as hors d'oeuvres or serve plain, drained asparagus spears as appetizer.

D. Jean Colburn, Zeta Nu
Boardman, Oregon

BREAD AND BUTTER CUCUMBER PICKLES

1 quart cucumbers	2 cups sugar
6 large onions, peeled	1 teaspoon mustard seed
1 tablespoon canning salt	1 teaspoon celery seed
1 cup vinegar	¼ teaspoon turmeric

Slice cucumbers and onions paper thin. Place in bowl. Cover with mixture of water and salt. Let stand for 2 hours. Drain. Combine vinegar, sugar and spices in saucepan. Bring to a boil. Add vegetables. Cook for 5 minutes. Spoon into hot sterilized jars, leaving ½-inch headspace; seal with 2-piece lids. Process in boiling water bath for 10 minutes. Yield: 2 quarts.

Reva J. Falk, Preceptor Alpha Epsilon
Tucson, Arizona

BREAD AND BUTTER PICKLES

4 quarts sliced cucumbers	5 cups sugar
6 medium white onions,	1½ teaspoons turmeric
sliced	1½ teaspoons celery seed
2 green peppers, chopped	2 tablespoons mustard
3 cloves of garlic	seed
⅓ cup medium-coarse salt	3 cups cider vinegar

Combine cucumbers, onions, green peppers and garlic in bowl. Sprinkle with salt. Cover with cracked ice; mix well. Let stand, covered, for 3 hours. Drain well. Remove and discard garlic. Place vegetables in large saucepan. Add mixture of sugar, turmeric, celery seed, mustard seed and vinegar. Bring just to a boil. Spoon into hot sterilized 1-pint jars, leaving ½-inch headspace; seal with 2-piece lids. Process in boiling water bath for 10 minutes. Yield: 8 pints.

Cheri Brown, Preceptor Sigma
Fort Washington, Maryland

MUSTARD PICKLES

8 cups chopped onions	12 small cucumbers,
Flowerets of 1 head	chopped
cauliflower	1 bunch celery, chopped
2 or 3 green tomatoes,	5 cups sugar
chopped	2 cups flour
12 red or green sweet	¼ cup mustard
peppers, chopped	1 tablespoon turmeric
1 head cabbage, chopped	6 cups vinegar

Combine all vegetables except celery with salted water to cover in large saucepan. Place celery in salted water to cover in saucepan. Let stand overnight. Cook in salted water until tender; drain. Combine sugar and flour in bowl. Combine mustard and turmeric in bowl. Add sugar mixture; mix well. Stir into heated vinegar in saucepan. Add vegetables; mix well. Cook over low heat for 2 hours. Spoon into hot sterilized jars, leaving ½-inch headspace. Cool. Seal with 2-piece lids. Yield: 10 quarts.

Mary Anne Johnson, Beta Lambda
Evanston, Wyoming

RED CINNAMON PICKLES

2 gallons large cucumbers	2 cups vinegar
2 cups pickling lime	10 cups sugar
8½ quarts water	3 cups water
1 cup vinegar	8 cinnamon sticks
1 1-ounce bottle of red	1 8-ounce package
food coloring	red hot cinnamon
1 tablespoon alum	candies

Peel and seed cucumbers; cut into sticks. Combine with lime and 8½ quarts water in large bowl. Let stand for 24 hours, stirring occasionally. Drain and rinse well. Cover with fresh water. Let stand for 3 hours. Drain. Combine cucumbers, 1 cup vinegar, food coloring and alum in saucepan. Add water to cover. Simmer for 2 hours. Drain. Combine 2 cups vinegar, sugar, 3 cups water, cinnamon sticks and candy in saucepan. Cook until candies dissolve. Pour over cucumbers. Let stand overnight. Drain into saucepan. Reheat syrup and repeat process 3 times. Pack into hot sterilized jars, leaving ½-inch headspace; seal with 2-piece lids. Process in boiling water bath for 10 minutes. Yield: 6 quarts.

Mary Seffert, Xi Sigma Pi
Hilltop Lakes, Texas

CRANBERRY-BLUEBERRY RELISH

1 12-ounce package	2 navel oranges
cranberries	1 20-ounce can crushed
1 16-ounce package	pineapple
frozen blueberries	1 cup sugar
2 Delicious apples, cored	

Chop cranberries, blueberries, apples and oranges coarsely 1 at a time in food processor. Combine with pineapple and sugar. Chill, covered, in refrigerator for 1 to 2 days. Yield: 10 cups.

Mary Seffert, Xi Sigma Pi
Hilltop Lakes, Texas

BRANDIED CRANBERRIES

| 1 12-ounce package | 2 cups sugar |
| cranberries | ½ cup Brandy |

Place cranberries in 9x13-inch baking dish. Sprinkle with sugar and Brandy. Cover with foil. Bake at 325 degrees for 1 hour, stirring occasionally. Store in covered containers in refrigerator. Serve as sauce with chicken or turkey. Yield: 4 cups.

Marjorie Haley, Preceptor Gamma Delta
Olalla, Washington

CRANBERRY-WINE SAUCE

3 cups cranberries	1½ tablespoons
1½ cups sugar	cornstarch
1¼ cups Port	¼ cup cold water

Bring cranberries, sugar and wine to a boil in large saucepan. Cook for 5 to 7 minutes or until cranberry skins pop. Dissolve cornstarch in water in small bowl. Stir into cranberry mixture. Bring to a boil, stirring constantly. Cook for 1 minute, stirring constantly. Pour into hot sterilized jars; seal with 2-piece lids. Serve warm sauce with pork or poultry. Yield: 3 cups.

Diane A. Burns, Xi Lambda Delta
Holiday, Florida

UNCOOKED RELISH

2 heads cabbage	½ cup salt
8 carrots	4 cups sugar
4 red sweet peppers	6 cups vinegar
4 green peppers	1 tablespoon celery seed
12 onions	1 tablespoon mustard
1 bunch celery	seed

Put all vegetables through food grinder. Place in bowl. Add salt; mix well. Let stand for 2 hours. Drain. Add sugar, vinegar and spices; mix well. Spoon into sterilized jars; seal. Store in refrigerator. Yield: 6 quarts.

Reva J. Falk, Preceptor Alpha Epsilon
Tuscon, Arizona

Relishes are beautiful in glass gift jars.

CRACKER CRISPIES

1 12-ounce package oyster crackers	½ teaspoon garlic powder
½ teaspoon lemon-pepper seasoning	1 4-ounce package Hidden Valley Original salad dressing mix
1 teaspoon (heaping) dillweed	1 cup oil

Spread crackers in 9x13-inch dish. Sprinkle with mixture of dry ingredients. Drizzle oil over crackers. Toss crackers lightly every 5 minutes until all oil is absorbed. Store in airtight container. Serve as snack or with soups or salads. Yield: 1¼ pounds.

Nancy Burns, Preceptor Alpha Gamma
Scottsdale, Arizona

CRAZY CRUNCH

½ cup all-purpose flour	1 12-ounce can mixed nuts
¼ cup Parmesan cheese	
2 tablespoons cornstarch	1 6-ounce box Brownberry rye croutons
2 teaspoons garlic salt	
½ cup beer	

Combine first 5 ingredients in bowl. Beat with rotary beater until blended. Fold in nuts and croutons; stir until coated. Spread in greased 10x15-inch baking pan. Bake at 300 degrees for 45 minutes, stirring occasionally. Cool. Yield: 6 cups.

Karen Wrenn, Xi Alpha Pi
Edgewater, Maryland

Package snack mixes in plastic bags. Place in serving basket, wrap with cellophane, and tie with pretty ribbon.

TV SNACK CRITTERS

1 envelope ranch-style salad dressing mix	¼ teaspoon garlic powder
¾ cup oil	¼ teaspoon onion powder
1 teaspoon lemon pepper	2 12-ounce packages oyster crackers

Combine salad dressing mix, oil and seasonings in bowl; mix well. Add crackers, stirring to coat well. Pour into 9x13-inch baking pan. Bake at 200 degrees for 1 hour, stirring every 15 minutes. Cool. Place in decorative airtight container.

Catherine Maulsby, Xi Epsilon Omicron
Claremore, Oklahoma

TEXAS TRASH

1 20-ounce box rice Chex cereal	2 cups salted nuts
1 20-ounce box wheat Chex cereal	1 cup oil
	¼ cup Worcestershire sauce
1 8-ounce package pretzel sticks	1 teaspoon hot sauce
1 package goldfish crackers	2 tablespoons seasoned salt

Combine cereals, pretzels, crackers and nuts in large shallow pan. Drizzle with mixture of oil, Worcestershire sauce, hot sauce and seasoned salt. Bake at 250 degrees for 20 minutes, stirring every 5 minutes. Turn off oven. Let stand in closed oven until cool. Spoon into 6 large-mouth 1-quart jars with 2-piece lids. Place lids on jars. Cover with 6-inch cloth circles. Seal with rims. Tie red or green bows around top. Yield: 6 quarts.

Dorothy Hartigan, Xi Sigma Pi
Hilltop Lakes, Texas

CURRIED NUTS

2 tablespoons butter	¼ teaspoon cayenne pepper
2 tablespoons oil	
1½ teaspoons Worcestershire sauce	½ teaspoon salt
	1 pound pecan or walnut halves
1½ tablespoons curry powder	

Combine butter, oil, Worcestershire sauce and seasonings in large heavy skillet. Heat until butter is melted; mix well. Stir in nuts, coating well. Spread on baking sheet lined with baking parchment. Bake at 300 degrees for 10 minutes. Turn off oven. Let nuts stand in closed oven until cool. Place in decorative airtight containers. Yield: 1 pound.

Pat Roether, Xi Eta
Ogden, Utah

MERINGUE BAKED NUTS

1 pound mixed whole nuts	Dash of salt
1 tablespoon sesame seed	1 cup sugar
2 egg whites	1 teaspoon ginger
	½ cup butter

Spread nuts and sesame seed in 9x13-inch baking pan. Toast at 325 degrees for 10 minutes. Beat egg whites with salt in mixer bowl until frothy. Add mixture of sugar and ginger, beating constantly at high speed until stiff peaks form. Stir in nuts, coating well. Melt butter in 9x13-inch baking dish. Drop nuts by spoonfuls into melted butter in pan. Bake for 40 minutes, stirring every 10 minutes. Remove to foil to cool. Place in decorated airtight container. Serve as appetizer or over ice cream.

Susan G. Riedel, Phi Eta
Niceville, Florida

GLAZED PEANUTS

1 cup water	4 cups peanuts
2 cups sugar	

Combine water and sugar in saucepan. Cook over high heat until sugar dissolves. Add peanuts. Bring to a boil; reduce heat. Cook over low heat for 30 to 45 minutes or until liquid evaporates. Spread peanuts on cookie sheet. Bake at 300 degrees for 30 minutes. Cool. Store in airtight container. Yield: 4 cups.

Peggy W. Cox, Preceptor Nu
Anniston, Alabama

SUGAR-COATED PEANUTS

2 cups sugar	4 cups raw peanuts
1 cup water	

Combine sugar and water in cast-iron skillet; mix well. Stir in peanuts. Cook over medium heat until mixture crystallizes; stir constantly. Spread on a greased baking sheet, separating peanuts with fork. Bake at 300 degrees for 20 to 25 minutes. Cool. Place in plastic Christmas tree containers. Yield: 4 cups.

Sally Finch, Xi Iota Zeta
Galesburg, Indiana

FROSTED PECANS

1 egg white	1 cup sugar
1 teaspoon cold water	1 teaspoon cinnamon
1 pound large pecan halves	1 teaspoon salt

Beat egg white with water in mixer bowl until frothy. Stir in pecans. Mix remaining ingredients in small bowl. Add to pecans; mix well. Spread on baking sheet. Bake at 225 degrees for 1 hour, stirring occasionally. Cool. Place in decorated containers. Yield: 1 pound.

Frances Brillian, Xi Delta
Rochester, New York

SPICED PECANS

1 egg white	½ cup sugar
1 teaspoon cold water	¼ teaspoon salt
1 pound pecans	½ teaspoon cinnamon

Beat egg white and water in mixer bowl until frothy. Add pecans, stirring to coat well. Add pecans to mixture of sugar, salt and cinnamon in bowl. Spread in buttered 10x15-inch baking pan. Bake at 225 degrees for 1 hour, stirring every 15 minutes. Cool. Place in decorated container. Yield: 1 pound.

Lisa Clark, Lambda Nu
Pattonsburg, Missouri

CHINESE FRIED WALNUTS

4 cups walnuts	Oil for deep frying
6 cups water	Salt to taste
½ cup sugar	

Combine walnuts and water in saucepan. Bring to a boil. Cook for 1 minute; drain. Rinse under running water; drain. Combine walnuts and sugar in bowl. Stir until sugar dissolves. Heat 1 inch oil to 350 degrees in electric skillet. Deep-fry walnuts ½ at a time for 5 minutes or until golden. Drain in sieve. Sprinkle with salt. Drain on paper towels. Pack in gift tins. Yield: 4 cups.

Tammy Mercer, Xi Gamma Xi
Corvallis, Oregon

Package spiced or sugared nuts in French canning jar. Arrange in decorated miniature bushel basket with whole nuts and nut cracker.

BAKED CARAMEL CORN

1 cup butter	1 teaspoon salt
2 cups packed brown	½ teaspoon soda
sugar	1 teaspoon vanilla extract
½ cup corn syrup	6 quarts popped popcorn

Melt butter in saucepan. Blend in brown sugar, corn syrup and salt. Bring to a boil, stirring constantly. Cook for 5 minutes; do not stir. Remove from heat. Stir in soda and vanilla. Pour gradually over popcorn in bowl, mixing well. Spread in 2 shallow baking pans. Bake at 250 degrees for 1 hour, stirring every 15 minutes. Cool completely. Break apart. Place popcorn in decorative airtight containers. Yield: 6 quarts.

Kathleen Clinton, Preceptor Alpha Lambda
Rochester, Michigan

BAKED CARAMEL CORN CLUSTERS

28 caramel candies	1 cup peanuts
¼ cup sugar	2 quarts popped popcorn
¼ cup water	

Combine caramels, sugar and water in saucepan. Bring to a boil over low heat, stirring constantly until smooth. Cook for 5 minutes, stirring constantly. Pour over peanuts and popcorn in bowl, tossing with forks to coat well. Spread on waxed paper. Cool. Break into clusters.

Kathleen Clinton, Preceptor Alpha Lambda
Rochester, Michigan

Package caramel corn in colored plastic bags according to the size of the recipients family and decorate with stickers and colorful ribbon ties. Or, package in metal canisters personalized or decorated with acrylic paint markers.

CARAMEL CORN

1 cup melted margarine	1 tablespoon vanilla
2 cups packed brown	extract
sugar	1 teaspoon soda
½ cup sugar	7½ quarts popped
1 teaspoon salt	popcorn

Combine first 4 ingredients in saucepan; mix well. Bring to a boil. Cook for 5 minutes; remove from heat. Stir in vanilla and soda. Pour over popped popcorn. Place in large baking pan. Bake at 200 degrees for 1 hour, stirring every 15 minutes. Cool. Package in gift containers. Yield: 7½ quarts.

Shirley Fitch, Xi Upsilon
Flagstaff, Arizona

CARAMEL CORN WITH NUTS

2 cups packed brown	1 teaspoon vanilla extract
sugar	6 quarts popped popcorn
1 cup margarine	1 cup almonds
½ cup light corn syrup	1 cup pecans
½ teaspoon soda	

Combine first 3 ingredients in saucepan; mix well. Bring to a boil. Cook for 5 minutes; remove from heat. Stir in soda and vanilla. Pour over popcorn. Add nuts; stir until popcorn and nuts are coated. Place in 2 greased 9x13-inch baking pans. Bake at 250 degrees for 1½ hours, stirring occasionally. Cool. Store in airtight containers. Yield: 6½ quarts.

Kayte Morton, Xi Upsilon Delta
Borrego Springs, California

CARAMEL CORN WITH CASHEWS

1 cup melted margarine	½ teaspoon soda
2 cups packed brown	1 teaspoon vanilla extract
sugar	6 or 7 quarts popped
½ cup light corn syrup	popcorn
½ teaspoon salt	Cashews

Combine first 4 ingredients in saucepan; mix well. Bring to a boil, stirring constantly. Cook for 5 minutes; do not stir. Remove from heat. Stir in soda and vanilla. Pour over popped popcorn; mix well. Add cashews; mix well. Place in large greased baking pan. Bake at 250 degrees for 1 hour, stirring every 10 minutes. Cool. Store in airtight container. Yield: 6 or 7 quarts.

Marilyn Christensen, Eta Alpha
Quincy, California

CARAMEL CORN WITH PEANUTS

2 cups packed brown sugar	1 cup raw peanuts
½ cup light corn syrup	6 to 8 quarts popped popcorn
1 cup butter	

Bring brown sugar, corn syrup and butter to a boil in saucepan. Cook for 5 minutes. Pour over peanuts and popcorn in bowl, tossing to coat well. Spread on greased baking sheet. Bake at 225 degrees for 45 minutes. Cool. Place in decorative airtight container. Yield: 6 to 8 quarts.

Wanda Odom, Preceptor Epsilon Upsilon
Denison, Texas

CARAMEL POPCORN

2 cups popcorn	¼ teaspoon soda
1 cup butter	1 teaspoon vanilla extract
½ cup dark syrup	

Pop popcorn according to package directions; spread in baking pan. Bring butter and syrup to a boil in saucepan. Cook for 5 minutes. Stir in soda and vanilla. Pour mixture gradually over popcorn; mix gently. Bake at 250 degrees for 1 hour, stirring occasionally. Cool. Store in airtight container.

Brenda Steakley, Epsilon Kappa
Nashville, Tennessee

POPCORN BALLS

¾ cup light corn syrup	2 tablespoons water
¼ cup butter	1 16-ounce package confectioners' sugar
1 cup chopped marshmallows	5 quarts popped popcorn

Combine corn syrup, butter, marshmallows, water and confectioners' sugar in saucepan. Bring to a boil over low heat, stirring constantly. Tint with red or green food coloring if desired. Pour over popcorn in large bowl, tossing to coat well. Shape quickly into balls with butter-coated hands. Place popcorn balls on waxed paper. Let stand until cool. Wrap individually in plastic wrap; tie with colorful curling ribbon.

Margaret A. Bohls, Preceptor Beta Lambda
Arvada, Colorado

JINGLE POPCORN BALLS

12 cups popped popcorn	1½ teaspoons vinegar
2 cups chopped gumdrops	¾ teaspoon salt
1 cup chopped nuts	1 tablespoon butter or margarine
1 cup light corn syrup	1½ teaspoons vanilla extract
½ cup honey	

Combine popcorn, gumdrops and nuts in bowl. Mix corn syrup, honey, vinegar and salt in saucepan. Bring to a boil over medium heat. Cook to 260 to 265 degrees on candy thermometer, hard-ball stage. Stir in butter and vanilla. Pour over popcorn mixture; mix well. Shape into 2-inch balls. Place on waxed paper-lined surface. Let stand until firm. Wrap in plastic wrap; tie with ribbon. Yield: 2½ dozen.

APRICOT LEATHER

1 pound dried apricots	2 cups confectioners' sugar
1 cup boiling water	
2 teaspoons grated lemon rind	

Combine apricots and boiling water in glass dish. Let stand for 12 hours. Put through food grinder fitted with fine blade. Combine apricots and lemon rind; mix well. Roll fruit into 12x16-inch rectangle on surface sprinkled with confectioners' sugar, sprinkling surface of candy with confectioners' sugar as necessary. Cut into 1¼x2-inch strips. Coat with confectioners' sugar. Store in aritight container.

PEACH LEATHER

10 cups sliced peeled peaches	1 cup sugar
	1 teaspoon ascorbic acid

Combine peaches, sugar and ascorbic acid in saucepan. Simmer until sugar is dissolved, stirring constantly. Purée in blender container. Cool to lukewarm. Spread ¼ inch thick on baking sheets lined with plastic wrap. Bake at 140 degrees until dry; leave oven door ajar. Cut into strips. Roll in plastic wrap. Pack in glass apothecary jars or tall mugs for gifts.

FRUIT AND NUT MIX

½ cup raisins	½ cup carob chips
½ cup dried banana flakes	½ cup cashews
½ cup coarsely chopped dates	½ cup sunflower seed
½ cup coarsely chopped dried apricots	½ cup coconut chips
½ cup coarsely chopped dried apples	1 cup granola

Combine raisins, bananas, dates, apricots and apples in bowl. Add carob chips, cashews, sunflower seed, coconut and granola; mix lightly. Store in airtight containers. Yield: 5½ cups.

HOLIDAY GRANOLA

6 cups oats	1 cup safflower oil
1 cup sesame seed	1 cup honey
1 cup sunflower seed	2 teaspoons vanilla extract
1 cup wheat germ	1 cup raisins
1 cup shredded coconut	2 cups small red and green gumdrops
1 cup chopped nuts	
1 cup nonfat dry milk powder	

Mix first 7 ingredients in large bowl. Combine safflower oil, honey and vanilla in blender container. Process until well blended. Add to oats mixture; mix well. Spread in 2 large baking pans. Bake at 300 degrees for 1 hour or until brown, stirring frequently. Cool. Mix in raisins and gumdrops. Store in airtight container. Yield: 16 cups.

CHRISTMAS CANDLE RING

30 large marshmallows	**3½ cups cornflakes**
½ cup margarine	**Teaberries**
1 teaspoon vanilla extract	**Yellow felt or construction**
2 teaspoons green food	**paper flame**
coloring	

Combine marshmallows, margarine, vanilla and food coloring in double boiler. Heat over hot water until melted and well blended, stirring frequently. Stir in cornflakes gradually; mix until coated. Drop by spoonfuls onto waxed paper; shape into wreath around Cinnamon Jelly Candles jar. Decorate with teaberries. Let stand until firm and dry. Glue flame to lid of jar. Yield: 1 ring.

CINNAMON JELLY CANDLES

3 cups unsweetened	**1 teaspoon red food**
apple juice	**coloring**
1 package Sure-Jel	**½ teaspoon oil of**
3½ cups sugar	**cinnamon**

Combine apple juice and Sure-Jel in large saucepan. Bring to a full boil. Stir in sugar. Bring to a full rolling boil. Boil for 2 minutes, stirring constantly. Remove from heat. Add food coloring and cinnamon. Let stand for several minutes or until skin forms on surface; skim. Pour into 4 hot sterilized tall slender jars such as olive jars; seal with lids. Let stand until cool. Yield: 4 cups.

June C. Hackett, Laureate Omicron
Sunbury, Pennsylvania

Edible candle rings are both decorative and delicious. Use as centerpiece, and serve during the party or at another meal.

SANTA LUCIA CANDLE RING

2 packages dry yeast	**½ cup chopped citron**
½ cup warm water	**½ cup chopped almonds**
½ cup sugar	**1 tablespoon grated**
1 teaspoon salt	**lemon rind**
2 eggs, beaten	**2 to 2½ cups flour**
2½ cups flour	**1 cup confectioners' sugar**
¼ cup butter, softened	**1 tablespoon (about) water**
Pinch of crushed saffron	**Red and green candied**
½ cup lukewarm milk	**cherries**

Dissolve yeast in ½ cup water in mixer bowl. Add next 5 ingredients and mixture of saffron and milk; beat until smooth. Stir in citron, almonds, lemon rind and 2 to 2½ cups flour to make easily handled dough. Knead on floured surface for 10 minutes or until smooth and elastic. Place in greased bowl, turning to grease surface. Let rise, covered, for 1½ hours or until doubled in bulk. Roll ⅔ of the dough into three 25-inch ropes on floured surface. Braid loosely on greased baking sheet. Shape into ring around 4-inch can; seal ends. Roll remaining dough into three 16-inch ropes. Braid on greased baking sheet. Shape into ring around 4-inch can; seal ends. Let rings rise, covered, for 45 minutes or until doubled in bulk. Remove cans. Bake at 375 degrees for 20 to 25 minutes. Mix confectioners' sugar and 1 tablespoon water in bowl. Drizzle over rings. Place small ring on larger ring. Place tapers into ring.

COFFEE CAKE CANDLE RING

½ cup sugar	**1½ to 2½ cups flour**
¼ cup margarine	**1 8-ounce package dried**
½ cup milk, scalded	**apricots**
2 packages dry yeast	**Sugar to taste**
½ cup warm water	**½ cup crushed pineapple**
3 cups flour	**1 cup confectioners' sugar**
1½ teaspoons salt	**¼ teaspoon vanilla extract**
2 eggs, beaten	**2 tablespoons water**

Combine first 3 ingredients in mixer bowl; cool to lukewarm. Dissolve yeast in ½ cup water. Add to milk mixture. Beat in 3 cups flour, salt and eggs. Stir in 1½ to 2½ cups flour to make stiff dough. Knead on floured surface for 9 minutes or until smooth and elastic. Place in greased bowl, turning to grease surface. Let rise, covered, for 1 hour or until doubled in bulk. Cook apricots with sugar to taste using package directions; drain. Purée with pineapple in blender container. Roll half the dough into 9x18-inch rectangle. Spread half the apricot mixture over 12 inches of length of dough. Fold unspread dough to cover half the filling. Fold again to cover remaining filling, forming 2 layers filling and 3 layers dough. Seal edges. Repeat process with remaining dough and filling. Place seam side down on greased baking sheet. Shape into rings around 4-inch cans; seal ends together. Cut ⅔ through ring from outer edge at 1-inch intervals; turn slices cut side down. Let rise, covered, for 1 hour. Remove cans. Bake at 350 degrees for 35 minutes. Combine remaining ingredients in bowl. Drizzle over warm coffee cakes. Place candles in center of each.

TURKEY CENTERPIECE

1 8x8-inch square red
   felt
1 1½x2-inch piece
   yellow felt
Glue
Polyester stuffing

2 plastic movable eyes
1 small oval basket
   without handle
Pine cones
8 to 12 large colorful
   fall leaves

Fold red felt in half. Pin turkey head pattern on felt; cut out. Cut beak from yellow felt. Insert beak between head pieces as indicated. Stitch as indicated. Stuff with polyester stuffing. Glue eyes as indicated. Fill basket with enough pine cones to form plump turkey body. Place turkey head at 1 end of basket. Arrange leaves at other end to resemble tail feathers.

Sharon Klingaman, Xi Delta Tau
Stillwater, Oklahoma

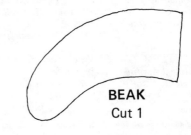

BEAK
Cut 1

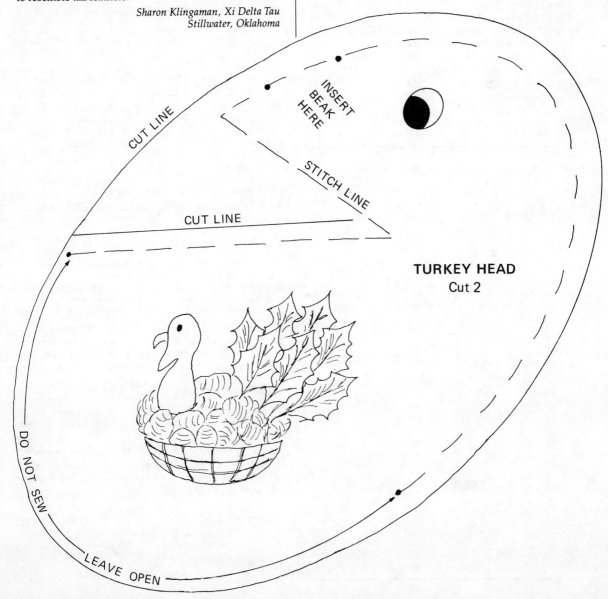

CUT LINE

INSERT BEAK HERE

STITCH LINE

CUT LINE

TURKEY HEAD
Cut 2

DO NOT SEW

LEAVE OPEN

CLOTHESPIN REINDEER ORNAMENT

3 flat wooden clothespins	*1 ⅜-inch gold jingle bell*
Tacky Glue	*1 9-inch gold metallic*
2 7-millimeter movable	*thread*
eyes	*1 ¾x3-inch piece green*
1 ¼-inch red cotton	*felt*
pompon	*1 ½x¾-inch piece*
2 small green leaf sequins	*brown felt*
6 5-millimeter red cup	*1 ½-inch white acrylic*
sequins	*pompon*

Turn 1 clothespin upside down. Glue on eyes and red pompon for nose. Glue leaf sequins and 3 red sequins above eyes (see diagram). Glue remaining 2 clothespins together at slotted sides for body. Glue head to body. Place bell on gold thread. Hang around reindeer's neck, knotting thread behind head and at ends. Round off corners of green felt. Glue on 3 red sequins. Glue felt across top of clothespins on reindeer's back. Cut four ¼x⅜-inch pieces of brown felt. Cut notch on 1 long side of each piece for hooves. Glue on ends of clothespins. Glue on white pompon for tail.

Barbara P. Fowler, Laureate Theta
Richland, Virginia

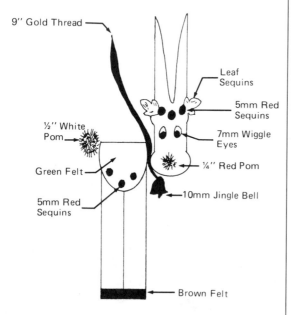

Use "Rudolph" on your tree or packages. Directions for the clothespin Reindeer Ornament are above.

SNOWFLAKE PLANTER

Broken brick, porous	*¼ cup ammonia*
rocks, foam rubber or	*Food coloring*
cellulose pieces	*¼ cup salt*
¼ cup water	*2 tablespoons water*
¼ cup bluing	*2 tablespoons ammonia*

Soak brick in water until damp but not dripping. Arrange in shallow glass bowl. Mix ¼ cup water, bluing and ¼ cup ammonia in bowl. Pour over brick pieces. Add drops of food coloring as desired. Sprinkle with salt. Crystals will begin forming in about 6 hours. Add mixture of 2 tablespoons water and 2 tablespoons ammonia every 2 days. Crystals will stop growing when water and ammonia evaporate.

Note: Do not allow snowflake crystals to touch furniture or marble.

Carole Chorlton, Preceptor Alpha Xi
Jacksonville, Florida

CANDLES AND CINNAMON CENTERPIECE

1 (9x13-inch)	*2 (6-inch) fat*
straw basket	*red candles*
2 (12-inch)fat	*2 (4-inch) fat*
white candles	*white candles*
2 (12-inch) fat	*1 (4-inch) fat*
red candles	*red candle*
3 (8-inch) fat	*24 (6-inch) cinnamon*
white candles	*sticks*

Arrange candles of varying heights in basket. Intersperse with cinnamon sticks.

POMANDER AND TAPER CENTERPIECE

6 to 8 oranges	*Several bunches dried*
6 to 8 limes	*herbs*
6 to 8 lemons	*9 (12-inch) white tapers*
2 or 3 small grapefruit	*1 (18-inch oval)*
1 box whole cloves	*wicker basket*

Stud fruit with cloves in decorative patterns to make pomanders. Arrange in basket. Interspersed with dried herbs. Place tapers between fruit to fit securely. Place tapers in candle holders first if necessary.

LIGHTS AND GLASS CENTERPIECE

1 5-foot long	*Flowers in season*
rectangular mirror	*Votive candles for floating*
Assorted glass dishes	

Place long rectangular mirror on table. Arrange a variety of clear or colored glass dishes on mirror. Fill with water. Float blossoms and votive candles in each. Vary flowers and scent of candles.

Beth Kuchen, Omega
Whidedish, Montana

SPICE SCENT

¼ cup crushed cardamom pods	6 peppercorns
1 (3-inch) cinnamon stick	1 whole nutmeg, crushed
	½ teaspoon whole cloves

Combine all ingredients in small saucepan. Add 1 to 2 cups water. Simmer over low heat to fill house with spicy scent. Package dry ingredients in small cloth bags to give as gifts.

CHRISTMAS POTPOURRI

6 cups fresh rose, honeysuckle, sweet pea or violet petals	1 teaspoon salt
¼ cup whole cloves	1 cup orrisroot
¼ cup broken cinnamon sticks	¾ teaspoon cinnamon oil
¼ cup whole allspice	¾ teaspoon lemon oil
	¾ teaspoon rose oil
	1½ teaspoons musk oil

Let flower petals stand for several weeks until completely dry. Combine flower petals, cloves, cinnamon, allspice, salt, orrisroot and fragrant oils in container. Let stand, covered, for 3 to 4 weeks. Store in airtight containers. Pack in glass jars or sew into sachets or pillows for gifts. Yield: 3 to 4 cups.

HOLIDAY POTPOURRI

6 drops oil of myrrh	6 cups mixed evergreens
6 drops citrus oil	3 tablespoons dried lavendar buds
2 tablespoons orrisroot	Tiny pine cones
Rind of 2 oranges	Tiny dried flowers
½ cup bay leaves	
2 ounces cinnamon sticks	

Sprinkle oils over orrisroot. Let stand until oils are absorbed. Cut orange rind into ⅛-inch strips. Crush bay leaves slightly. Break cinnamon into small pieces. Combine orrisroot, orange rind, bay leaves, cinnamon, evergreens and lavendar in large plastic bag; shake to mix well. Let stand in closed bag at 60 to 70 degrees for 2 weeks. Add pine cones and dried flowers for bulk and color. Divide into small decorative jars or baskets for gifts. Yield: 8 cups.

Barbara T. Redman, Xi Alpha Theta
Chestertown, Maryland

WOODSY POTPOURRI

Acorns	Whole cloves
Small pine cones and needles	Gingerroot
Sweet gum balls	Star anise
Chestnuts	Patchouli leaves
Whole nutmeg, cracked	Small pieces of sandalwood
Eucalyptus leaves	Sandalwood oil
Bay leaves	Spruce or pine oil
Coriander seed	Patchouli oil
Rose hips	

Combine 4 cups dried materials and 2 drops of each oil in bowl; mix well. Let stand, covered, for 4 to 6 weeks. Place in large decorative bowl. Yield: 4 cups.

POTPOURRI HOOP

1 (4-inch) wooden embroidery hoop	½ yard ruffled lace
1 (6-inch) square sheer fabric backing	¼ yard (⅛-inch wide) ribbon
Potpourri	½ yard (½-inch wide) ribbon
¼ yard flat lace	

Open hoop. Place sheer fabric over inner loop. Place potpourri on sheer fabric. Top with flat lace. Place outer loop over inner loop; push half way down. Turn hoop over. Trim excess fabric and lace. Close hoop completely; tighten screw. Glue ruffled lace around hoop edge. Tie ⅛-inch ribbon through screw for hanging. Tie bow with ½-inch ribbon. Glue to top of hoop. May make miniature hoops to use for tree ornaments.

SCENTED COOKIE CUTTER ORNAMENTS

1-inch wide print ribbon	Netting
Large 1-inch thick holiday cookie cutters open on both sides	Silver rickrack
	Potpourri
	Narrow ribbon

Glue print ribbon around outside of cookie cutters to cover edge. Glue netting across one open side; trim. Glue silver rickrack to cover raw edges. Fill with potpourri. Repeat process with netting and rickrack to cover open side. Attach ribbon hanger made of narrow ribbon to top of cookie cutter.

SPICED KISSING BALL

1 (4-inch) styrofoam ball	Whole celery seed
Whole cloves	Ground mustard
Whole anise seed	Whole caraway seed
Ground cinnamon	Curry powder
Whole poppy seed	1 sprig of mistletoe
Ground paprika	7½ inches velvet ribbon

Mark ball into 8 equal sections with pencil. Outline sections with cloves. Work on 1 section at a time. Spread each section with glue. Cover 1 section with each seed or spice, alternating sections of whole and ground spices. Let stand until dry. Attach mistletoe to 1 end and pin ribbon loop to top for hanging.

CHRISTMAS FRAGRANCE

Rind of ½ orange	Rind of ½ lemon
⅛ large cinnamon stick	¼ cup whole cloves
2 bay leaves	1½ cups water

Combine all ingredients in saucepan. Bring to a boil; reduce heat. Simmer as long as desired, adding water as necessary Gives the whole house a lovely fragrance.
Yield: Enough scent for 1 use.
Note: Give mixture of first 5 ingredients with instructions for use as gift.

Gloria Hayungs, Rho Rho
Granville, Illinois

PLAY CLAY HEART WREATH

PLAY CLAY

1 cup cornstarch	*3 tablespoons ground*
2 cups baking soda	*ginger*
1½ cups cold water	*Ground cinnamon*

Combine cornstarch and soda in saucepan; mix well. Stir in mixture of water and ginger. Cook over medium heat until very thick, stirring constantly. Mixture will come to a boil, thicken in lumps, then form thick mixture which holds its shape. Spoon onto plate; cover with damp cloth. Cool. Divide into 2 portions. Keep 1 portion covered with damp cloth. Knead enough cinnamon into remaining portion on surface sprinkled with cornstarch to color deep brown. Knead until smooth and pliable. Cover with damp cloth. Knead uncolored portion until smooth and pliable. Store in airtight container or plastic bag in cool place for up to 2 weeks.

HEART WREATH

1 recipe Play Clay	*Foam wreath form*
16 paper clips	*9 (3-inch) cinnamon*
3 yards (1-inch wide)	*sticks*
plaid ribbon	
1 yard (¾-inch wide)	
red ribbon	

Roll each portion Play Clay separately to ½-inch thickness. Stack portions. Roll as for jelly roll from narrow side. Cut into 1½-inch slices. Roll each slice to ¼-inch thickness. Cover unused Play Clay with damp cloth. Cut each slice with 2-inch heart-shaped cookie cutter. Punch hole in top with straw. Place on waxed paper-lined wire rack. Let stand for several hours to overnight or until tops of hearts are dry. Turn hearts. Dry until hardened, turning occasionally. Straighten paper clips. Bend in half to V-shape. Cut plaid ribbon into 6-inch lengths. Cut red ribbon into 12-inch lengths. Thread plaid ribbon through hearts. Tie with knot toward back. Insert paper clip into knot with V at knot. Insert clips into wreath. Tie red ribbon around V's in remaining clips. Tie 3 cinnamon sticks with each ribbon. Insert into wreath.

CINNAMON ORNAMENTS

1 1-ounce can cinnamon	*Waxed paper*
1 plastic bag	*Cookie cutters*
1 16-ounce can	*Toothpick*
applesauce	*Yarn or ribbon*
Rolling pin	

Empty cinnamon into plastic bag. Add applesauce gradually, holding bag closed at top and kneading applesauce and cinnamon to doughy consistency. Shape into ball on waxed paper. Roll between waxed paper to ¼-inch thickness. Cut with cookie cutters; make holes for hanging using toothpick. Let dry for 24 hours or longer, turning frequently. Loop yarn through holes.
Yield: 10 ornaments.

Carol Brakeall, Eta Alpha
Shawnee, Kansas

Linda Robinson, Beta Alpha
Mount Vernon, Ohio

GINGERBREAD ADVENT CALENDAR

Frosting and decorating tubes	*1 (3½-inch wide x 1½-yard long) burlap strip*
1 large gingerbread man	
25 small gingerbread men (See page 173 for Gingerbread People recipe)	*1 (23-inch long) strand red yarn*
	25 (9-inch long) strands red yarn

Pipe numbers onto gingerbread men using frosting and decorating tubes. Large gingerbread man should be number 25 and smaller ones, numbers 1 to 24. Wrap gingerbread men individually in plastic wrap or bags, gathering at top and securing with tape. Fringe ½ inch on each long side and on 1 end of burlap. Stitch unfringed edge under 1 inch. Thread long yarn strand through hem for hanger; knot ends securely. Stitch 9-inch yarn strand 9-inches from top through burlap so that both ends are on right side and are centered on burlap strip. Add remaining yarn strands in rows of two, each row 3 inches beneath the row above, beginning ½ inch from each edge. Tie large gingerbread man at top. Tie smaller gingerbread men to remaining yarn strands in descending order with numbers 1 and 2 at bottom. Attach holiday card and bow at top.

GINGERBREAD STARBURST

1 14-ounce package gingerbread mix	*4 green candied cherries*
⅓ cup lukewarm water	*4 walnut halves*
1 egg white	*6 to 7 dozen whole blanched almonds*
5 red candied cherries	

Combine gingerbread mix and water in bowl; mix well. Chill for 1 hour. Roll dough into 12-inch square on foil-lined cookie sheet. Cut into 8-point star. Remove excess dough. Brush star with egg white. Cut red cherries into quarters. Arrange cherry pieces on star to resemble petals; center with whole green cherries. Place walnut halves between cherry flowers. Outline star and center cut-out with almonds. Bake at 300 degrees for 18 to 20 minutes or until firm. Cool on wire rack. Remove foil. Loop ribbon through center. Hang from window or door.

NEW MEXICO PEPPER WREATH

80 pepper pods	*String*
Wire coat hanger	

Dry peppers in 200-degree oven for 3 hours. Straighten coat hanger and reshape into circle. Bend last 2 inches of hanger into right angle. Thread each pepper pod through center onto wire. Push pepper pod to end of wreath. Thread first pepper pod with stem toward center of wreath; turn second pepper pod in opposite direction. Alternate direction of pepper pods around entire wreath. Thread pepper pods as tightly as possible around wreath. Leave 2 inches of wire at end of wreath; bend at a right angle. Twist 2 ends of wire together. Tie a loop of string to wire to hang wreath.

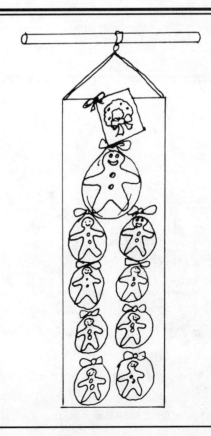

THANKSGIVING BASKET

Take along a basket as a hostess gift if you're lucky enough to be the guest at a Thanksgiving dinner. Start with our Turkey Centerpiece (page 51), a delicious pie (pages 177 to 185), and perhaps packages of Wild Rice Pilaf Mix (page 44) for an unusual dressing. A cheese ball (page 58) and a bottle of homemade wine (page 74) will make everyone thankful.

SUNSHINE FRUIT BASKET

Fill this basket with fruit and treats for any occasion. **Mae Warren of Preceptor Nu, Anniston, Alabama,** arranges fruit such as apples, oranges, plums, pears, grapes, peaches, strawberries, bananas, nectarines and lemons in an attractive basket. She adds wrapped candies and gum, a bow and gift card.

HOLIDAY BREAD BASKET

Holiday breads from your own kitchen are one of the pleasures of the season, and a basket full of tempting varieties will make a sensational gift. Include Bread Sticks (page 128), Spudnuts (page 129), a loaf of Cranberry-Walnut Bread (page 130), a smaller basket of French Breakfast Puffs (page 134), a beribboned loaf of French bread (page 134), and a crock of flavored butter (page 131). Add a jar of Spiced Cider Jelly (page 43). The lucky recipient will remember your thoughtfulness at every meal throughout the holidays.

A Souper New Year's Basket (See instructions below.)

SOUPER NEW YEAR'S BASKET

A basket full of makings for a lucky New Year's supper can be given any time during the holidays. Fill with a jar of our New Year's Day Bean Soup Mix (page 43), along with fixings of onions, garlic, a 1-pound canned ham, and a packet of the seasonings. Add packages of corn bread mix and a box of homemade brownies (page 168). Slip in soup bowls or mugs and a party horn or two.

THE CHILDREN'S HOUR BASKET

Christmas is for children, and this basket will be a special gift for the members of the younger set on your list. Presented at the first of December, the basket will provide hours of pleasure. Include a container of Play Clay with directions for making ornaments (page 54), our Gingerbread Advent Calendar (page 55) for happy counting, Jingle Popcorn Balls (page 49), the ingredients to make peanut butter fudge (page 36), Hot Chocolate Mix (page 43), and a tin of Christmas Kiss Candies (page 35).

MERRY OLDE DICKENS BASKET

Give a basket of English treats to your friends who would love to be in England during the holidays or to celebrate a Victorian Christmas. Include a cheesecloth-wrapped steamed pudding and a crock of flavored hard sauce (page 148), miniature fruitcakes (page 40), and a jar of English Wassail for holiday cheer (page 78). Tuck in packages of toffee and English tea along with walnuts and fresh fruit. Pack all in a fireside basket or coal scuttle and present with a copy of *A Christmas Carol.*

A Holiday Bread Basket (See instructions above.)

Holiday Appetizers

CHEESE BALL

1   5-ounce jar Old English
   cheese, softened
2½ cups shredded
   Cheddar cheese,
   softened
48 ounces cream cheese,
   softened
1 ounce Roquefort cheese
1 ounce bleu cheese
1 medium onion, grated
4 or 5 green onions,
   finely chopped
¼ cup finely chopped
   parsley

Garlic salt to taste
Worcestershire sauce
   to taste
Tabasco sauce to taste
3 tablespoons
   mayonnaise
½ cup finely chopped
   pecans
1   2-ounce package
   chopped walnuts
½ cup finely chopped
   pecans
½ cup finely chopped
   parsley

Combine cheeses, onion, ¼ cup parsley, seasonings, mayonnaise, ½ cup pecans and walnuts in bowl; mix well. Chill in refrigerator. Shape in balls. Roll in remaining ½ cup pecans and parsley. Serve with assorted crackers. Yield: 3 cheese balls.
Note: May put hard cheeses, onions and nuts through food grinder.

Jenelle Harris, Preceptor Delta Upsilon
Dayton, Ohio

CHEESE LOGS

2 pounds Velveeta
   cheese, softened
16 ounces cream cheese,
   softened
2 ounces Roquefort cheese
1 teaspoon garlic salt

2 tablespoons
   Worcestershire sauce
1 teaspoon onion salt
8 ounces pecans,
   finely chopped

Combine first 6 ingredients in bowl; mix well. Divide into 3 portions; wrap each in waxed paper. Chill in refrigerator. Shape into logs. Roll in pecans; place on serving plate. Serve with crackers. Yield: 3 logs.
Note: May roll in paprika or parsley before rolling in pecans if desired.

Mae Dell Crawford, Preceptor Eta Beta
Boerne, Texas

HOLIDAY CHEESE BALL

12 ounces sharp cheese,
   shredded
8 ounces cream cheese
5 ounces bleu cheese

1 teaspoon hot sauce
Garlic powder to taste
1 cup chopped nuts

Combine cheeses in mixer bowl. Let stand until softened. Add hot sauce and garlic powder; mix well. Chill until firm. Shape into ball. Roll in nuts. Let stand at room temperature to soften for easier spreading. Serve with crackers. Yield: 1 cheese ball.

Wanda McMahon, Preceptor Epsilon Alpha
Winter Haven, Florida

JALAPEÑO CHEESE ROLL

10 ounces Cheddar cheese	1/4 teaspoon garlic powder
8 to 16 ounces American cheese	2 or 3 jalapeño peppers, minced
8 ounces cream cheese	1 cup chopped pecans

Melt Cheddar and American cheeses in top of double boiler. Add cream cheese; stir until melted. Add remaining ingredients; mix well. Shape into logs on waxed paper. Chill, covered, for 24 to 48 hours. Serve with butter crackers. Yield: 15-20 servings.

Chris Richardson, Xi Zeta Eta
Pasadena, Texas

MOM'S CHEESE BALL

8 ounces cream cheese, softened	3 tablespoons steak sauce
Dash of Tabasco sauce	1 clove of garlic, crushed
	Finely chopped pecans

Combine cream cheese, sauces and garlic in bowl; mix well. Shape into ball. Roll in pecans; wrap in plastic wrap. Chill until serving time. Place on serving plate. Serve with butter crackers. Yield: 1 cheese ball.

Pam Feldhaus, Epsilon Psi
Shelbyville, Tennessee

TASTY CHEESE BALL

16 ounces cream cheese, softened	1/4 cup finely chopped green pepper
2 cups crushed pecans	2 tablespoons chopped onion
1 8-ounce can crushed pineapple, drained	1 teaspoon seasoned salt

Combine all ingredients in bowl; mix well. Shape into ball. Garnish with additional crushed pecans. Serve with crackers or bread sticks. Yield: 1 cheese ball.

Kate Williams, Xi Epsilon Sigma
Oscoda, Minnesota

THREE-CHEESE BALL

1 5-ounce jar Old English cheese spread	Grated onion to taste
8 ounces cream cheese, softened	Dash of Worcestershire sauce
1 ounce bleu cheese	Chopped nuts

Combine first 5 ingredients in bowl; mix well. Chill for 2 hours. Shape into ball; roll in nuts. Chill until firm. Serve with crackers. Yield: 1 cheese ball.

Bev Wallstrum, Preceptor Zeta Lambda
Santa Rosa, California

HAM AND CHEESE BALL

16 ounces cream cheese, softened	8 green onions, chopped
8 ounces boiled ham, chopped	3 tablespoons MSG
	1 teaspoon Worcestershire sauce

Combine all ingredients in bowl; mix well. Shape into 1 large or 2 small balls. Garnish with ham strips. Serve with crackers. Yield: 1 cheese ball.

Pamela Dunleavy, Iota Iota
Jersey Shore, Pennsylvania

PARTY CHEESE LOG

8 ounces cream cheese, softened	1 tablespoon Worcestershire sauce
8 ounces mild Cheddar cheese, shredded	Dash of Tabasco sauce
2 tablespoons milk	Crushed pecans

Combine first 5 ingredients in bowl; mix well. Shape into log; roll in crushed pecans to coat. Chill, wrapped in foil, until serving time. Yield: 1 cheese log.

Karen Thrasher, Epsilon Psi
Shelbyville, Tennessee

PINEAPPLE-CHEESE BALL

16 ounces cream cheese, softened	1/2 cup chopped onion
1 3-ounce can crushed pineapple	Seasoned salt to taste
1 cup chopped celery	3/4 cup finely chopped walnuts

Combine all ingredients in bowl; mix well. Shape into ball. Chill, covered with damp cloth, overnight. Roll in additional chopped walnuts. Yield: 1 cheese ball.

Barbara Champion, Beta Omega
Overland Park, Kansas

SALMON BALL

1 16-ounce can salmon, drained, flaked	1/2 cup chopped pecans
8 ounces cream cheese, softened	1 tablespoon lemon juice
	1 tablespoon horseradish
2 tablespoons grated onion	1/4 teaspoon salt
	1/4 cup chopped fresh parsley

Combine all ingredients except parsley in bowl; mix well. Chill in refrigerator. Shape into ball; roll in parsley. Serve with assorted crackers. Yield: one 6-inch cheese ball.

June B. Fuller, Preceptor Beta Eta
Bradenton, Florida

SALMON PARTY BALL

1 16-ounce can pink salmon, drained, flaked	1 teaspoon onion powder
	1/4 teaspoon liquid smoke
16 ounces cream cheese, softened	1/4 teaspoon salt
1 tablespoon lemon juice	1/4 cup parsley flakes
1 teaspoon horseradish	1/2 cup chopped nuts

Combine all ingredients in bowl; mix well. Shape into ball. Chill for 1 hour. Serve with crackers and bite-sized fresh vegetables or use as sandwich spread. May be frozen or stored tightly covered in refrigerator. Yield: 1 large cheese ball.

Mary Garrett, Xi Beta Mu
Deming, New Mexico

SALMON CHEESE BALLS

1 8-ounce can salmon	1 teaspoon prepared
8 ounces cream cheese,	horseradish
softened	½ teaspoon liquid smoke
1 tablespoon lemon juice	½ cup chopped pecans
2 teaspoons grated onion	3 tablespoons minced
¼ teaspoon salt	parsley

Drain salmon; flake in bowl. Add remaining ingredients except pecans and parsley; mix well. Chill for several hours. Shape into 2 balls; roll in mixture of parsley and pecans. Place on serving plate. Chill until serving time. Serve with crackers. Yield: 2 cheese balls.

Virginia Demarais, Xi Upsilon Delta
Borrego Springs, California

SHRIMP CHEESE BALL

8 ounces cream cheese,	1 6-ounce can shrimp
softened	Cocktail sauce

Blend cream cheese in bowl until smooth. Add shrimp; mix well. Shape into ball; place on serving plate. Make indentation in top. Fill with cocktail sauce.
Yield: 1 cheese ball.

Betty Ann Osborne, Epsilon Psi
Shelbyville, Tennessee

NUTTY SHRIMP CHEESE BALLS

8 ounces cream cheese,	½ teaspoon onion salt
softened	½ teaspoon garlic salt
1 6-ounce can shrimp,	1 cup crushed nuts
drained	

Combine cream cheese, shrimp, onion salt and garlic salt in bowl; mix well. Shape into small balls; roll in nuts to coat. Chill, covered, until serving time. Serve with assorted crackers. Yield: 25 servings.

B.J. Tueller, Beta Lambda
Evanston, Wyoming

STRAWBERRIES AND CHEESE

4 cups shredded Cheddar	1 bunch green onions,
cheese	chopped
3 cups mayonnaise	2 teaspoons seasoned salt
1 cup chopped pecans	1 teaspoon seasoned
4 slices crisp-fried bacon,	pepper
crumbled	1 jar strawberry preserves

Combine cheese, mayonnaise, pecans, bacon, green onions, salt and pepper in large bowl; mix well. Spoon into springform pan. Melt strawberry preserves in saucepan, stirring constantly. Pour over cheese mixture. Chill for 4 hours or until firm. Remove side of pan. Place on serving platter. Serve with crackers. Yield: 35-40 servings.

Sandra Sharp, Gamma Epsilon
Clarksville, Arkansas

CHEESE RING

16 ounces sharp Cheddar	Pepper to taste
cheese, shredded	1 cup chopped nuts
1 tablespoon mayonnaise	Strawberry jam

Combine cheese, mayonnaise and pepper in bowl; mix well. Shape into ring. Press nuts evenly over ring. Place small bowl filled with jam in center of ring. Serve with favorite crackers. Yield: 20 servings.

Linda Robinson, Beta Alpha
Mt. Vernon, Ohio

TACO BALL

1 envelope taco seasoning	Onion, minced
mix	Black olives, finely
8 ounces cream cheese,	chopped
softened	Green pepper, finely
8 ounces small curd	chopped
cottage cheese	Cheddar cheese, shredded
Tomato, finely chopped	

Combine seasoning mix and cheeses in mixer bowl; beat until smooth. Shape into ball. Press mixture of tomato, onion, olives and green pepper over cheese ball. Top with Cheddar cheese. Serve with chips.
Yield: 1 cheese ball.

Elizabeth A. Cooper, Epsilon Omicron
Portage, Michigan

HOT ARTICHOKE DIP

1 14-ounce can	Lemon juice to taste
artichoke hearts	1 cup mayonnaise
1 cup Parmesan cheese	Dash of salt

Drain artichokes; squeeze dry. Break artichokes into small pieces in bowl. Add remaining ingredients; mix well. Spoon into shallow baking dish. Bake at 350 degrees for 20 minutes or until brown on top. Blot top with paper towel. Serve hot with crackers or corn chips.
Yield: 12 to 15 servings.

Brenda Steakley, Epsilon Kappa
Nashville, Tennessee

MARGE'S ARTICHOKE DIP

2 jars marinated	6 tablespoons
artichokes, drained,	mayonnaise
chopped	1½ cups shredded
1 4-ounce can chopped	Cheddar cheese
green chilies	

Layer artichokes and chilies in 8-inch baking dish. Spread mayonnaise over top, sealing to edge. Sprinkle with cheese. Bake at 350 degrees for 10 minutes. Serve with tortilla chips. Yield: 8 to 10 servings.

Jill R. Scott, Eta Phi
Sunnyside, Washington

MICROWAVE HOT ARTICHOKE DIP

2 14-ounce cans artichoke hearts, drained, mashed	1 cup margarine
2 cups Parmesan cheese	½ teaspoon garlic powder
	Dash of lemon juice

Combine all ingredients in bowl; mix well. Pour into glass baking dish. Microwave on High for 10 minutes; mix well. Microwave for 5 to 10 minutes longer. Garnish with paprika. Serve with Triscuits. Yield: 4 cups.

Katherine S. Hill, Xi Gamma Zeta
Denver, Colorado

SPICY HOT ARTICHOKE DIP

1 14-ounce can artichoke hearts	¼ teaspoon garlic powder
1 cup Parmesan cheese	¼ teaspoon pepper
1 cup mayonnaise	1 loaf French bread
1 tablespoon onion flakes	Paprika to taste

Drain and mash artichoke hearts in bowl. Add cheese, mayonnaise, onion, garlic powder and pepper; mix well. Scoop out center of loaf to form shell. Cut center into bite-sized pieces and set aside. Spoon artichoke mixture into bread shell. Sprinkle with paprika. Bake at 350 degrees for 30 minutes. Serve with reserved bread pieces. Yield: 18 to 24 servings.

Suzanne Bobo, Epsilon Psi
Shelbyville, Tennessee

HOT BEEF DIP

2 cups sour cream	¼ cup chopped green pepper
16 ounces cream cheese	¼ teaspoon pepper
½ cup milk	½ cup chopped walnuts
8 ounces dried beef	
¼ cup minced onion	

Combine first 7 ingredients in bowl; mix well. Spoon into 1½-quart casserole. Bake at 350 degrees until heated through. Sprinkle with walnuts. Serve with Triscuits. Yield: 4½ cups.

Linda Gizienski, Xi Alpha
Providence, Rhode Island

CARAMEL DIP FOR APPLES

8 ounces cream cheese, softened	¼ cup sugar
¾ cup packed brown sugar	1 teaspoon vanilla extract

Combine all ingredients in mixer bowl. Beat until creamy. Serve with fresh apple slices. Yield: 1 cup.

Jean Rucker, Alpha Rho
Maryville, Missouri

CHILI RELLENO DIP

1 tablespoon olive oil	1 small can chopped olives, drained
1 large tomato, peeled, chopped	½ cup chopped green onions
1 4-ounce can chopped chili peppers	

Mix all ingredients in bowl. Chill, covered, for 1 hour or longer. Serve with tortilla chips. Yield: 2 cups.

Mary Anne Johnson, Beta Lambda
Evanston, Wyoming

CHILI DIP

8 ounces cream cheese, softened	1 4-ounce can chopped green chilies
1 tablespoon minced onion	

Combine all ingredients in blender container. Process until well mixed. Pour into serving bowl. Chill until serving time. Serve with tortilla chips. Yield: 1 cup.

Carol Plemmons, Xi Alpha
Providence, Rhode Island

CHIPPED BEEF DIP

1 small jar chipped beef	¼ cup finely chopped green pepper
½ cup sour cream	2 tablespoons minced onion
8 ounces cream cheese, softened	Chopped pecans
2 tablespoons milk	
½ teaspoon garlic salt	

Combine first 5 ingredients in bowl; mix well. Add green pepper and onion; mix well. Spread in 8-inch pie plate. Sprinkle with pecans. Bake at 350 degrees for 20 minutes. Serve with crackers or corn chips. Yield: 2 cups.

Pam Brasher, Epsilon Psi
Shelbyville, Tennessee

SPICY BEEF DIP

1 small onion, finely chopped	3 tablespoons chili powder
1 to 2 tablespoons butter	1 7-ounce bottle of catsup
1 pound ground beef	Salt and pepper to taste
1 15-ounce can pinto beans	1 cup shredded cheese

Sauté onion in butter in skillet until brown; drain and set aside. Brown ground beef in skillet, stirring until crumbly; drain. Combine ground beef, sautéed onion, beans, chili powder and salt and pepper in skillet; mix well. Simmer for 20 minutes. Pour into ovenproof serving dish. Sprinkle with cheese. Bake at 250 degrees for 10 minutes. Serve with tortilla chips. Yield: 6 cups.

Sissy Smith, Epsilon Psi
Shelbyville, Tennessee

HOT CHEESE DIP

2 pounds cheese, cubed	Jalapeño peppers to taste
1 10-ounce can Ro-Tel tomatoes	Milk

Combine cheese and Ro-Tel in glass bowl. Microwave on Medium-High until cheese melts, stirring frequently. Add chopped jalapeño peppers and enough milk to make of desired consistency; mix well. Yield: 2 to 3 cups.

Patsy Taylor, Epsilon Psi
Shelbyville, Tennessee

HOT CHILI SCOOP

1 1-pound can chili con carne	3 ounces cream cheese, softened
1 4-ounce can diced green chilies	

Combine chili con carne, green chilies and cream cheese in fondue pot. Heat until well mixed, stirring constantly. Serve hot with corn chips. Yield: 3 cups.

Mary Anne Johnson, Beta Lambda
Evanston, Wyoming

CHUTNEY CHICKEN SPREAD

8 ounces chopped cooked chicken	2 tablespoons grated onion
8 ounces cream cheese, softened	¼ cup mayonnaise
3 tablespoons chutney	Pinch of pepper
1 teaspoon curry powder	¼ cup toasted slivered almonds

Place chicken in food processor container. Process with steel blade for 5 seconds. Add cream cheese, chutney, curry powder, onion, mayonnaise and pepper. Process for 5 to 10 seconds or until well blended. Place in shallow baking dish. Sprinkle with almonds. Bake at 350 degrees for 15 minutes. Yield: 2 cups.

Sara Hunt, Epsilon Psi
Shelbyville, Tennessee

CHUTNEY DIP

8 ounces cream cheese, softened	¼ jar finely chopped Major Grey's chutney
1 teaspoon curry powder	Toasted slivered almonds

Combine cream cheese, curry powder and chutney in bowl; mix well. Chill for 24 hours. Let stand at room temperature for 3 hours before serving. Sprinkle with toasted almonds. Yield: 1½ cups.

Sue Mock, Xi Alpha
Providence, Rhode Island

CLAM DIP

16 ounces cream cheese, softened	3 or 4 drops of Tabasco sauce
2 teaspoons lemon juice	1 7-ounce can minced clams
1 teaspoon grated onion	
1 teaspoon Worcestershire sauce	1 tablespoon minced parsley
¼ teaspoon salt	

Combine first 6 ingredients in mixer bowl; beat until light and fluffy. Drain clams, reserving juice. Stir clams and parsley into cream cheese mixture. Add enough reserved clam juice to make of desired consistency. Spoon into serving dish. Serve with potato chips. Yield: 2 cups.

Kim Churas, Xi Alpha
Providence, Rhode Island

CONFETTI DIP

8 ounces cream cheese, softened	Cucumber, finely chopped
1½ teaspoons horseradish	Radishes, finely chopped
1 teaspoon lemon juice	Green onions, finely chopped
½ teaspoon garlic powder	

Combine cream cheese, horseradish, lemon juice and garlic powder in bowl; mix well. Stir in vegetables. Serve with crackers, chips and assorted fresh vegetables for dipping. Yield: 1 cup.

Cameron Stinson, Xi Theta
Mayfield, Kentucky

CRAB DIP DIVINE

1 12-ounce bottle of catsup	⅛ teaspoon hot sauce
1 12-ounce bottle of chili sauce	⅛ teaspoon Worcestershire sauce
¼ cup horseradish	2 6½-ounce cans crab meat, flaked
Juice of 1 lemon	1 fresh pineapple shell

Combine first 6 ingredients in bowl; blend well. Add crab meat. Chill until serving time. Serve in pineapple shell with assorted crisp crackers. Yield: 4 to 5 cups.

Linda Hawkins, Preceptor Delta
Cookeville, Tennessee

CRAB MEAT DELIGHT

16 ounces cream cheese, softened	1 small onion, grated
2 teaspoons Worcestershire sauce	Lettuce leaves
	¾ cup chili sauce
1 teaspoon lime juice	1 6-ounce can crab meat, drained
2 teaspoons mayonnaise	

Combine cream cheese, Worcestershire sauce, lime juice and mayonnaise in bowl; mix well. Stir in onion. Chill until serving time. Line serving tray with lettuce. Spoon cream cheese mixture into 1½-inch thick mound on lettuce. Drizzle with chili sauce. Sprinkle crab meat over top. Serve with crackers. Yield: 12 to 16 servings.

Pat Thomas, Epsilon Psi
Shelbyville, Tennessee

CRAB AND SHRIMP DIP

16 ounces cream cheese, softened	1 6-ounce can small shrimp
1 6-ounce can crab meat	1 teaspoon mayonnaise

Combine all ingredients in mixer bowl; beat until well mixed. Spoon into casserole. Bake at 350 degrees until heated through. Serve hot with crackers or fresh vegetables. Yield: 2 cups.

Pat Blasbalg, Xi Alpha
Providence, Rhode Island

DELICASEAS CRAB DIP

8 ounces cream cheese, softened
½ cup mayonnaise
½ cup chopped onion
½ cup chopped celery
3 tablespoons lemon juice
2 tablespoons creamed horseradish
1 tablespoon Worcestershire sauce
8 ounces chopped crab meat

Blend cream cheese and mayonnaise in bowl. Add remaining ingredients except crab meat; mix well. Stir in crab meat. Chill, covered, for 2 hours or longer. Serve with chips or crackers. May be used as topping for baked potato, filling for celery sticks or spread on hot English muffin. Yield: 3 cups.

Gladys Simonson, Preceptor Beta Rho
Spokane, Washington

DILL DIP

1 cup sour cream
1 cup mayonnaise
2 tablespoons onion flakes
1 tablespoon dillweed
1 tablespoon seasoned salt
Worcestershire sauce to taste
1 round loaf bread

Mix sour cream, mayonnaise, onion flakes, dillweed, salt and Worcestershire sauce in bowl. Chill for several hours. Scoop out center of loaf to form shell; cut center into bite-sized pieces. Spoon dip into bread shell. Place on serving platter with bread pieces and assorted fresh vegetables or chips for dipping. Yield: 2 cups.

Judy Kephart, Xi Theta Omicron
Holden, Missouri

DILLED VEGETABLE DIP

⅔ cup sour cream
⅔ cup mayonnaise
1 teaspoon dillweed
1 tablespoon parsley flakes
1 tablespoon onion flakes
1 teaspoon Beau Monde seasoning

Combine all ingredients in bowl; mix well. Chill until serving time. Spoon into serving dish. Serve with chips or bite-sized fresh vegetables. Yield: 1 cup.

Jean White, Xi Alpha
Providence, Rhode Island

DILLWEED DIP

1 cup mayonnaise
1 cup sour cream
1 cup cottage cheese
2 tablespoons chopped parsley
1½ tablespoons onion flakes
1½ tablespoons dillweed
1½ teaspoons Worcestershire sauce
1½ teaspoons seasoned salt
1 large green pepper

Combine mayonnaise, sour cream, cottage cheese, parsley, onion flakes, dillweed, Worcestershire sauce and seasoned salt in bowl; mix well. Chill, covered, until serving time. Scoop out center of green pepper. Spoon dip into pepper shell. Place on serving dish with assorted

fresh vegetables for dipping. Yield: 8 to 10 servings.
Note: May store for several days in covered container in refrigerator.

Carol Jarman, Beta Sigma
New Bern, North Carolina

PUMPERNICKEL DILL DIP

1⅓ cups sour cream
1⅓ cups mayonnaise
2 teaspoons minced parsley
1 teaspoon garlic salt
2 teaspoons dillweed
2 teaspoons Beau Monde seasoning
2 teaspoons onion flakes
2 round loaves pumpernickel bread

Combine first 7 ingredients in bowl; mix well. Cut 1 loaf into cubes. Scoop out center of remaining loaf to form bowl. Cut scooped out center into cubes. Spoon dip into bread bowl. Serve with bread cubes for dipping. Yield: 3 cups.

Ann Kesley, Epsilon Kappa
Nashville, Tennessee

ENSALADA DE FELIZ NAVIDAD

1 16-ounce can refried beans
1 4-ounce jar salsa
2 6-ounce cans guacamole dip
1 4-ounce can chopped green chilies
2 large tomatoes, chopped
1 4-ounce can sliced black olives, drained
8 ounces Monterey Jack cheese, shredded

Layer ingredients in order listed in 9x9-inch glass dish. Chill until serving time. Serve with corn chips. Yield: 12 servings.

Virginia De Marais, Xi Upsilon Delta
Borrego Springs, California

CINNAMON FRUIT DIP

8 ounces cream cheese, softened
8 ounces honey
1 teaspoon vanilla extract
1 teaspoon cinnamon

Combine all ingredients in bowl; mix well. Chill for 2 hours. Serve with fresh strawberries and bite-sized melon, banana, pineapple and other fresh fruit. Yield: 1 cup.

Kaye Crouch, Tau
Wilmington, Delaware

Arrange chilled vegetable crudités such as asparagus, blanched green beans, cauliflowerets, broccoli flowerets, baby carrots, radishes, pea pods, cucumber, squash, mushrooms, cooked Brussels sprouts, cherry tomatoes and endive in large basket or grouped on trays. Serve dips in hollowed out giant peppers, red or savoy cabbage, radicchio, pattypan squashes or Bibb lettuce.

FRUIT DIP

2 7-ounce jars	Assorted fruit, cut into
marshmallow creme	bite-sized pieces
16 ounces cream cheese,	
softened	

Soften marshmallow creme in microwave for several seconds. Blend with cream cheese in bowl. Place in serving bowl in center of tray. Arrange assorted bite-sized pieces of fresh fruit such as strawberries, bananas, apples and pineapple around dip. Yield: 3 cups.
Note: This is also good for topping pie.

Roberta DeNegre, Preceptor Gamma Upsilon
Blue Springs, Missouri

PIÑA COLADA FRUIT DIP

1 8-ounce can crushed	1 3-ounce package
pineapple	coconut instant
¾ cup milk	pudding mix
½ cup sour cream	

Combine all ingredients in blender container. Process until blended. Chill, covered, overnight. Pour into serving bowl. Serve with fresh fruit such as melon, cherries, apples and pears. Yield: 2 cups.

Anne Beirth, Laureate Rho
Norristown, Pennsylvania

GUACAMOLE

1 avocado	1 teaspoon lemon juice
2 tablespoons	¼ teaspoon salt
picante sauce	

Mash avocado in bowl. Add picante sauce, lemon juice and salt; mix well. Spoon into serving dish. Serve with chips. Yield: 1 cup.

Sarah Thacker, Epsilon Kappa
Nashville, Tennessee

JEZEBEL SAUCE

1 10-ounce jar apple	½ 1½-ounce can dry
jelly	mustard
1 10-ounce jar apricot	1 teaspoon pepper
preserves	1 8-ounce package
1 6-ounce jar horseradish	cream cheese, softened

Combine first 5 ingredients in saucepan. Bring to a boil, stirring constantly. Cool. Place cream cheese in shallow serving dish. Pour sauce over top. Serve with snack crackers. Shredded wheat crackers are particularly good. Yield: 8 to 10 servings.

Kimberly L. Birch, Eta Nu
Charles City, Iowa

K.C. COUNTRY CLUB DIP

16 ounces sour cream	1 teaspoon Tabasco sauce
4 slices crisp-fried bacon,	1 envelope ranch
crumbled	dressing mix
1 tablespoon horseradish	

Combine all ingredients in small bowl; mix well. Chill, covered, in refrigerator for 1 to 7 days. Serve with corn chips or assorted fresh vegetables for dipping. Yield: 2½ cups.

Beth Ann Steuerwald, Kappa Omicron
Saylorsburg, Pennsylvania

LOW-CALORIE DIP FOR VEGGIES

1 cup low-calorie	1 envelope ranch
mayonnaise	dressing mix
1 cup low-fat milk	

Combine all ingredients in bowl; mix well. Pour into serving dish. Serve with bite-sized fresh vegetables. Yield: 2 cups.

Carol Payne, Xi Alpha
Providence, Rhode Island

PARTY SPREAD

1 8-ounce container	2 tablespoons chopped
French onion dip	green onion tops
2 5-ounce jars	Party rye bread
pineapple-cream	
cheese spread, softened	

Combine onion dip and pineapple-cream cheese spread in bowl; mix well. Spoon into serving dish. Sprinkle with green onion tops. Serve with party rye bread. Yield: 2 cups.

Mickey McLean, Epsilon Psi
Shelbyville, Tennessee

FRESH RADISH DIP

8 ounces cream cheese,	1 clove of garlic, minced
softened	¼ teaspoon dillweed
1 tablespoon lemon juice	1 cup chopped radishes
1 teaspoon salt	

Combine cream cheese, lemon juice, salt, garlic and dillweed; mix until creamy. Stir in radishes. Chill, covered, for 2 hours or longer. Serve with assorted vegetables for dipping. Yield: 2 cups.

Susan G. Riedel, Phi Eta
Niceville, Florida

ROUND RYE AND DIP

1 cup sour cream	1 small onion, chopped
8 ounces cream cheese,	1 tablespoon dillweed
softened	Salt and pepper to taste
2 stalks celery, chopped	1 round loaf rye bread
1 6-ounce can shrimp	

Blend sour cream and cream cheese in bowl. Add celery, shrimp, onion and seasonings; mix well. Scoop out center of loaf to form shell; cut center into pieces. Spoon shrimp mixture into bread shell. Serve with bread pieces. Yield: 2 cups.

Carol Plemmons, Xi Alpha
Providence, Rhode Island

RYE PARTY DIP

1 cup sour cream	2 tablespoons onion
1 cup mayonnaise	flakes
2 teaspoons dillweed	2 teaspoons seasoned salt
2 tablespoons parsley	12 black olives, chopped
flakes	1 round loaf rye bread

Mix sour cream, mayonnaise, dillweed, parsley flakes, onion flakes, seasoned salt and black olives in bowl. Chill, covered, overnight. Scoop out center of loaf to form shell; cut center into bite-sized pieces. Spoon dip into bread shell. Place on serving platter with bread pieces for dipping. Yield: 2½ cups.

Sharon Forbes, Tau
Wilmington, Delaware

SHRIMP BUTTER

8 ounces cream cheese,	2 tablespoons chopped
softened	onion
¾ cup butter, softened	¼ cup mayonnaise
2 6-ounce cans shrimp	Juice of 1 lemon

Combine cream cheese and butter in bowl; mix well. Add shrimp, onion, mayonnaise and lemon juice; mix well. Spoon into serving dish. Serve with crackers. Yield: 2½ cups.

Shedra Sells, Epsilon Psi
Shelbyville, Tennessee

ITALIAN SHRIMP DIP

8 ounces cream cheese,	1 envelope Italian
softened	salad dressing mix
8 ounces sour cream	1 6½-ounce can shrimp,
2 teaspoons lemon juice	drained

Combine cream cheese, sour cream, lemon juice and dressing mix in bowl; mix well. Stir in shrimp. Chill, covered, for 24 to 48 hours. Serve with bite-sized fresh vegetables or wheat thins. Yield: 2½ cups.

Carolyn Wyckoff, Preceptor Lambda
Arvada, Colorado

SHRIMP DIP

1 can cream of shrimp	8 to 16 ounces shrimp,
soup	chopped
8 ounces cream cheese,	Garlic powder and
softened	paprika to taste

Blend soup and cream cheese in bowl. Add shrimp and seasonings; mix well. Spoon into serving dish. Chill until serving time. Serve with crackers. Yield: 4 cups.

Xi Alpha
Providence, Rhode Island

TAMALE DIP

2 pounds Velveeta cheese	1 16-ounce can tamales,
1 16-ounce can chili	mashed
without beans	

Melt cheese in double boiler. Add chili and tamales; mix well. Heat to serving temperature. Serve warm with tortilla chips. Yield: 6 cups.

Susan Oerman, Xi Phi Iota
Victorville, California

TEX-MEX DIP

3 avocados	1 bunch green onions,
2 tablespoons lemon juice	chopped
Salt and pepper to taste	2 cans black olives,
1½ cups sour cream	chopped
½ cup mayonnaise	3 medium tomatoes,
1 envelope taco	chopped
seasoning mix	2 cups shredded sharp
2 16-ounce cans spicy	Cheddar cheese
refried beans	

Mash avocados in bowl. Add lemon juice and salt and pepper; mix well. Blend sour cream, mayonnaise and taco seasoning mix in small bowl. Spread refried beans in 9x13-inch pan. Layer avocado mixture, sour cream mixture and green onions and olives over beans. Chill until serving time. Add tomatoes and cheese just before serving. Serve with chips. Yield: 20 servings.

Connie M. Pierce, Preceptor Pi
Douglas, Wyoming

VEGETABLE DIP

⅔ cup mayonnaise	1 tablespoon
⅔ cup sour cream	Worcestershire sauce
1 tablespoon dry	1 teaspoon garlic salt
minced onion	1 teaspoon dillweed
1 tablespoon parsley	1 teaspoon MSG
flakes	2 drops hot sauce

Combine all ingredients in bowl; mix well. Refrigerate overnight. Serve with assorted bite-sized fresh vegetables for dipping. Yield: 15 to 20 servings.

Marianne Hays, Xi Alpha Mu
Terre Haute, Indiana

ARTICHOKE SQUARES

2 6-ounce jars marinated	Dash of Tabasco sauce
artichokes	½ teaspoon oregano
1 onion, chopped	Salt and pepper to taste
1 clove of garlic, minced	2 cups shredded
4 eggs, beaten	Cheddar cheese
¼ cup bread crumbs	

Drain and chop artichokes, reserving half the marinade. Sauté onion and garlic in reserved marinade in skillet. Combine eggs, bread crumbs, Tabasco sauce and seasonings in bowl; mix well. Stir in sautéed vegetables, cheese and artichokes. Pour into greased 9x13-inch baking pan. Bake at 325 degrees for 30 minutes. Cut into squares. Serve hot. Yield: 2½ dozen.

Brenda Segroves, Epsilon Psi
Shelbyville, Tennessee

BAMBINI

1 cup ricotta cheese	1 10-ounce package large
½ cup grated mozzarella	flaky refrigerator
cheese	biscuits
¼ cup Parmesan cheese	20 thin slices pepperoni

Combine cheeses in bowl; mix well. Separate biscuits into 20 thin biscuits. Shape each biscuit into oval. Place 1 slice pepperoni on each biscuit. Top each with 1 level tablespoon cheese mixture. Moisten edges of biscuits; fold to enclose filling. Pinch edges to seal. Place on lightly greased baking sheet. Bake at 350 degrees for 20 minutes. Serve warm. Yield: 20 servings.

Lynne Farrar, Epsilon Psi
Shelbyville, Tennessee

BROCCOLI-CHEESE STRUDEL

¼ cup melted butter	1 10-ounce package
¼ cup all-purpose flour	frozen chopped
Salt to taste	broccoli, thawed,
½ teaspoon cayenne	drained
pepper	8 ounces phyllo dough
1¼ cups milk	Melted butter
4 ounces Swiss cheese,	½ cup dry bread crumbs
shredded	

Blend butter, flour, salt and cayenne pepper in 2-quart saucepan. Stir milk in gradually. Cook over medium heat until thickened, stirring constantly. Add cheese and broccoli. Heat until cheese is melted, stirring constantly; remove from heat. Unroll phyllo sheets on waxed paper-lined surface in 12x20-inch rectangle. Brush each of bottom 2 sheets generously with melted butter; sprinkle second sheet with 1 tablespoon bread crumbs. Repeat with remaining phyllo sheets, butter and crumbs. Spoon broccoli mixture lengthwise over half the phyllo rectangle; roll as for jelly roll from broccoli side. Place seam side down on baking sheet. Brush with melted butter. Bake at 375 degrees for 30 minutes or until golden brown. Cool on baking sheet on wire rack for 20 minutes. Remove to wire rack to cool completely. Cut into 1-inch slices. Serve as first course. Yield: 10 servings.

Janet Sullivan, Xi Chi
Waterbury, Connecticut

CHEESE CRISPIES

2 cups flour	10 ounces Cheddar
¼ teaspoon salt	cheese, shredded
½ teaspoon cayenne	2 cups crisp rice cereal
pepper	¼ cup toasted sesame
1 cup margarine	seed

Mix flour, salt and cayenne pepper in bowl. Cut in margarine until crumbly. Add cheese, cereal and sesame seed; mix well. Shape by tablespoonfuls into balls; flatten on ungreased baking sheet. Bake at 350 degrees for 15 minutes. Remove to wire rack. Serve warm or cool. Store in covered container in refrigerator. Yield: 4 dozen.

Alma Bakko, Xi Upsilon Delta
Borrego Springs, California

STUFFED CELERY

3 ounces cream cheese,	2 tablespoons chili sauce
softened	¼ cup chopped pecans
Milk	1 bunch celery, trimmed
1 teaspoon grated onion	¼ cup chopped pecans

Blend cream cheese with a small amount of milk to make of desired consistency. Add onion, chili sauce and ¼ cup pecans; mix well. Cut celery into bite-sized pieces. Fill with cream cheese mixture; sprinkle with remaining pecans. Yield: 6 to 8 servings.

Ann Kesley, Epsilon Kappa
Nashville, Tennessee

NEW YEAR'S CHEESE SQUARES

3 jalapeño peppers,	1 pound Cheddar cheese
chopped	6 eggs

Sprinkle peppers in greased 9x9-inch baking pan. Shred cheese, spread evenly over peppers. Beat eggs in mixer bowl until light. Pour over cheese and peppers. Bake at 250 degrees for 30 minutes. Cool. Cut into small squares. Serve with toothpicks.

Bonnie Russell, Xi Delta Theta

CHEESE PASTRY HORS D'OEUVRES

2½ cups flour	3 cups shredded Cheddar
1 cup butter, softened	cheese
1 cup sour cream	Paprika
Seasoned salt and pepper	
to taste	

Combine flour, butter and sour cream in large bowl; mix well. Divide into 4 portions. Chill, wrapped in plastic wrap, for 1 hour. Roll each portion into a 6x12-inch rectangle on floured surface. Sprinkle with seasoned salt and pepper and ¾ cup shredded cheese. Roll as for jelly roll from long side; seal edges and ends. Place seam side down on ungreased baking sheet. Slice rolls halfway through at 1-inch intervals. Sprinkle with paprika. Bake at 350 degrees for 30 to 35 minutes or until golden brown. Slice at markings. Yield: 4 dozen.

Beth Rush, Xi Kappa
Rawlins, Wyoming

Baked Brie cheese makes a delicious appetizer. Place on baking sheet. Bake at 275 degrees for 5 to 10 minutes. Place on wooden Brie container. Top with sugared nuts or frosted fruit. Or, wrap 16-ounce wheel of Brie in puff pastry or buttered layers of phyllo. Bake on baking sheet at 350 degrees until puffed and brown. Serve at room temperature. Slice Brie horizontally and spread apricot preserves and sprinkle with sliced almonds between layers before wrapping in pastry for variation.

CHEESE LOUISE

6 to 8 bread slices, crusts trimmed	1 cup grated Parmesan cheese
2 cups salad dressing	½ cup minced onion

Cut each bread slice into 4 squares. Arrange on baking sheet. Combine salad dressing, cheese and onion in bowl; mix well. Spread on bread squares. Broil for 2 to 5 minutes or until brown. Serve hot. Yield: 24 to 32 slices.

Linda Rostenberg, Omega
Kansas City, Missouri

CHICKEN PUFFS

1 cup boiling water	4 eggs
1 stick margarine	1 recipe chicken salad
1 cup sifted flour	

Combine boiling water and margarine in saucepan. Cook until margarine melts. Stir in flour. Remove from heat, stirring constantly. Add eggs 1 at a time, mixing well after each addition. Stir until mixture forms glazed ribbon. Drop by teaspoonfuls 2 inches apart onto ungreased baking sheet. Bake at 425 degrees for 15 to 20 minutes or until golden brown. Cut off tops. Cool. Fill with chicken salad. Yield: 6 dozen.

Pam Feldhaus, Epsilon Psi
Shelbyville, Tennessee

PEANUTTY CHICKEN WINGS

3 pounds chicken wings	3 tablespoons oil
6 tablespoons chunky peanut butter	¾ teaspoon soy sauce
3 tablespoons lime juice	¾ teaspoon chili powder
¾ teaspoon Kitchen Bouquet	¾ teaspoon salt
	Garlic powder to taste

Separate wings at joints. Combine remaining ingredients in large bowl; mix well. Marinate wings overnight, turning occasionally. Drain. Arrange in single layer on baking sheet; do not allow wings to touch. Bake at 325 degrees for 45 to 60 minutes; do not turn. Serve with wine or cocktails. May be frozen after baking. Yield: 8 to 10 servings.

Elizabeth Brennan, Preceptor Delta Mu
Titusville, Florida

CRAB MOLD

1 envelope unflavored gelatin	5 green onions, finely chopped
3 tablespoons water	8 ounces cream cheese, softened
1 can cream of chicken soup	1 cup mayonnaise
7 ounces crab meat	1 teaspoon Worcestershire sauce
1 cup finely chopped celery	Pimento

Soften gelatin in water in saucepan. Add soup. Heat until gelatin dissolves, stirring constantly. Cool. Add crab meat and next 5 ingredients; mix well. Pour into fish-shaped mold. Chill until set. Unmold onto lettuce-lined serving plate. Garnish with pimento. Serve with assorted crackers. Yield: 16 to 20 servings.

Katherine S. Hill, Xi Gamma Zeta
Denver, Colorado

CRAB MEAT MOLD

1 envelope unflavored gelatin	1 cup mayonnaise
3 tablespoons water	1 teaspoon horseradish
1 10-ounce can cream of mushroom soup	¼ teaspoon salt
8 ounces cream cheese, softened	⅛ teaspoon pepper
1 cup chopped celery	2 tablespoons lemon juice
	Pimento

Soften gelatin in water in saucepan. Add soup. Heat until gelatin dissolves, stirring constantly. Add cream cheese; beat until smooth. Add celery and next 5 ingredients; mix well. Tint with green food coloring if desired. Arrange pimento in 4-cup mold. Add crab mixture carefully. Chill until set. Unmold onto lettuce-lined serving plate. Serve with assorted crackers. Yield: 8 to 10 servings.

Norma Risley, Preceptor Alpha Eta
Kokomo, Indiana

CRAB MOUSSE

2 tablespoons unflavored gelatin	1 8-ounce can crab meat
½ cup cold water	1 cup mayonnaise
1 can cream of shrimp soup	2 tablespoons minced onion
8 ounces cream cheese, softened	1 cup finely chopped celery

Soften gelatin in water. Heat soup in saucepan over low heat. Add cream cheese. Heat until cheese melts; beat until smooth. Add gelatin; mix well. Cool. Rinse and drain crab meat. Add to soup mixture with remaining ingredients; mix well. Pour into 1-quart mold sprayed with nonstick cooking spray. Cover with waxed paper and foil. Chill overnight. Unmold onto serving platter. Garnish with lemon slices and green olives. Serve with crackers. Yield: 16 to 20 servings.

Connie Leetsch, Zeta Iota
Abilene, Texas

CRAB MUFFIN TOASTIES

8 ounces cooked crab meat	½ cup butter, softened
5 ounces Old English cheese spread	¼ teaspoon onion salt
1½ tablespoons mayonnaise	⅛ teaspoon garlic salt
	6 English muffins, split

Combine first 6 ingredients in bowl; mix well. Spread on muffin halves. Cut each into 6 wedges. Arrange on baking sheet. Broil until brown. Serve immediately. Yield: 72 toasties.

Donna Gayle Miller, Zeta Nu
Monroeville, Alabama

CHRISTMAS HORS D'OEUVRE WREATH

1 12-inch styrofoam
   wreath
2 bunches parsley
Florists' pins or
   hair pins
1 silk poinsettia

1 package 2½-inch
   toothpicks
Bite-sized fresh fruit,
   vegetables, pickles,
   olives, cheese cubes
   and shrimp

Place wreath in center of large round tray. Cover with parsley, securing with florists' pins. Place silk poinsettia in center of wreath. Place toothpick in each bite-sized morsel. Insert toothpicks in wreath to cover in attractive pattern or at random. Yield: 12 servings.
Note: May place 2 wreaths as for double wedding rings when preparing for wedding reception.

Mitzi Smirl, Delta Lambda
Bedford, Texas

CREAM CHEESE-DATE-NUT SPREAD

8 ounces cream cheese,
   softened
Salt to taste

¾ cup chopped dates
½ cup chopped walnuts
Milk

Blend cream cheese and salt in bowl. Add dates and walnuts. Mix well. Add enough milk to make of spreading consistency. Serve with party crackers or use as filling for celery stalks. Yield: 2½ cups.

Dorothy A. Kramer, Laureate Theta
Omaha, Nebraska

GREEN SQUARES

1 cup chopped onion
2 cloves of garlic, chopped
½ cup margarine
3 eggs, beaten
¼ cup half and half
2 tablespoons flour
2½ cups shredded
   Cheddar cheese
¾ cup dry bread crumbs
1 10-ounce can cream
   of mushroom soup

1 10-ounce package
   frozen chopped
   broccoli, cooked,
   drained
1 10-ounce package
   frozen chopped
   spinach, cooked,
   drained
¼ teaspoon oregano
¼ teaspoon nutmeg
Salt and pepper to taste

Sauté onion and garlic in margarine in skillet. Mix eggs, half and half and flour in bowl until smooth. Add cheese and bread crumbs; mix well. Add soup, broccoli, spinach, seasonings and sautéed vegetables; mix well. Pour into greased 9x13-inch baking dish. Bake at 375 degrees for 30 minutes. Cool. Cut into 1-inch squares. Yield: 8 dozen.

Frances M. Jeffers, Preceptor Gamma Delta
Port Orchard, Washington

HAM AND CHEESE ROLL-UPS

¼ cup shredded Cheddar
   cheese
3 ounces cream cheese,
   softened
¼ cup margarine,
   softened

4 ⅛-inch slices boiled
   ham
Party crackers

Combine cheese, cream cheese and margarine in bowl; mix until creamy. Spread on ham slices. Roll from short side as for jelly roll. Chill until firm. Cut into ½-inch slices. Serve on crackers. Yield: 3 to 3½ dozen.
Note: May be frozen; thaw for 20 minutes before serving.

Debbie Crosiar, Xi Xi
Caldwell, Idaho

JALAPEÑO PIE

2 cups grated sharp cheese
2 or 3 fresh jalapeño
   peppers

6 eggs, beaten

Spread cheese in greased 9-inch glass pie plate. Seed peppers; cut into narrow strips. Arrange over cheese. Pour eggs over cheese and peppers. Bake at 275 degrees for 45 minutes. Cool. Slice into small wedges. Serve with margaritas. Yield: 6 servings.

Cynthia A. Welch, Xi Alpha Pi
Albuquerque, New Mexico

LIVERWURST PÂTÉ

1 pound liverwurst
1 clove of garlic, crushed
½ teaspoon basil
¼ cup minced onion
8 ounces cream cheese,
   softened

1 clove of garlic, crushed
⅛ teaspoon red pepper
   sauce
1 teaspoon mayonnaise
Red or black caviar or
   anchovy paste, optional

Mash liverwurst with fork in bowl. Add 1 clove of garlic, basil and onion in bowl; mix well. Shape into mound on plate. Chill, covered, in refrigerator. Combine cream cheese, 1 clove of garlic, red pepper sauce and mayonnaise in bowl; mix well. Frost liverwurst mound with cream cheese mixture. Chill, covered, for 8 hours. Top with caviar or anchovy paste. Garnish with parsley before serving. Yield: 12 to 16 servings.

Denys D. Dellapé, Beta Alpha Pi
Garden Grove, California

AUNT BEA'S SWEET MEATBALLS

1 pound ground beef
20 crackers, crushed
1 egg, beaten
Salt and pepper to taste
1 clove of garlic, minced

1 12-ounce bottle of
   chili sauce
1 10-ounce jar grape
   jelly

Combine ground beef, cracker crumbs, egg, salt, pepper and garlic in bowl; mix well. Shape into small balls. Bring chili sauce and jelly to a simmer in saucepan. Add meatballs. Simmer for 45 minutes. Spoon into chafing dish. Yield: 2 dozen.

Mary Ann Mader, Laureate Alpha Delta
Elizabeth Township, Pennsylvania

COCKTAIL MEATBALLS

2 pounds ground beef	1 16-ounce bottle of
Salt and pepper to taste	cocktail sauce
Dash of soy sauce	1 16-ounce jar jellied
Dash of Worcestershire	cranberry sauce
sauce	

Combine ground beef and seasonings in bowl; mix well. Shape into small balls. Place in baking pan. Bake at 325 degrees for 20 minutes; drain. Combine cocktail and cranberry sauces in saucepan. Cook over low heat until thickened. Pour over meatballs. Bake for 15 minutes longer. Yield: 4 dozen.

Sissy Smith, Epsilon Psi
Shelbyville, Tennessee

CRAZY MEATBALLS

2½ pounds ground beef	1 can whole cranberry
¼ cup dry bread crumbs	sauce
3 eggs	1 cup packed brown sugar
1 envelope dry onion	1 8-ounce bottle of chili
soup mix	sauce
1 14-ounce can Bavarian-	1 chili sauce bottle of
style sauerkraut,	water
drained, rinsed	

Combine ground beef, bread crumbs, eggs and soup mix in bowl; mix well. Shape into 1-inch balls. Place in rows in 9x13-inch baking dish. Combine remaining ingredients in bowl; mix well. Pour over meatballs. Bake at 350 degrees for 1½ hours. Spoon into serving dish.
Yield: 20 to 24 servings.

Trudy Jacobson, Xi Gamma Upsilon
Sycamore, Illinois

HAWAIIAN MEATBALLS

1½ pounds ground beef	2 tablespoons soy sauce
⅔ cup cracker crumbs	2 tablespoons lemon juice
⅔ cup evaporated milk	½ cup vinegar
½ cup chopped onion	½ cup packed brown
1 teaspoon salt	sugar
⅓ cup flour	1 cup chopped green
3 tablespoons shortening	pepper
1 13-ounce can	2 tablespoons chopped
pineapple chunks	pimento
2 tablespoons cornstarch	

Combine ground beef, cracker crumbs, evaporated milk, onion and salt in bowl; mix well. Shape into small balls. Roll in flour. Brown on all sides in shortening in skillet; drain. Arrange in serving dish. Drain pineapple, reserving juice. Add enough water to reserved juice to measure 1 cup. Add cornstarch; stir until smooth. Combine with soy sauce, lemon juice, vinegar and brown sugar in saucepan. Cook until thickened, stirring constantly. Add pineapple, green pepper and pimento. Simmer, covered, for 15 minutes. Pour over meatballs. Yield: 2½ dozen.

B.J. Tueller, Beta Lambda
Evanston, Wyoming

HAPPY HOLIDAY MEATBALLS

1½ pounds ground beef	2 tablespoons brown
1 envelope dry onion soup	sugar
mix	1½ tablespoons cornstarch
½ cup soft bread crumbs	¼ cup vinegar
1 egg, beaten	¼ cup water
1 16-ounce can	2 green peppers, coarsely
pineapple chunks	chopped

Combine ground beef, soup mix, bread crumbs and egg in bowl; mix well. Shape into 1-inch balls. Brown on all sides in skillet; drain. Arrange in serving dish. Drain pineapple chunks, reserving juice. Combine juice with brown sugar, cornstarch, vinegar and water in saucepan; blend well. Add pineapple and green peppers. Cook over medium heat until thickened, stirring constantly. Pour over meatballs. Yield: 3 dozen.

Dottie Fortson, Gamma Theta
Baltimore, Maryland

FONDUE MEATBALLS

2 to 3 pounds ground beef	Salt to taste
1 cup bread crumbs	1 teaspoon
⅔ cup chopped onion	Worcestershire sauce
½ cup milk	½ cup oil
2 eggs	2 12-ounce bottles of
2 tablespoons parsley	chili sauce
flakes	2 10-ounce jars grape
2 teaspoons pepper	jelly

Combine first 9 ingredients in large bowl; mix well. Shape into small balls. Brown in oil in skillet; drain well. Combine chili sauce and jelly in skillet. Heat until well blended. Add meatballs. Simmer for 30 minutes. Spoon into chafing dish. Serve with toothpicks.
Yield: 5 to 6 dozen.
Note: May omit oil and cook meatballs in oven or Crock•Pot.

Ann J. Cazer, Xi Alpha Iota
Custer, South Dakota

PARTY MEATBALLS

2 pounds ground chuck	1 10-ounce jar apple jelly
1 envelope onion soup	1 15-ounce can tomato
mix	sauce
¼ cup bread crumbs	1 15-ounce can pizza
1 egg	sauce
2 tablespoons MSG	

Combine ground chuck, soup mix, bread crumbs, egg and MSG in bowl; mix well. Shape into 1-inch balls. Brown on all sides in skillet; drain. Mix jelly, tomato sauce and pizza sauce in saucepan. Add meatballs. Simmer, covered, for 30 minutes. Serve in chafing dish.
Yield: 8 to 10 servings.
Note: May serve over rice as main dish.

Marianne Hays, Xi Alpha Mu
Terre Haute, Indiana

MEXICAN NACHOS

1 16-ounce package nacho cheese tortilla chips	⅓ cup chopped onion
	2 tablespoons milk
	2 cups shredded lettuce
8 ounces Mexican Velveeta cheese, cubed	1 cup chopped tomato
	½ cup sliced black olives

Cover large platter with tortilla chips. Combine cheese, onion and milk in saucepan over low heat. Heat until cheese melts, stirring constantly. Top with lettuce, tomato and olives. Drizzle cheese mixture over top. Yield: 4 to 6 servings.
Note: May microwave cheese mixture in ½-quart dish on Medium for 6 minutes, stirring every 2 minutes.

Beverly Davis, Epsilon Kappa
Nashville, Tennessee

FREEZER STUFFED MUSHROOMS

8 4-inch fresh mushrooms	1 teaspoon Worcestershire sauce
4 ounces sausage	½ teaspoon dry mustard
2 tablespoons butter	Dash of MSG
2 stalks celery, finely chopped	1 cup crushed herb stuffing mix
½ cup finely chopped onion	1 cup strong beef broth
½ teaspoon lemon juice	2 tablespoons melted butter

Wash mushrooms; pat dry. Remove and chop enough mushroom stems to measure 6 tablespoons. Brown sausage in skillet in 2 tablespoons butter, stirring until crumbly. Add chopped mushroom stems, celery and onion. Sauté until tender. Remove from heat. Stir in lemon juice, Worcestershire sauce, mustard, MSG and stuffing mix. Add enough broth to make of stuffing consistency. Brush mushroom caps with melted butter. Place right side up in broiler pan. Broil for 1 minute. Fill with stuffing mixture. Arrange on flat dish; freeze until firm. Store in freezer bags or covered container. Partially thaw mushrooms; place on baking sheet. Dot with additional butter. Broil for 5 minutes or until lightly browned and heated through. Serve as appetizer or accompaniment for roast or turkey. Yield: 8 servings.

Alta Gable, Preceptor Beta Omega
Fort Worth, Texas

MUSHROOMS À LA MIDNIGHT

36 medium mushrooms	2 tablespoons Worcestershire sauce
1 7-ounce can deviled ham	
	½ teaspoon garlic salt
3 ounces cream cheese, softened	⅛ teaspoon pepper
	½ cup melted butter
2 cups fresh bread crumbs	

Rinse mushrooms; pat dry. Remove stems; chop finely. Combine chopped stems with deviled ham, cream cheese, bread crumbs and seasonings in bowl; mix well. Dip each mushroom cap in butter to coat. Fill with deviled ham mixture; place in 9x13-inch baking dish. Bake at 375 degrees for 15 minutes. Yield: 3 dozen.

Coralie R. Clary, Xi Xi
Rapid City, South Dakota

OLIVE-CHEESE PUFFS

4 ounces sharp Cheddar cheese, shredded	½ cup sifted flour
	½ teaspoon paprika
¼ cup margarine, softened	¼ teaspoon salt
	24 green olives, pitted

Combine cheese and margarine in bowl; mix well. Add flour, paprika and salt; mix well. Shape 1 teaspoonful dough around each olive. Place on ungreased baking sheet. Chill, covered, until 30 minutes before serving. Bake at 400 degrees for 10 to 15 minutes. Arrange on serving plate. Serve hot. Yield: 24 servings.

Kate Williams, Xi Epsilon Sigma
Oscoda, Michigan

OYSTER CRACKERS DELICIOSO

1 12-ounce package oyster crackers	½ cup oil
	½ teaspoon garlic powder
1 envelope milk-recipe ranch dressing mix	½ teaspoon dillweed
	1 teaspoon lemon pepper

Place crackers in plastic bag. Mix remaining ingredients in bowl. Pour over crackers. Shake bag for 5 minutes or until crackers are coated. Store in airtight container at room temperature or in freezer. Yield: 1 pound.

Carol Sassin, Xi Psi Beta
Beeville, Texas

POTATO SKINS

Baked potatoes	Crisp-fried bacon, crumbled
Grated Cheddar cheese	
Chopped green onions	

Cut potatoes into halves. Scoop out potatoes, leaving ½-inch shells. Reserve potato for another purpose. Cut potato skins into halves. Arrange on glass serving plate. Sprinkle with cheese, green onions and bacon. Microwave on High for several minutes or until cheese melts.

Mary Shapard, Epsilon Psi
Shelbyville, Tennessee

To serve large groups easily, use such pastry-based foods as quiche or pizza. Recipes can be doubled, baked on cookie sheets, and cut into bite-sized pieces. Or, roll 2 sheets thawed puff pastry to fit baking sheet. Layer 1 sheet pastry, Dijon mustard, boiled ham, Swiss cheese and remaining pastry on baking sheet. Cut steam vents. Bake in 450-degree oven for about 15 minutes or until golden brown.

MINI REUBENS

24 slices party rye bread	1 15-ounce can
¼ cup catsup	sauerkraut, drained
¾ cup mayonnaise	16 ounces Swiss cheese,
2½ ounces dried beef	sliced

Spread bread slices with mixture of catsup and mayonnaise. Place on foil-lined baking sheet. Place folded beef slice on each bread slice. Top with 1 teaspoon sauerkraut and ¼ slice cheese. Bake at 350 degrees for 15 minutes. Arrange on serving dish. Yield: 24 servings.

Barbara Mills, Xi Chi
Stephens City, Virginia

PARTY PIZZAS

1 pound ground chuck	1 cup shredded
1 egg, slightly beaten	mozzarella cheese
1 loaf party rye bread	1 6-ounce can sliced
1 6-ounce can pizza	mushrooms, drained
sauce	Parmesan cheese

Combine ground chuck and egg in bowl; mix well. Spread ¼ inch thick on rye slices. Layer pizza sauce, mozzarella cheese and mushrooms on top. Sprinkle with Parmesan cheese. Place on baking sheet. Bake at 350 degrees for 15 minutes or until bubbly. Yield: 3 to 4 dozen.

Barbara Boot, Xi Mu Chi
Corning, California

PARTY RYES

1 cup shredded Swiss	¼ cup chopped onion
cheese	¼ cup mayonnaise
½ cup crumbled crisp-	1 teaspoon
fried bacon	Worcestershire sauce
½ to ⅔ cup chopped	¼ teaspoon salt
black olives	1 loaf party rye bread

Combine cheese, bacon, olives, onion, mayonnaise, Worcestershire sauce and salt in bowl; mix well. Spread on bread slices; arrange on baking sheet. Bake at 350 degrees for 10 to 12 minutes or until bubbly. Serve hot. Yield: 15 to 20 servings.

Mary Meddles, Preceptor Delta Tau
Richwood, Ohio

RYE ROUNDS

1 pound process cheese	1 tablespoon
1 pound ground beef	Worcestershire sauce
1 pound hot sausage	1 loaf party rye

Cut cheese into pieces. Brown ground beef and sausage in large skillet, stirring until crumbly; drain well. Stir in Worcestershire sauce. Add cheese. Cook until cheese melts, stirring constantly. Spoon onto party rye bread. Place on baking sheet. Bake at 350 degrees for 10 minutes. Yield: 4 dozen.

Note: Rye Rounds may be frozen before baking.

Pat Cromwell, Epsilon Psi
Shelbyville, Tennessee

EASY DOGS

1 10-count package	1 cup packed brown sugar
hot dogs	½ cup grape jelly
25 bacon slices, cut into	
halves	

Cut each hot dog into 5 pieces; wrap each with ½ bacon slice. Place seam side down on baking sheet. Broil until brown; drain. Place into 2-quart baking dish. Combine brown sugar and jelly in small bowl; mix well. Pour over hot dogs. Bake at 300 degrees for 2 hours. Serve hot. Yield: 10 to 15 servings.

Margaret A. Bohls, Preceptor Beta Lambda
Arvada, Colorado

PARTY SANDWICHES

8 ounces cream cheese,	¼ cup chopped onion
softened	3 tablespoons pimento
¾ cup chopped nuts	1 tablespoon catsup
3 hard-boiled eggs,	1 teaspoon salt
chopped	Pepper to taste

Combine all ingredients in bowl; mix well. Chill in refrigerator. Serve with crackers or use as sandwich spread. Yield: 2½ cups.

Peggy W. Cox, Preceptor Nu
Anniston, Alabama

CHEESE AND SAUSAGE BISCUITS

1 pound extra-sharp	3 cups buttermilk
Cheddar cheese	baking mix
1 pound sausage	

Melt cheese in top of double boiler. Combine sausage and baking mix in bowl; mix well. Add melted cheese; mix well. Drop by spoonfuls onto ungreased baking sheet. Bake at 325 degrees for 20 minutes. Drain on paper towels. Serve hot. Yield: 2 to 3 dozen.

Rachel Ollar, Beta Lambda
Evanston, Wyoming

SAUSAGE-ONION SNACKS

1 pound bulk sausage	1 tablespoon caraway seed
1 large onion, chopped	1½ cups sour cream
2 cups buttermilk	¼ teaspoon salt
baking mix	1 egg, beaten
¾ cup milk	Paprika
1 egg, beaten	

Brown sausage and onion in skillet, stirring until crumbly; drain. Combine baking mix, milk and 1 egg in bowl; mix well. Pat into ungreased 9x13-inch baking dish. Sprinkle with caraway seed. Spoon in sausage mixture. Combine sour cream, salt and 1 egg in bowl; mix well. Pour over sausage layer. Sprinkle with paprika. Bake at 350 degrees for 25 to 30 minutes or until set. Cut into rectangles. Yield: 32 servings.

Dottie Fortson, Gamma Theta
Baltimore, Maryland

SCALLOP BITES

8 ounces sea scallops	Brown sugar to taste
8 ounces sliced bacon	

Rinse and drain scallops; pat dry. Wrap each scallop in ½ slice bacon; secure with toothpick. Place in foil-lined baking sheet. Sprinkle with brown sugar. Broil for 3 to 4 minutes or until bacon is crisp. Drain on paper towel. Yield: 2 dozen.

Xi Alpha
Providence, Rhode Island

SHRIMP CANAPÉ

1 pound large shrimp	½ teaspoon curry powder
½ lemon, sliced	1 loaf party rye bread
1 clove of garlic	Parsley sprigs
½ cup mayonnaise	Pimento strips
¼ cup Major Grey's chutney	Caviar

Cook shrimp with lemon and garlic in water to cover in saucepan until pink; drain and peel. Chill in refrigerator. Combine mayonnaise, chutney and curry powder in bowl; mix well. Spread on party rye bread. Cut shrimp in half lengthwise. Place 1 half, cut side down, on each canapé. Garnish with parsley, pimento and caviar. Yield: 3 dozen.

Jackie Vogler, Xi Sigma Phi
Hilltop Lakes, Texas

SPINACH BALLS

2 10-ounce packages frozen chopped spinach, cooked	6 eggs, well beaten
	¾ cup butter, melted
	½ cup grated Parmesan cheese
3 cups herb-flavored stuffing mix	1 tablespoon pepper
1 large onion, finely chopped	1½ teaspoons garlic salt
	½ teaspoon thyme

Drain spinach well; squeeze dry. Combine spinach with remaining ingredients in large bowl; mix well. Shape into ¾-inch balls. Place on lightly greased baking sheet. Bake at 325 degrees for 15 to 20 minutes or until golden brown. Place on serving plate. Serve hot. Garnish with parsley. Yield: 10 to 11 dozen.
Note: May be frozen before baking, thawed slightly and baked as above.

Nina Slaton, Preceptor Gamma Nu
Lubbock, Texas

SPRING ROLLS

½ cup chopped onion	1 pound bean sprouts
1 tablespoon oil	¾ cup chopped carrots
1 pound ground pork	24 won ton wrappers, separated
1 tablespoon soy sauce	
¾ teaspoon garlic salt	Oil for deep frying

Sauté onion in 1 tablespoon oil in skillet. Stir in ground pork, soy sauce and garlic salt. Cook until crumbly, stirring frequently. Stir in bean sprouts and carrots. Drain and cool. Spoon 1 tablespoon filling onto lower center of each won ton wrapper; fold up from bottom to just cover filling. Fold sides to center; roll up. Moisten edge with water; press to seal. Deep-fry several at a time in 375-degree oil for 2 to 3 minutes or until golden brown. Remove with slotted spoon; drain on paper towels. Serve hot with catsup and mustard. Yield: 12 to 14 servings.

Deneen Phelps, Eta
Auburn, Washington

SWEET TORTILLA CHIPS

10 flour tortillas	¼ cup sugar
Oil for deep frying	½ teaspoon cinnamon

Cut each tortilla into 6 wedges. Fry in 375-degree oil for 45 seconds on each side or until slightly puffed and golden brown. Drain on paper towels. Sprinkle warm chips with mixture of sugar and cinnamon. Yield: 5 dozen.

Lorrie Spidel, Alpha Kappa
Angola, Indiana

INSTANT MEXICAN PIZZA

8 ounces cream cheese, softened	Sliced jalapeño peppers
	Sliced green olives
1 16-ounce jar chunky salsa	1 cup shredded sharp Cheddar cheese
Sliced ripe olives	

Spread cream cheese on serving plate. Spoon salsa over cream cheese. Sprinkle ripe olives, peppers, green olives and Cheddar cheese on top. Serve with chips. Yield: 12 to 16 servings.

Pat Cromwell, Epsilon Psi
Shelbyville, Tennessee

TACO PIE

8 ounces cream cheese, softened	¼ cup chopped green pepper
½ cup sour cream	¼ cup chopped onion
1 8-ounce jar taco sauce	1½ cups grated Cheddar cheese
2 cups shredded lettuce	
2 tomatoes, chopped	Black olives, chopped

Blend cream cheese and sour cream in bowl. Spread in 10-inch pie plate. Spread taco sauce over cheese mixture. Add layers of lettuce and mixture of tomatoes, green pepper and onion over top. Cover with cheese. Top with black olives. Chill until serving time. Serve with tortilla chips for dipping. Yield: 12 servings.

Jan Perigard, Xi Chi
Waterbury, Connecticut

Fill won ton wrappers with Monterey Jack cheese cubes and ½ teaspoon chopped green chilies. Fold and deep-fry as for Spring Rolls on this page.

TORTILLA ROLLS

3 8-ounce packages cream cheese, softened	12 green onions, chopped
8 ounces sour cream	Juice of ½ lime
4 jalapeño peppers, seeded, chopped	18 flour tortillas
	1 jar picante sauce

Combine cream cheese and sour cream in bowl. Beat until smooth. Add jalapeño peppers, green onions and lime juice; mix well. Spread tortillas with cream cheese mixture. Roll as for jelly roll. Wrap in plastic wrap. Chill for several hours. Cut into bite-sized pieces. Arrange on serving plate. Place bowl of picante sauce in center. Yield: 20 servings.

VEGETABLE PÂTÉ

2 envelopes unflavored gelatin	¼ cup sour cream
½ cup cold water	2 tablespoons minced celery
1 cup hot water	2 tablespoons chopped green pepper
4 teaspoons instant chicken bouillon	½ cup chopped mushrooms
¼ cup vegetable juice cocktail	2 tablespoons butter
1 cup shredded Cheddar cheese	4 ounces liverwurst
2 tablespoons crumbled bleu cheese	2 teaspoons lemon juice
	1 tablespoon Brandy
	½ cup chopped pecans

Soften gelatin in ½ cup cold water. Combine with 1 cup hot water in saucepan. Heat until gelatin dissolves, stirring constantly. Add bouillon, stirring until dissolved. Combine ¼ cup gelatin mixture with vegetable juice. Pour into oiled 4½-cup mold. Chill until set. Combine cheeses and sour cream in bowl; beat until smooth. Stir in ½ cup gelatin mixture, celery and green pepper. Spoon over congealed layer. Chill until set. Sauté mushrooms in butter in skillet. Combine liverwurst and lemon juice in bowl; mix well. Add mushrooms; mix well. Stir in remaining gelatin mixture, Brandy and pecans. Spoon over congealed layers. Chill until firm. Unmold onto serving plate. Serve with assorted breads and crackers. Yield: 24 servings.

VEGETABLE PIZZA

16 ounces cream cheese, softened	1 cup mayonnaise
1 package dry vegetable soup mix	2 packages refrigerator crescent rolls
	Fresh vegetables

Combine cream cheese, soup mix and mayonnaise in small bowl; mix well. Chill in refrigerator. Place roll dough in 11x14-inch baking pan; seal edges and perforations. Bake according to package directions. Cool. Spread with cream cheese mixture. Arrange fresh vegetables such as cauliflower and broccoli flowerets and chopped green pepper, green onions and mushrooms over top; press lightly into cream cheese mixture. Cut into squares. Yield: 4 to 6 servings.

Dorothy A. Kramer, Laureate Theta
Omaha, Nebraska

VEGETABLE SNAPPIES

2 packages refrigerator crescent rolls	½ cup salad dressing
8 ounces cream cheese, softened	2 tablespoons dillweed
½ cup sour cream	Onion, minced
	Fresh vegetables
	Grated cheese

Place roll dough in greased 10x15-inch baking pan; seal edges and perforations. Bake at 400 degrees for 10 minutes. Cool. Combine cream cheese, sour cream, salad dressing, dillweed and onion in bowl; mix well. Spread over baked layer. Top with assorted chopped fresh vegetables such as broccoli, cauliflower, green pepper, carrots, radishes and mushrooms. Sprinkle with cheese. Cut into 2-inch squares. Yield: 30 squares.

Sally Finch, Xi Iota Zeta
Galesburg, Illinois

VEGGIE BARS

2 packages refrigerator crescent rolls	1 envelope ranch dressing mix
16 ounces cream cheese, softened	½ cup mayonnaise

Place roll dough on ungreased baking sheet; seal edges and perforations. Bake at 300 degrees for 10 minutes. Cool. Combine cream cheese, dressing mix and mayonnaise in small bowl; mix well. Spread over baked layer. Top with chopped assorted vegetables such as celery, carrots, broccoli, cauliflower, radishes and red cabbage. Chill, covered, for several hours. Cut into squares. Yield: 4 to 6 servings.

Joyce Wood, Preceptor Lambda
Parkersburg, West Virginia

BARBECUED WATER CHESTNUTS

1 pound sliced bacon	½ cup mayonnaise
2 cans whole water chestnuts, drained	1 cup packed brown sugar
	1 cup chili sauce

Cut bacon slices into halves. Wrap each chestnut with bacon; fasten with toothpick. Arrange in 9x13-inch baking pan. Combine remaining ingredients in small bowl; mix well. Pour over chestnuts carefully; do not pour on toothpick skewers. Bake at 350 degrees for 1 hour. Place on serving plate. Yield: 10 servings.

Pamela Miller, Iota Iota
Antes Fort, Pennsylvania

LIGHT ZUCCHINI ROUNDS

8 ounces cream cheese, softened	1 tomato, seeded, chopped
2 tablespoons minced onion	¼ cup ground walnuts
	4 zucchini

Mix first 4 ingredients in bowl. Chill for 1 to 4 hours. Slice zucchini ¾ inch thick. Spread with cream cheese mixture; arrange on serving plate.

Marge Hefty, Preceptor Alpha Epsilon
Tucson, Arizona

Holiday Beverages

BOURBON SLUSH

*2 tablespoons instant
tea powder*
2 cups water
*1 12-ounce can frozen
lemonade concentrate,
thawed*

*1 6-ounce can frozen
orange juice
concentrate, thawed*
1 cup sugar
7 cups water
1½ cups Bourbon

Dissolve tea powder in 2 cups water. Combine with remaining ingredients in large container; mix well. Freeze, covered, until firm. Thaw for 30 minutes before serving. Spoon into glasses. May add chilled 7-Up or ginger ale if desired. Yield: 20 servings.

Paula Disterhaupt, Preceptor Alpha Pi
Glenwood, Iowa

CAPE CANAVERAL PUNCH

*5 bottles of Champagne,
chilled*
1 pint applejack Brandy
1 quart ginger ale, chilled

3 lemons, sliced
3 oranges, sliced
*Confectioners' sugar
to taste*

Mix Champagne, Brandy and ginger ale in punch bowl. Stir in lemon and orange slices and sugar to taste. Add decorative ice cubes. Yield: 21 servings.
Note: Freeze ice cubes decorated with lemon and orange slices and maraschino cherries.

Dorothy (Dottie) Hall, Preceptor Alpha Lambda
Williamsburg, Virginia

CHRISTMAS PUNCH

1 quart light rum
1 pint Brandy
1 pint peach Brandy
1 pint dark rum
*1 6-ounce bottle of
lemon juice*

*4 6-ounce cans frozen
lemonade concentrate,
thawed*
3 quarts water
*1 package frozen sliced
peaches*

Combine first 6 ingredients in punch bowl. Add water. Stir in peaches gently. Ladle into punch cups.
Yield: 1½ gallons.

Paula Middleton, Xi Mu Eta
Houston, Texas

GRASSHOPPER PUNCH

*5 ounces green Crème de
Menthe*
*3 ounces white Crème de
Menthe*

1 quart vanilla ice cream

Combine liqueurs in blender container. Add vanilla ice cream 1 spoonful at a time, processing until smooth after each addition. Serve immediately as punch or after-dinner drink.

Eloise Hood, Preceptor Epsilon Alpha
Winter Haven, Florida

ORANGE SLUSH

2 to 3 cups blended whiskey	1 12-ounce can frozen lemonade concentrate, thawed
2 cups strong tea	
1 12-ounce can frozen orange juice concentrate, thawed	1 cup sugar
	4 cups water
	Grapefruit soda

Combine whiskey, tea, concentrates and sugar with water in freezer container; mix well. Freeze until slushy. Mix with grapefruit soda in punch bowl. Yield: 20 to 25 servings.

Mary Ann Cavalier, Xi Kappa Beta
Follansbee, West Virginia

STRAWBERRY SLUSH

3 cups sugar	1 12-ounce can frozen orange juice concentrate, thawed
9 cups water	
1 package strawberry drink mix	
2 cups vodka	1 bottle of 7-Up, chilled

Bring sugar and water to a boil in saucepan. Cool. Add remaining ingredients; mix well. Process ¼ at a time in blender until smooth. Pour into freezer container. Freeze for 12 to 24 hours, stirring occasionally. Spoon into frosted glasses. Add chilled 7-Up if desired. Yield: 15 to 20 servings.

Mary Ann Cavalier, Xi Kappa Beta
Follansbee, West Virginia

ROSÉ PUNCH

3 12-ounce cans frozen fruit punch concentrate, thawed	½ cup sugar
	2 teaspoons grated orange rind
2 12-ounce cans frozen grapefruit juice concentrate, thawed	2 quarts Rosé, chilled
	1 quart club soda, chilled

Reconstitute concentrates using package directions. Chill until serving time. Combine with sugar, orange rind and wine in punch bowl. Add ice ring. Garnish with orange slices or other fresh fruit. Add soda just before serving.

Mary Lee Hunt, Xi Xi Theta
Palos Verdes Peninsula, California

FESTIVE WINE PUNCH

2½ cups orange juice	1 tablespoon honey
1 cup unsweetened pineapple juice	6 whole cloves
	½ teaspoon cinnamon
½ cup sifted confectioners' sugar	½ teaspoon nutmeg
	2 cups water
2 tablespoons grated lemon rind	1½ quarts ginger ale, chilled
1 quart dry white wine	

Combine first 10 ingredients in large pitcher. Refrigerate, covered, for 3 hours. Strain into punch bowl over ice ring. Add ginger ale just before serving. Yield: 20 servings.

Janet Shipe, Epsilon Chi
Chamblee, Georgia

WINE PUNCH

1 bottle of white wine	½ gallon orange or lime sherbet
1 2-liter bottle of 7-Up	

Chill wine and 7-Up. Pour into punch bowl. Add sherbet; mix lightly. Chill until serving time. Add ice cubes just before serving. Ladle into punch cups. Yield: 24 servings.

Deneen Phelps, Eta
Auburn, Washington

RED WINE

1 package dry yeast	Sugar
6 pounds sugar	
5 12-ounce cans frozen grape juice concentrate, thawed	

Dissolve yeast in a small amount of warm water. Dissolve sugar in several cups lukewarm water in 5 gallon cubitainer. Add grape juice concentrate diluted with warm water according to package directions. Stir in dissolved yeast and enough lukewarm water to fill cubitainer to 1½ inches from base of neck; mix well. Fill water seal valve ½ full; place on cubitainer. Let stand in area with constant 65 to 80 degree temperature. Mixture will "burp" 60 or more times per minute by the following day. Let stand for 12 days or until count is reduced to 12 to 15 times per minute. Pour into bottles. Add 1 teaspoon sugar to each. Seal with metal caps. Store in cool place for 30 days or longer.

Billy Jane Gabel, Xi Mu Eta
Houston, Texas

WHITE WINE SANGRIA

3¼ cups dry white wine, chilled	1 small lime, thinly sliced
	1 small orange, thinly sliced
½ cup orange juice	
¼ cup lime juice	1 small red Delicious apple, thinly sliced
¼ cup Brandy	
⅓ cup sugar	1 7-ounce bottle of club soda, chilled
1 cup strawberry halves	

Combine wine, orange and lime juices and Brandy in large pitcher. Add sugar; stir until dissolved. Stir in strawberries and fruit slices. Chill until serving time. Mix in club soda and ice just before serving time. Yield: 8 to 9 servings.

Lois Maine, Laureate Zeta
Duluth, Minnesota

Create special party spritzers and punches by mixing 1 bottle of white wine with one of the following: an equal amount of soda water plus lemon, lime or kiwifruit slices; 2 bottles of champagne plus 3 thinly sliced oranges; ½ cup sweet Sherry plus 1 cup sliced peaches, apricots, pineapple or strawberries.

WHISKEY SLUSH

2 cups water	1 6-ounce can frozen
7 tea bags	lemonade concentrate
2½ cups whiskey	1 cup sugar
2 6-ounce cans frozen	6 cups water
orange juice	7-Up
concentrate	

Bring 2 cups water to a boil in large pan. Add tea bags; steep until strong. Add whiskey, concentrates, sugar and 6 cups water; mix well. Pour into large freezer container. Freeze until slushy. Mix ¾ cup slush with ¼ cup 7-Up in glass. Yield: 10 to 12 servings.

Mary M. Dalton, Xi Kappa Beta
Steubenville, Ohio

FROZEN WHISKEY SOURS

1 6-ounce can frozen	6 to 10 ice cubes
lemon juice concentrate	Sugar to taste
4½ ounces Bourbon	

Combine lemon juice, Bourbon, ice cubes and sugar to taste in blender container. Process until blended. Serve in frosted glasses. Yield: 3 to 4 servings.

Sandi Davison, Preceptor Gamma Upsilon
Kansas City, Missouri

CAMERON'S PUNCH

1 3-ounce package grape	2 cups sugar
gelatin	1 quart pineapple juice
1 cup boiling water	1 10-ounce bottle of
2 quarts warm water	ginger ale
1 package grape drink mix	2 pints pineapple sherbet

Dissolve gelatin in boiling water in large container. Add warm water, drink mix and sugar. Stir until dissolved. Stir in pineapple juice. Chill until serving time. Mix gently with ginger ale and sherbet in punch bowl just before serving. Yield: 1 gallon.
Note: Vary the flavor and color of gelatin and drink mix with the holiday. Strawberry is good for Christmas.

Cameron Stimson, Xi Theta
Mayfield, Kentucky

HOLIDAY EGGNOG

6 egg whites	2 cups milk
¼ cup sugar	2 cups CocoRibe coconut
6 egg yolks	rum liqueur
2 tablespoons sugar	Nutmeg to taste
2 cups heavy cream	

Beat egg whites in large mixer bowl until foamy. Add ¼ cup sugar gradually, beating constantly until stiff peaks form. Beat egg yolks with 2 tablespoons sugar in mixer bowl for 5 minutes or until thick and lemon-colored. Fold gently into egg whites. Stir in cream, milk and liqueur. Chill in refrigerator. Pour into punch bowl. Sprinkle with nutmeg. Yield: 20 servings.

Photograph for this recipe on page 1.

EGGNOG BRASILIA

4 eggs, separated	¼ cup light corn syrup
3 cups milk	½ cup Brandy
2 cups light cream	¼ cup light corn syrup
3 tablespoons instant	¼ cup water
coffee powder	Nutmeg to taste

Beat egg yolks in large saucepan; stir in milk, cream, coffee powder and ¼ cup corn syrup. Cook just to the scalding point over low heat, stirring frequently. Remove from heat; stir in Brandy. Combine ¼ cup corn syrup and ¼ cup water in small saucepan; bring to a boil. Simmer for 5 minutes. Beat egg whites until foamy; beat in hot syrup gradually until soft peaks form. Fold in egg yolk mixture. Ladle into punch bowl; sprinkle with nutmeg.

Wenda Robertson, Theta Sigma
Boise City, Oklahoma

EGGNOG

12 eggs, separated	1 teaspoon vanilla extract
4 to 6 cups confectioners'	Nutmeg to taste
sugar	Milk

Beat egg whites in large mixer bowl until foamy. Add 2 to 3 cups confectioners' sugar gradually, beating constantly until stiff peaks form. Fold in vanilla extract and nutmeg. Beat egg yolks and remaining confectioners' sugar in bowl until thick and lemon-colored. Fold into egg white mixture. Fill punch bowl ⅓ full, add enough warm or cold milk to make of desired consistency; blend well. Sprinkle with additional nutmeg. Yield: 24 to 30 servings.

Jean Koehl, Xi Zeta Mu
Eldridge, Iowa

PEPPERMINT EGGNOG PUNCH

1 pint pink peppermint	1 cup whipping cream,
stick ice cream	whipped
2 cups eggnog	16 small candy canes
1 28-ounce bottle of	⅓ cup crushed
club soda, chilled	peppermint candy
Red food coloring	

Spoon ice cream into punch bowl. Add eggnog and club soda; mix well. Tint pink with food coloring. Spoon whipped cream over top. Place candy cane in each cup. Ladle eggnog into cups. Sprinkle crushed candy on top. Yield: 16 servings.
Note: Tie bow around handle of punch ladle.

Linda Hawkins, Preceptor Delta
Cookeville, Tennessee

SOUTHERN COFFEE PUNCH

2 quarts strong cold coffee	½ cup sugar
2 cups cold milk	1 quart vanilla ice cream
2 teaspoons vanilla extract	Nutmeg to taste

Combine coffee, milk, vanilla and sugar in punch bowl; stir until sugar is dissolved. Add small scoops of ice cream. Sprinkle lightly with nutmeg. Yield: 20 servings.

Janie Carpenter, Gamma Lambda
Sanford, Florida

CRANBERRY SPARKLE

½ cup fresh cranberries	6 cups cranberry juice
1 6-ounce can frozen	cocktail
orange juice	½ cup lemon juice
concentrate, thawed	2 quarts ginger ale

Place cranberries in 5-cup ring mold. Add enough water to fill mold. Freeze until firm. Reconstitute orange juice using package directions. Chill juices for several hours. Pour juices into punch bowl. Dip frozen mold into warm water for 1 minute; unmold. Float ring in punch; add ginger ale just before serving. Yield: 20 servings.

Rita A. Roycraft, Xi Delta
Wheaton, Illinois

FROSTY GOLDEN PUNCH

1 6-ounce can frozen	1 12-ounce can apricot
lemonade concentrate	nectar, chilled
1 6-ounce can frozen	½ cup lemon juice
orange juice	1 quart lemon sherbet
concentrate	2 quarts ginger ale, chilled
1 6-ounce can frozen	
pineapple juice	
concentrate	

Reconstitute thawed concentrates using package directions. Combine with apricot nectar and lemon juice in punch bowl. Spoon in sherbet and add ginger ale just before serving. Yield: 20 to 25 servings.

Mary Schreiner, Theta Zeta
Tiffin, Ohio

SPIRITED PUNCH

Juice of 10 lemons	¾ cup dark rum
Juice of 6 limes	¾ cup light rum
¼ cup sugar	¾ cup Brandy
¼ cup grape juice	1 fifth of Bourbon
¼ cup grenadine	3 quarts club soda

Combine all ingredients except soda in punch bowl. Add soda just before serving.

Betty Clark, Xi Beta Epsilon
Lakeland, Florida

BUBBLING CHRISTMAS PUNCH

1 3-ounce package	1 6-ounce can frozen
lime gelatin	lemonade concentrate
1 cup boiling water	1 quart ginger ale
2 cups cold water	15 to 20 small scoops
1 cup pineapple juice	sherbet

Dissolve gelatin in boiling water in bowl. Add cold water, pineapple juice and thawed lemonade; mix well. Pour over ice in punch bowl. Add ginger ale and sherbet just before serving. Yield: 15 to 20 servings.

Florence Brennan, Xi Beta Nu
Joseph, Oregon

HOLIDAY PUNCH

1 3-ounce package	4 cups cranberry
cherry gelatin	juice cocktail
1 cup boiling water	1 16-ounce bottle of
1 6-ounce can frozen	ginger ale
lemonade concentrate	½ gallon vanilla
3 cups cold water	ice cream

Dissolve gelatin in boiling water in bowl. Add lemonade concentrate and cold water; mix well. Stir in cranberry juice cocktail. Chill until serving time. Pour into punch bowl. Add ginger ale. Scoop ice cream into balls. Add to punch. Ladle into punch cups. Yield: 24 servings.

Carol Williams, Theta Theta
Hayden, Colorado

MAGIC QUENCHER

3 to 4 cups favorite mixed	1 cup orange juice
fruit punch	Juice of 3 lemons
Canned pineapple slices	3 tablespoons honey
Maraschino cherries	3 cups ginger ale
1 cup unsweetened	1 quart ice milk
pineapple juice	

Partially freeze fruit punch. Arrange pineapple slices and cherries in ring mold. Spoon fruit punch carefully over fruit. Freeze until firm. Combine pineapple juice, orange juice, lemon juice and honey in pitcher; mix well. Chill until serving time. Add ginger ale and ice milk; mix well. Pour into punch bowl; add ice ring.

Dorothy Scott, Xi Epsilon Zeta
Sikeston, Missouri

PARTY PUNCH

1 16-ounce can	1 6-ounce can frozen
pineapple tidbits	lemonade concentrate,
1 16-ounce package	thawed
individually frozen	1 6-ounce can frozen
whole strawberries	limeade concentrate,
Sections of 2 peeled	thawed
oranges	1 46-ounce can
1 12-ounce can frozen	pineapple juice
orange juice	6 cups cold water
concentrate, thawed	1 to 2 quarts club soda

Drain pineapple, reserving juice. Arrange fruit in ring mold. Pour reserved juice carefully around fruit. Fill mold with cold water. Freeze until firm. Mix concentrates and pineapple juice in pitcher. Chill until serving time. Mix with 6 cups cold water in punch bowl. Add club soda. Unmold ice ring; place in punch bowl.
Yield: 4 to 5 quarts.
Note: May add mint or lemon leaves to ice ring.

Jean Sego, Kappa Lambda
Greenwood, Indiana

RITUAL PUNCH

1 12-ounce can frozen orange juice concentrate	1 46-ounce can pineapple juice
1 12-ounce can frozen lemonade concentrate	2 quarts ginger ale

Reconstitute thawed concentrates in punch bowl using package directions. Stir in pineapple juice. Add ginger ale just before serving. Yield: 15 cups.

Lois Sanner, Tau
Silver Bay, Minnesota

SHERRY'S DIET DELIGHT PUNCH

1 ripe banana	1 12-ounce can frozen orange juice concentrate, thawed
1 3-ounce package sugar-free gelatin	
1 cup pineapple juice	3 cans diet cranberry juice
1 12-ounce can frozen apple juice concentrate, thawed	4 cups cold water
	32 ounces sugar-free 7-Up

Purée banana in blender container. Add gelatin; mix well. Combine banana mixture and juices in large container. Chill until serving time. Pour into punch bowl. Add cold water; mix well. Stir in 7-Up.
Yield: 24 to 32 servings.
Note: Sugar-free ginger ale may be substituted for 7-Up and any flavor gelatin may be used.

Sharon Tabor, Xi Beta Phi
Marion, Illinois

SNOW PUNCH

3 cups mashed bananas	1 3-liter bottle of lemon-lime soda
1 cup lemon juice	
2 cups sugar	1 quart lemon sherbet
2 cups light cream	1/3 cup flaked coconut

Blend bananas, lemon juice and sugar in bowl. Chill until serving time. Pour into punch bowl; stir in cream. Add soda gradually. Float spoonfuls of sherbet in punch. Sprinkle sherbet with coconut. Yield: 40 servings.

Maud Heilman, Xi Nu Alpha
San Jose, California

FORMAL TEA PUNCH

4 cups sugar	3 12-ounce cans frozen lemonade concentrate, thawed
4 cups water	
2 cups strong black tea	
1 46-ounce can pineapple juice	1 16-ounce package frozen strawberries
1 12-ounce can frozen orange juice concentrate, thawed	4 quarts cold water
	1 bottle of Chablis
	2 quarts ginger ale

Bring sugar and 4 cups water to a boil in saucepan. Boil for 10 minutes. Cool. Add tea, pineapple juice, orange juice and lemonade; mix well. Place in punch bowl. Thaw strawberries partially. Add to tea mixture in punch bowl. Add 4 quarts water, Chablis and ginger ale just before serving. Yield: 50 to 60 servings.

Mrs. James G. Lewis, Kappa Theta
South Haven, Michigan

HOT CIDER

4 cups cider	2 cinnamon sticks
3 cups cranapple juice	

Combine cider and cranapple juice in large saucepan. Add cinnamon sticks. Bring to a boil; reduce heat. Simmer for 1 hour. Ladle into cups. Yield: 10 servings.

Colette Iberg, Rho Chi
Pocahantas, Illinois

SPICED CIDER

3 cups sweet apple cider	1/2 teaspoon grated lemon rind
20 whole cloves	
3 cinnamon sticks	1/2 teaspoon grated orange rind
3 cups sweet apple cider	

Bring 3 cups cider and spices to a boil over low heat in saucepan. Simmer for 5 minutes; remove from heat. Let stand for 30 minutes; strain. Add remaining cider and lemon and orange rinds; mix well. Serve warm in mugs garnished with cinnamon stick or chilled over ice in chilled glasses garnished with orange or lemon slices. Yield: 8 to 10 servings.

Colleen Scott, Iota Alpha
Independence, Louisiana

SPICED HOLIDAY PUNCH

2 lemons, quartered	1 quart cranberry juice cocktail, chilled
3/4 cup packed brown sugar	
4 2-inch cinnamon sticks	1 quart apple cider, chilled
1 tablespoon whole allspice	2 quarts unsweetened pineapple juice, chilled
1 tablespoon whole cloves	1 quart cold water

Combine lemons, brown sugar and spices in percolator basket. Place juices and water in percolator. Perk for 30 minutes. Serve hot. Yield: 30 servings.

Roberta DeNegre, Preceptor Gamma Upsilon
Blue Springs, Missouri

Make a decorative ice mold to chill punches. Pour 1½ inches water in ring mold. Freeze until almost solid. Add strawberry, lemon, orange or kiwifruit slices in pretty pattern. Cover with ice cold water. Freeze until firm. Repeat if necessary to fill mold. Unmold into punch bowl.

HOT PUNCH

6 cups apple cider	¼ cup honey
1 cinnamon stick	3 tablespoons lemon
1 20-ounce can	juice
unsweetened pineapple	¼ teaspoon nutmeg
juice	

Bring cider and cinnamon stick to a boil in saucepan. Simmer, covered, for 5 minutes. Add remaining ingredients. Simmer, uncovered, for 5 minutes. Serve hot. Yield: 10 to 12 servings.

Lucile Davis, Preceptor Nu
Anniston, Alabama

HOT CRANBERRY TEA

4 cups fresh cranberries	Juice of 1 lemon
4 cups water	Juice of 3 oranges
2½ cups sugar	½ cup red hot
4 quarts water	cinnamon candies

Combine cranberries with 4 cups water in saucepan. Cook berries until skins pop. Strain; return pulp to saucepan. Add sugar and 2 quarts water. Bring mixture to a boil. Cook, stirring constantly, until sugar is dissolved. Add lemon and orange juice and candies. Heat until candies are dissolved. May be served cold. Yield: 1 gallon.

Betty John, Preceptor Alpha Alpha
Mt. Carmel, Illinois

HOT CRANBERRY ROSÉ CUP

1 quart cranberry-apple	12 whole cloves
drink	Peel of ½ lemon, cut
2 cups water	in strips
1 cup sugar	2 fifths rosé wine
4 1-inch cinnamon sticks	¼ cup lemon juice

Combine cranberry-apple drink, water, sugar, cinnamon, cloves and lemon peel in saucepan; bring to a boil, stirring until sugar is dissolved. Reduce heat; simmer for 15 minutes. Strain; add wine and lemon juice. Heat through; pour into punch bowl. Garnish with lemon slices and fresh cranberries, if desired. Serve in preheated mugs or cups. Yield: 20 servings.

Jean Lombardi, Alpha Alpha Chi
Santa Rosa, California

MULLED GRAPEFRUIT CIDER

1 cup sugar	12 whole cloves
½ cup water	1 48-ounce can
2 ½-inch cinnamon	grapefruit juice
sticks	1 quart sweet cider

Combine sugar, water and spices in saucepan; simmer for 10 minutes. Strain. Combine with grapefruit juice and cider. Reheat; serve hot from punch bowl. Yield: 12 servings.

Sylvia Stenbol, Theta Kappa
Escanaba, Michigan

HOT SPICED GRAPE PUNCH

1 tablespoon whole cloves	½ cup water
1 2-inch cinnamon stick	¾ cup orange juice
1 quart grape juice	¼ cup lemon juice

Tie cloves and cinnamon in small cloth bag. Place grape juice, spice bag and water in saucepan; bring to a boil. Remove from heat; remove spice bag. Stir in orange juice and lemon juice. Yield: 10 servings.

Yvonne Louthan, Epsilon
Montesano, Washington

CAROLERS' WASSAIL

1 gallon sweet cider	4 cinnamon sticks
½ teaspoon nutmeg	2 cups sugar
1 teaspoon cloves	Juice of 8 oranges
1 tablespoon allspice	Juice of 4 lemons

Combine all ingredients in large saucepan. Bring to a boil. Serve hot.

Joan Payne, Iota Theta
Concord, California

ENGLISH WASSAIL

1¾ cups sugar	2 tablespoons chopped
4 cups water	ginger
2 whole cloves	2 cups lemon juice
4 cinnamon sticks	2 quarts apple cider
4 whole allspice	3 cups orange juice

Bring sugar and water to a boil in saucepan. Boil for 10 minutes. Add spices. Let stand, covered, in warm place for 1 hour. Strain into large kettle; stir in lemon juice, cider and orange juice. Heat to serving temperature.

JoAnn Bonner, Delta
San Francisco, California

PINEAPPLE WASSAIL

4 cups unsweetened	1 cup orange juice
pineapple juice	6 1-inch cinnamon
1 12-ounce can	sticks
apricot nectar	1 teaspoon whole cloves
2 cups apple cider	1 orange, sliced

Combine all ingredients in large saucepan. Bring to a boil; reduce heat. Simmer for 15 minutes. Strain into large punch bowl or pitcher. Float orange slices on top. Serve hot.

Shirley Berrard, Xi Epsilon Pi
Paris, Illinois

Garnish hot fruit beverages in punch bowls with baked apple halves, candied orange slices, or clove-studded orange slices. Garnish individual servings with cinnamon stick stirrers or clove-studded lemon or lime slices. Garnish mugs of hot chocolate with whipped cream, marshmallow creme, or candy cane stirrers.

Holiday Salads

APRICOT SALAD

1 6-ounce package
   apricot gelatin
1 20-ounce can crushed
   pineapple
2 cups boiling water
8 ounces cream cheese,
   softened

1 20-ounce can apricot
   halves, drained,
   chopped
1 cup chopped celery
1 cup chopped pecans
2 envelopes whipped
   topping mix, prepared

Combine gelatin, pineapple and water in saucepan; mix well. Cook for 10 minutes, stirring constantly. Add cream cheese; stir until melted. Pour into bowl. Chill until partially set. Add apricots, celery and pecans. Fold in whipped topping. Pour into 9x13-inch dish. Chill until firm. Cut into squares. Serve on lettuce-lined plates. Yield: 16 to 20 servings.

Dorothy Henderson, Preceptor Gamma Sigma
Gonzales, Texas

BLUEBERRY SALAD

3 ounces cream cheese,
   softened
1 cup light mayonnaise
2 cups miniature
   marshmallows
1½ cups strawberries

1 cup blueberries
1 8-ounce can crushed
   pineapple, drained
½ cup chopped pecans
1 cup whipped cream

Blend cream cheese and mayonnaise in bowl. Add marshmallows, fruit and pecans; mix well. Fold in whipped cream. Pour into 1-pound coffee can. Freeze until firm. Cut bottom from can with can opener; push out salad and slice. Serve on lettuce-lined salad plates. Yield: 10 to 12 servings.

Angie Cyr, Xi Delta Tau
Stillwater, Oklahoma

CHERRY SALAD

1 20-ounce can cherry
   pie filling
1 8-ounce can pineapple
   chunks, drained
1 14-ounce can
   sweetened condensed
   milk

1 12-ounce package
   miniature
   marshmallows
½ cup chopped nuts
8 ounces whipped topping

Combine pie filling, pineapple and condensed milk in 2-quart bowl; mix well. Stir in marshmallows and nuts. Fold in whipped topping. Chill until firm. Yield: 8 to 10 servings.

Dora Sheerer, Eta Mu
Woodstock, Georgia

CHERRY COTTON CANDY SALAD

1   21-ounce can cherry
    pie filling
1   16-ounce can crushed
    pineapple, drained
1 cup chopped nuts

1   14-ounce can
    sweetened condensed
    milk
16 ounces whipped
    topping

Combine all ingredients in bowl; mix well. Chill until serving time. Yield: 20 servings.

Brenda Evans, Alpha Omega
Overland Park, Kansas

FROZEN CHERRY CUP SALAD

2 cups sour cream
2 tablespoons lemon
    juice
½ cup sugar
Dash of salt
1   8-ounce can crushed
    pineapple

1 large banana, chopped
½ cup chopped pecans
1   16-ounce can pitted
    Bing cherries, drained
5 drops of red food
    coloring

Combine all ingredients in bowl; mix well. Spooon into paper-lined muffin cups. Freeze overnight or until firm. Remove to plastic bags. Store in freezer. Thaw for 30 minutes before serving. Remove paper liners. Arrange on lettuce-lined serving tray. Garnish with holly sprigs. Yield: 16 to 18 servings.

Lou Alexander, Xi Xi Rho
Ft. Worth, Texas

CONGEALED SALAD

1   3-ounce package
    strawberry gelatin
2 cups boiling water
1   12-ounce can crushed
    pineapple
1   3-ounce package
    lemon gelatin
1 cup boiling water

8 ounces cream cheese,
    softened
20 marshmallows,
    chopped
1   3-ounce package
    lime gelatin
2 cups boiling water
1 cup chopped nuts

Dissolve strawberry gelatin in 2 cups boiling water. Add pineapple; mix well. Pour into 7x12-inch dish. Chill until firm. Dissolve lemon gelatin in 1 cup boiling water. Melt cream cheese and marshmallows in top of double boiler; remove from heat. Stir in lemon gelatin mixture. Cool. Pour over congealed strawberry layer. Chill until firm. Dissolve lime gelatin in 2 cups boiling water. Cool. Add nuts. Spoon over congealed lemon layer. Chill until firm. Cut into 1-inch squares. Yield: 10 to 12 servings.

Wanda Odom, Preceptor Epsilon Upsilon
Denison, Texas

CRANBERRY FLUFF SALAD

1 envelope unflavored
    gelatin
½ cup cold water
¾ cup boiling water
1 pound cranberries,
    ground
¾ cup sugar

1 cup chopped celery
1 cup miniature
    marshmallows
1 cup coarsely chopped
    nuts
1 cup whipped topping

Soften gelatin in cold water in large bowl. Add boiling water; stir until dissolved. Cool. Add mixture of cranberries, sugar, celery, marshmallows and nuts; mix well. Fold in whipped topping. Pour into serving dish. Chill until firm. Yield: 10 to 12 servings.

Ann Corrigan, Preceptor Gamma Epsilon
Blue Springs, Missouri

CRANBERRY FREEZE

1 pound cranberries,
    ground
1 package miniature
    marshmallows
1   29-ounce can crushed
    pineapple, drained

1½ cups sugar
½ cup coarsely chopped
    walnuts
½ cup sugar
1 pint whipping cream,
    whipped

Combine cranberries, marshmallows, pineapple and 1½ cups sugar in bowl; mix well. Chill overnight. Add walnuts and ½ cup sugar; mix well. Fold in whipped cream. Pour into 9x13-inch dish. Freeze until firm. Cut into squares. Serve with assorted crackers. Yield: 10 to 12 servings.

Norma L. Gibson, Xi Eta
LaGrande, Oregon

CRANBERRY-FRUIT FREEZE

6 ounces cream cheese,
    softened
2 tablespoons sugar
2 tablespoons
    mayonnaise
2 cups whole cranberry
    sauce

½ cup chopped walnuts
1   9-ounce can crushed
    pineapple, drained
1 cup whipping cream,
    whipped
4 drops of red food
    coloring

Blend cream cheese with sugar and mayonnaise in bowl. Add cranberry sauce, walnuts and pineapple; mix well. Fold in whipped cream and food coloring. Pour into 3½x4½-inch loaf pan. Freeze until firm. Let stand at room temperature for 10 to 15 minutes before serving. Unmold onto serving plate; cut into slices.
Yield: 8 to 10 servings.
Note: May double recipe and freeze in tube pan.

Maureen Warren, Preceptor Alpha Gamma
Scottsdale, Arizona

CRANBERRY SALAD

1 pound cranberries,
    chopped
1 cup sugar
12 ounces miniature
    marshmallows

2 cups whipping cream,
    whipped
1   8-ounce can crushed
    pineapple

Mix cranberries and sugar in bowl. Let stand for 2 hours. Fold marshmallows into stiffly whipped cream. Let stand for 2 hours. Fold cranberries into whipped cream mixture. Fold in pineapple. Pour into 9x13-inch dish. Chill overnight. Yield: 15 servings.

Janice Venrick, Preceptor Beta Psi
Akron, Colorado

CRANBERRY JELL-O SALAD

1   3-ounce package
cherry gelatin
1   8-ounce can crushed
pineapple

1   16-ounce can whole
cranberry sauce

Prepare gelatin according to package directions, using slightly less water. Add pineapple and cranberry sauce; mix well. Pour into mold. Chill until firm. Unmold onto serving plate. Yield: 6 servings.

Cameron Stimson, Xi Theta
Mayfield, Kentucky

CREAMY CRANBERRY SALAD

1 pound cranberries,
frozen
3 medium apples, cored
20 large marshmallows
1 cup sugar

½ cup chopped celery
½ cup chopped nuts
1 cup whipping cream,
whipped

Put cranberries, apples and marshmallows through food grinder. Place in large glass bowl. Add sugar, celery and nuts; mix well. Chill for 30 minutes. Fold in whipped cream. Chill, covered, for 24 hours. Yield: 20 servings.

Marita Carter, Preceptor Lambda Iota
San Jose, California

FROZEN CRANBERRY SALAD

12 ounces cranberries,
ground
2 cups sugar
1 large can crushed
pineapple

16 ounces miniature
marshmallows
8 ounces whipped
topping

Combine cranberries and sugar in bowl; mix well. Chill, covered, overnight, stirring occasionally. Add pineapple and marshmallows; mix well. Chill, covered, overnight, stirring occasionally. Fold in whipped topping. Pour into two 1-quart molds. Freeze until firm. Unmold onto serving dish. Serve with turkey. Yield: 8 to 10 servings.

Sandy Tingley, Zeta Nu
Boardman, Oregon

CRANBERRY-ORANGE SALAD

3 cups cranberries
1 large orange
1½ cups sugar
2   3-ounce packages
lemon gelatin

3 cups boiling water
1 cup chopped celery
1 cup chopped pecans

Put cranberries and orange through food chopper. Sprinkle with sugar. Let stand for 1 hour. Dissolve gelatin in boiling water. Cool. Stir in celery and pecans. Add to cranberry and orange mixture; mix well. Pour into 10x13-inch dish. Chill for 3 hours or longer. Yield: 12 servings.
Note: Garnish with whipped cream to serve as dessert.

Lois Renfro, Alpha Chi Mu
Azle, Texas

CRANBERRY RELISH

2 apples
2 oranges
1   8-ounce package
fresh cranberries
1   3-ounce package
lemon gelatin
1   3-ounce package
orange gelatin

3 cups boiling water
1 cup canned crushed
pineapple
1 cup chopped pecans
2 cups sugar

Peel 1 apple and 1 orange. Grind apples, oranges and cranberries. Dissolve gelatins in boiling water in bowl. Add ground fruit, pineapple, pecans and sugar; mix well. Pour into serving bowl. Chill for several hours. Yield: 16 to 18 servings.

Mary Helen Buttman, Xi Gamma Zeta
Bartlesville, Oklahoma

FRUITY CRANBERRY SALAD

1   12-ounce package
fresh cranberries,
ground
1   15-ounce can crushed
pineapple, drained
1 cup sugar

⅓ to ½ package miniature
marshmallows
1 pint whipping cream,
whipped
2 bananas, sliced
⅔ cup chopped walnuts

Combine cranberries, pineapple, sugar and marshmallows in bowl; mix well. Chill in refrigerator overnight. Divide into 2 portions. Stir remaining ingredients into 1 portion. Pour into serving dish. Freeze remaining portion for another time. Yield: 8 to 10 servings.

Stella Davis, Xi Mu Chi
Corning, California

FROSTED CRANBERRY SALAD

1   6-ounce package
raspberry gelatin
2 cups boiling water
1   11-ounce can
mandarin oranges
1   16-ounce can whole
cranberry sauce
¼ cup chopped nuts

1   8-ounce can crushed
pineapple
¼ cup sugar
1 tablespoon all-purpose
flour
1 egg, beaten
½ cup whipping cream,
whipped

Dissolve gelatin in boiling water in bowl. Drain oranges, reserving ⅓ cup juice. Chop oranges coarsely. Add juice and cranberry sauce to gelatin mixture. Chill until partially set. Drain pineapple, reserving ⅓ cup juice. Add oranges, ¼ cup nuts and pineapple to gelatin mixture; mix gently. Pour into 8-inch glass dish. Chill until firm. Combine pineapple juice, sugar, flour and egg in saucepan. Cook until thickened, stirring constantly. Cool. Fold in whipped cream. Spread over congealed layer. Garnish with additional nuts. Serve on lettuce-lined plates. Yield: 8 to 10 servings.

Linda Robinson, Beta Alpha
Mt. Vernon, Ohio

FROZEN CRANBERRY SALAD

1 pound cranberries	1 20-ounce can crushed
1 pound miniature	pineapple, drained
marshmallows	½ cup sugar
1½ cups sugar	1 pint whipping cream,
¾ cup chopped walnuts	whipped

Freeze cranberries. Put through food grinder. Combine cranberries, marshmallows and 1½ cups sugar in bowl; mix well. Chill overnight. Add walnuts, pineapple and ½ cup sugar; mix well. Fold in whipped cream. Spoon into individual molds. Freeze until firm. May be kept frozen for up to 2 weeks. Unmold onto serving plates. Yield: 10 to 12 servings.
Note: Excellent with turkey.

Shirley Fitch, Xi Upsilon
Flagstaff, Arizona

DESSERT SALAD

2 or 3 3-ounce	1 20-ounce can crushed
packages lemon gelatin	pineapple
1 cup boiling water	1 6-ounce jar maraschino
8 ounces cream cheese,	cherries, drained,
softened	chopped
1 package slivered	2 cups whipping cream,
almonds	whipped

Dissolve gelatin in boiling water. Add 2 cups mixed crushed ice and water; stir until ice is melted. Chill until partially set. Combine cream cheese, almonds, pineapple and cherries in bowl; mix well. Fold in whipped cream. Add gelatin mixture. Pour into large springform pan. Chill until firm. Place on serving plate; remove side of pan. Cut into wedges. Yield: 12 servings.

Gerry Matisek, Preceptor Kappa Nu
San Bruno, California

DIRT SALAD

1 4-ounce package	8 to 9 ounces whipped
banana instant	topping
pudding mix	15 to 20 Oreo cookies,
1 12-ounce can crushed	crushed
pineapple	
2 cups miniature	
marshmallows	

Combine dry pudding mix and pineapple with juice in bowl; mix well. Stir in marshmallows and whipped topping. Spoon into clean 8-inch flower pot. Cover with crushed cookies. Chill until serving time. Place artificial flower in pot just before serving. Yield: 6 to 8 servings.

Dotty Cline, Xi Eta Omicron
Loda, Illinois

HARVEST FRUIT CUP

1 16-ounce can fruit	1 orange, peeled
cocktail, chilled	1 avocado
1 red apple	

Drain fruit cocktail. Cut apple into wedges and orange into sections. Scoop avocado pulp into small balls. Combine all ingredients in bowl; mix gently. Spoon into sherbet dishes. Serve with cheese crackers.
Yield: 4 servings.

Bettie Plummer, Laureate Pi
Independence, Missouri

DREAM BUFFET SALAD

2 8-ounce cans mandarin	1 10-ounce package
oranges	miniature
2 eggs, beaten	marshmallows
½ cup sugar	1 20-ounce can crushed
2 tablespoons all-purpose	pineapple
flour	1 envelope whipped
8 ounces cream cheese,	topping mix, prepared
softened	

Drain oranges, reserving juice. Combine 1 cup reserved juice, eggs and mixture of sugar and flour in saucepan. Cook until thickened and bubbly, stirring constantly. Remove from heat. Stir in cream cheese and marshmallows. Pour into bowl. Chill for 1 hour. Mix in oranges and pineapple. Fold in whipped topping. Chill for 24 hours. Yield: 10 to 12 servings.

Vera Wilson, Preceptor Lambda
Parkersburg, West Virginia

FALL FRUIT SALAD

2 cups ground	2 cups chopped
cranberries	red apples
3 cups miniature	½ cup seedless green
marshmallows	grapes
¾ cup sugar	¼ teaspoon salt
¼ cup chopped walnuts	1 cup whipped topping

Combine cranberries, marshmallows and sugar in 1½-quart bowl; mix well. Chill, covered, overnight. Add walnuts, remaining fruit and salt; mix well. Fold in whipped topping. Yield: 12 servings.

Cathy Wallace, Xi Kappa Beta
Wintersville, Ohio

FROZEN FRUIT CUP

2 16-ounce cans apricots,	1 cup (scant) sugar
drained, chopped	1 17-ounce can
1 12-ounce can water	pineapple tidbits
1 12-ounce can frozen	6 bananas, sliced
orange juice	2 tablespoons lemon
concentrate, thawed	juice

Combine all ingredients in large bowl; mix well. Spoon into individual serving dishes. Freeze, covered with plastic wrap, until firm. Thaw at room temperature for 1½ hours before serving. Yield: 8 to 12 servings.
Note: May microwave on Low for several seconds for quick thawing.

Ann Corrigan, Preceptor Gamma Epsilon
Blue Springs, Missouri

FROZEN FRUIT SALAD

2 eggs, beaten
2 tablespoons vinegar
10 marshmallows, cut up
1   15-ounce can fruit
    cocktail, drained

1 cup whipping cream,
   whipped
Chopped pecans

Mix eggs, vinegar and marshmallows in double boiler.
Cook until marshmallows are melted, stirring constantly.
Cool. Add fruit cocktail; mix well. Fold in whipped cream
and pecans. Pour into freezer container. Freeze until firm.
Thaw for 30 minutes before serving. Yield: 8 servings.

Betty Jo Hunter, Laureate Pi
Huntington, West Virginia

MARY ANN'S FROZEN SALAD

1   14-ounce can
    sweetened condensed
    milk
1   20-ounce can cherry
    pie filling

1   8-ounce can crushed
    pineapple
16 ounces whipped
   topping

Combine condensed milk, pie filling and pineapple in
bowl; mix well. Fold in whipped topping. Pour into
shallow dish. Freeze until firm. Let stand at room
temperature for 30 minutes before serving. Cut into
squares. Yield: 6 to 8 servings.

Mary Ann Mader, Laureate Alpha Delta
Elizabeth Township, Pennsylvania

FRUIT SALAD

1 medium watermelon,
   cubed
2 cantaloupes, cubed
3 oranges, sliced

1½ pounds seedless
    grapes, halved
1½ pounds strawberries,
    halved

Combine watermelon, cantaloupes, oranges, grapes and
strawberries in large bowl; mix lightly. Chill, covered, for
2 to 3 hours. Yield: 20 servings.

Gloria Hayungs, Rho Rho
Granville, Illinois

JELL-O SALAD

1   3-ounce package
    orange gelatin
8 ounces cream cheese,
   cubed
10 large marshmallows,
   chopped
2 tablespoons salad
   dressing

1   10½-ounce can
    crushed pineapple,
    drained
1 pint whipping cream,
   whipped
1   3-ounce package
    raspberry gelatin

Prepare orange gelatin according to package directions.
Stir in cream cheese, marshmallows and salad dressing.
Chill until partially set. Fold pineapple and partially congealed gelatin into whipped cream. Pour into 8x8-inch
dish. Chill until set. Prepare raspberry gelatin according
to package directions. Chill until partially set. Spoon
over congealed layer. Chill until set. Yield: 9 servings.

Tina K. McLemore, Theta Kappa
Minden, Louisiana

MANDARIN ORANGE SALAD

1   3-ounce package
    orange gelatin
1 cup boiling water

⅓ cup shredded cheese
2 bananas, sliced
1 cup mandarin oranges

Dissolve gelatin in boiling water in bowl. Add cheese,
bananas and oranges; mix well. Pour into mold. Chill
until firm. Unmold onto serving plate.
Yield: 8 to 10 servings.

Rachel Ollar, Beta Lambda
Evanston, Wyoming

PEACH PIE FRUIT SALAD

1   20-ounce can
    pineapple chunks
1 pint strawberries,
   sliced

2 bananas, sliced
1   20-ounce can peach
    pie filling

Drain pineapple, reserving ½ cup juice. Combine fruit,
pie filling and reserved juice in large bowl; cover. Chill
overnight. Yield: 10 servings.

Lois Renfro, Alpha Chi Mu
Azle, Texas

PEAR SALAD

1   6-ounce package
    lime gelatin
1 cup hot pear juice
1   29-ounce can pears,
    drained, mashed

8 ounces cream cheese,
   softened
12 ounces whipped
   topping

Dissolve gelatin in hot pear juice. Chill until partially set.
Combine pears and cream cheese in bowl; mix until
creamy. Stir into gelatin mixture. Fold in whipped
topping. Spoon into 9x13-inch glass dish. Chill until
firm. Yield: 12 servings.

Cheryl Ledger, Xi Kappa Beta
Wintersville, Ohio

PRETZEL SALAD

12 ounces cream cheese,
   softened
¾ cup sugar
2⅔ cups coarsely chopped
   pretzels
¾ cup margarine, melted
8 ounces whipped topping

1   6-ounce package
    sugar-free strawberry
    gelatin
2 cups pineapple juice,
   heated
1   10-ounce package
    frozen strawberries

Combine cream cheese and sugar in bowl; mix well. Mix
pretzels and margarine in bowl. Press into 9x13-inch
baking dish. Bake at 400 degrees for 8 minutes. Spread
cream cheese mixture over warm crust. Spread with
whipped topping. Chill in refrigerator. Dissolve gelatin
in hot pineapple juice; stir in strawberries. Chill until
partially set. Pour over whipped topping layer. Chill until
firm. Yield: 24 servings.

Lucille Greenfield, Laureate Theta
Richland, Washington

RASPBERRY PRETZEL SALAD

2½ cups crushed pretzels
¾ cup margarine, softened
8 ounces cream cheese, softened
1 cup sugar
8 ounces whipped topping
1 6-ounce package raspberry gelatin
2 cups boiling water
1 10-ounce package frozen raspberries

Mix pretzels and margarine in bowl. Press into 9x13-inch baking dish. Bake at 350 degrees for 10 to 12 minutes. Cool. Combine cream cheese and sugar in bowl; mix well. Fold in whipped topping. Spread over crust, sealing to edge. Dissolve gelatin in boiling water; stir in raspberries. Cool. Pour over cream cheese layer. Chill until firm. Garnish with parsley. Yield: 10 servings.

Edith Craig, Xi Phi
Butte, Montana

VIV'S RASPBERRY SALAD

2 3-ounce packages raspberry gelatin
2 cups boiling water
2 10-ounce packages frozen raspberries
1 13-ounce can crushed pineapple
2 tablespoons lemon juice
1 cup sour cream

Dissolve gelatin in boiling water in bowl. Add raspberries, pineapple and lemon juice; mix well. Pour half the mixture into 9 x13-inch dish. Chill until firm. Spread sour cream over congealed layer. Chill until firm. Spoon remaining gelatin mixture over sour cream layer. Chill until firm. Serve with turkey or ham. Yield: 8 servings.

Joanna Akers, Chi
Laramie, Wyoming

RAINBOW SALAD

1 3-ounce package cherry gelatin
1 3-ounce package lime gelatin
1 3-ounce package orange gelatin
3 cups boiling water
1½ cups cold water
1 cup pineapple juice
¼ cup sugar
1 3-ounce package pineapple gelatin
1 envelope whipped topping mix
2 cups fine vanilla wafer crumbs
¼ cup melted margarine

Place cherry, lime and orange gelatin in separate bowls. Add 1 cup boiling water to each; stir to dissolve. Add ½ cup cold water to each. Pour each into separate 8x8-inch dishes. Chill until firm. Cut each flavor into small cubes. Heat pineapple juice and sugar in saucepan until sugar dissolves. Add pineapple gelatin; stir until dissolved. Let stand until syrupy. Prepare whipped topping mix according to package directions. Fold in pineapple mixture. Fold in gelatin cubes. Mix crumbs and margarine in bowl. Reserve a small amount for topping. Pat remaining mixture into 9x13-inch dish. Spoon gelatin mixture over crumbs. Sprinkle with reserved crumbs. Chill for 8 hours or longer. Cut into squares. Yield: 15 to 20 servings.

Carol Williams, Theta Theta
Hayden, Colorado

RED HOT HOLIDAY SALAD

1 cup apple juice
½ cup red hot cinnamon candies
1 3-ounce package raspberry gelatin
1 16-ounce can fruit cocktail

Bring apple juice and red hots to a boil in saucepan, stirring until candies dissolve. Add gelatin; stir until dissolved. Drain fruit cocktail, reserving juice. Add enough water to reserved juice to measure 1 cup. Add to gelatin mixture. Add fruit. Pour into 9x9-inch dish. Chill until set. Yield: 6 servings.
Note: May substitute spiced apple slices, pineapple or bananas for fruit cocktail.

Mary K. Heitt, Preceptor Gamma Lambda
Tekoa, Washington

RIBBON SALAD

1 6-ounce package lime gelatin
2 cups boiling water
1½ cups cold water
1 3-ounce package lemon gelatin
1 cup boiling water
1 cup miniature marshmallows
2 3-ounce packages cream cheese, softened
½ cup mayonnaise
1 12-ounce can crushed pineapple
1 cup whipped cream
1 6-ounce package cherry gelatin
2 cups boiling water
1½ cups cold water

Dissolve lime gelatin in 2 cups boiling water. Stir in 1½ cups cold water. Pour into large glass bowl. Chill until firm. Dissolve lemon gelatin in 1 cup boiling water in bowl. Add marshmallows, mix well. Add cream cheese; beat until blended. Chill until thick. Add mayonnaise and pineapple; mix well. Chill until thick. Spoon over congealed lime layer. Chill until firm. Dissolve cherry gelatin in 2 cups boiling water. Stir in 1½ cups cold water. Pour over congealed lemon layer. Chill until firm. Yield: 12 to 15 servings.

Cheryl Huntoon, Preceptor Theta
Sparks, Nevada

RUBY RED SALAD MOLD

3 3-ounce packages strawberry gelatin
2 cups boiling water
1 16-ounce package frozen strawberries
1 16-ounce can whole cranberry sauce
1 20-ounce can crushed pineapple
½ cup chopped pecans
½ cup chopped celery
1 16-ounce jar cranberry relish

Dissolve gelatin in boiling water in bowl. Add remaining ingredients; mix well. Pour into 3-quart mold. Chill until firm. Unmold onto serving plate. Yield: 12 to 15 servings.

Rosalind Ratchford, Preceptor Beta Eta
Ellenton, Florida

SNOWFLAKE FRUIT MOLD

1 envelope unflavored gelatin	6 ounces cream cheese, softened
½ cup cold water	1 5-ounce can mandarin oranges, drained
1 15-ounce can crushed pineapple	½ cup chopped pecans
Juice of 1 lemon	½ cup flaked sweetened coconut
3 tablespoons sugar	

Soften gelatin in cold water in saucepan. Drain pineapple, reserving juice. Add enough water to reserved juice to measure 1 cup. Add to softened gelatin; mix well. Heat until dissolved; remove from heat. Add lemon juice, sugar and cream cheese; beat with wire whisk until smooth. Chill until partially set. Fold in remaining ingredients. Pour into lightly greased 1-quart mold. Chill until firm. Unmold onto lettuce-lined plate. Garnish with lemon slices. Yield: 8 servings.

Carole Chorlton, Preceptor Alpha Xi
Jacksonville, Florida

FRUITED SPAGHETTI SALAD

7 ounces spaghetti, broken	½ cup lemon juice
1 16-ounce can pineapple chunks, drained	2 cups confectioners' sugar
	6 apples, peeled, chopped
4 eggs, beaten	12 ounces whipped topping

Cook spaghetti according to package directions, adding red food coloring to water. Rinse in cool water; drain. Combine with pineapple in salad bowl; mix well. Chill in refrigerator. Combine eggs, lemon juice and confectioners' sugar in double boiler; mix well. Cook until thickened, stirring constantly. Cool. Stir in apples. Mix with spaghetti. Chill overnight. Fold in whipped topping just before serving. Yield: 12 servings.

Connie Sharp, Preceptor Upsilon
Omaha, Nebraska

STRAWBERRY PRETZEL SALAD

2 3-ounce packages strawberry gelatin	3 tablespoons sugar
2 cups boiling water	¾ cup margarine, melted
2 10-ounce packages frozen sweetened strawberries	8 ounces cream cheese, softened
	1 cup sugar
1 9-ounce package pretzels	2 cups whipped topping

Dissolve gelatin in boiling water; stir in strawberries. Chill until partially set. Crush pretzels in dish with potato masher. Add 3 tablespoons sugar and margarine; mix well. Press into 9x13-inch dish. Bake at 400 degrees for 10 minutes. Cool. Combine cream cheese and 1 cup sugar in bowl; mix well. Fold in whipped topping. Spread over crust. Pour gelatin over cream cheese layer. Chill until firm. Cut into squares. Yield: 12 servings.

Carol Allison, Zeta Nu
Boardman, Oregon

STRAWBERRY GELATIN MOLD

2 3-ounce packages strawberry gelatin	2 10-ounce packages frozen strawberries, thawed
1 cup boiling water	
1 cup cold water	8 ounces sour cream

Prepare gelatin according to package directions, using 1 cup boiling water and 1 cup cold water. Chill until partially set. Stir in strawberries and juice. Add sour cream; mix well. Pour into 2-quart mold. Chill until set. Unmold onto lettuce-lined plate. Garnish with whipped topping. Yield: 7 to 10 servings.

Jacquie Vancil, Xi Gamma Upsilon
Sycamore, Illinois

SWEETHEART CHRISTMAS SALAD

2 cups crushed pineapple	2 tablespoons lemon juice
½ cup sugar	6 ounces cream cheese, softened
1½ tablespoons unflavored gelatin	12 maraschino cherries, chopped
¼ cup cold water	1 cup whipping cream, whipped
2 tablespoons maraschino cherry juice	

Heat pineapple and sugar in saucepan. Soften gelatin in cold water. Stir into hot pineapple mixture until dissolved. Add cherry and lemon juices; mix well. Combine cream cheese and cherries in bowl; mix well. Add pineapple mixture gradually, mixing well after each addition. Chill until partially set. Fold in whipped cream. Pour into mold. Chill until firm. Unmold onto serving plate. Garnish with parsley sprigs and additional red and green cherries cut to resemble petals and placed to form poinsettias. Yield: 8 servings.

Doris Reher, Laureate Gamma Phi
Arvada, Colorado

WALDORF SALAD

4 red apples, chopped	1 cup chopped celery
1 tablespoon lemon juice	¼ cup mayonnaise
1 cup miniature marshmallows	½ cup whipping cream, whipped
1 cup seedless grape halves	½ cup chopped nuts
	1 large banana, sliced

Sprinkle apples with lemon juice. Combine with marshmallows, grapes, celery and mayonnaise in bowl; mix gently. Fold in whipped cream. Chill until serving time. Fold in nuts and banana just before serving. Serve in lettuce-lined salad bowl. Garnish with additional whipped cream, nuts and grapes. Yield: 15 to 20 servings.

Bettie Plummer, Laureate Pi
Independence, Missouri

WINTER FRUIT BOWL

Sections of 4 grapefruit	2 cups cranberries
1 cup sugar	3 medium bananas, sliced
½ cup orange marmalade	

Drain grapefruit sections, reserving juice. Add enough water to juice to measure 1 cup. Combine wtih sugar and marmalade in saucepan. Bring to a boil. Cook until sugar is dissolved, stirring constantly. Add cranberries. Cook for 5 to 8 minutes or until cranberries burst, stirring constantly. Cool. Add grapefruit sections; mix well. Chill, covered, until serving time. Add bananas; mix well. Spoon into serving bowl. Serve immediately. Yield: 10 servings.

Diane Burns, Xi Lambda Delta
Holiday, Florida

APPLE AND TUNA TOSS

4 cups torn romaine and iceberg lettuce	1 6½-ounce can tuna, drained
2 cups chopped unpeeled apples	⅓ cup chopped walnuts
1 10-ounce can mandarin oranges, drained	½ cup mayonnaise
	2 teaspoons soy sauce
	1 teaspoon lemon juice

Combine lettuce, apples, oranges, tuna and walnuts in salad bowl. Blend mayonnaise, soy sauce and lemon juice in small bowl. Add to lettuce mixture; toss gently. Yield: 4 to 6 servings.

Geraldine Reed, Preceptor Upsilon
Omaha, Nebraska

DEVILED EGGS

12 eggs	Salt
¼ cup finely minced onion	Pepper
Crushed butter crackers	Parsley flakes
Mayonnaise	Paprika
	Celery salt

Boil eggs in water to cover in saucepan for 10 minutes; drain. Cool in ice water. Peel eggs and cut into halves lengthwise. Remove yolks; mash in bowl. Stir in onion and desired amounts of cracker crumbs, mayonnaise, salt, pepper, parsley flakes, paprika and celery salt. Spoon into egg whites. Sprinkle with additional parsley flakes and paprika. Yield: 12 servings.

Linda Gizienski, Xi Alpha
Providence, Rhode Island

MEXICAN SALAD

1 pound ground chuck	1 or 2 green peppers, chopped
Garlic salt to taste	
Onion salt to taste	1 8-ounce bottle of French dressing
1 head lettuce, shredded	
4 tomatoes, chopped	1 8-ounce package corn chips, crushed
1 purple onion, chopped	

Brown ground chuck in skillet, stirring until crumbly; drain. Add garlic salt and onion salt; mix well. Steam, covered, for 5 to 7 minutes; cool. Combine lettuce, tomatoes, onion and green pepper in salad bowl. Add ground chuck mixture and French dressing; toss lightly. Chill, covered, until serving time. Add corn chips. Serve immediately. Yield: 12 servings.

Billie McKee, Laureate Chi
Carthage, Texas

TACO SALAD

1 pound ground chuck	½ green pepper, chopped
1 package taco seasoning mix	1 large onion, chopped
	1 carrot, grated
½ head lettuce, shredded	1 cup fresh mushrooms, sliced
1 16-ounce can kidney beans, drained	
	1 8-ounce bottle of Caesar salad dressing
1 large tomato, chopped	
1 cucumber, sliced	Cheddar cheese, shredded

Brown ground chuck in skillet, stirring until crumbly; drain. Add taco seasoning mix; mix well. Combine lettuce, kidney beans, tomato, cucumber, green pepper, onion, carrot and mushrooms in large bowl. Add salad dressing; toss lightly. Spoon ground chuck mixture over top. Sprinkle with cheese. Serve with nacho or tortilla chips. Yield: 8 servings.
Note: Sauté onion with chuck for milder onion flavor.

Janean C. Baker, Precpetor Beta Delta
Orange Park, Florida

FRUITED TURKEY SALAD

4 cups chopped cooked turkey	1 cup seedless grapes
	1 cup chopped apple
1 cup drained pineapple tidbits	1 cup chopped nuts
	1½ cups mayonnaise

Combine turkey, fruit and nuts in bowl. Add mayonnaise; mix gently. Serve on lettuce-lined salad plates. Yield: 8 servings.

Sissy Smith, Epsilon Psi
Shelbyville, Tennessee

DALE'S SHRIMP SALAD

1 envelope unflavored gelatin	1 to 1½ cups salad dressing
¼ cup cold water	½ small onion, chopped
2 to 2½ cups minced cooked shrimp	3 tablespoons lemon juice

Soften gelatin in cold water in bowl. Microwave gelatin and water for 1 to 2 minutes or until gelatin is dissolved. Cool. Add shrimp, salad dressing, onion and lemon juice; mix well. Add red food coloring if desired; mix well. Pour into mold. Chill for 24 hours. Unmold onto lettuce-lined serving plate. Serve with snack crackers. Yield: 15 to 20 servings.

Kim Thorn, Beta Sigma
Vanceboro, North Carolina

EXOTIC SHRIMP SALAD

2 pounds peeled cooked shrimp	2 cups drained chopped grapefruit sections
1/2 cup toasted almonds	1 cup mayonnaise
1/4 cup minced green onions	2 teaspoons curry powder
1/4 cup chopped celery	2 tablespoons soy sauce

Combine first 5 ingredients in bowl. Add mixture of mayonnaise, curry powder and soy sauce; mix gently. Serve in large shell-shaped bowl. Garnish with orange wedges placed to resemble butterfly wings and green pepper strips for antennae. Yield: 8 servings.

Mitzi Smirl, Delta Lambda
Bedford, Texas

SHRIMP-TOMATO ASPIC

2 envelopes unflavored gelatin	1 teaspoon lemon juice
1/2 cup cold water	1/4 cup chopped onion
2 cups tomato juice	1/4 cup chopped celery
1 teaspoon Worcestershire sauce	1/4 cup chopped green pepper
Dash of Tabasco sauce	1 6-ounce can shrimp, drained

Soften gelatin in cold water in saucepan. Add tomato juice, Worcestershire sauce and Tabasco sauce. Bring to a boil, stirring until gelatin dissolves. Cool. Add lemon juice. Chill until partially set. Add vegetables and shrimp. Pour into lightly oiled mold. Chill until firm. Unmold onto serving plate. Yield: 6 servings.

Mrs. Robert L. Scofield, Laureate Eta
Clarksville, Tennessee

PASTA SEAFOOD SALAD

8 ounces rotini, cooked, drained	1 package seatails, chopped
Flowerets of 1 bunch broccoli	1 8-ounce bottle of Italian dressing
4 to 6 tomatoes, cut in wedges	

Combine rotini, broccoli, tomatoes and seatails in large salad bowl; mix well. Add dressing; toss lightly. Yield: 24 to 30 servings.

Ruth M. Rosenke, Xi Gamma Upsilon
Sycamore, Illinois

ROTINI SALAD

1 16-ounce package rotini	1 bunch broccoli, chopped
1 large green pepper, chopped	1 6-ounce can sliced black olives, drained
4 stalks celery, chopped	2 pounds peeled boiled shrimp
1 bunch green onions, chopped	1 8-ounce bottle of Italian salad dressing
1 head cauliflower, chopped	Salt and pepper to taste

Cook rotini according to package directions; drain. Combine with remaining ingredients in bowl; mix well. Chill until serving time. Yield: 12 servings.

Note: May substitute 2 cups chopped cooked chicken or ham for shrimp.

Bobbi L. Cart, Xi Alpha
Lake Charles, Louisiana

MOLDED SHRIMP SALAD

2 3-ounce packages lemon gelatin	1 cup sliced olives
2 cups boiling water	2 4½-ounce cans shrimp, drained
1 cup whipping cream	2 tablespoons chopped green onions
8 ounces cream cheese, softened	1 cup mayonnaise
1/2 cup chopped celery	

Dissolve gelatin in 2 cups boiling water in bowl. Chill until partially set. Whip cream in bowl until soft peaks form. Add cream cheese, celery and olives. Mix in partially congealed gelatin. Spoon into 9x13-inch dish. Chill for several hours or until set. Combine shrimp, green onions and mayonnaise in bowl; mix well. Spread over congealed layer. Cut into squares. Serve on lettuce-lined plate. Yield: 15 servings.

Jennifer Holden, Xi Beta Mu
Baker, Oregon

SHRIMP SALAD

3/4 to 1 cup mayonnaise	5 stalks celery, chopped
2 tablespoons catsup	1 small red onion, chopped
1 tablespoon taco sauce	4 to 6 hard-boiled eggs, chopped
Garlic powder, basil, poppy seed, paprika, salt and pepper to taste	2 to 3 6-ounce cans tiny shrimp, drained
1 large head lettuce, shredded	

Combine mayonnaise, catsup and taco sauce in bowl; mix well. Add seasonings to taste. Chill in refrigerator. Combine remaining ingredients in bowl. Add dressing; toss to coat. Yield: 6 to 10 servings.

Georgia Standridge, Xi Mu Chi
Corning, California

SPRING TUNA SALAD

2 hard-boiled eggs	1/2 cup chopped celery
1/2 cup low-fat yogurt	1/4 cup chopped green onions
1/2 teaspoon mustard	
1/4 teaspoon pepper	1 tablespoon minced onion
1/2 teaspoon Old Bay spice	1 tablespoon chopped parsley
1 7-ounce can water-pack tuna	
1/2 cup sliced apple	

Mash egg yolks in bowl. Blend in yogurt, mustard and spices. Add chopped egg whites and remaining ingredients; mix well. Chill for 1 hour. Serve with crackers, bagels or toast. Yield: 6 servings.

Mareke Campbell, Theta Kappa
Belleville, Illinois

SPAGHETTI SALAD

1 16-ounce package spaghetti	1 green pepper, chopped
1 16-ounce bottle of Italian dressing	1 large onion, chopped
	⅓ bottle of McCormick's salad seasoning

Cook spaghetti using package directions; drain. Add dressing, green pepper, onion and seasoning; mix well. Chill, covered, overnight. Yield: 8 to 10 servings.

Marilyn Kelly, Xi Gamma Upsilon
Dunedin, Florida

WON TON SALAD

½ package won ton wrappers	1 onion, chopped
Oil for deep frying	¼ cup sliced almonds
4 chicken breasts, cooked, shredded	¼ cup sugar
½ head lettuce, chopped	¼ cup vinegar
	¼ cup oil
	½ teaspoon salt

Deep-fry won ton wrappers in hot oil using package directions; drain. Combine chicken, lettuce, onion, almonds and won ton wrappers in large bowl; mix well. Combine vinegar, oil and salt in small bowl; mix well. Pour over salad mixture; toss lightly. Spoon into individual salad bowls. Yield: 8 to 10 servings.

Sue Thomson, Xi Gamma Upsilon
DeKalb, Illinois

ASPARAGUS SALAD

1 16-ounce can cut asparagus	2 teaspoons grated onion
2 envelopes unflavored gelatin	2 tablespoons lemon juice
1 can water chestnuts, drained, chopped	1 cup water
½ cup chopped celery	½ cup vinegar
1 2-ounce jar chopped pimento, drained	½ teaspoon salt
	⅔ cup sugar
	Ranch dressing

Drain asparagus, reserving liquid. Soften gelatin in reserved asparagus liquid. Combine asparagus, water chestnuts, celery, pimento, onion and lemon juice in 9x13-inch glass dish; toss lightly. Bring mixture of water, vinegar, salt and sugar to a boil in saucepan. Add softened gelatin; mix until dissolved. Cool. Pour over asparagus mixture. Chill until firm. Cut into squares. Place on lettuce-lined plates. Serve with ranch dressing. Yield: 8 servings.

Dorothy M. Durrett, Preceptor Nu
Anniston, Alabama

ASPIC SALAD

1 3-ounce package lemon gelatin	½ cup mayonnaise
1 cup boiling water	¼ cup mixed chopped onion and green pepper
1 10-ounce can tomato soup	½ cup chopped celery
8 ounces cream cheese, softened	1 teaspoon lemon juice

Dissolve gelatin in boiling water in bowl. Chill until partially set. Beat soup, cream cheese and mayonnaise in mixer bowl until well blended. Add soup mixture, vegetables and lemon juice to gelatin; mix well. Pour into mold. Chill until set. Unmold onto serving plate. Yield: 10 servings.

Barbara Ball, Xi Alpha Kappa
Grand Junction, Colorado

BROCCOLI AND SUNFLOWER SEED

1 cup mayonnaise	12 slices crisp-fried bacon, crumbled
⅓ cup sugar	Flowerets of 2 bunches broccoli
2 tablespoons white vinegar	1 cup sunflower seed
1 onion, chopped	

Combine mayonnaise, sugar and vinegar in small bowl; mix well. Combine onion, bacon, broccoli and sunflower seed in large bowl. Add mayonnaise mixture; toss lightly. Yield: 8 servings.

Evelyn Tallyn, Iota Chi
Creve Coeur, Missouri

BROCCOLI SALAD

Flowerets of 1 bunch broccoli	1 cup chopped celery
¼ cup chopped onion	1 cup mayonnaise
1 7-ounce jar stuffed olives, drained, sliced	1 teaspoon lemon juice
	1 teaspoon dillweed

Steam broccoli in a small amount of water in saucepan until tender-crisp; drain. Combine with onion, olives and celery in bowl. Combine mayonnaise, lemon juice and dillweed in small bowl; mix well. Stir into broccoli mixture. Chill overnight. Yield: 6 to 8 servings.

Geneva Lanman, Laureate Alpha Beta
Princeton, Indiana

BEET SALAD

1 3-ounce package lemon gelatin	1 teaspoon vinegar
1 cup beet juice	1 teaspoon salt
⅔ cup orange juice	1 16-ounce can diced beets
1 teaspoon grated onion	1 cup chopped celery
2 teaspoons horseradish	

Dissolve gelatin in boiling beet juice. Add orange juice, onion and seasonings; mix well. Chill until slightly thickened. Stir in beets and celery. Pour into ring mold. Chill until firm. Unmold on serving plate. Fill center with fruit if desired. Yield: 6 servings.

For an easy holiday salad, remove core from large head of Boston lettuce. Rinse and drain. Place on serving plate; spread leaves apart. Arrange drained canned sliced beets between leaves. Drizzle with vinaigrette dressing flavored with Dijon-style mustard.

WARM GREEN BEANS AND POTATOES

1 pound green beans,
  trimmed
1¼ pounds small red
  new potatoes
6 ounces slab bacon,
  finely chopped
⅓ cup chopped leek
½ cup Sherry vinegar

1 teaspoon Dijon-style
  mustard
½ cup olive oil
½ cup corn oil
¾ teaspoon salt
½ teaspoon coarsely
  ground pepper
2 cucumbers, peeled

Cook beans in boiling salted water in saucepan until tender-crisp. Drain; pat dry. Cook potatoes in water to cover in saucepan just until tender; drain. Cut into quarters. Fry bacon in heavy skillet until brown; remove bacon, reserving ¼ cup drippings. Sauté leek in reserved drippings for 2 to 3 minutes or until tender, stirring constantly. Stir in vinegar and mustard. Cook until heated through. Stir in olive oil and corn oil. Add salt and pepper; remove from heat. Mound potatoes in center of serving platter. Pour ⅓ of the dressing over potatoes. Add beans to remaining dressing. Cook until heated through, stirring gently. Remove with slotted spoon; arrange around potatoes. Cut cucumbers lengthwise; remove seed. Slice ¼-inch thick. Add to remaining dressing. Cook until heated through, stirring constantly. Remove with slotted spoon; arrange around beans. Pour remaining dressing over salad.
Yield: 6 to 8 servings.

Kimberly L. Birch, Eta Nu
Charles City, Iowa

APPLE-PINEAPPLE SLAW

3 cups shredded cabbage
1 9-ounce can pineapple
  tidbits, drained
1 cup chopped unpeeled
  apples

1 cup miniature
  marshmallows
½ cup chopped celery
½ cup mayonnaise

Combine all ingredients in bowl; mix well. Spoon into lettuce-lined serving bowl. Garnish with additional apple wedges sprinkled with lemon juice.
Yield: 4 to 6 servings.

Bettie L. Plummer, Laureate Pi
Independence, Missouri

CABBAGE SALAD

1 small head cabbage,
  chopped
¼ cup low-fat milk
¼ cup white vinegar

1 6-ounce can crushed
  pineapple
1 cup raisins

Combine all ingredients in bowl. Chill, tightly covered, until serving time. Serve with hot cabbage rolls.
Yield: 4 to 6 servings.

Mary Hinton, Preceptor Lambda
East Rochester, New York

MIMI'S SALAD

1 small head cabbage,
  shredded
1 medium tomato,
  chopped
1 avocado, chopped

4 green onions, chopped
  Shrimp
2 tablespoons salad
  dressing
Salt and pepper to taste

Combine cabbage, tomato, avocado, green onions and shrimp in salad bowl; mix well. Combine salad dressing with salt and pepper to taste in bowl. Add to salad; toss lightly. Let stand for 10 minutes before serving.
Yield: 4 servings.

Virginia Trethewey, Nu Chi
Napa, California

NINE-DAY COLESLAW

1 4-pound head
  cabbage, shredded
2 onions, chopped
2 green peppers, chopped
1 small jar chopped
  pimento, drained

1½ cups sugar
1 cup oil
1 cup vinegar
1 tablespoon salt
1 tablespoon celery seed

Combine cabbage, onions, green peppers and pimento in large bowl; mix well. Combine remaining ingredients in saucepan. Bring to a boil, stirring constantly. Pour over cabbage mixture; mix well. Chill, covered, for several hours. May store in refrigerator for 1 week.
Yield: 15 servings.

Eleanor Taylor, Sigma Lambda
Bridgeview, Illinois

ORIENTAL CABBAGE SALAD

2 cups chopped cooked
  chicken
1 medium head cabbage,
  chopped
1 bunch green onions,
  chopped
1 package uncooked
  Ramen noodles,
  crushed

3 tablespoons slivered
  almonds
3 tablespoons sesame
  seed, toasted
½ cup oil
3 tablespoons vinegar
1 teaspoon salt
¼ teaspoon pepper
2 tablespoons sugar

Combine chicken, cabbage, green onions, noodles, almonds and sesame seed in large bowl; toss lightly. Combine oil, vinegar, salt, pepper and sugar in small bowl; mix well. Pour over salad; toss gently to coat. Serve immediately. Yield: 8 servings.

Jody Lorash, Beta Omicron
Red Lodge, Montana

Garnish slaw with green onion frills. Slice root end from green onions. Remove all but 2 inches green tops. Make slashes at root end and green end with sharp paring knife. Soak in ice water until ends curl.

SUMI SALAD

½ large head cabbage, sliced
4 green onions, chopped
¼ cup sugar
½ teaspoon white pepper
½ cup oil
1 teaspoon salt
6 tablespoons rice vinegar

2 packages uncooked oriental-flavored Ramen noodles, crushed
½ cup sesame seed, toasted
½ cup slivered almonds, toasted

Mix cabbage and green onions in large salad bowl. Combine sugar, white pepper, oil, salt and rice vinegar in small bowl; mix well. Pour over cabbage mixture; toss lightly. Chill for 1 hour. Add noodles, sesame seed and almonds just before serving; toss gently. Yield: 6 servings.

Norma L. Gibson, Xi Eta
La Grande, Oregon

CARROT-PINEAPPLE SALAD

1 16-ounce can pineapple chunks, drained
1 pound carrots, grated

1 16-ounce jar applesauce
1 cup raisins

Combine all ingredients in bowl; mix well. Chill, covered, overnight. Yield: 6 to 8 servings.

Sara Easton, Xi Tau
Clarkston, Michigan

KRAUT SLAW

1 20-ounce can chopped sauerkraut
1 cup chopped celery
1 medium green pepper, chopped

1 sweet red pepper, chopped
½ cup sugar
½ cup oil
½ cup red wine vinegar

Combine sauerkraut and chopped vegetables in bowl. Add mixture of sugar, oil and vinegar; mix well. Chill overnight. Yield: 10 servings.

Mary Williams, Xi Theta Omicron
Holden, Missouri

CHRIS' CREAM-STYLE POTATO SALAD

2 hard-boiled eggs, chopped
½ cup chopped celery
¼ cup chopped onion
1 tablespoon mustard
½ cup salad dressing
1½ tablespoons chopped dill pickle

2 tablespoons sweet relish
6 potatoes, cooked, peeled, sliced
1 tablespoon celery seed
1 tablespoon parsley flakes
½ teaspoon celery salt
Salt and pepper to taste

Combine eggs, celery, onion, mustard, salad dressing, pickles and relish in large bowl; mix gently. Add warm potatoes and remaining ingredients; mix well. Garnish with sprinkle of paprika. Spoon into serving bowl. Chill, covered, until serving time. Yield: 8 servings.

Norma Wright, Gamma Theta
Baltimore, Maryland

SPINACH-MANDARIN SALAD

Fresh spinach, torn
Romaine lettuce, torn
Iceberg lettuce, torn
1 8-ounce can mandarin oranges, drained
1 red onion, sliced into rings

½ cup chopped pecans
⅓ cup wine vinegar
½ cup sugar
1 cup oil
1 teaspoon salt
1 teaspoon dry mustard
2 tablespoons water

Combine spinach, lettuces, oranges, onion rings and pecans in salad bowl; toss lightly. Add mixture of vinegar and remaining ingredients. Pour over salad; toss lightly. Yield: 6 to 8 servings.

Mary Elizabeth Reinhart, Laureate Eta
Fox Point, Wisconsin

MOLDED SPINACH SALAD

2 3-ounce packages sugar-free lemon gelatin
2 cups boiling water
1 cup mayonnaise
2 tablespoons vinegar
1 10-ounce package frozen chopped spinach, thawed, drained

¾ cup chopped celery
1 tablespoon chopped onion
1 cup small curd cottage cheese
Chopped green or red pepper
Sliced stuffed olives
½ teaspoon salt

Dissolve gelatin in boiling water in bowl. Stir in mayonnaise and vinegar gradually. Add remaining ingredients; mix well. Spoon into 9x11-inch dish. Chill until set. Cut into squares. Serve on lettuce-lined plates. Yield: 8 to 10 servings.

Connie Sharp, Preceptor Upsilon
Omaha, Nebraska

SPINACH SALAD

2 10-ounce packages frozen chopped spinach, thawed
3 hard-boiled eggs, chopped
1 cup shredded sharp Cheddar cheese

½ cup chopped celery
1¼ cups mayonnaise
½ teaspoon hot red pepper sauce
½ teaspoon salt
1½ teaspoons vinegar
1 tablespoon bacon bits

Drain spinach; squeeze dry. Combine with eggs, cheese and celery in bowl. Blend mayonnaise, pepper sauce, salt and vinegar in bowl. Pour over spinach mixture; mix well. Chill for several hours. Sprinkle with bacon bits just before serving. Yield: 6 to 8 servings.

Mary Williams, Xi Theta Omicron
Holden, Missouri

For a beautiful holiday spinach salad, combine torn fresh spinach leaves and sliced fresh strawberries in salad bowl or salad plates. Serve with poppy seed dressing.

CRISP SPINACH SALAD

1 cup oil	1 20-ounce can bean
¼ to ½ cup sugar	sprouts
⅓ cup catsup	1 7-ounce can sliced
¼ cup vinegar	water chestnuts
1 medium onion, grated	2 hard-boiled eggs, sliced
2 teaspoons	5 slices crisp-fried bacon,
Worcestershire sauce	crumbled
1 pound fresh spinach,	
torn	

Combine oil and next 5 ingredients in bowl; mix well. Chill overnight. Combine well-drained spinach, bean sprouts and water chestnuts in salad bowl. Chill until serving time. Add eggs, bacon and dressing just before serving; toss until well mixed. Yield: 8 servings.

Diana Bal, Xi Delta Xi
Rochester, New York

CRUNCHY SPINACH SALAD

½ cup sugar	1 pound spinach, torn
1 cup oil	7 slices crisp-fried bacon,
⅓ cup catsup	crumbled
¼ cup wine vinegar	1 8-ounce can sliced
1 small onion, grated	water chestnuts,
2 tablespoons	drained
Worcestershire sauce	1 16-ounce can bean
¼ teaspoon salt	sprouts, drained
Seasoned pepper to taste	

Combine first 8 ingredients in blender container. Process until smooth. Chill, tightly covered, overnight. Combine remaining ingredients in salad bowl. Pour dressing over spinach mixture; toss lightly. Serve immediately. Yield: 10 servings.
Note: 8 ounces fresh bean sprouts may be substituted for canned sprouts.

Lisa Fay, Alpha Omicron
Williston, North Dakota

LAYERED SALAD

1 head lettuce, chopped	2 cups salad dressing
¾ cup chopped green	2 tablespoons sugar
pepper	½ cup shredded Cheddar
¾ cup chopped celery	cheese
1 purple onion, sliced	1 pound bacon, crisp-
into rings	fried, crumbled
1 10-ounce package	
frozen peas, thawed	

Layer lettuce, green pepper, celery, onion and peas in 9x13-inch glass dish. Spread salad dressing over top, sealing to edge. Sprinkle sugar, cheese and bacon over top. Chill, covered with foil, overnight. Yield: 8 to 10 servings.

Jowahna Hill, Upsilon
Claremore, Oklahoma

TWENTY-FOUR HOUR SALAD

2 cups sour cream	½ cup chopped onion
½ cup mayonnaise	¼ cup chopped green
Lettuce, torn	pepper
1 10-ounce package	½ cup shredded cheese
frozen peas, thawed	Bacon bits
½ cup chopped celery	

Blend sour cream and mayonnaise in bowl. Layer lettuce, peas, celery, onion and green pepper in 9x13-inch dish. Spread sour cream mixture over salad, sealing to edge of dish. Sprinkle with cheese and bacon bits. Chill, covered, overnight. Yield: 6 servings.

Barbara Ball, Xi Alpha Kappa
Grand Junction, Colorado

SEVEN-LAYER LETTUCE SALAD

1 head lettuce, torn	8 ounces bacon, crisp-
2 stalks celery, finely	fried, crumbled
chopped	½ cup mayonnaise
1 red onion, thinly sliced	Vinegar to taste
1 cup sour cream	Parmesan cheese
½ cup sugar	

Layer lettuce, celery and onion in salad bowl. Spread with mixture of sour cream and sugar. Sprinkle with bacon. Mix mayonnaise and vinegar in small bowl. Pour over bacon. Sprinkle with cheese. Chill, covered with foil, for 3 hours or longer. Yield: 8 servings.

Andrea Ryan, Zeta Alpha
Williamsport, Pennsylvania

BASIC VEGETABLE SALAD

2 cups chopped carrots	½ cup chopped radishes
2 cups chopped celery	¼ cup chopped onion
1 cup chopped cucumber	1 cup mayonnaise
½ cup chopped green	1½ teaspoons salt
pepper	1½ cups cottage cheese

Combine vegetables in large bowl; mix lightly. Blend mayonnaise, salt and cottage cheese in small bowl; mix well. Pour over vegetable mixture; mix well. Serve with corn chips. Yield: 6 servings.

Benjie Thomas, Laureate Chi
Carthage, Texas

Vegetable roses make pretty garnishes for layered salads. For tomato roses, peel large firm tomato in one continuous ¾-inch wide strip. Use sharp knife and begin at top of tomato. Coil peel into shape of rose. Place on salad. Add herb leaves to resemble rose leaves. For radish roses, cut off root and top of radish. Slice 4 or 5 thin petal-shaped pieces from sides of radishes, to but not through end. Chill in ice water until the petals open.

EIGHT-LAYER SALAD

1 medium red onion, chopped	1 large head lettuce, torn
6 hard-boiled eggs, chopped	1 10-ounce package frozen peas
½ cup crumbled crisp-fried bacon	2 cups mayonnaise
	1 cup sour cream
1 16-ounce package fresh spinach, torn	1 cup shredded Swiss cheese

Combine onion, eggs and bacon in bowl; toss lightly. Layer half the spinach, half the lettuce and half the onion mixture in 3-quart salad bowl. Spread peas over layers. Layer remaining spinach, lettuce and onion mixture over peas. Spread mixture of mayonnaise and sour cream over layers, sealing to edge of bowl. Top with cheese. Chill until serving time. Yield: 10 servings.

Dianne Peters, Xi Alpha
Providence, Rhode Island

SEVEN-LAYER SALAD

1 head lettuce, chopped	6 hard-boiled eggs, sliced
½ cup chopped green pepper	2 cups mayonnaise
½ cup sliced onion	2 teaspoons vinegar
½ cup sliced carrots	Salt and pepper to taste
1 10-ounce package frozen peas, thawed	¼ cup evaporated milk
1½ cups shredded Cheddar cheese	2 teaspoons sugar

Layer lettuce, green pepper, onion, carrots and peas in large salad bowl. Sprinkle cheese and eggs over top. Chill, covered, overnight. Combine remaining ingredients in bowl; mix well. Pour over salad just before serving; toss lightly. Yield: 10 to 12 servings.

Sandra McDonald, Xi Kappa Beta
Wintersville, Ohio

MARINATED VEGETABLES

1 cup carrot sticks	1 cup oil
1 cup celery sticks	¾ cup vinegar
1 medium zucchini, sliced	½ cup sugar
Flowerets of 1 bunch broccoli	1 teaspoon onion salt
	¼ teaspoon garlic powder
Flowerets of 1 cauliflower	¼ teaspoon ginger
	½ teaspoon salt
½ cup green pepper sticks	¼ teaspoon pepper
1 cup pitted black olives	

Combine vegetables and olives in salad bowl. Mix remaining ingredients in small bowl. Pour over vegetables; mix well. Marinate in refrigerator overnight. Yield: 12 to 15 servings.

Connie Sharp, Preceptor Upsilon
Omaha, Nebraska

MARINATED VEGETABLE SALAD

1 head cauliflower, chopped	12 cherry tomatoes, cut into halves
1 bunch broccoli, chopped	1 8-ounce bottle of Italian salad dressing
½ medium onion, sliced	
1 4-ounce can artichoke hearts, drained	1 cup mayonnaise
	3 to 4 tablespoons chili sauce
12 fresh mushrooms	
1 6-ounce can pitted ripe olives	2 teaspoons dillweed
	1 teaspoon salt

Combine cauliflower, broccoli, onion, artichoke hearts, mushrooms, olives and cherry tomatoes in bowl. Add Italian salad dressing; mix well. Marinate in refrigerator for 24 hours. Drain. Combine remaining ingredients in small bowl. Add to vegetables. Refrigerate for several hours before serving. Yield: 12 servings.

Connie Sharp, Preceptor Upsilon
Omaha, Nebraska

PARTY PIZAZZ VEGETABLE SALAD

2 cups chopped broccoli	½ cup sliced almonds
2 cups chopped cauliflower	1 cup mayonnaise
	2 tablespoons cider vinegar
1 cup golden raisins	
5 slices crisp-fried bacon, crumbled	½ cup sugar

Combine broccoli, cauliflower, raisins, bacon and almonds in bowl; mix well. Mix mayonnaise, vinegar and sugar in bowl. Pour over vegetables; mix well. Chill until serving time. Yield: 6 servings.

Pat Arthaud, Xi Zeta Theta
Hazleton, Iowa

VEGETABLE SALAD

1 16-ounce can small green peas	1 2-ounce jar pimento
	1 small onion, chopped
1 16-ounce can cut green beans	½ teaspoon salt
	½ cup sugar
1 16-ounce can whole kernel corn	½ cup oil
	⅓ cup water
½ cup chopped celery	½ cup vinegar
1 green pepper, chopped	

Drain canned vegetables. Combine with celery, green pepper, pimento and onion in large dish. Mix salt, sugar, oil, water and vinegar in bowl. Pour over vegetables. Chill, covered, in refrigerator. Yield: 12 to 15 servings. Note: Salad may be made several days in advance.

Layer marinated vegetable or salad ingredients in pretty glass jar. Pour mixture of marinade ingredients over vegetables. Store in refrigerator. Tie decorative bow on jar. Give with recipe as gift.

Holiday Main Dishes

BARBECUED BEEF

1 2 to 3-pound chuck roast	1 tablespoon Worcestershire sauce
1 small onion, chopped	2 tablespoons mustard
2 tablespoons vinegar	½ cup celery seed
¾ cup catsup	

Combine roast with water to cover in saucepan. Simmer, covered, for 4 hours or until beef is very tender, adding water if necessary. Drain and shred beef, reserving 1 cup broth. Combine beef, reserved broth and remaining ingredients in saucepan. Simmer for 1 hour. Chill overnight; reheat at serving time. Serve on sandwich buns. Yield: 8 to 10 servings.

Joanne Golebiowski, Sigma Eta
Chesterfield, Missouri

BEEF BURGUNDY

2½ pounds ¼-inch thick round steak	1 clove of garlic, crushed
¼ cup all-purpose flour	1 large bay leaf
¼ cup butter or margarine	1 teaspoon salt
½ cup coarsely chopped onion	Dash of pepper
2 tablespoons finely chopped parsley	1 6-ounce can whole mushrooms, drained
	1 cup Burgundy
	¾ cup water

Cut steak into bite-sized pieces. Coat with flour; use all flour. Brown in butter in skillet. Remove from heat. Add remaining ingredients. Simmer, covered, over medium-low heat for 1 hour or until steak is tender. Remove bay leaf. Serve over hot cooked noodles. Yield: 8 servings. Note: Partially frozen steak is easier to cut.

Kimberly L. Birch, Eta Nu
Charles City, Iowa

BEEF STROGANOFF TOPPING

1 pound ½-inch thick steak	1 10-ounce can beef broth
8 ounces mushrooms, sliced	2 tablespoons catsup
½ cup minced onion	1 clove of garlic, minced
2 tablespoons butter or margarine	1 teaspoon salt
	3 tablespoons flour
	1 cup sour cream

Cut steak into strips. Sauté mushrooms and onion in butter in skillet until tender; remove from skillet. Cook steak in pan juices until light brown. Reserve ⅓ cup broth. Stir remaining broth, catsup, garlic and salt into skillet. Simmer, covered, for 15 minutes. Blend flour with reserved broth. Stir into steak mixture. Add sautéed vegetables. Bring to a boil, stirring constantly. Cook for 1 minute, stirring constantly. Reduce heat. Stir in sour cream. Heat to serving temperature; do not boil. Serve over baked potatoes or noodles.

Susan Foster, Xi Alpha
Grand Rapids, Michigan

BRISKET OF BEEF

1 5 to 6-pound beef brisket	½ teaspoon garlic powder
3 tablespoons oil	1 teaspoon paprika
2 cups chopped onions	½ teaspoon pepper
4 stalks celery, chopped	1 teaspoon dried dillweed
1 green pepper, cut into strips	2 cups red wine
2 beef bouillon cubes, crushed	2 tablespoons vinegar
	2 bay leaves, cut into halves

Brown brisket on all sides in Dutch oven. Sauté onions, celery and green pepper in skillet. Place half the sautéed vegetables in Dutch oven around brisket; sprinkle brisket with mixture of bouillon, garlic powder, paprika, pepper and dill. Top with remaining sautéed vegetables. Add wine, vinegar and bay leaves. Bake, covered, at 325 degrees for 3 to 3½ hours or until brisket is tender. Let stand for 15 minutes. Remove to serving platter. Slice cross grain.

Ruth M. Scoggins, Laureate Beta Omicron
San Benito, Texas

CROCK•POT ROAST

Carrots, split lengthwise	1 10-ounce can golden mushroom soup
Potatoes, cut into quarters	1 cup sliced mushrooms
1 3 to 4½-pound beef roast	2 envelopes dry onion soup mix
½ cup red wine	

Place carrots and potatoes in Crock•Pot. Place roast on vegetables. Mix wine, and mushroom soup in bowl. Pour around roast. Sprinkle mushrooms and dry soup mix over soup. Cook on High for 7 to 8 hours or on Low for 10 to 12 hours or until roast and vegetables are tender.
Note: May omit carrots and potatoes and place roast on rack in Crock•Pot. May substitute cream of mushroom soup for golden mushroom soup.

Jerry Wright, Xi Alpha
Providence, Rhode Island

BEEF BARBECUE

1 stalk celery, chopped	1½ cups water
3 onions, chopped	2 teaspoons salt
1 green pepper, chopped	½ teaspoon pepper
1 16-ounce bottle of catsup	½ teaspoon chili powder
3 tablespoons vinegar	1 6-pound boneless chuck roast

Combine first 9 ingredients in roasting pan; mix well. Add roast. Bake at 300 degrees for 5 hours. Cool for 30 minutes. Shred roast; discard fat. Combine with pan juices in roasting pan; mix well. Bake for 1 hour longer. Serve in semihard rolls. Yield: 20 to 25 servings.

Eileen Carfang, Eta Mu
Marietta, Georgia

OVEN-STYLE MEXICAN FAJITAS

5 to 8 pounds skirt steak	1 16-ounce bottle of barbecue sauce
1 or 2 cans light beer	

Trim and tenderize steak. Place in foil-lined roaster. Pour mixture of beer and barbecue sauce over steak. Marinate for several hours to overnight. Bake, uncovered, at 350 degrees for 1½ to 2 hours or until tender. Slice steaks cross grain into fajita strips. Serve in hot flour tortillas.

Ruth M. Scoggins, Laureate Beta Omicron
San Benito, Texas

CAJUN SWISS STEAK

2 pounds cube steaks	⅓ cup chopped carrot
1 tablespoon flour	1 clove of garlic, minced
¼ teaspoon pepper	¾ cup beef broth
2 tablespoons oil	¾ cup tomato juice
1 small onion, sliced	1 teaspoon Worcestershire sauce
1 green pepper, sliced	
⅓ cup chopped celery	

Sprinkle steaks with mixture of flour and pepper. Brown steaks several at a time in hot oil in large skillet over medium heat for 3 minutes on each side. Drain on paper towel. Sauté onion, green pepper, celery, carrot and garlic in pan drippings for 2 minutes. Add steaks and remaining ingredients. Reduce heat. Simmer, covered, for 45 to 60 minutes or until tender. Yield: 8 servings.

Carol Williams, Theta Theta
Hayden, Colorado

CREOLE STEAK STRIPS

1½ pounds boneless round steak	⅛ teaspoon garlic powder
Salt and pepper to taste	1 medium green pepper, chopped
1 onion, chopped	1 10-ounce package frozen okra, partially thawed
1 cup sliced celery	
1 cup seasoned tomato juice	1 2½-ounce can sliced mushrooms, drained
2 teaspoons Worcestershire sauce	

Cut steak into ½x2-inch strips. Sprinkle with salt and pepper. Place in 3½-quart Crock•Pot. Add onion, celery, tomato juice, Worcestershire sauce and garlic powder. Cook on Low for 6 to 8 hours. Add green pepper, okra and mushrooms. Cook on High for 30 minutes or until okra is tender. Serve over rice with fresh vegetable salad, French bread and iced tea. Garnish with carrot curls. Yield: 5 to 6 servings.

Nina Slaton, Preceptor Gamma Mu
Lubbock, Texas

SPICY ORANGE BEEF

1 pound lean round steak, sliced ¼ inch thick	3 tablespoons orange juice
1 tablespoon Sherry	1 clove of garlic, minced
2 tablespoons catsup	1 teaspoon crushed red pepper
½ cup water	1 teaspoon salt
2 tablespoons honey	2 tablespoons oil
2 teaspoons sugar	2 tablespoons cornstarch
4 pieces orange rind	2 tablespoons water
1 slice gingerroot	

Cut steak into 2x3-inch strips. Combine with Sherry, catsup, ½ cup water, honey, sugar, orange rind, gingerroot, orange juice, garlic, red pepper and salt in bowl; mix well. Marinate for 1 to 2 hours. Drain, reserving marinade. Remove orange rind and set aside. Strain marinade. Heat wok. Add oil. Heat for 30 seconds, swirling to coat well. Add orange rind. Stir-fry until light brown. Sprinkle beef with 1 tablespoon cornstarch. Add to wok. Stir-fry until brown. Stir in reserved marinade. Bring to a boil. Add mixture of remaining 1 tablespoon cornstarch and 2 tablespoons water. Cook until thickened. Serve with steamed rice. Yield: 4 servings.

Laura Ross, Zeta
Kansas City, Missouri

STUFFED STEAK

3 pounds round steak	Bread crumbs
Salt, pepper and	1 egg, beaten
paprika to taste	½ cup melted butter
4 ounces fresh	1 tablespoon boiling
mushrooms, sliced	water
¼ cup sliced pimento-	4 ounces fresh mushrooms
stuffed olives	3 small onions
1 sweet onion, sliced	1 cup red wine

Pound round steak thin with meat mallet. Overlap pieces to form 1 large steak. Sprinkle with salt, pepper and paprika. Layer sliced mushrooms, olives and onion on steak. Cover with crumbs. Drizzle mixture of egg, butter and water over crumbs. Roll as for jelly roll; tie in several places. Coat with flour. Brown in oil in skillet. Place in baking dish. Add whole mushrooms and onions. Sprinkle with additional salt, pepper and paprika. Add wine. Bake, covered, at 350 degrees for 2 hours. Place on serving platter; remove string. Slice into serving portions. Yield: 4 servings.

Mary Elizabeth Reinhart, Laureate Eta
Fox Point, Wisconsin

SWISS STEAK

1½ to 2 pounds round	1 12-ounce can
steak	mushrooms, drained
Flour	1 6-ounce can tomato
Oil	paste
1 large onion, chopped	2 cups (about) mixed
2 to 3 stalks celery,	vegetable juice cocktail
chopped	1 tablespoon
½ 18-ounce bottle of	Worcestershire sauce
catsup	

Cut steak into serving pieces. Pound with meat mallet to tenderize. Coat with flour. Brown on both sides in a small amount of oil in Dutch oven. Add remaining ingredients. Bake at 325 degrees for 45 to 60 minutes or until tender. Yield: 6 to 8 servings.

Jean Kuhn, Xi Iota
Wyoming, Michigan

SKEWERED STEAK AND MUSHROOMS

½ cup Burgundy	½ teaspoon MSG
½ cup oil	½ teaspoon rosemary
2 tablespoons catsup	½ teaspoon marjoram
1 teaspoon	½ teaspoon salt
Worcestershire sauce	1½ pounds 2-inch steak
1 tablespoon vinegar	cubes
1 teaspoon sugar	12 large fresh mushrooms
1 clove of garlic, crushed	

Combine first 11 ingredients in bowl; mix well. Add steak cubes and mushrooms. Marinate for 2 hours. Drain, reserving marinade. Alternate steak and mushrooms on skewers. Place on broiler pan. Broil until brown on all sides, basting frequently with reserved marinade. Yield: 4 servings.

Andrea Ryan, Zeta Alpha
Williamsport, Pennsylvania

OLD-FASHIONED PARTY STEW

1 3-pound boneless	½ cup water
chuck roast, cut	1 envelope dry onion
into cubes	soup mix
3 tablespoons oil	1 10-ounce can golden
2 large onions, chopped	mushroom soup
1 small green pepper,	¼ cup wine
chopped	2 bunches carrots, sliced
2 stalks celery, chopped	8 small whole potatoes
2 small cloves of garlic,	1 cup sour cream
minced	

Brown beef cubes on all sides in oil in stockpot. Add chopped onions, green pepper, celery and garlic. Sauté until vegetables are translucent; drain. Stir in water and dry onion soup mix. Cook, covered, for 2 hours or longer. Add mushroom soup, wine, carrots and potatoes. Cook for 1 hour or until carrots and potatoes are tender. Stir in sour cream. Cook for 20 minutes longer. Serve with salad and biscuits. Yield: 10 servings.

Wanda McMahon, Preceptor Epsilon Alpha
Winter Haven, Florida

ROAST BEEF BURRITOS

1 onion, chopped	2 to 3 cups chopped
1 10-ounce can beef	cooked roast beef
bouillon	2 medium potatoes,
1 4-ounce can chopped	peeled, finely chopped
green chilies	12 flour tortillas

Combine onion and beef bouillon in saucepan. Bring to a boil. Add green chilies and beef; reduce heat. Simmer for 10 minutes. Add potatoes. Cook until potatoes are the consistency of mashed potatoes, stirring frequently. Season with salt and pepper to taste. Spoon mixture onto tortillas. Roll to enclose filling. Place in greased 9x13-inch baking dish. Bake, covered, at 300 degrees for 30 minutes. Yield: 12 servings.

Note: May microwave burritos on High for 30 seconds. May be frozen individually and thawed before baking.

Lennie Bates, Preceptor Mu
Neosho, Missouri

BLACK-EYED PEAS AND CORN BREAD

1 pound ground beef	1 teaspoon salt
1 small onion, chopped	½ cup oil
1 cup flour	1 cup buttermilk
1 cup cornmeal	1 15-ounce can corn
½ teaspoon soda	1 15-ounce can
1 cup shredded mild	black-eyed peas
Cheddar cheese	

Brown ground beef and onion in skillet, stirring until crumbly; drain. Combine flour, cornmeal, soda, cheese and salt in bowl. Add oil and buttermilk; mix well. Stir in corn, black-eyed peas and ground beef mixture. Pour into greased 9x13-inch baking dish. Bake at 350 degrees for 45 minutes. Yield: 15 to 20 servings.

Deborah J. Butcher, Xi Psi Beta
Beeville, Texas

BURGER PINWHEELS

1½ pounds ground beef	¼ cup chopped onion
⅔ cup evaporated milk	1 tablespoon prepared
1 egg	mustard
½ cup fine cracker crumbs	1 teaspoon lemon pepper
½ cup chopped green	1 15-ounce jar pimento
pepper	cheese spread

Combine first 8 ingredients in bowl; mix well. Pat into 12-inch square on waxed paper. Cover with cheese spread. Roll as for jelly roll; seal edge. Cut into 1-inch slices. Broil for 7 minutes on each side or to desired degree of doneness. Serve on buns or hard rolls if desired. Yield: 6 servings.

Alice P. Castaneda, Preceptor Zeta Delta
Rio Grande City, Texas

CHEESY CABBAGE ROLLS

1½ pounds ground beef	½ teaspoon Italian
1 egg	seasoning
1 medium onion, chopped	1 large head cabbage
½ cup catsup	½ cup shredded Colby
1 cup minute rice	cheese
½ cup Parmesan cheese	2 cups tomato sauce
¼ teaspoon cumin	

Combine ground beef, egg, onion, catsup, rice, Parmesan cheese, cumin and Italian seasoning in bowl; mix well. Chill for 30 minutes. Core cabbage, discarding dark outer leaves. Place in boiling water to cover in saucepan. Cook until outer leaves are loosened. Remove outer leaves. Spoon ½ to ¾ cup ground beef mixture onto each cabbage leaf. Roll to enclose filling. Place seam side down in 9x11-inch baking dish. Sprinkle with Colby cheese. Pour tomato sauce over top. Bake, loosely covered, at 350 degrees for 1 hour. Yield: 4 to 6 servings.

Mary Hinton, Preceptor Lambda
East Rochester, New York

STUFFED CABBAGE ROLLS

1 pound ground beef	½ teaspoon marjoram
2 green peppers, chopped	½ teaspoon salt
2 medium onions,	Pinch of pepper
chopped	1 head cabbage
2 tablespoons oil	1 8-ounce can tomato
1 cup soft bread crumbs	sauce
⅓ cup chili sauce	2 tablespoons butter
2 teaspoons	½ cup sour cream
Worcestershire sauce	

Brown ground beef with green peppers and onions in oil in skillet, stirring until beef is crumbly; drain. Add bread crumbs, chili sauce, Worcestershire sauce and seasonings; mix well. Core cabbage. Cook in boiling salted water to cover in saucepan for 7 minutes; drain. Cool. Remove 12 outer leaves gently. Spoon ground beef mixture onto leaves. Roll to enclose filling; secure with toothpicks. Place in large skillet. Pour tomato sauce over top. Dot with butter. Simmer, covered, for 1 hour. Remove to serving plate. Stir sour cream into sauce in skillet. Heat to serving temperature. Spoon half the sauce over cabbage rolls. Spoon remaining sauce into serving bowl. Serve with rolls. Serve over noodles or rice. Yield: 6 servings.

Alta Gable, Preceptor Beta Omega
Ft. Worth, Texas

GOULASH

1½ cups egg noodles	½ cup catsup
1 10-ounce package	1 2½-ounce jar sliced
frozen mixed	mushrooms, drained
vegetables in butter	1 14½-ounce can
1 pound ground beef	tomatoes, chopped
½ cup chopped onion	2 teaspoons salt
½ cup sliced celery	¼ teaspoon pepper

Cook noodles according to package directions; rinse and drain. Cook mixed vegetables according to package directions; drain. Brown ground beef with onion and celery in skillet, stirring until beef is crumbly; drain. Stir in catsup, noodles, mixed vegetables, mushrooms, tomatoes, salt and pepper. Spoon into 2-quart baking dish. Bake, covered, at 350 degrees for 30 minutes. Serve with garden salad and hot bread. Yield: 6 servings.

Dorothy Hall, Preceptor Alpha Lambda
Newport News, Virginia

LAZY LASAGNA

1 pound ground beef	1 cup shredded mozzarella
1 32-ounce jar spaghetti	cheese
sauce	8 ounces medium or
1 cup Parmesan cheese	wide noodles, cooked

Brown ground beef in skillet, stirring until crumbly; drain. Add spaghetti sauce; mix well. Combine cheeses and noodles; mix well. Layer sauce and noodles alternately in greased 9x13-inch baking dish. Bake at 375 degrees for 25 to 30 minutes. Yield: 4 servings.

Andrea Ryan, Zeta Alpha
Williamsport, Pennsylvania

LASAGNA-STYLE SIRLOIN CASSEROLE

1 pound ground sirloin	8 ounces cream cheese,
1 tablespoon butter	softened
3 8-ounce cans tomato	½ cup sour cream
sauce	⅓ cup chopped green
12 ounces wide lasagna	pepper
noodles	⅓ cup chopped green
1½ cups cottage cheese	onion

Brown ground sirloin in butter in skillet, stirring until crumbly; drain. Stir in tomato sauce. Cook noodles according to package directions. Combine cheeses, sour cream and vegetables in bowl; mix well. Layer noodles and cottage cheese mixture ½ at a time in 9x13-inch baking dish. Pour beef mixture over layers. Bake at 350 degrees for 30 minutes. Yield: 8 to 10 servings.

Lorraine Kirkpatrick, Xi Eta Kappa
Barstow, California

LASAGNA ROLL-UPS

¾ pound ground beef	Salt and pepper to taste
¼ cup chopped onion	1 cup drained chopped
2 cups medium	tomatoes
white sauce	⅓ cup grated carrots
½ cup shredded	12 lasagna noodles,
mozzarella cheese	cooked

Brown ground beef and onion in skillet, stirring until crumbly; drain. Add ⅔ cup white sauce, cheese and salt and pepper; mix well. Cool slightly. Stir tomatoes and carrots into remaining white sauce. Simmer for 10 minutes. Spoon ¼ cup ground beef mixture onto each lasagna noodle; roll to enclose filling. Place seam side down in shallow baking dish. Spoon sauce over top. Sprinkle with additional cheese. Bake at 375 degrees for 25 minutes or until bubbly. Yield: 6 servings.

CARROT MEAT LOAF

1 medium onion, chopped	Dash of garlic powder
1 tablespoon margarine	Dash of pepper
1½ cups shredded carrots	1½ pounds lean ground
¼ teaspoon salt	beef
1 egg, beaten	1 16-ounce jar spiced
2 tablespoons milk	crab apples
¾ teaspoon salt	⅓ cup pineapple
1½ cups bread crumbs	preserves
¾ teaspoon thyme	1 teaspoon mustard

Sauté onion in margarine in skillet. Cook carrots in a small amount of water in saucepan for 5 minutes; drain. Stir in half the onion and ¼ teaspoon salt. Combine egg, milk, ¾ teaspoon salt, bread crumbs, remaining onion and seasonings in bowl; mix well. Mix in ground beef. Shape into 8x10-inch rectangle on waxed paper. Spread carrot mixture to within 1 inch of edge. Roll as for jelly roll; seal edges. Place seam side down in 9x13-inch baking dish. Bake at 350 degrees for 1 hour. Drain crab apples, reserving 1 cup liquid. Bring reserved liquid, preserves and mustard to a boil in saucepan. Cook for 15 minutes. Spoon over meat loaf. Bake for 15 minutes longer. Remove to serving plate. Arrange sliced crab

apples around meat loaf. Garnish with parsley. Let stand for 10 minutes before serving. Yield: 6 servings.

Gladys Simonson, Preceptor Beta Rho
Spokane, Washington

LUMPIA

1 2-ounce package dried	1 cup chopped cabbage
shrimp	2 cups fresh bean sprouts
1 pound ground beef	1 teaspoon salt
¼ cup finely chopped	1 teaspoon paprika
onion	1 teaspoon MSG
1 clove of garlic, minced	1 package lumpia
1 tablespoon oil	wrappers
1 carrot, finely chopped	2 eggs, beaten
2 stalks celery, finely	2 tablespoons water
chopped	Oil for deep frying

Soak shrimp in water using package directions. Drain and chop. Brown ground beef in skillet, stirring until crumbly; drain. Sauté onion and garlic in 1 tablespoon oil in skillet. Add carrot and celery. Cook until tender. Add cabbage. Cook until cabbage is tender. Add bean sprouts. Cook for 2 minutes. Add seasonings, ground beef and shrimp; remove from heat. Separate lumpia wrappers. Brush ends of wrappers 1 at a time with mixture of eggs and water. Fill with 1 tablespoon ground beef mixture. Fold in sides; roll to enclose filling. Deep-fry in hot oil until golden brown, turning as necessary. Serve with sweet and sour sauce. Yield: 30 servings.

Cathy Vins, Xi Alpha
Honolulu, Hawaii

COTTAGE NOODLE BAKE

1 8-ounce package	⅛ teaspoon pepper
medium noodles	1½ cups cottage cheese
1 pound ground beef	½ cup sour cream
2 tablespoons butter	6 green onions, chopped
1 8-ounce can tomato	¾ cup shredded Monterey
sauce	Jack cheese
1¼ teaspoons garlic salt	

Cook noodles according to package directions; drain. Brown ground beef in butter in skillet, stirring until crumbly; drain. Add tomato sauce, garlic salt and pepper. Simmer for 5 minutes. Mix noodles with cottage cheese, sour cream and green onions in bowl. Alternate layers of noodle mixture and ground beef mixture in 2-quart baking dish until all ingredients are used, ending with ground beef mixture. Top with Monterey Jack cheese. Bake at 350 degrees for 30 minutes.
Yield: 6 to 8 servings.

Margaret E. Niemeyer, Preceptor Xi
Aberdeen, South Dakota

To make fancier meat loaf, pat half the meat loaf mixture into loaf pan. Top with one of these fillings: sliced mushrooms, 1 cup shredded cheese, sliced hard-boiled eggs, knockwurst slices or 1 package thawed spinach. Add remaining meat loaf mixture and bake as directed.

SPAGHETTI PIE

6 ounces spaghetti	1 6-ounce can tomato
2 tablespoons margarine	paste
1/3 cup Parmesan cheese	1 8-ounce can tomatoes,
2 eggs, beaten	chopped
8 ounces cottage cheese	1 teaspoon oregano
1 pound ground beef	1/2 teaspoon garlic salt
1/2 cup chopped onion	1/2 cup shredded
1 teaspoon sugar	mozzarella cheese

Cook spaghetti according to package directions; drain well. Stir in margarine, Parmesan cheese and eggs. Shape into crust in buttered 10-inch pie plate. Spread cottage cheese over spaghetti. Brown ground beef with onion in skillet, stirring until beef is crumbly; drain. Add next 5 ingredients; mix well. Cook until heated through. Spoon over cottage cheese. Bake at 350 degrees for 20 minutes. Sprinkle with mozzarella cheese. Bake for 5 minutes longer. Yield: 8 servings.

Roberta DeNegre, Preceptor Gamma Upsilon
Blue Springs, Missouri

HOMEMADE SALAMI

2 pounds ground chuck	1/8 teaspoon garlic powder
1 tablespoon mustard seed	1/4 teaspoon salt
1 tablespoon liquid smoke	1/4 teaspoon pepper
2 tablespoons tender-	3/4 cup water
quick salt	

Combine all ingredients in bowl; mix well. Shape into 3 rolls. Wrap each roll in foil. Chill for 24 hours. Pierce holes in foil along 1 side of each roll. Place pierced side down on rack in baking dish. Bake at 350 degrees for 1 hour. Cool. Replace foil. Store in refrigerator or freezer. Yield: 3 rolls.

Diane Ashworth, Beta Sigma
New Bern, North Carolina

TACORITTOS

2 pounds lean ground beef	1 teaspoon each oregano,
1 16-ounce can refried	sage and cumin
beans	10 small flour tortillas
2 10-ounce cans cream of	Shredded lettuce
chicken soup	Chopped onion
2 soup cans water	Chopped mushrooms
2 tablespoons chili	1 pound Longhorn
powder	cheese, shredded
Dash of garlic powder	

Brown ground beef in skillet, stirring until crumbly; drain. Stir in beans. Combine soup, water and seasonings in bowl; mix well. Add 1 cup mixture to ground beef; mix well. Spoon ground beef mixture onto tortillas. Sprinkle with lettuce, onion, mushrooms and half the cheese. Roll to enclose filling. Place in baking dish. Top with remaining soup mixture and cheese. Bake at 350 degrees for 20 to 30 minutes or until bubbly. Garnish with sour cream and black olives. Yield: 6 to 8 servings.

Connie Sharp, Preceptor Upsilon Xi
Omaha, Nebraska

ITALIAN SOUP

1 pound extra-lean	1 16-ounce can mixed
ground beef	vegetables
1 onion, chopped	1/2 to 3/4 cup orzo
1 16-ounce can tomatoes	Garlic powder, oregano
4 cups water	and basil to taste

Brown ground beef in saucepan, stirring until crumbly; drain. Add remaining ingredients; mix well. Simmer for 20 minutes. Ladle into serving bowls. Garnish with sprinkle of Parmesan cheese. Yield: 4 to 6 servings.
Note: May substitute other small pasta for orzo.

Joan White, Xi Alpha
Providence, Rhode Island

EASY HOLIDAY WEDDING SOUP

1 pound ground beef	1/4 cup Parmesan cheese
1/4 cup minced onion	1 32-ounce can chicken
1 clove of garlic, minced	stock
1/2 cup (or more) Italian	1 large bunch endive
bread crumbs	3 eggs
1 egg	1/4 cup Parmesan cheese
1/4 cup catsup	

Combine ground beef, onion, garlic, bread crumbs, egg, catsup and 1/4 cup Parmesan cheese in bowl; mix well. Shape into marble-sized balls. Bring chicken broth to a boil in saucepan. Add meatballs 1 at a time. Reduce heat. Cook until meatballs are cooked through. Cook endive in a small amount of water in saucepan until tender; drain. Chop endive, discarding core. Stir into soup. Bring to a boil over high heat. Beat 3 eggs with 1/4 cup Parmesan cheese in bowl. Stir eggs into hot mixture. Reduce heat. Simmer for 30 minutes. Serve with spaghetti and salad. Yield: 6 to 8 servings.

Candy DeStefano, Xi Kappa Beta
Wintersville, Ohio

SUPER BOWL STEW

1 pound ground beef	1 teaspoon MSG
1 medium onion, chopped	1 teaspoon oregano
1 8-ounce can tomato	1 teaspoon chili powder
sauce	1 teaspoon cumin
1 6-ounce can tomato	2 teaspoons garlic salt
paste	1 teaspoon salt
3 6-ounce cans water	Tortilla chips
1 tablespoon sugar	

Brown ground beef with onion in saucepan, stirring until beef is crumbly; drain. Add tomato sauce, tomato paste, water, sugar and seasonings. Simmer for 45 minutes. Place tortilla chips in individual serving bowls. Ladle stew into bowls. Garnish with grated cheese or chopped tomato, lettuce, green pepper, onion or cucumber if desired. Yield: 3 to 4 servings.

Patsy Taylor, Epsilon Psi
Shelbyville, Tennessee

CHINESE FRUITED PORK

6 ½-inch thick loin pork chops	1 tablespoon oil
2 tablespoons soy sauce	1 10-ounce package frozen snow peas, partially thawed
1 teaspoon oil	
¼ teaspoon pepper	¼ cup water
1 tablespoon cornstarch	1 teaspoon cornstarch
1 16-ounce can apricots	3 cups hot cooked rice
¾ cup oil	

Bone and trim pork chops. Pound ¼ inch thick between waxed paper with meat mallet. Cut into ½x1-inch pieces. Combine with soy sauce, 1 teaspoon oil, pepper and 1 tablespoon cornstarch in bowl; mix well. Let stand for 15 minutes. Drain apricots, reserving ¼ cup syrup. Heat ¾ cup sesame oil in wok. Add pork. Stir-fry for 3 to 4 minutes. Remove with slotted spoon. Drain wok and wipe with paper towel. Heat 1 tablespoon oil in wok. Add snow peas. Stir-fry for 30 seconds. Add apricots and pork. Stir-fry for 30 seconds. Add 1 teaspoon cornstarch dissolved in reserved apricot syrup. Cook until thickened, stirring constantly. Serve over rice. Yield: 8 servings.

Preceptor Beta Delta
Calmar, Iowa

PORK CHOPS AND RICE

1 cup minute rice	2½ cups water
4 to 6 pork chops	4 to 6 green pepper rings
1 envelope dry onion soup mix	3 to 4 tablespoons chili sauce

Sprinkle rice in 9x13-inch baking dish. Brown pork chops on both sides in skillet. Arrange over rice. Add soup mix and water to pan drippings, stirring to deglaze skillet. Bring to a boil. Pour over pork chops. Place 1 green pepper ring on each pork chop. Place 2 teaspoons chili sauce in center of each pepper ring. Bake at 350 degrees for 1 hour. Yield: 4 to 6 servings.

Patricia McCormick, Xi Gamma Upsilon
Sycamore, Illinois

STUFFED PORK CHOPS À LA JERRY

1 package herb-flavored stuffing mix	4 slices onion
½ cup chopped celery	4 slices lemon
12 dates, chopped	¼ cup packed brown sugar
4 ¾-inch thick pork chops	¼ cup barbecue sauce

Prepare stuffing mix according to package directions, adding celery and dates. Slit pork chops to form pockets. Spoon stuffing into pockets; secure with toothpicks. Place in shallow baking dish. Top each pork chop with onion slice, lemon slice, 1 tablespoon brown sugar and 1 tablespoon barbecue sauce. Bake, covered, at 350 degrees for 30 minutes. Bake, uncovered, for 30 minutes longer. Yield: 4 servings.

Betty J. Bowers, Preceptor Beta Omega
Ft. Worth, Texas

BARBECUED RIBS

¼ cup packed brown sugar	1½ teaspoons salt
¼ cup Bourbon	1 medium onion, sliced
¼ cup soy sauce	3 to 4 pounds spareribs

Combine first 5 ingredients in bowl; mix well. Pour over ribs in shallow dish. Marinate for 2 hours or longer at room temperature or in refrigerator overnight, turning occasionally. Drain. Grill 6 to 8 inches from hot coals for 45 to 60 minutes or until tender, turning frequently. Serve with assorted sauces for dipping and extra cloth napkins. Yield: 4 servings.

Diana Bal, Xi Delta Xi
Rochester, New York

HONEY AND GARLIC SPARERIBS

2 pounds country-style spareribs	¼ cup catsup
Garlic powder to taste	¼ cup soy sauce
½ cup honey	2 tablespoons brown sugar

Simmer spareribs in water to cover in saucepan for 20 minutes. Drain and rinse under hot water. Cut into serving pieces. Place in baking dish. Sprinkle with garlic powder. Combine remaining ingredients in bowl; mix well. Spoon over ribs. Bake, covered, at 300 to 350 degrees for 30 minutes. Bake, uncovered, for 30 minutes, basting occasionally.

Linda Gizienski, Xi Alpha
Providence, Rhode Island

CHERRY-GLAZED ROAST LOIN OF PORK

1 5-pound pork loin roast	¼ teaspoon dry mustard
Salt	¼ cup packed brown sugar
1 20-ounce can sour red cherries	½ teaspoon salt
2 tablespoons all-purpose flour	1 clove of garlic, minced
	3 tablespoons vinegar
	10 whole cloves

Rub pork with salt. Drain cherries, reserving juice. Combine flour, dry mustard, brown sugar, ½ teaspoon salt, reserved juice, garlic, vinegar and cloves in bowl; mix well. Pour into roasting pan. Place roast, fat side up, in pan. Roast at 325 degrees to 160 degrees on meat thermometer, basting frequently. Add cherries. Roast to 170 degrees on meat thermometer, basting occasionally. Remove roast to serving platter; slice. Spoon cherry sauce over slices. Yield: 10 to 12 servings.

Mrs. Robert L. Scofield, Laureate Eta
Clarksville, Tennessee

For easy holiday pork roast, pierce through center of 5-pound pork loin center rib roast with long, narrow sharp knife, twisting to make pocket. Pack plumped prunes into pocket with handle of wooden spoon. Sprinkle with salt, pepper and ginger. Roast at 325 degrees to 170 degrees on meat thermometer. Flavor gravy with ginger and 1 teaspoon currant jelly.

HERBED ROAST PORK

1 3½ to 4-pound pork loin	½ teaspoon pepper
2 teaspoons thyme	¼ cup water
1 teaspoon cumin	1 tablespoon all-purpose flour
1 teaspoon garlic powder	¼ cup dry white wine
Salt to taste	1 cup water

Trim fat from top of roast in 1 piece and reserve. Rub all surfaces with mixture of thyme, cumin, garlic powder, salt and pepper. Replace fat. Place on rack in roasting pan. Add ¼ cup water. Bake at 400 degrees for 20 minutes. Reduce temperature to 350 degrees. Bake for 1 hour and 40 minutes longer or to 170 degrees on meat thermometer, basting occasionally. Remove roast to warm platter. Drain pan, reserving 2 tablespoons pan drippings. Blend flour and pan drippings in roaster. Add wine and 1 cup water. Cook until thickened, stirring constantly. Slice roast. Serve with gravy and hot noodles. Yield: 4 servings.

Mary Bess Maltby, Preceptor Iota Omicron
Morro Bay, California

JAPANESE YAKITORI

1 cup soy sauce	2 pounds pork tenderloin, sliced
½ cup wine vinegar	
¼ cup peanut oil	12 scallions
2 ounces dry Sherry	4 green peppers, cut into 1-inch squares
¼ cup sugar	
1 clove of garlic, crushed	12 small mushrooms
1 teaspoon ginger	

Combine soy sauce, vinegar, peanut oil, Sherry, sugar, garlic and ginger in saucepan. Bring to a boil. Combine with pork in bowl. Marinate for 4 hours to overnight. Drain, reserving marinade. Thread pork onto skewers. Thread each kind of vegetable onto separate skewers. Pour reserved marinade over skewered pork and vegetables in shallow dish. Marinate for 30 miunutes. Drain, reserving marinade. Place pork skewers on grill over hot coals. Cook for 5 minutes, turning and basting frequently with reserved marinade. Add scallion and mushroom skewers. Cook for 10 minutes, turning and basting frequently. Add green peppers. Cook all skewers for 5 minutes or until tender, turning and basting frequently. Remove to serving plate. Serve with steamed rice and fresh fruit for dessert.
Note: May substitute 2 pounds chicken, cut into 1-inch cubes, for pork.

Carol Brakeall, Eta Alpha
Shawnee, Kansas

SAUERKRAUT WITH PORK (SAUERKRAUT UND SPECK)

3 pounds fresh pork	4 cups sauerkraut
1 tablespoon salt	

Place pork in roasting pan. Add water to cover and salt. Bake at 300 degrees for 1 hour. Add sauerkraut and enough additional water to make of desired consistency.

Cook for 1 hour longer or until pork is tender. Season to taste with additional salt and pepper. Serve with mashed potatoes and green beans. Yield: 6 servings.

Patricia Hudson, Xi Alpha Psi
Superior, Wisconsin

GAIL'S PORK TERIYAKI

1 10-ounce bottle (or more) of teriyaki sauce	Sliced green onions
	Sliced carrots
	Sliced mushrooms
1 to 3 cloves of garlic, crushed	Flowerets and sliced stems of broccoli
Grated fresh ginger to taste	Snow peas
	½ cup water
Black pepper to taste	1 teaspoon cornstarch
1 to 1½ pounds pork, partially frozen	

Combine teriyaki sauce, garlic, ginger and pepper in bowl. Slice pork thinly. Add to sauce. Marinate in refrigerator for 4 hours to overnight, stirring occasionally. Place in heated electric skillet. Stir-fry until brown. Cook, covered, for 10 to 20 minutes or until no longer pink. Add vegetables and ½ cup water; reduce heat. Steam, covered, for 5 to 10 minutes or to desired degree of tenderness. Stir in mixture of cornstarch and a small amount of water. Cook until thickened, stirring constantly. Serve over rice. Yield: 4 servings.

Gail E. Frics, Preceptor Upsilon
Omaha, Nebraska

PORK TENDERLOIN WITH GINGERED FRUIT SAUCE

1 pound pork tenderloin	Dash of red pepper
1 8-ounce can juice-pack pineapple tidbits	Soy sauce to taste
	4 green onions
⅔ cup orange juice	1 medium carrot
1 tablespoon cornstarch	1 clove of garlic, minced
1 tablespoon grated gingerroot	1 tablespoon butter or margarine

Place pork tenderloin in shallow roasting pan. Roast at 325 degrees for 1 hour or to 170 degrees on meat thermometer. Cover and keep warm. Drain pineapple, reserving juice. Combine reserved juice, orange juice, cornstarch, gingerroot, red pepper and soy sauce in bowl; mix well. Cut onions diagonally into 1-inch pieces. Cut carrot into thin slivers. Sauté onions, carrots and garlic in butter in saucepan for 3 to 4 minutes. Stir in juice mixture. Cook until thickened, stirring constantly. Cook for 2 minutes longer. Add pineapple. Cook until heated through. Slice pork; arrange on serving plate. Spoon sauce over top. Yield: 4 to 6 servings.

Sissy Smith, Epsilon Psi
Shelbyville, Tennessee

BAKED HAM IN CIDER

1 11-pound fully-cooked ham	4 cups apple cider
20 whole cloves	2 small onions
1 cup boiling water	1 tablespoon lemon juice
2 tablespoons brown sugar	1 tablespoon flour

Sear ham; stud with cloves. Place in roaster. Combine water, brown sugar, cider and onions in saucepan. Bring to a boil. Cook for 10 minutes; strain. Pour over ham. Bake at 350 degrees for 1 hour, basting every 15 minutes. Place ham on heated serving platter. Strain cooking liquid. Stir mixture of lemon juice and flour into strained liquid. Cook until thickened, stirring constantly. Serve with ham. Yield: 20 servings.

Velda M. Kloke, Xi Gamma Zeta
Harvard, Nebraska

HOLIDAY HAM

1 10-pound fully-cooked ham	1 4-ounce bottle of maraschino cherries, drained
1 8-ounce can sliced pineapple, drained	

Remove and discard any gelatin from ham; place in baking pan. Arrange pineapple slices and cherries on ham. Bake at 350 degrees for 2½ hours or for 15 minutes per pound. Yield: 20 servings.

Shirley Jones, Preceptor Iota Theta
Clayton, California

SPICED HAM GLAZED WITH GUAVA JELLY

1 7 to 8-pound ready-to-eat ham	1 cup guava jelly
Whole cloves	2 tablespoons light corn syrup
1 teaspoon dry mustard	1 tablespoon white vinegar
1 teaspoon warm water	

Place ham on rack in baking pan. Bake at 325 degrees for 12 to 15 minutes per pound. Score diagonally into 1-inch diamonds. Place whole clove in each diamond. Blend dry mustard and warm water in small bowl. Let stand for 10 minutes. Melt jelly in 3-cup saucepan. Stir in corn syrup, vinegar and mustard; mix well. Cook just until heated through. Brush generously over ham. Bake at 350 degrees for 10 minutes. Brush with glaze. Bake for 15 minutes longer or until brown. Place on serving platter. Garnish with parsley and pineapple rings centered with cherries. Let stand for 20 to 30 minutes before slicing. Yield: 12 to 15 servings.
Note: May use tenderized ham and bake for 25 minutes per pound.

Mrs. Robert L. Scofield, Laureate Eta
Clarksville, Tennessee

HAM LOAF

2 pounds ground ham	½ teaspoon mustard
12 ounces ground fresh pork	2½ cups bread crumbs
1 egg	1 cup packed brown sugar
½ cup milk	¾ cup pineapple juice
½ cup pineapple juice	1 teaspoon mustard

Combine ham, pork, egg, milk, ½ cup pineapple juice, ½ teaspoon mustard and bread crumbs in bowl; mix well. Shape into loaf. Place in baking pan. Combine brown sugar and remaining ingredients in bowl; mix well. Bake ham loaf at 350 degrees for 1 hour, basting occasionally with brown sugar mixture.

Norma Jean Engler, Laureate Alpha Beta
Princeton, Indiana

HAM LOAVES

2 eggs, beaten	8 ounces ground beef
1½ cups milk	½ cup packed brown sugar
⅔ cup cracker crumbs	⅓ cup cider or wine vinegar
1 tablespoon minced onion	¼ cup water
⅓ cup tapioca	1 tablespoon dry mustard
1 pound ground ham	
1 pound sausage	

Combine eggs, milk, cracker crumbs, onion and tapioca in bowl; mix well. Let stand for 30 minutes. Add ham, sausage and ground beef; mix well. Shape by ⅔ cupfuls into loaves. Place in 9x13-inch baking dish. Combine brown sugar and remaining ingredients in saucepan. Bring to a boil. Cook for 3 minutes. Baste ham loaves with brown sugar mixture. Bake at 350 degrees for 30 minutes. Baste with remaining brown sugar mixture. Bake for 30 minutes longer. Yield: 12 servings.

Betty Spurgeon, Preceptor Beta Beta
Columbus, Indiana

CENTER CUT HAM WITH APRICOTS AND BROWN SUGAR

1 ¾ to 1-inch thick center cut ham slice	1 16-ounce can apricot halves
1 cup packed brown sugar	

Trim and bone ham slice. Place in shallow baking dish. Cover with brown sugar. Drain apricots, reserving ¼ cup juice. Place apricots, cut side up, on ham. Pour reserved juice over top. Bake at 350 degrees for 20 minutes or until bubbly. Yield: 6 to 8 servings.

Dorothy M. Durrett, Preceptor Nu
Anniston, Alabama

Make an easy fruit sauce to turn ham slices into company fare. Simmer 1 cup each dried prunes and apricots with 1¾ cups orange juice and ¼ cup sugar in saucepan for 20 minutes. Stir in mixture of 1 tablespoon cornstarch and 2 tablespoons water. Cook until thickened, stirring constantly.

HAM AND RICE CASSEROLE

Thinly sliced ham	*1 10-ounce can Cheddar*
1½ cups rice, cooked	*cheese soup*
1 10-ounce package	*½ soup can milk*
frozen peas	*Crushed cheese crackers*
Chopped onion	

Combine ham, rice, peas, onion, soup and milk in bowl; mix well. Spoon into 8x8-inch baking dish. Top with cracker crumbs. Bake at 350 degrees for 30 minutes. Yield: 4 servings.

Marjorie A. Green, Preceptor Alpha
Abilene, Kansas

HAM BALLS

1 pound ground ham	*1 10-ounce can tomato*
1 pound ground pork	*soup*
¾ cup milk	*1¼ cups packed brown*
1 cup graham cracker	*sugar*
crumbs	*1 tablespoon mustard*
¼ cup vinegar	

Combine ham, pork, milk and cracker crumbs in bowl; mix well. Shape into 2-inch balls. Place in 7x11-inch baking dish. Mix remaining ingredients in bowl. Pour over meatballs. Bake at 350 degrees for 1 hour, basting every 15 minutes. Yield: 5 servings.

Kathy Reid, Xi Gamma Alpha
Dubuque, Iowa

FOUR-FOOT SUBMARINE SANDWICH

1 4-foot loaf French	*1½ heads lettuce,*
bread	*shredded*
1½ pounds ham	*2 cucumbers*
1½ pounds summer	*2 green peppers*
sausage	*3 tomatoes*
1½ pounds bologna	*1 onion*
8 ounces sliced	*1 bottle of Italian*
American cheese	*salad dressing*
8 ounces sliced Swiss-	
American cheese	

Split French bread lengthwise. Slice ham, summer sausage and bologna thinly. Arrange on bottom half of bread. Layer cheeses and lettuce on top. Slice vegetables thinly. Layer on top of lettuce. Brush with Italian salad dressing. Replace top of loaf. Cut into serving-sized sandwiches. Yield: 8 servings.

Iota Phi
West Bend, Indiana

BREAKFAST PIZZA

1 8-count package	*⅛ teaspoon pepper*
refrigerator crescent	*1 cup frozen hashed*
rolls	*brown potatoes, thawed*
1 pound pork sausage	*1 cup shredded sharp*
5 eggs	*Cheddar cheese*
¼ cup milk	*2 tablespoons Parmesan*
½ teaspoon salt	*cheese*

Separate roll dough into triangles. Arrange on 12-inch pizza pan to form crust; seal edges. Brown sausage in skillet, stirring until crumbly; drain. Combine eggs, milk, salt and pepper in bowl; beat until smooth. Layer sausage, potatoes and Cheddar cheese in prepared pan. Pour egg mixture over layers. Sprinkle with Parmesan cheese. Bake at 375 degrees for 25 to 30 minutes or until set. Yield: 6 to 8 servings.

Ann Campbell, Xi Beta Psi
Topeka, Kansas

SPINACH QUICHE

4 green onions, chopped	*3 eggs, beaten*
2 slices boiled ham,	*2 teaspoons lemon juice*
chopped	*1 tablespoon flour*
½ cup shredded Swiss	*1 tablespoon melted*
cheese	*butter*
1 unbaked 9-inch	*⅛ teaspoon nutmeg*
pie shell	*Pepper to taste*
8 ounces fresh spinach,	*1 cup buttermilk*
cooked	

Sauté green onions in skillet. Place ham and cheese in pie shell. Add well-drained spinach and sautéed green onions. Combine eggs and remaining ingredients in bowl; beat until smooth. Pour into pie shell. Bake at 375 degrees for 25 to 30 minutes or until knife inserted in center comes out clean. Yield: 6 to 8 servings.

Dolores R. Seward, Xi Epsilon Alpha
Muskogee, Oklahoma

BUFFET CASSEROLE

4 slices bread	*2 cups milk*
1 pound bulk sausage	*1 teaspoon dry mustard*
1 cup shredded Cheddar	*1 teaspoon salt*
cheese	*Pepper to taste*
6 eggs	

Crumble bread into 9x12-inch baking dish. Brown sausage in skillet, stirring until crumbly; drain. Layer sausage and cheese in prepared dish. Combine remaining ingredients in bowl; mix well. Pour over layers. Refrigerate overnight. Bake at 350 degrees for 40 minutes. Yield: 6 to 8 servings.

A. Marie Connolly, Preceptor Delta Kappa
Springfield, Ohio

BUFFET HAM SANDWICHES

1 5-pound ham	*¾ cup mustard*
2 cups honey	*Whole cloves*

Score ham diagonally; place in roaster. Baste with mixture of honey and mustard; stud with cloves. Bake at 325 degrees for 2 to 2½ hours. Serve buffet-style with assorted breads, cheeses, lettuce and garnishes for self-serve sandwich making.
Yield: Enough ham for 20 sandwiches.

Deneen Phelps, Eta
Auburn, Washington

BRUNCH SAUSAGE CASSEROLE

1 pound bulk sausage	2½ cups milk
4 slices bread	1 teaspoon mustard
1 cup shredded sharp	1 teaspoon salt
Cheddar cheese	Pepper to taste
4 eggs	

Brown sausage in skillet, stirring until crumbly; drain. Trim crusts from bread; cut bread into cubes. Layer bread cubes, sausage and cheese in greased 9x13-inch baking dish. Beat remaining ingredients in bowl until smooth. Pour over layers. Refrigerate, covered, overnight. Bake at 350 degrees for 45 minutes. Yield: 12 to 15 servings.

Bonnie Jean Maylone, Preceptor Alpha
Carson City, Nevada

SPECIAL BREAKFAST

6 slices bread	6 eggs
6 slices process cheese	⅓ cup milk
8 ounces sausage	Salt and pepper to taste

Trim crusts from bread. Arrange in 9x11-inch baking dish sprayed with nonfat cooking spray. Top each with cheese slice. Brown sausage in skillet, stirring until crumbly; drain. Sprinkle over cheese. Beat eggs with milk, salt and pepper in bowl. Pour over sausage. Bake at 300 degrees for 45 minutes to 1 hour or until set. Yield: 6 servings.

Linda Sterba, Sigma Lambda
Bridgeview, Illinois

BEAUFORT STEW

2 packages shrimp and	2 ears corn, shucked
crab boil	7 pounds shrimp
20 sausages	

Bring generous amount of water to a boil in large kettle. Add shrimp boil and sausages. Cook until sausage is almost cooked through. Add corn. Cook for several minutes. Add shrimp. Cook until shrimp turn pink. Drain in large colander. Arrange on large platter. Yield: 20 servings.

Brenda Pringle, Xi Alpha Nu
Florence, South Carolina

CHEESE AND EGG CASSEROLE

10 slices bread	2 cups milk
Butter, softened	¼ teaspoon dry mustard
12 ounces sharp white	Salt and pepper to taste
cheese, cubed	Crumbled crisp-fried
3 eggs, slightly beaten	bacon

Trim crusts from bread. Butter bread; cut into cubes. Toss with cheese cubes in bowl. Place mixture in buttered 1½-quart baking dish. Combine eggs, milk, dry mustard, salt and pepper in bowl; mix well. Add bacon. Pour over bread and cheese. Chill for 3 hours to overnight. Bake at 325 degrees for 1 hour or until golden brown. Yield: 5 to 6 servings.

Harriett D. Hall, Xi Alpha Theta
Chestertown, Maryland

EASY BREAKFAST CASSEROLE

6 eggs	1 cup shredded
2 cups milk	Cheddar cheese
1 teaspoon dry mustard	8 cooked sausage
1 teaspoon salt	links, chopped
6 slices bread, cubed	

Combine eggs, milk, dry mustard and salt in bowl. Beat until smooth. Mix in bread cubes, cheese and sausage. Spoon into 9x12-inch baking dish. Refrigerate for 8 hours to overnight. Bake at 350 degrees for 45 minutes. Serve with toasted English muffins. Yield: 4 to 6 servings.

Barbara Mills, Xi Chi
Stephens City, Virginia

EGG SOUFFLÉ

12 slices bread, torn	6 eggs, beaten
1 pound Velveeta cheese,	4 cups milk
chopped	1 teaspoon dry mustard
2 cups chopped cooked	½ teaspoon salt
bacon	¼ cup melted margarine

Layer bread, cheese and bacon in greased 9x13-inch baking dish. Combine eggs, milk, dry mustard and salt in bowl; mix well. Pour over layers. Drizzle margarine over top. Refrigerate, covered, overnight to 24 hours. Bake at 350 degrees for 45 to 60 minutes or until set. Yield: 12 servings.

Ann Corrigan, Preceptor Gamma Epsilon
Blue Springs, Missouri

NO-CRUST SAUSAGE AND CHEESE PIE

2 ounces summer sausage,	4 eggs
chopped	¾ cup milk
8 ounces mozzarella	¼ teaspoon basil
cheese, shredded	

Sprinkle sausage and cheese in deep-dish pie plate. Combine remaining ingredients in bowl; beat until smooth. Pour into prepared pie plate. Bake at 400 degrees for 25 minutes or until set. Yield: 4 to 6 servings.

Jill R. Scott, Eta Phi
Sunnyside, Washington

SAUSAGE AND EGG CASSEROLE

6 thick slices bread	6 eggs, beaten
Butter, softened	2 cups half and half
1 pound bulk sausage	1 teaspoon salt
1½ cups shredded cheese	

Trim crusts from bread. Butter 1 side lightly. Place buttered side up in buttered 9x12-inch baking dish. Brown sausage in skillet, stirring until crumbly; drain. Layer sausage and cheese over bread. Combine remaining ingredients in bowl; mix well. Pour over layers. Refrigerate, covered, overnight. Let stand at room temperature for 15 minutes. Bake, uncovered, at 350 degrees for 45 minutes. Yield: 8 servings.

D. Jean Colburn, Zeta Nu
Boardman, Oregon

EASY OMELET SOUFFLÉ

3 slices bread, buttered, cubed	*4 eggs, beaten*
	2 cups milk
12 ounces Cheddar cheese, shredded	*½ teaspoon dry mustard*
	Dash of cayenne pepper
Chopped sausage	

Combine bread cubes, cheese and sausage in 7x9-inch baking dish; mix lightly. Pour mixture of eggs, milk and seasonings over mixture. Chill, covered with foil, overnight. Bake, uncovered, at 325 degrees for 1 hour. Let stand for 10 minutes before serving. Cut into squares. Yield: 4 servings.

Note: May use cooked ham, bacon or shrimp in place of sausage.

Dorothy A. Kramer, Laureate Theta
Omaha, Nebraska

SAUSAGE AND POTATOES AU GRATIN

1 pound hot sausage	*½ teaspoon salt*
1 10-ounce can cream of mushroom soup	*Pepper to taste*
	4 cups thinly sliced potatoes
½ cup milk	
½ cup chopped onion	*1 tablespoon butter or margarine*
¼ cup chopped green pepper	
	½ cup shredded Cheddar cheese
1 tablespoon chopped pimento	

Cut sausage into bite-sized pieces. Brown on all sides in skillet; drain. Combine soup, milk, onion, green pepper, pimento, salt and pepper to taste in bowl; mix well. Layer potatoes, sausage and soup mixture ½ at a time in 2-quart casserole. Dot with butter. Bake, covered, at 350 degrees for 1 hour and 15 minutes. Sprinkle with cheese. Bake, uncovered, for 10 minutes longer or until potatoes are tender. Yield: 3 to 4 servings.

Anita M. Wilson, Laureate Alpha Mu
Mansfield, Ohio

SAUSAGE ZUCCHINI BOATS

4 ounces hot sausage	*½ teaspoon MSG*
¼ cup chopped onion	*¼ teaspoon salt*
4 medium zucchini	*Dash of pepper*
1 egg, slightly beaten	*½ cup Parmesan cheese*
½ cup cracker crumbs	*Paprika*
¼ teaspoon thyme	

Brown sausage and onion in skillet, stirring frequently; drain. Cook whole zucchini in salted boiling water to cover in saucepan for 7 to 10 minutes or until tender. Cut zucchini in half lengthwise. Scoop out pulp, reserving shells. Mash zucchini in bowl. Add sausage, egg, cracker crumbs, thyme, MSG, salt and pepper; mix well. Reserve 2 teaspoons Parmesan cheese. Stir remaining cheese into sausage mixture. Spoon into zucchini shells. Place in shallow baking dish. Sprinkle with reserved cheese and paprika. Bake at 350 degrees for 25 to 30 minutes. Yield: 2 to 3 servings.

Anita M. Wilson, Laureate Alpha Mu
Mansfield, Ohio

SAUSAGE QUICHES

1½ pounds sausage links	*2½ cups milk*
8 slices bread, cubed	*¾ teaspoon dry mustard*
2 cups shredded sharp Cheddar cheese	*1 10-ounce can cream of mushroom soup*
4 eggs, beaten	*½ cup milk*

Cut sausage links into thirds. Brown in skillet; drain. Layer bread cubes, cheese and sausage in 8x12-inch baking dish. Beat eggs with 2½ cups milk and dry mustard. Pour over layers. Chill, covered, overnight. Blend soup with ½ cup milk in bowl. Pour over top of chilled mixture. Bake at 300 degrees for 1½ hours or until set. Let stand for several minutes before cutting into squares. Yield: 6 to 8 servings.

Gladys Simonson, Preceptor Beta Rho
Spokane, Washington

SAUSAGE SOUFFLÉ

2 pounds sausage	*2 cups milk*
1½ cups shredded cheese	*4 slices bread, crumbled*
12 eggs, beaten	*2 teaspoons dry mustard*

Brown sausage in skillet, stirring until crumbly; drain. Combine all ingredients in bowl; mix well. Pour into 9x13-inch baking dish. Refrigerate overnight. Bake at 325 degrees for 45 minutes. Yield: 12 servings.

Ann Corrigan, Preceptor Gamma Epsilon
Blue Springs, Missouri

MOSTACCIOLI

1 pound sausage links	*¼ teaspoon pepper*
½ cup chopped onion	*¼ teaspoon oregano*
½ cup chopped green pepper	*½ cup water*
	8 ounces curly macaroni, cooked
1 16-ounce can tomatoes	
1 6-ounce can tomato paste	*2 cups shredded Cheddar cheese*
½ teaspoon salt	*¼ cup Parmesan cheese*

Cut sausage into 1-inch pieces. Brown in skillet; remove sausage. Sauté onion and green pepper in pan drippings until tender. Add tomatoes, tomato paste, seasonings and water; mix well. Layer macaroni, sausage, tomato mixture and Cheddar cheese ½ at a time in 2-quart casserole. Sprinkle with Parmesan cheese. Bake at 350 degrees for 30 minutes. Yield: 6 servings.

Leilani Thomas, Xi Zeta Zeta
Colby, Kansas

For an easy cassoulet, brown 8 ounces sausage with ½ cup onion, 1 garlic clove; drain. Combine with two 16-ounce cans navy beans, 1½ cups chopped cooked ham, ¼ cup white wine and bay leaf in casserole. Bake, covered, at 325 degrees for 45 minutes and uncovered for 45 minutes. Remove bay leaf.

CASHEW CHICKEN

2 chicken breast filets	1 teaspoon sugar
1 tablespoon sugar	½ cup chicken broth
1 tablespoon cornstarch	1 tablespoon hoisin sauce
1 egg white	Oil for frying
¼ teaspoon garlic powder	1 stalk celery, chopped
¼ teaspoon salt	½ cup bamboo shoots
2 tablespoons soy sauce	1 teaspoon cornstarch
1 tablespoon Sherry	1 tablespoon water
1 teaspoon sesame oil	½ cup cashews

Wash chicken filets and pat dry. Cut into 1-inch pieces. Combine with 1 tablespoon sugar, 1 tablespoon cornstarch, egg white, garlic powder and salt in bowl; mix well. Marinate for 1 to 2 hours. Combine soy sauce, Sherry, sesame oil, 1 teaspoon sugar, chicken broth and hoisin sauce in bowl; mix well. Set aside. Heat oil in wok. Add chicken 1 piece at a time. Fry until golden brown. Remove to paper towel. Drain oil, reserving 1 tablespoon. Add celery. Stir-fry for several minutes. Add bamboo shoots and soy sauce mixture. Bring to a boil; reduce heat. Add chicken. Cook until heated through, stirring constantly. Stir in mixture of 1 teaspoon cornstarch and water. Cook until thickened, stirring constantly. Stir in cashews. Serve with steamed rice. Yield: 4 to 6 servings.

Laura Ross, Zeta
Kansas City, Missouri

CREAMY CHICKEN BREASTS

8 chicken breast filets	¼ cup dry white wine
8 4x4-inch slices	1 cup crushed herb-
Swiss cheese	seasoned stuffing mix
1 10-ounce can cream of	¼ cup melted butter
chicken soup	

Wash chicken filets and pat dry. Arrange chicken breast filets in greased 9x13-inch baking dish. Place cheese slices over filets. Mix soup and wine in small bowl. Pour over filets. Sprinkle with stuffing mix. Drizzle with butter. Bake at 350 degrees for 45 to 55 minutes or until chicken is tender. Yield: 8 servings.

Sammie Wilder Nichols, Beta Sigma
New Bern, North Carolina

LEMON THYME CHICKEN

4 chicken breasts	¼ cup oil
4 chicken thighs	1 teaspoon thyme
1 cup finely chopped	¼ teaspoon garlic powder
onion	½ teaspoon cracked
½ cup fresh lemon juice	pepper

Wash chicken pieces and pat dry. Combine remaining ingredients in bowl; mix well. Add chicken. Marinate in refrigerator overnight; drain. Place chicken, skin side down, in shallow baking dish. Bake at 400 degrees for 40 minutes or until tender, turning once. Garnish with lemon slices. Yield: 4 servings.
Note: May grill over hot coals.

Mary B. Maltby, Preceptor Iota Omicron
Morro Bay, California

OVEN CHICKEN BREASTS

10 chicken breast filets	1 10-ounce can cream of
3 ounces dried beef	chicken soup
10 slices bacon	4 ounces cream cheese,
1 cup sour cream	softened

Wash chicken filets and pat dry. Cut dried beef into small pieces; spread over bottom of 9x13-inch baking dish. Roll up each chicken breast; wrap with bacon slice, securing with toothpick. Arrange over dried beef. Blend sour cream, soup, and cream cheese in bowl. Pour over chicken. Bake, covered, at 300 degrees for 2 hours. Bake, uncovered, for 1 hour longer. Serve with rice cooked in chicken bouillon. Yield: 10 servings.

Jean M. Rucker, Alpha Rho
Maryville, Missouri

PINEAPPLE-CHICKEN STIR-FRY

1 pound chicken breasts	2 cups broccoli flowerets
Garlic salt and pepper	¼ cup vinegar
to taste	2 tablespoons Sherry
1 fresh pineapple	1 tablespoon soy sauce
½ cup slivered almonds	1 tablespoon sugar
1 tablespoon oil	2 teaspoons cornstarch
2 green onions, sliced	1 teaspoon minced
1 sweet red pepper,	gingerroot
chopped	½ teaspoon garlic salt

Wash chicken breasts and pat dry. Slice thinly. Sprinkle with garlic salt and pepper to taste. Cut pineapple into quarters; peel and core quarters. Chop fruit into bite-sized pieces. Sauté almonds in oil in wok until golden brown; remove with slotted spoon. Add chicken. Stir-fry for 5 minutes or until well browned. Add green onions, red pepper and broccoli. Stir-fry until tender-crisp. Add mixture of remaining ingredients. Cook until thickened. Stir in pineapple. Serve with rice. Yield: 6 servings.

Preceptor Beta Delta
Calmar, Iowa

CHICKEN AND RICE

8 to 10 chicken breast filets	24 fresh mushrooms,
2 cups cream of chicken	sliced
soup	2 envelopes dry onion
2 cups brown rice	soup mix
1½ cups water	Pinch of pepper

Wash chicken filets and pat dry. Place in 9x13-inch baking dish. Combine remaining ingredients in bowl; mix well. Pour over chicken. Bake, covered, at 350 degrees for 45 minutes. Bake, uncovered, for 45 minutes, adding water if casserole becomes too dry.
Yield: 8 to 10 servings.

Laura Alverson, Preceptor Laureate Nu
Olympia, Washington

Frosted cranberries or grapes make a pretty garnish for poultry dishes. Dip fruit into mixture of egg white and a small amount of water. Coat with sugar and let stand until dry.

STUFFED CHICKEN BREASTS

6 medium chicken breasts	1¼ teaspoons poultry
⅓ cup chopped celery	seasoning
⅓ cup chopped green	⅛ teaspoon pepper
pepper	2 tablespoons butter
3 tablespoons chopped	2 tablespoons cornstarch
onion	½ teaspoon salt
3 tablespoons butter	1¼ cups cold milk
2 cups cooked long	¼ to 1 cup shredded
grain rice	sharp cheese

Wash chicken breasts and pat dry. Sauté celery, green pepper and onion in 3 tablespoons butter in skillet. Add rice, poultry seasoning and pepper; mix well. Slit chicken breasts to form pocket. Spoon rice mixture into pockets; secure with toothpicks. Place in shallow baking dish. Melt 2 tablespoons butter in saucepan. Stir in cornstarch and salt. Stir in milk gradually. Cook until thickened, stirring constantly; remove from heat. Add cheese; stir until cheese melts. Pour over chicken. Bake at 350 degrees until chicken is tender. Yield: 6 servings.

Mary C. Shapard, Epsilon Psi
Shelbyville, Tennessee

GREEK CHICKEN

1 chicken	1 tablespoon basil
⅓ cup olive oil	1 tablespoon rosemary
½ cup melted butter	1 tablespoon oregano
1 tablespoon garlic salt	

Wash chicken and pat dry. Place in 8x8-inch baking dish. Combine remaining ingredients in bowl; mix well. Drizzle over chicken. Bake at 350 degrees for 1 hour. Yield: 5 servings.

Annette Lauer, Xi Alpha Epsilon
Greensboro, North Carolina

CHICKEN AND SPAGHETTI

2 large chickens	1 12-ounce can tomatoes
1 large onion, chopped	and chilies
2 large greeen peppers,	1 16-ounce can green
chopped	peas
Butter	1 16-ounce can tomatoes
16 ounces spaghetti	1 16-ounce can
1 pound Old English	mushrooms
cheese, chopped	2 teaspoons
1 pound Velveeta cheese,	Worcestershire sauce
chopped	Parmesan cheese

Cook chicken in water to cover in large stockpot until tender. Drain, reserving 8 cups broth. Cut chicken into bite-sized pieces. Sauté onion and green peppers in a small amount of butter in skillet. Cook spaghetti *al dente* in reserved broth in saucepan; do not drain. Stir in Old English and Velveeta cheeses until melted. Drain next 4 ingredients. Add to spaghetti with Worcestershire sauce, sautéed vegetables and chicken; mix well. Spoon into 9x13-inch baking dish. Sprinkle with Parmesan cheese. Bake at 350 degrees for 30 minutes. Yield: 12 servings.

Vergie Stockton, Preceptor Beta Omega
Ft. Worth, Texas

SWISS CHICKEN

8 chicken breast filets	1 10-ounce can cream of
1 cup fine bread crumbs	chicken soup
8 slices Swiss cheese	¼ cup dry white wine

Wash chicken filets and pat dry. Coat with bread crumbs. Place in 8x8-inch baking dish sprayed with nonstick cooking spray. Top with cheese slices. Mix soup and wine in bowl. Pour over chicken. Bake at 350 degrees for 45 to 55 minutes or until tender. Yield: 4 servings.
Note: May add mushrooms to sauce if desired.

Sally Adams, Xi Xi
Caldwell, Idaho

LAZY DAISY CHICKEN

4 chicken legs	1 teaspoon onion flakes
4 chicken thighs	1 teaspoon brown sugar
2 tablespoons oil	½ teaspoon garlic powder
½ cup low-calorie zesty	⅛ teaspoon pepper
Italian salad dressing	1 4-ounce can
½ cup water	mushrooms, drained
¼ cup soy sauce	1⅓ cups instant rice

Remove skin from chicken; wash and pat dry. Heat oil in large skillet over medium heat. Add chicken. Cook until brown on both sides; drain. Combine salad dressing, ½ cup water, soy sauce, onion flakes, brown sugar, garlic powder and pepper in bowl; mix well. Pour over chicken. Cook, covered, over low heat for 45 minutes or until tender, turning and basting chicken occasionally and adding enough water to make of desired consistency if necessary. Remove chicken to warm plate. Pour sauce from skillet into 2-cup measure. Add enough water to measure 1⅓ cups liquid. Combine with mushrooms in skillet. Bring to a boil. Stir in rice; remove from heat. Let stand, covered, for 5 minutes; fluff with fork. Spoon rice onto round serving plate. Arrange chicken legs and thighs with smaller ends toward center alternately on rice. Garnish with parsley. Yield: 4 servings.

Helen J. Beidelschies, Preceptor Delta Alpha
Bucyrus, Ohio

HAWAIIAN CHICKEN

1 2½-pound chicken,	⅓ cup steak sauce
cut up	3 tablespoons brown
Salt and pepper to taste	sugar
1 8½-ounce can sliced	
pineapple	

Wash chicken and pat dry. Place in 8x12-inch baking dish. Sprinkle with salt and pepper. Bake at 400 degrees for 15 minutes. Drain pineapple, reserving 2 tablespoons liquid. Combine reserved liquid, steak sauce and brown sugar in small bowl. Pour over chicken. Bake for 25 minutes longer, basting occasionally. Arrange pineapple slices over chicken. Bake for 10 minutes longer. Skim sauce. Spoon over chicken to serve. Yield: 4 servings.

Darlene Burchinal, Preceptor Beta
Bismarck, North Dakota

POLYNESIAN CHICKEN

1 chicken, cut up	1 7-ounce can bamboo
Garlic powder to taste	shoots
Oil for frying	1 small onion, chopped
Brown sugar	1 7-ounce can sliced
1 20-ounce can	water chestnuts
pineapple chunks	1 small piece gingerroot
1 green pepper, sliced	Pineapple juice

Wash chicken and pat dry. Sprinkle with garlic powder. Brown on both sides in a small amount of oil in large deep skillet; drain. Sprinkle both sides of chicken with brown sugar. Add pineapple, green pepper, bamboo shoots, onion, water chestnuts, gingerroot and pineapple juice to cover. Simmer for 1 hour or until chicken is tender and sauce is of desired consistency. Sprinkle chicken with brown sugar and turn frequently.

Yield: 6 to 8 servings.

Note: May thicken sauce with cornstarch if desired.

Patricia Cornwall, Xi Gamma Upsilon
Sycamore, Illinois

POPOVER CHICKEN

1 2½ to 3-pound chicken,	3 tablespoons oil
cut up	1 teaspoon tarragon
Salt and pepper to taste	1 3-ounce can
2 tablespoons oil	mushrooms, drained
3 eggs	1 tablespoon butter
1½ cups milk	1 10-ounce can cream of
1½ cups all-purpose flour	chicken soup
¾ teaspoon salt	¼ cup milk

Wash chicken and pat dry. Sprinkle with salt and pepper to taste. Brown on both sides in 2 tablespoons oil in skillet. Place in greased shallow 2-quart baking dish. Combine eggs, 1½ cups milk, flour and ¾ teaspoon salt in mixer bowl. Beat for 1½ minutes. Add 3 tablespoons oil and tarragon. Beat for 30 seconds. Pour over chicken. Bake at 350 degrees for 50 to 60 minutes or until puffed and brown. Sauté mushrooms in butter in skillet for 4 to 5 minutes. Stir in soup. Add ¼ cup milk gradually. Cook until heated through. Serve with chicken.

Yield: 4 to 6 servings.

Shirley Carnine, Xi Tau
New Haven, Connecticut

CHICKEN CURRY

1 medium onion, minced	2 cups cream
⅔ cup sliced mushrooms	2 cups chicken broth
2 tablespoons chopped	Salt and pepper to taste
green pepper	2 cups (or more) chopped
2 tablespoons chopped	cooked chicken
sweet red pepper	1 5-ounce can sliced
¼ cup butter	water chestnuts
5 tablespoons all-purpose	½ cup toasted almonds
flour	1 large apple, chopped
2 tablespoons curry	
powder	

Sauté onion, mushrooms and peppers in 3 tablespoons butter in saucepan. Add remaining 1 tablespoon butter, flour and curry powder; mix well. Stir in cream and chicken broth gradually. Cook until thickened, stirring constantly. Season to taste. Stir in remaining ingredients. Cook until heated through.

Note: May spoon into baking dish and bake in moderate oven until bubbly.

Pat Blasbalg, Xi Alpha
Providence, Rhode Island

CHICKEN TAMALE PIE

1 2-pound chicken,	1 medium onion, chopped
cut up	¼ cup oil
2 cloves of garlic, crushed	½ cup tomato sauce
Juice of 1 lime	¼ cup dry Sherry
Salt and pepper to taste	2 cups grated fresh corn
1 medium green pepper,	3 cups chicken broth
chopped	

Wash chicken pieces and pat dry. Season with garlic, lime juice, salt and pepper. Sauté green pepper and onion in oil in skillet. Add chicken. Cook until brown on both sides. Stir in tomato sauce and Sherry. Cook for 5 minutes. Spoon into baking dish. Add corn and chicken broth. Bake at 300 degrees for 60 minutes or until chicken is tender and sauce is thickened, stirring occasionally.

Jerry Wright, Xi Alpha
Providence, Rhode Island

LUANNE'S FESTIVE CHICKEN CASSEROLE

2 10-ounce cans cream of	2 4-ounce cans
chicken soup	mushrooms, drained
1 cup mayonnaise	Pimento
½ cup chopped onion	Oregano to taste
½ cup chopped celery	5 cups chopped
1 7-ounce can water	cooked chicken
chestnuts, drained	2 cups cooked rice

Heat soup in saucepan. Stir in mayonnaise, onion, celery, water chestnuts, mushrooms, pimento and oregano; mix well. Fold in chicken and rice. Spoon into 9x13-inch baking dish. Bake at 375 degrees for 45 minutes.

Yield: 8 servings.

LuAnne Becker, Preceptor Beta Delta
Fort Atkinson, Iowa

Serve roast or baked poultry with one of these easy sauces for special main dishes: mixture of 1 cup crushed pineapple, 2 tablespoons jelly and 2 tablespoons each orange rind and chopped mint; mixture of 1 cup orange marmalade, ½ cup chopped walnuts and 3 tablespoons lemon juice. Heat all sauces until blended.

SCALLOPED CHICKEN CASSEROLE

1 2½ to 3-pound chicken	1 cup shredded
1 cup chopped celery	Cheddar cheese
2 eggs, beaten	1 10-ounce can cream of
2 cups crushed	chicken soup
butter crackers	1 10-ounce can cream of
1 cup chicken broth	mushroom soup

Wash chicken and pat dry inside and out. Cook chicken in boiling salted water to cover in saucepan until tender. Bone and skin chicken; cut into bite-sized pieces. Combine with remaining ingredients in bowl; mix well. Spoon into 9x13-inch baking dish. Bake at 350 degrees for 45 minutes. Yield: 15 servings.

Marjorie K. E. Lessman, Xi Alpha Kappa
Dalton, Nebraska

CHICKEN ENCHILADAS

1 chicken	1 4-ounce can chopped
1 small onion, chopped	green chilies
Butter	Corn tortillas
1 10-ounce can cream of	1 pound longhorn cheese,
chicken soup	shredded
1 10-ounce can cream of	
mushroom soup	

Wash chicken and pat dry. Place in saucepan. Add water to cover. Cook until tender. Drain, reserving 1 cup broth. Chop chicken. Sauté onion in a small amount of butter in large skillet. Add soups, green chilies and reserved broth; mix well. Stir in chicken. Layer tortillas, chicken mixture and cheese ½ at a time in 9x13-inch baking dish. Bake at 350 degrees for 30 minutes. Yield: 6 servings.

Rachel Ollar, Beta Lambda
Evanston, Wyoming

CHICKEN LOAF

4 pounds chicken pieces	1½ teaspoons salt
2 cups fresh bread crumbs	1 10-ounce can
1 cup cooked rice	mushroom soup
1 tablespoon chopped	4 eggs, well beaten
onion	2 hard-boiled eggs,
⅓ cup chopped pimento	chopped
3 cups milk	

Wash chicken and pat dry. Cook chicken in water to cover in saucepan until tender. Drain, reserving 1½ cups broth. Chop chicken into bite-sized pieces. Combine with bread crumbs, rice, onion, pimento, milk and salt in bowl; mix well. Reserve ½ cup soup for gravy. Stir remaining soup into chicken mixture. Add beaten eggs; mix well. Spoon into greased 9x12-inch baking pan. Bake at 350 degrees for 1 hour. Combine reserved broth and reserved soup in saucepan. Cook until heated through. Stir in hard-boiled eggs. Cut chicken loaf into squares. Arrange on serving platter. Garnish with parsley and crab apples. Serve with mushroom gravy. Yield: 10 to 12 servings.

Jenelle Harris, Preceptor Delta Upsilon
Dayton, Ohio

CHICKEN SOPA

1 2½-pound chicken	½ teaspoon salt
2 10-ounce cans cream of	12 tortillas
chicken soup	2 tablespoons shortening
1 12-ounce can	4 cups shredded
evaporated milk	Cheddar cheese
1 4-ounce can chopped	2 medium onions,
green chilies	chopped

Wash chicken and pat dry. Cook chicken in water to cover in large saucepan. Remove chicken; reserve ¾ cup stock. Bone and chop chicken. Combine with reserved stock, soup, evaporated milk, green chilies and salt in bowl; mix well. Cut tortillas into halves. Soften in hot shortening in skillet for several seconds. Alternate layer of tortillas, chicken mixture, cheese and onions in 9x13-inch baking dish until all ingredients are used. Bake at 350 degrees for 30 minutes or until bubbly. Yield: 12 servings.

Edith I. Craig, Xi Phi
Butte, Montana

DUCKLING WITH KUMQUAT SAUCE

1 duckling	¼ cup sugar
1½ teaspoons salt	¼ teaspoon salt
1 teaspoon pepper	1 teaspoon instant
2 teaspoons paprika	chicken bouillon
2 teaspoons poultry	½ cup hot water
seasoning	Pinch each of nutmeg,
½ cup puréed preserved	cloves, thyme and
kumquats	allspice
½ cup Burgundy	2 teaspoons cornstarch
1 teaspoon lemon juice	1 tablespoon green
1 tablespoon butter	peppercorns

Cut duckling into quarters. Rinse and pat dry. Rub with 1½ teaspoons salt, pepper, paprika and poultry seasoning. Place skin side down in skillet. Cook over medium heat for 1 hour, turning every 20 minutes. Do not drain during cooking. Combine kumquat purée, wine, lemon juice, butter, sugar and ¼ teaspoon salt in saucepan. Stir in bouillon dissolved in hot water and spices. Cook until mixture is reduced by half. Add mixture of cornstarch and a small amount of water. Cook until thickened, stirring constantly. Rinse and drain peppercorns. Stir into sauce. Place duckling on serving plate. Spoon hot sauce over top. Yield: 4 servings.
Note: May cook in electric skillet at 350 degrees.

Rosanna Fahl, Preceptor Alpha Epsilon
Oroville, California

Brush poultry with one of the following glazes during last 10 to 20 minutes roasting time: mixture of ½ cup quince jelly, 1 tablespoon butter and 1 teaspoon cinnamon; mixture of ½ cup each apple jelly and orange juice; mixture of ½ cup honey, 1 tablespoon soy sauce and ½ teaspoon ginger.

HOLIDAY DUCKLING AND ORANGE STUFFING

1 4 to 5-pound duckling	1 teaspoon Kitchen
Salt	Bouquet
2 tablespoons honey	

Wash duckling and pat dry. Discard wing tips. Rub cavity with salt; stuff lightly with Orange Stuffing. Secure opening with skewers; lace with cord. Place breast side up on rack in shallow baking pan. Bake, uncovered, at 325 degrees for about 1½ hours. Brush with mixture of honey and Kitchen Bouquet. Bake for 30 minutes longer or until meaty part of leg feels tender and leg moves up and down easily. Yield: 4 servings.

ORANGE STUFFING

3 cups toasted bread cubes	¾ teaspoon salt
2 cups finely chopped celery	½ teaspoon poultry seasoning
1 tablespoon grated orange rind	Dash of pepper
¾ cup chopped orange sections	1 egg, beaten
	⅓ cup melted butter or margarine

Combine first 7 ingredients in bowl; toss to mix. Add egg and butter; mix well.

Bettie Plummer, Laureate Pi
Independence, Missouri

ROAST CORNISH GAME HENS

4 1-pound Rock Cornish game hens	½ can condensed chicken consommé
Salt and pepper to taste	½ cup light corn syrup
½ cup melted butter or margarine	

Wash hens and pat dry. Sprinkle inside and out with salt and pepper. Place breast side up on rack in shallow baking pan. Brush generously with melted butter. Bake, uncovered, at 400 degrees for 45 to 60 minutes or until tender, basting frequently during final 15 minutes of baking time with mixture of consommé and syrup. Yield: 4 servings.

Bettie Plummer, Laureate Pi
Independence, Missouri

BAKED TURKEY WITH CORN BREAD DRESSING

1 16 to 18-pound turkey	2 to 3 tablespoons oil
Salt	2 sticks margarine

Wash turkey; pat dry. Place in large roaster. Rub with salt; brush with oil. Place margarine sticks in cavity. Bake, covered, at 250 degrees for 7 hours or until tender. Remove to serving platter. Serve with Corn Bread Dressing and Giblet Gravy. Yield: 16 servings.
Note: Simmer turkey neck, heart and gizzard in 3 cups salted water in saucepan for 2 hours. Add liver and simmer for 30 minutes longer. Use broth for dressing and chopped giblets for gravy.

CORN BREAD DRESSING

3 cups chopped celery hearts	6 slices toasted bread
2 cups chopped green onions with tops	6 eggs, beaten
Giblet broth	6 hard-boiled eggs, chopped
1 recipe Mother Cheek's Corn Bread (page 128)	Salt and pepper to taste
	Turkey drippings

Sauté celery and green onions in giblet broth in saucepan until tender. Break corn bread and toasted bread into coarse pieces. Combine corn bread, beaten eggs, hard-boiled eggs, salt, pepper and toast in bowl in order listed. Add enough drippings to moisten. Spoon into roasting pan. Bake at 300 degrees for 40 minutes to 1 hour. Dressing will be very moist. Yield: 16 servings.

GIBLET GRAVY

½ cup all-purpose flour	Salt and pepper to taste
½ cup hot bacon drippings	Chopped cooked giblets
1 cup turkey drippings	6 hard-boiled eggs, sliced
3 to 4 cups (about) water	

Combine flour and bacon drippings in cast-iron skillet. Cook over low heat until light brown. Stir in turkey drippings and enough water to make of desired consistency. Cook until smooth, stirring constantly. Add salt, pepper and giblets. Simmer for 15 minutes. Add eggs. Simmer for 5 minutes longer. Yield: 6 cups.

Deann Walters, Delta Kappa
Ellisville, Missouri

CURRIED TURKEY AND SAFFRON RICE

2 to 3 cups rice	½ cup all-purpose flour
⅛ teaspoon saffron	2 tablespoons curry powder
1 large onion, chopped	1¼ cups turkey broth
2 stalks celery, chopped	1¼ cups milk
1 apple, peeled, chopped	½ cup cream
1 carrot, shredded	4 cups chopped cooked turkey
2 cloves of garlic, crushed	
½ cup butter	

Cook rice according to package directions, adding saffron. Sauté onion, celery, apple, carrot and garlic in butter in saucepan. Stir in flour and curry powder. Stir in broth, milk and cream gradually. Cook over low heat until thickened, stirring constantly. Add turkey. Simmer until heated through. Serve over rice. Serve with bowls of toppings such as raisins, coconut, peanuts, cashews, chopped green onions, chopped hard-boiled eggs, chutney and crumbled bacon for individual garnishing. Yield: 8 servings.

Claire Hebert, Preceptor Delta
Sulphur, Louisiana

Use leftover baked breads of various types for all or part of bread crumbs or cubes in stuffing recipes. Corn bread, biscuits, rolls, raisin bread, English muffins or cheese bread make good additions.

TURKEY BURRITOS

1 onion, chopped	3 to 3½ cups chopped
1 clove of garlic, minced	cooked turkey
1 tablespoon oil	Salt and pepper to taste
1 10-ounce can tomatoes	12 flour tortillas
1 4-ounce can chopped	4 cups shredded Monterey
green chilies	Jack cheese

Sauté onion and garlic in oil in saucepan. Add tomatoes and green chilies. Bring to a boil; reduce heat. Simmer for 1 hour. Add turkey; mix well. Season with salt and pepper. Spoon mixture onto tortillas. Sprinkle with cheese. Roll to enclose filling. Place in greased 9x12-inch baking dish. Bake, covered, at 300 degrees for 30 minutes. Yield: 12 servings.
Note: May microwave burritos on High for 30 seconds.

Lennie Bates, Preceptor Mu
Neosho, Missouri

GOBBLER MUSHROOM BRUNCH

½ cup chopped onion	1 10-ounce can cream of
½ cup chopped celery	mushroom soup
½ teaspoon basil	½ cup milk
½ teaspoon salt	2 tablespoons Sherry
¼ teaspoon pepper	3 cups chopped cooked
2 tablespoons margarine	turkey
8 ounces mushrooms,	
sliced	

Sauté onion, celery, basil, salt and pepper in margarine in deep skillet. Add mushrooms. Cook, covered, over medium heat for 3 minutes. Mix soup, milk, Sherry and turkey in bowl. Stir into mushroom mixture. Cook over low heat until heated through. Serve over rice, toast points or leftover turkey dressing. Yield: 8 servings.

Claire Hebert, Preceptor Delta
Sulphur, Louisiana

HOLIDAY LIGHT TURKEY LASAGNA

2½ cups skim milk	1½ cups chopped cooked
3 tablespoons flour	turkey
Salt and pepper to taste	¼ cup (or more) Parmesan
Nutmeg to taste	cheese
2 10-ounce packages	¼ cup (or more) dry bread
frozen chopped spinach	crumbs
8 lasagna noodles, cooked	Paprika to taste
7 to 8 ounces ricotta	
cheese	

Blend milk and flour in saucepan. Cook over low heat until thickened, stirring constantly. Season with salt, pepper and nutmeg. Cook spinach using package directions; drain and squeeze dry. Pour a small amount of sauce into 8x12-inch baking dish. Stir spinach into remaining sauce. Alternate layers of noodles, sauce, ricotta and turkey in prepared dish, ending with sauce. Sprinkle with mixture of Parmesan cheese and bread crumbs. Sprinkle with paprika. Bake at 375 degrees for 30 to 40 minutes or until bubbly and golden on top. Let stand for 10 minutes before serving. Yield: 6 servings.

ONE-PAN TURKEY AND STUFFING

1 cup buttermilk baking	½ teaspoon poultry
mix	seasoning
1¼ cups milk	½ teaspoon salt
3 eggs	2 cups chopped cooked
1 teaspoon parsley flakes	turkey
1 teaspoon sage	1 cup chopped celery
¾ teaspoon thyme	½ cup chopped onion

Combine baking mix, milk, eggs and seasonings in bowl; mix until smooth. Stir in turkey, celery and onion. Spoon into baking dish. Bake at 400 degrees for 30 to 35 minutes or until brown. Yield: 6 servings.

Wanda Odom, Preceptor Epsilon Upsilon
Denison, Texas

SMOKED TURKEY

1 18 to 20-pound turkey,	Salt to taste
split	Hickory chips, twigs
Shortening	or nuts

Wash turkey and pat dry. Coat skin generously with shortening. Sprinkle inside and out with salt. Place breast side up in foil-lined pan on rack in smoker or covered grill. Place coals at 1 end of smoker. Add hickory chips, twigs or nuts to coals every hour to maintain smoke. Smoke turkey for 3 to 4 hours or until turkey tests done. Skin will be brown and meat slightly pink.
Yield: 16 to 20 servings.
Note: Cook giblets in water, adding ½ cup margarine to produce rich stock for other purposes.

Dorothy M. Durrett, Preceptor Nu
Anniston, Alabama

TURKEY SOPA

4 cups chopped cooked	1 onion, finely chopped
turkey	8 to 10 corn tortillas,
3 10-ounce cans	cut into halves
tomatoes and green	Oil
chilies	1 cup shredded Monterey
2 cups sour cream	Jack cheese

Combine turkey, tomatoes and chilies, sour cream and onion in bowl; mix well. Soften tortillas in small amount of hot oil in skillet. Layer tortillas and turkey mixture ½ at a time in greased 3-quart casserole. Top with cheese. Bake at 325 degrees for 1 hour. Yield: 8 servings.
Note: May freeze casserole and let stand at room temperature for 2 hours before baking.

Lennie Bates, Preceptor Mu
Neosho, Missouri

Add a holiday touch to stuffings by including one of these festive ingredients: 12 ounces chopped mixed dried fruit; 16 ounces fresh cranberries; 1½ pounds cooked chestnuts; 8 ounces crisp-fried bacon; 1 cup raisins; 8 ounces cooked Italian sausage; 8 ounces cooked sausage plus 3 chopped apples.

CHRISTMAS EVE FISH

1 pound haddock or cod	1 clove of garlic
2 tablespoons lemon juice	¼ cup butter
1 teaspoon salt	1 tablespoon chopped parsley
½ cup bread crumbs	¼ teaspoon tarragon
1 small onion, chopped	

Cut fish into serving pieces. Cook in boiling salted water in saucepan for 5 to 8 minutes or until fish flakes easily; drain. Place in 1½-quart baking dish. Sprinkle with lemon juice, salt and bread crumbs. Sauté onion and garlic in butter in skillet. Add parsley and tarragon; mix well. Discard garlic. Pour over fish. Bake, covered, at 400 degrees for 20 minutes. Bake, uncovered, for 10 minutes longer. Yield: 4 servings.

Emily Lancia, Xi Kappa Beta
Wintersville, Ohio

FLAVORFUL FLOUNDER

Butter	1 10-ounce can cream of celery soup
2 or 3 flounder fillets	
1 green onion, chopped	½ cup shredded Cheddar cheese
4 or 5 large mushrooms, sliced	

Melt butter in shallow baking dish. Cut flounder fillets into serving-sized pieces. Place in single layer in dish, turning to coat well with butter. Sprinkle with green onion and mushrooms. Spread soup evenly over top. Bake at 350 degrees for 20 minutes or until fish flakes easily. Sprinkle with cheese. Bake until cheese is melted. Serve with rice, green peas and crisp garden salad. Yield: 3 or 4 servings.

Donna Blankenship, Xi Gamma Pi
Lafayette, Tennessee

CHAR-BROILED SWORDFISH

Swordfish steaks	Mayonnaise

Spread both sides of swordfish steaks with mayonnaise. Place on grill over hot coals. Grill for 20 minutes on each side or until fish flakes easily.

Dolores Snyder, Xi Alpha Pi
Hagerstown, Maryland

HOT OYSTER STEW

2 cups oysters, drained	1 teaspoon paprika
¼ cup butter	⅛ teaspoon pepper
4 cups milk	½ pint whipping cream, at room temperature
1½ teaspoons salt	

Cook oysters in butter in nonstick saucepan for 3 minutes or until edges curl. Remove from heat. Stir in milk and seasonings. Heat just to the boiling point. Stir in whipping cream. Serve immediately. Yield: 4 to 6 servings.

Bettie Plummer, Laureate Pi
Independence, Missouri

SCALLOPED OYSTERS

1 17-ounce can cream-style corn	1 cup cracker crumbs
	½ cup butter, melted
1 medium onion, chopped	1 cup half and half
¼ cup chopped celery	Salt and pepper to taste
1 egg, slightly beaten	Fresh oysters
1 10-ounce can oyster stew	½ cup butter cracker crumbs
1 tablespoon chopped pimento	2 tablespoons melted butter

Combine corn, onion, celery, egg, oyster stew, pimento, 1 cup cracker crumbs, ½ cup melted butter, half and half, salt and pepper in bowl; mix well. Spoon into 9x13-inch baking dish. Add oysters. Top with mixture of butter cracker crumbs and 2 tablespoons melted butter. Bake at 350 degrees for 1 hour. Yield: 12 to 15 servings.

Barbara Leach, Xi Sigma
Kansas City, Missouri

CRAB IMPERIAL

1 teaspoon dry mustard	½ cup mayonnaise
1 teaspoon Worcestershire sauce	1 tablespoon capers
	1 pound crab meat
½ teaspoon salt	Paprika

Blend dry mustard, Worcestershire sauce and salt in bowl. Stir in ½ cup mayonnaise and capers. Fold in crab meat. Spoon into scallop shells or small shallow baking dish. Spread additional mayonnaise on top. Sprinkle with paprika. Bake at 375 degrees for 20 minutes or until golden brown. Yield: 4 servings.

Dolores Snyder, Xi Alpha Pi
Hagerstown, Maryland

CRAB PIE

½ cup chopped onion	Garlic salt to taste
½ cup chopped celery	Pinch of mixed herbs
½ cup margarine	10 to 12 slices stale bread
1 pound crab meat	1 cup milk
1 4-ounce can mushrooms, drained	Cracker crumbs
	Margarine
½ cup chopped parsley	1 10-ounce can cream of mushroom soup
6 to 8 drops of Tabasco sauce	Nutmeg to taste

Sauté onion and celery in ½ cup margarine in skillet until tender. Stir in crab meat, mushrooms, parsley, Tabasco sauce, garlic salt and mixed herbs; mix well. Cut bread slices into halves. Dip bread in milk 1 half at a time. Alternate layers of bread and crab meat mixture in buttered baking dish until all ingredients are used. Sprinkle with cracker crumbs. Dot with margarine. Bake at 350 degrees for 30 to 35 minutes or until brown. Heat mixture of soup and nutmeg to taste in saucepan. Serve with casserole. Yield: 8 to 10 servings.

Claire Hebert, Preceptor Delta
Sulphur, Louisiana

CRÊPES WITH CURRIED CRAB MEAT

1 recipe crêpe batter	⅜ teaspoon cayenne
1½ teaspoons onion	pepper
powder	1½ teaspoons salt
6 tablespoons melted	3 cups light cream
butter	¾ cup Parmesan cheese
6 tablespoons flour	3 pounds crab meat
1 tablespoon dry mustard	1½ cups mixed minced
3 tablespoons curry	celery, green pepper,
powder	onion and pimento

Prepare and bake 30 crêpes according to recipe directions, adding onion powder. Blend butter and flour in saucepan. Add spices. Stir in cream and cheese. Cook until thickened, stirring constantly. Reserve 1½ cups sauce. Stir crab meat and chopped vegetables into remaining sauce. Spoon onto crêpes. Fold each to enclose filling; place seam side down in baking dish. Top with reserved sauce. Bake at 350 degrees for 30 minutes. Yield: 4 to 6 servings.
Note: May substitute chicken or turkey for crab meat.

Nancy Burns, Preceptor Alpha
Scottsdale, Arizona

IMPERIAL CRAB

1 tablespoon margarine	1½ teaspoons
1 tablespoon all-purpose	Worcestershire sauce
flour	½ cup mayonnaise
½ cup milk	½ teaspoon lemon juice
2 tablespoons minced	2 tablespoons margarine
green pepper	1 pound crab meat
1 teaspoon minced onion	Paprika
2 slices bread, cubed	

Melt 1 tablespoon margarine in medium saucepan. Blend in flour. Stir in milk gradually. Cook until thickened, stirring constantly. Add green pepper, onion, bread cubes and Worcestershire sauce; mix well. Cool. Fold in mayonnaise and lemon juice. Melt 2 tablespoons margarine in saucepan. Cook until light brown. Stir in crab meat. Add to cream sauce; mix lightly. Spoon into 1½-quart baking dish. Sprinkle with paprika. Bake at 400 degrees for 25 to 30 minutes or until bubbly. Yield: 4 servings.
Note: May spoon into clean crab shells or individual ramekin to bake.

Norma Wright, Gamma Theta
Baltimore, Maryland

NOODLES ROMANOFF WITH SHRIMP

8 ounces egg noodles	1 8-ounce can tiny
2 cups sour cream	shrimp, drained
¼ cup Parmesan cheese	2 tablespoons melted
1 tablespoon chopped	butter
chives	¼ cup toasted bread
1 clove of garlic, crushed	crumbs
1 teaspoon salt	¼ cup Parmesan cheese
⅛ teaspoon pepper	

Cook noodles according to package directions; drain. Combine sour cream, ¼ cup cheese, chives, garlic, salt and pepper in saucepan; mix well. Stir in shrimp and melted butter. Cook, covered, over low heat for 10 minutes or just until mixture begins to simmer; remove from heat. Rinse noodles in hot water. Place in serving dish. Pour sauce over noodles. Top with bread crumbs and ¼ cup cheese. Yield: 8 servings.

Sheri Schlemper, Omicron Phi
Union, Missouri

BROCCOLI-CHEDDAR STEW WITH SHRIMP

2 11-ounce cans	1 cup frozen hashed
Cheddar cheese soup	brown potatoes
3 cups milk	1 small onion, chopped
1 10-ounce package	1 7-ounce can small
frozen chopped broccoli	shrimp

Blend soup and milk in saucepan. Stir in broccoli, potatoes and onion. Cook over medium heat until bubbly, stirring occasionally. Simmer, covered, for 30 minutes. Stir in shrimp. Yield: 4 to 6 servings.

Wendy T. Kirchner, Zeta Eta
Ann Arbor, Michigan

SHRIMP STEW

¾ cup all-purpose flour	½ teaspoon liquid
⅔ cup oil	crab boil
2 medium onions,	1 tablespoon salt
finely chopped	½ teaspoon pepper
1 cup chopped green	5 cups water
onion tops	2 pounds peeled shrimp
½ cup chopped parsley	

Stir flour into oil in 3-quart saucepan. Cook over low heat until medium brown, stirring constantly. Add onions. Sauté until transparent. Add green onion tops, parsley, crab boil, salt, pepper and water. Simmer for 1 hour. Add shrimp. Cook for 1 hour longer. Serve over rice. Yield: 10 servings.

Norma Risley, Preceptor Alpha Eta
Kokomo, Indiana

SHRIMP VICTORIA

1 pound peeled shrimp	1 tablespoon all-purpose
½ cup chopped onion	flour
¼ cup margarine	1 teaspoon salt
1 6-ounce can	Dash of red pepper
mushrooms, drained	1 cup sour cream
¼ teaspoon garlic powder	

Sauté shrimp and onion in margarine in skillet for 10 minutes. Add mushrooms. Cook for 10 minutes longer. Sprinkle with garlic powder, flour, salt and red pepper. Stir in sour cream. Cook over low heat for 10 minutes; do not boil. Serve over rice. Yield: 4 to 6 servings.

Cynthia A. Welch, Xi Alpha Pi
Albuquerque, New Mexico

TWENTY-FOUR HOUR SHRIMP AND WINE BAKE

1 loaf day-old French bread	1/4 cup dry white wine
1/4 cup melted butter	1 tablespoon Dijon mustard
1 cup shredded sharp Cheddar cheese	2 tablespoons Worcestershire sauce
2 pounds peeled shrimp	Salt to taste
8 eggs	Dash of cayenne pepper
1 3/4 cups milk	1 cup sour cream
6 green onions with tops, chopped	1 cup Parmesan cheese

Tear bread into bite-sized pieces. Place in 9x13-inch baking dish. Drizzle with melted butter. Layer Cheddar cheese and shrimp over bread. Combine eggs, milk, green onions, wine, mustard, Worcestershire sauce, salt and cayenne pepper in bowl. Beat until foamy. Pour over layers. Refrigerate, covered, for 24 hours or longer. Let stand at room temperature for 1 hour. Bake, covered, at 325 degrees for 1 hour or until set. Spread with mixture of sour cream and Parmesan cheese. Bake for 10 minutes longer. Yield: 6 to 8 servings.

Glenda Ing, Preceptor Alpha Epsilon
Nashville, Tennessee

HOT SEAFOOD SALAD

1 cup cooked shrimp	1 cup mayonnaise
1 cup cooked crab meat	1 teaspoon Worcestershire sauce
1 cup chopped celery	
1/2 cup chopped green pepper	1/2 teaspoon salt
1/4 cup grated onion	1/4 teaspoon pepper
3 hard-boiled eggs, chopped	Buttered bread crumbs
	Slivered almonds

Combine shrimp, crab meat, vegetables, eggs, mayonnaise and seasonings in 2-quart casserole; mix well. Sprinkle bread crumbs and almonds on top. Bake at 350 degrees for 35 minutes. Yield: 6 to 8 servings.

Ann J. Cazer, Xi Alpha Iota
Custer, South Dakota

SEAFOOD CASSEROLE

1 cup chopped onion	1 2-ounce jar chopped pimento, drained
1 cup chopped celery	
1/2 cup chopped green pepper	1 6 1/2-ounce can shrimp
2 tablespoons margarine	1 6 1/2-ounce can crab meat
1 10-ounce can cream of celery soup	1 cup cooked rice
8 ounces cream cheese, softened	1/2 cup milk
	3/4 cup cracker crumbs

Sauté onion, celery and green pepper in margarine in saucepan. Add soup, cream cheese and pimento. Heat over low heat until blended, stirring constantly. Add shrimp, crab meat, rice and milk; mix well. Spoon into 2-quart casserole. Bake at 350 degrees for 30 minutes. Sprinkle with cracker crumbs. Bake for 2 minutes longer. Yield: 6 servings.

Dorothy M. Durrett, Preceptor Nu
Anniston, Alabama

SEAFOOD NEWBURG

1/2 cup butter	8 ounces mushrooms, sliced
9 tablespoons all-purpose flour	8 ounces lobster
4 teaspoons paprika	12 ounces cooked shrimp
Salt and pepper to taste	1 8-ounce can crab meat
6 cups milk	1/4 to 1/2 cup Sherry

Melt 1/2 cup butter in saucepan. Blend in flour, paprika, salt and pepper. Stir in milk gradually. Cook until thickened, stirring constantly. Sauté mushrooms in a small amount of butter in skillet. Add sautéed mushrooms, lobster, shrimp and crab meat to cream sauce. Cook until heated through. Stir in Sherry just before serving. Yield: 8 servings.

Catherine Benitez, Xi Alpha
Providence, Rhode Island

SEAFOOD GUMBO

1 cup butter	3 tomatoes, peeled, chopped
2 cups all-purpose flour	1 10-ounce can tomatoes and green chilies
3 large onions, chopped	
3 stalks celery, chopped	5 pounds shrimp, peeled
1 large green pepper, chopped	Salt, black pepper and cayenne pepper to taste
4 cloves of garlic, minced	1 1/2 pounds crab meat
6 quarts water	1 pint oysters
1 10-ounce package frozen okra	7 to 14 cups cooked rice

Melt butter in heavy stockpot over medium heat. Blend in flour. Cook for 15 minutes or until mixture is copper-colored, stirring constantly. Add onions, celery, green pepper and garlic. Cook over low heat until vegetables are tender, stirring frequently; do not scorch. Stir in water gradually, mixing well after each addition. Add okra, fresh tomatoes and tomatoes and chilies. Devein shrimp. Chop enough shrimp to measure 1 cup. Add to gumbo. Bring to a boil; reduce heat. Simmer for 3 hours, stirring occasionally. Season with salt and peppers. Add remaining shrimp. Simmer for 10 minutes. Add crab meat and oysters with liquid. Adjust seasoning. Simmer for 15 minutes longer. Serve over rice in bowls.
Yield: 12 to 14 servings.
Note: May thicken servings with a small amount of gumbo filé if desired.

Fran Sullivan, Xi Beta Zeta
Brookfield, Wisconsin

CHILI EGG PUFF

10 eggs, well beaten	½ teaspoon salt
½ cup flour	1 pound Monterey Jack
1 teaspoon baking powder	cheese, shredded
16 ounces small curd	½ cup melted margarine
cream-style cottage	1 4-ounce can chopped
cheese	green chilies

Combine all ingredients in bowl; mix well. Pour into buttered 9x13-inch baking dish. Bake at 350 degrees for 45 minutes or until top is brown and center is firm. Cut into squares. Yield: 6 servings.

Maureen Laurence, Alpha Epsilon
Wrangell, Arkansas

EGG ENCHILADAS

1 small onion, chopped	5 eggs
½ cup chopped green	2 tablespoons milk
pepper	¼ cup chopped green
1½ tablespoons oil	chilies
1 15-ounce can tomato	Salt and pepper to taste
sauce	2 tablespoons butter
1½ teaspoons chili	4 corn tortillas
powder	Parmesan cheese

Sauté onion and green pepper in oil in small skillet over medium heat. Stir in tomato sauce and chili powder; reduce heat. Simmer for several minutes. Beat eggs in bowl. Add milk, green chilies, salt and pepper; mix well. Melt butter in skillet over low heat. Pour in egg mixture. Cook until set, lifting edges and allowing unset portion to flow into bottom of skillet. Remove from heat. Soften tortillas in hot tomato sauce mixture. Spoon egg mixture onto tortillas; roll to enclose filling. Place in baking dish. Spoon sauce over top. Sprinkle with Parmesan cheese. Bake at 325 to 350 degrees for 15 minutes. Yield: 4 servings.

Michele Sylvester, Chi Phi
Lompoc, California

QUICK QUICHE

Shredded Swiss and	Butter
Cheddar cheese	3 eggs
1 unbaked pie shell	1 cup milk
Chopped onion	Dash of nutmeg
Chopped green pepper	Chopped ham
Sliced mushrooms	

Sprinkle enough cheese into pie shell to cover bottom. Sauté onion, green pepper and mushrooms in a small amount of butter in skillet. Beat eggs, milk and nutmeg in bowl. Stir in sautéed vegetables and ham. Pour into prepared pie shell. Bake at 350 degrees for 35 to 45 minutes or until set and brown. Yield: 6 servings.

Pam Harr, Xi Alpha Pi
Hagerstown, Maryland

EGGS OLÉ

9 eggs	1 4-ounce can chopped
½ cup milk	green chilies
⅛ teaspoon salt	1 teaspoon onion powder
2 cups shredded	¼ teaspoon garlic powder
Cheddar cheese	¼ teaspoon cumin
1 16-ounce can	½ teaspoon chili powder
tomatoes, chopped	

Beat eggs, milk and salt in bowl. Pour into greased 9x13-inch baking dish. Bake at 325 degrees for 20 minutes or until set. Sprinkle with cheese. Bake for 5 minutes longer. Combine tomatoes and remaining ingredients in saucepan. Simmer for 30 minutes or until thickened. Serve warm salsa over eggs. Garnish with avocado slices and sliced black olives. Yield: 6 servings.

SAUCY BROCCOLI PUFF

1 10-ounce package	3 tablespoons melted
frozen chopped	margarine
broccoli, thawed	1 teaspoon dry mustard
¼ teaspoon salt	2 cups milk
Pepper to taste	2 cups shredded
6 eggs, separated	Cheddar cheese
½ teaspoon cream of tartar	1 tablespoon
3 tablespoons flour	Worcestershire sauce

Combine broccoli, salt, pepper and egg yolks in blender container. Process until well-mixed. Beat egg whites with cream of tartar in mixer bowl until stiff peaks form. Fold in broccoli mixture. Pour into ungreased 1-quart baking dish. Bake at 350 degrees for 20 minutes or until puffed and set. Blend flour, margarine and dry mustard in saucepan. Cook over medium heat until bubbly, stirring constantly. Stir in milk gradually. Cook over medium heat until thickened, stirring constantly. Add cheese and Worcestershire sauce; stir until cheese melts. Spoon broccoli puff onto plates. Top with hot cheese sauce. Yield: 4 to 6 servings.

CONFETTI SPAGHETTI

1 16-ounce package	⅛ teaspoon nutmeg
frozen mixed vegetables	1 cup milk
½ cup chopped onion	⅓ cup minced red and
½ cup sliced mushrooms	green pepper
3 tablespoons margarine	16 ounces spaghetti
2 to 3 tablespoons flour	¼ cup Parmesan cheese
¼ teaspoon salt	

Cook mixed vegetables using package directions; drain, reserving liquid. Sauté onion and mushrooms in margarine in skillet. Mix in flour, salt and nutmeg. Stir in milk and reserved liquid gradually. Cook until thickened, stirring constantly. Stir in mixed vegetables, peppers, onion and mushrooms. Heat to serving temperature. Cook spaghetti according to package directions just until tender; drain. Place in heated serving bowl. Add sauce; toss until coated. Sprinkle Parmesan cheese over top. Serve with additional cheese. Yield: 6 servings.

Holiday Vegetables and Side Dishes

ASPARAGUS PARMESAN

2 pounds fresh asparagus	2 teaspoons seasoned salt
½ cup water	¼ teaspoon dry mustard
1½ teaspoons seasoned salt	¼ teaspoon pepper
1 cup coarse cracker crumbs	⅛ teaspoon onion powder
3 tablespoons butter	1½ cups milk
3 tablespoons all-purpose flour	1 4-ounce can chopped mushrooms
	Parmesan cheese

Cook asparagus in water with 1½ teaspoons seasoned salt in saucepan for 10 minutes or until tender; drain. Sprinkle crumbs over bottom of 1½-quart baking dish. Arrange asparagus in prepared dish. Melt butter in saucepan over medium heat. Stir in flour, 2 teaspoons seasoned salt, dry mustard, pepper and onion powder. Cook until bubbly, stirring constantly. Remove from heat. Stir in milk. Cook over low heat until thickened, stirring constantly. Stir in mushrooms. Pour over asparagus; sprinkle with Parmesan cheese. Bake at 350 degrees for 30 minutes. Yield: 6 to 8 servings.

Deb Walker, Xi Xi
Caldwell, Idaho

PECAN-ASPARAGUS CASSEROLE

2 16-ounce cans asparagus, drained	¼ teaspoon pepper
5 hard-boiled eggs, sliced	1 cup shredded Monterey Jack cheese
1 can cream of mushroom soup	1 cup butter cracker crumbs
½ cup asparagus liquid	¼ cup melted margarine
⅛ teaspoon salt	½ cup chopped pecans

Layer asparagus and eggs in buttered 9x13-inch baking dish. Combine soup, asparagus liquid, salt and pepper in bowl; mix well. Pour over eggs. Sprinkle with cheese and mixture of crumbs and butter. Top with pecans. Bake at 325 degrees for 45 minutes. Yield: 6 servings.

Diann Walters, Delta Kappa
Ellisville, Missouri

DILLED GREEN BEANS

1 pound fresh green beans	½ teaspoon salt
6 slices bacon	¼ teaspoon pepper
1 small onion, chopped	2 tomatoes, quartered
1 teaspoon dillweed	

Cook green beans, bacon and onion in a small amount of water in saucepan until beans are tender. Add dillweed, salt and pepper. Add tomatoes. Heat until tomatoes are hot but not cooked. Yield: 6 to 8 servings.

Jean Kuhn, Xi Iota
Wyoming, Michigan

BAKED BEANS

8 15-ounce cans Great	1 teaspoon dry mustard
Northern beans	1 stick margarine, sliced
1 pound bacon	½ cup molasses
1 small onion, cut into	1 cup packed brown sugar
quarters	

Drain 4 cans of beans. Combine drained and undrained beans, bacon, onion, mustard, margarine, molasses and brown sugar in large roaster; mix well. Bake, covered, at 350 degrees for 1 hour. Reduce heat to 250 degrees. Bake, covered, for 4 hours. Bake, uncovered, for 1 hour longer. Yield: 20 servings.

Kim Nelson, Xi Rho
Glendive, Montana

FRIED RED BEETS

2 cups sliced cooked beets	¼ cup all-purpose flour
¼ cup butter	2½ cups milk

Brown beets in butter in heavy skillet. Mix in flour. Stir in milk gradually. Cook until thickened, stirring constantly. Serve over toast. Yield: 6 servings.

Jean Spaide, Laureate Upsilon
Allentown, Pennsylvania

PICKLED BEETS AND EGGS

2 16-ounce cans sliced	2 tablespoons pickling
beets	spices
2 cups vinegar	1½ teaspoons salt
¾ cup sugar	12 hard-boiled eggs

Drain beets, reserving 1½ cups beet liquid. Combine reserved liquid, vinegar, sugar, pickling spices and salt in saucepan. Bring to a boil; reduce heat. Simmer, covered, for 5 to 10 minutes. Layer beets and eggs in 1-gallon jar. Add hot liquid. Chill, covered, for 24 hours to 1 week. Yield: 12 servings.

Barbara Ball, Xi Alpha Kappa
Grand Junction, Colorado

Beet consommé is a beautiful first course holiday soup. Combine 1 cup each beet juice, consommé and minced canned beets in saucepan. Add 1 tablespoon lemon juice. Heat to serving temperature. Garnish each serving with a lemon slice topped with sour cream and caviar or minced tarragon.

BAKED BROCCOLI AND ONIONS DELUXE

2 10-ounce packages	Dash of pepper
frozen chopped	1 cup milk
broccoli	3 ounces cream cheese,
2 cups frozen small	chopped
onions	½ cup shredded sharp
2 tablespoons melted	American cheese
butter	2 tablespoons melted
2 tablespoons all-purpose	butter
flour	1 cup soft bread crumbs
¼ teaspoon salt	

Cook broccoli and onions in separate saucepans using package directions; drain. Blend 2 tablespoons butter and flour in saucepan. Add salt and pepper. Stir in milk. Cook until thickened, stirring constantly. Reduce heat. Add cream cheese. Cook until blended, stirring constantly. Place broccoli and onions in 1½-quart casserole. Pour sauce over top. Sprinkle with shredded cheese and mixture of 2 tablespoons butter and bread crumbs. Bake at 350 degrees for 40 to 45 minutes or until heated through. Yield: 6 servings.

Mrs. Robert L. Scofield, Laureate Eta
Clarksville, Tennessee

BROCCOLI SOUP

2 tablespoons chopped	1 10-ounce package
onion	frozen chopped broccoli
2 tablespoons butter	1 16-ounce can chicken
2 tablespoons all-purpose	broth
flour	1 bay leaf
2 cups milk	Salt and pepper to taste
4 ounces American	
cheese, shredded	

Sauté onion in butter in large skillet until tender. Add flour. Stir in milk. Cook until thickened, stirring constantly. Add cheese; stir until melted. Cook broccoli in broth with bay leaf, salt and pepper in saucepan until tender. Discard bay leaf. Add broccoli and broth to cheese mixture. Heat to serving temperature, stirring frequently. Ladle into serving bowls. Garnish with additional cheese or crumbled crisp-fried bacon. Yield: 4 to 5 servings.

Brenda Pringle, Xi Alpha Nu
Florence, South Carolina

BROCCOLI WREATH

14 cups broccoli	½ teaspoon pepper
flowerets	Butter
1 teaspoon salt	1 cup cherry tomatoes

Steam broccoli in 1 inch boiling water for 5 minutes; drain. Cover with cold water; drain. Season with salt and pepper. Arrange in 12-cup ring mold. Dot with butter. Cover with foil. Chill in refrigerator. Let stand until broccoli comes to room temperature. Bake at 325 degrees for 25 minutes. Invert onto serving plate. Fill center with cherry tomatoes. Yield: 20 servings.

Jackie Vogler, Xi Sigma Pi
Hilltop Lakes, Texas

CHEESY BAKED BRUSSELS SPROUTS

2 10-ounce packages frozen Brussels sprouts	½ cup soft bread crumbs
2 eggs, beaten	2 tablespoons chopped onion
1 10-ounce can cream of mushroom soup	Pepper to taste
½ cup shredded sharp cheese	1 tablespoon butter, melted
	1 cup soft bread crumbs

Cook Brussels sprouts using package directions; drain and cool. Cut into quarters. Combine eggs, soup, cheese, ½ cup bread crumbs, onion and pepper in bowl; mix well. Stir in Brussels sprouts. Pour into 1½-quart casserole. Sprinkle with mixture of butter and 1 cup bread crumbs. Bake at 350 degrees for 50 to 55 minutes. Good served with turkey or ham. Yield: 6 to 8 servings.

Kimberly L. Birch, Eta Nu
Charles City, Iowa

CANDIED CARROTS

2 16-ounce packages carrots	¼ cup butter
2 tablespoons lemon juice	½ cup packed brown sugar

Cut carrots into halves crosswise. Bring 1 inch water to a boil in 3-quart saucepan over medium heat; add carrots. Bring to a boil; reduce heat. Simmer for 20 minutes or until tender; drain. Stir in remaining ingredients. Cook over medium heat for 5 minutes or until brown sugar is dissolved and carrots are glazed, stirring gently. Spoon into serving dish. Garnish with lemon rind.
Yield: 10 to 12 servings.

Linda Gizienski, Xi Alpha
Providence, Rhode Island

CARROT AND CAULIFLOWER BAKE

1 pound carrots	1 teaspoon salt
Flowerets of 1 head cauliflower	¼ teaspoon nutmeg
¼ cup butter	Parmesan cheese

Cut carrots into ¼x2-inch pieces. Layer carrots and cauliflower in 7x11-inch baking dish. Dot with butter; sprinkle with salt and nutmeg. Bake at 375 degrees for 50 to 55 minutes or until vegetables are tender. Sprinkle with Parmesan cheese. Garnish with parsley.
Yield: 10 servings.

Denise Biastre, Xi Alpha
Providence, Rhode Island

COPPER PENNIES

2 pounds carrots, sliced	1 cup vinegar
1 medium onion, sliced into rings	1 cup sugar
1 green pepper, sliced into rings	1 teaspoon Worcestershire sauce
1 10-ounce can tomato soup	1 teaspoon prepared mustard
½ cup oil	Salt and pepper to taste

Cook carrots in a small amount of water in saucepan until tender; drain. Layer carrots, onion and green pepper in serving dish. Combine remaining ingredients in bowl; mix well. Pour over vegetables. Chill, covered, overnight. Yield: 6 servings.

Nancy Proveaux, Chi Pi
Bay City, Texas

ZESTY CARROTS

6 to 8 carrots	¼ teaspoon salt
2 tablespoons grated onion	⅛ teaspoon pepper
½ cup horseradish	¼ cup cracker crumbs
¼ cup water	1 tablespoon melted butter
½ cup mayonnaise	Dash of paprika

Scrape carrots; cut into halves lengthwise. Cook in water to cover in saucepan until tender-crisp; drain. Place in shallow baking dish. Combine onion, horseradish, ¼ cup water, mayonnaise, salt and pepper in bowl; mix well. Pour over carrots. Mix cracker crumbs, butter and paprika in bowl. Sprinkle over carrots. Bake at 375 degrees for 15 to 20 minutes. Yield: 6 servings.

Mary Fox, Epsilon Kappa
Nashville, Tennessee

MICROWAVE CREAMY CAULIFLOWER

1 head cauliflower	1 teaspoon celery powder
1 large onion, chopped	1 10-ounce can cream of mushroom soup
¼ cup butter	1 cup sour cream
1 teaspoon paprika	
1 teaspoon garlic powder	

Cook cauliflower until tender. Cut into flowerets; place in 3-quart glass casserole. Sauté onion in butter in large saucepan. Add paprika, garlic powder, celery powder, soup and sour cream; mix well. Add water if necessary to make of desired consistency. Cook until bubbly, stirring frequently. Pour over cauliflower. Microwave on Medium for 15 minutes. Garnish with chopped chives. Serve with meat loaf, baked chicken or ham. Yield: 6 to 8 servings.

Mary W. Breerwood, Gamma Lambda
Houma, Louisiana

CELERY CASSEROLE

2 cups chopped celery	½ cup melted margarine
1 7-ounce can water chestnuts	1 3-ounce package slivered almonds
1 10-ounce can mushroom soup	32 butter crackers, crushed

Cook celery in boiling water in saucepan for 7 minutes; drain. Place in casserole. Add water chestnuts and soup. Mix margarine, almonds and cracker crumbs in bowl. Sprinkle over celery mixture. Bake at 350 degrees for 15 to 20 minutes. Yield: 6 servings.

Jane Koehn, Laureate Alpha Zeta
Jacksonville, Florida

CORN CASSEROLE

1 16-ounce can cream-style corn	1 8-ounce package corn bread mix
1 16-ounce can whole kernel corn	2 eggs, beaten
½ cup melted butter	¼ cup shredded cheese

Combine all ingredients except cheese in bowl; mix well. Pour into 2½-quart casserole. Bake at 350 degrees for 50 minutes. Sprinkle with cheese. Bake for 10 minutes longer. Yield: 12 servings.

Judith J. Swope, Alpha Tau
Kansas City, Missouri

CORN CHOWDER

8 large potatoes, peeled, quartered	1 cup heavy cream, whipped
1 large yellow onion, shredded	4 slices crisp-fried bacon, crumbled
Chicken broth	1 cup sour cream
1 stick butter	1 10-ounce package frozen corn
1 quart milk	

Combine potatoes and onion in stockpot. Add enough chicken broth to cover. Simmer for 30 minutes. Add butter. Beat with electric mixer until creamy. Mix in milk and cream. Simmer for 30 minutes. Add remaining ingredients. Bring just to the simmering point, stirring frequently; do not boil. Yield: 8 to 12 servings.

Sandra Sharp, Gamma Epsilon
Clarksville, Arkansas

CORN FRITTERS

1 cup all-purpose flour	1 tablespoon melted butter
½ teaspoon salt	1½ cups fresh or frozen corn
1 teaspoon baking powder	
1 teaspoon sugar	Oil for deep frying
2 eggs, beaten	
¼ cup milk	

Sift flour, salt, baking powder and sugar into bowl. Add eggs and milk; mix well. Stir in butter and corn. Drop by spoonfuls into 365-degree oil. Deep-fry until golden brown. Drain on paper towel. Serve hot with butter and honey or syrup. Yield: 1½ dozen.

Dolores R. Seward, Xi Epsilon Alpha
Muskogee, Oklahoma

UNUSUAL CORN CASSEROLE

1 egg, beaten	1 8-ounce can corn
1 cup sour cream	1 8-ounce can cream-style corn
½ cup melted butter	
¼ teaspoon butter flavoring	1 8-ounce package corn muffin mix

Combine all the ingredients in order given in bowl; mix well. Pour into greased 9x9-inch baking dish. Bake at 350 degrees for 40 to 55 minutes or until toothpick inserted in center comes out clean. Serve hot. Yield: 6 servings.

Mary Ann Eisenmann, Preceptor Alpha Omega
Mason City, Iowa

MUSHROOMS PROVENÇALE

Chopped onion	¼ cup fresh bread crumbs
2 cloves of garlic, crushed	¼ cup chopped parsley
¼ cup olive oil	Salt and pepper to taste
1 pound fresh mushrooms	

Sauté onion and garlic in olive oil in skillet until tender. Add mushrooms. Sauté just until tender. Add remaining ingredients. Toss lightly. Spoon into serving dish. Yield: 4 to 6 servings.

Claire Hebert, Preceptor Delta
Sulphur, Louisiana

CREAMED ONIONS

15 medium onions	1 cup shredded mild Cheddar cheese
⅓ cup oil	
3 tablespoons flour	½ cup chopped peanuts
1¼ cups milk	

Peel and slice onions. Cook in a large amount of boiling salted water in saucepan until tender; drain. Blend oil and flour in saucepan. Stir in milk. Cook over medium heat until thickened, stirring constantly. Add cheese. Cook until cheese melts, stirring constantly. Add onions. Cook until heated through. Spoon into serving bowl. Sprinkle with peanuts. Yield: 6 servings.

Bettie Plummer, Laureate Pi
Independence, Missouri

FRENCH ONION SOUP

2½ cups thinly sliced onions	1 teaspoon Worcestershire sauce
3 tablespoons butter or margarine	Salt and pepper to taste
3 cans condensed beef broth	2 French rolls, sliced, toasted
	Grated Parmesan cheese

Sauté onions in butter in saucepan until light brown. Add broth and Worcestershire sauce. Bring to a boil. Season with salt and pepper. Pour soup into bowls. Place 1 toast slice in each bowl. Sprinkle with cheese. Yield: 4 to 6 servings.

Bettie Plummer, Laureate Pi
Independence, Missouri

ONION PIE

2½ pounds onions, thinly sliced	3 eggs, beaten
	¼ cup Sherry
3 tablespoons butter, softened	Salt, pepper, nutmeg, thyme and cloves to taste
1 cup sour cream	1 unbaked 9-inch pie shell

Sauté onions in butter in skillet until transparent. Cool. Combine butter, sour cream, eggs, Sherry and seasonings in bowl; mix well. Add onions; mix well. Pour into pie shell. Bake at 350 degrees for 45 to 60 minutes or until filling is firm and crust is light brown. Serve immediately. Yield: 6 to 8 servings.

Diana Bal, Xi Delta Xi
Rochester, New York

VIDALIA ONION CASSEROLE

4 cups sliced Vidalia
  onions
½ cup butter
1 10-ounce can cream
  of mushroom soup

½ cup sour cream
1¼ cups corn bread
  stuffing mix
Buttered bread crumbs

Sauté onions in butter in skillet. Stir in soup, sour cream and stuffing mix. Spoon into baking dish. Top with buttered bread crumbs. Bake at 300 degrees until brown. Yield: 4 servings.

Woody Markert, Member at Large
Roswell, Georgia

CHEESY NEW POTATOES

12 medium new potatoes
Salt and pepper to taste
2 cups shredded Old
  English cheese

16 slices crisp-fried
  bacon, crumbled
½ cup melted butter
¼ cup chopped parsley

Chop potatoes; do not peel. Cook in water to cover in saucepan until tender; drain. Season with salt and pepper. Layer potatoes, cheese, bacon and butter ½ at a time in casserole. Bake at 350 degrees for 25 minutes. Garnish with parsley. Yield: 6 to 8 servings.

Jackie Vogler, Xi Sigma Pi
Hilltop Lakes, Texas

CREAMED POTATOES PLUS

5 cups chopped cooked
  potatoes
1 teaspoon salt
1 10-ounce package
  frozen peas with pearl
  onions, thawed
3 slices American cheese,
  cut into ¼-inch strips

1 10-ounce can cream of
  celery soup
3 ounces cream cheese,
  softened
⅓ cup milk
¼ teaspoon savory

Sprinkle potatoes with salt. Combine with peas and half the cheese in buttered 2-quart casserole. Heat soup, cream cheese, milk and savory in saucepan over low heat until well blended, stirring constantly. Pour over vegetables; mix gently. Top with remaining cheese. Chill, covered, overnight. Bake, uncovered, at 350 degrees for 45 minutes. Serve with baked ham dinner. Yield: 6 servings.

June C. Hackett, Laureate Omicron
Sunbury, Pennsylvania

DOUBLE POTATO CASSEROLE

7 to 10 potatoes
1½ cups shredded
  Cheddar cheese
1 10-ounce can cream
  of mushroom soup
2 cups sour cream

¼ cup butter, softened
½ cup chopped green
  onions
1 teaspoon garlic salt
½ teaspoon pepper
1 cup crushed potato chips

Cook potatoes in boiling water until tender. Let stand overnight. Peel and shred potatoes into large bowl. Add remaining ingredients except potato chips; mix well. Spoon into 9x13-inch baking dish. Bake at 350 degrees for 40 minutes. Sprinkle potato chips over top. Bake for 5 minutes longer. Yield: 12 servings.

Sandy Tingley, Zeta Nu
Boardman, Oregon

EASY CHEESY POTATOES

1 2-pound package
  frozen hashed brown
  potatoes
1 cup chopped onion
1 10-ounce can cream
  of mushroom soup

16 ounces sour cream
1 stick butter, melted
8 ounces sharp cheese,
  shredded
Bacon bits

Combine potatoes, onion, soup, sour cream, butter and cheese in bowl; mix well. Spoon into 9x13-inch baking dish. Sprinkle with additional cheese if desired. Top with bacon bits. Bake at 350 degrees for 1 hour. Yield: 8 servings.

Barbara Ball, Xi Alpha Kappa
Grand Junction, Colorado

GOLDEN POTATO CASSEROLE

6 medium potatoes,
  cooked
2 cups sour cream
10 ounces sharp Cheddar
  cheese, shredded
1 bunch green onions,
  chopped

3 tablespoons milk
Salt and pepper to taste
2 tablespoons melted
  butter
⅓ cup seasoned bread
  crumbs

Peel and coarsely chop potatoes. Combine with sour cream, cheese, onions, milk, salt and pepper in bowl; mix well. Spoon into 9x13-inch glass baking dish. Mix butter and bread crumbs in small bowl; sprinkle over potato mixture. Bake at 300 degrees for 50 to 60 minutes. Yield: 8 servings.

Beth Ann Steuerwald, Kappa Omicron
Saylorsburg, Pennsylvania

GRATIN DAUPHINOIS

5 to 6 cups sliced
  peeled potatoes
2 cups milk
1½ cups whipping cream
1 clove of garlic, puréed

¾ teaspoon salt
½ teaspoon freshly
  ground white pepper
1 tablespoon butter
½ cup grated Swiss cheese

Place potatoes in saucepan. Add milk, cream, garlic, salt and pepper. Bring to a boil over medium heat, stirring gently. Spread butter in shallow baking dish. Pour in potato mixture. Sprinkle with cheese. Bake at 400 degrees for 1 hour. Let stand for 15 minutes before serving. Yield: 6 to 8 servings.

Jackie Vogler, Xi Sigma Pi
Hilltop Lakes, Texas

HASHED BROWN BAKE

2 pounds hashed brown potatoes, thawed	2 cups shredded Cheddar cheese
½ cup margarine, softened	1 teaspoon salt
1 can cream of chicken soup	¼ teaspoon pepper
2 cups sour cream	2 cups cornflake crumbs
	¼ cup melted margarine

Combine first 7 ingredients in bowl; mix well. Pour into 9x13-inch baking dish. Toss crumbs with melted margarine. Sprinkle over potato mixture. Bake at 400 degrees for 40 minutes. Yield: 10 servings.

Roberta DeNegre, Preceptor Gamma Upsilon
Blue Springs, Missouri

OVER-STUFFED BAKED POTATOES

2 medium baking potatoes	1 tablespoon diet margarine
3 small yellow squash, coarsely chopped	¼ cup skim milk
4 ounces small mushrooms, sliced	½ cup shredded mozzarella cheese
1 medium onion, chopped	2 tablespoons chopped parsley

Prick potatoes. Bake at 425 degrees for 50 minutes or until tender. Sauté squash, mushrooms and onion in margarine in saucepan for 5 minutes or until tender. Split potatoes; scoop out pulp, reserving shells. Whip potato pulp with milk in bowl. Stir in cheese. Spoon into potato shells; place on serving plate. Spoon sautéed vegetables over top. Garnish with chopped parsley.
Yield: 2 servings.

Andrea Ryan, Zeta Alpha
Williamsport, Pennsylvania

PIZZA POTATOES

1 16-ounce can tomatoes	1 4-ounce package sliced pepperoni
1½ cups water	
¼ teaspoon oregano	1 4-ounce package shredded mozzarella cheese
1 package scalloped potatoes	

Bring tomatoes, water and oregano to a boil in saucepan. Add potatoes and seasoning packet; mix well. Spoon into baking dish. Top with pepperoni and mozzarella cheese. Bake, uncovered, at 400 degrees for 30 to 35 minutes or until bubbly. Yield: 6 servings.

Jerry Wright, Xi Alpha
Providence, Rhode Island

POTATO CASSEROLE

4 or 5 red potatoes	1 teaspoon salt
½ cup melted butter	Pepper to taste
½ package dry onion soup mix	½ cup water

Slice unpeeled potatoes. Combine butter, onion soup mix, salt and pepper in bowl; mix well. Pour water into 2-quart casserole. Layer ⅕ of the potatoes and 1 tablespoon onion mixture alternately in prepared casserole. Bake, covered, at 350 degrees for 45 to 60 minutes. Yield: 4 to 6 servings.

Jan Perigard, Xi Chi
Waterbury, Connecticut

POTATO CASSEROLE WITH CORNFLAKE TOPPING

½ cup melted margarine	1 10-ounce can cream of chicken soup
2 cups sour cream	
½ cup chopped green onions	1 teaspoon salt
	½ teaspoon pepper
2 pounds frozen hashed brown potatoes, thawed	2 cups crushed cornflakes
	½ cup melted margarine
2 cups shredded cheese	

Combine ½ cup margarine, sour cream, green onions, potatoes, cheese, soup, salt and pepper in large bowl; mix well. Pour into 9x13-inch casserole. Mix cornflakes and ½ cup margarine in bowl until crumbly. Sprinkle over potato mixture. Bake at 350 degrees for 45 minutes. Yield: 16 to 20 servings.

Jennifer Rivenbark, Epsilon Chi
Wallace, North Carolina

SCALLOPED POTATOES WITH HAM

6 to 8 potatoes, thinly sliced	1 10-ounce can Cheddar cheese soup
1 to 2 tablespoons minced onion	8 ounces chopped ham

Combine all ingredients in Crock•Pot; mix well. Cook on Low for 7 to 8 hours. Yield: 8 servings.

Joan White, Xi Alpha
Providence, Rhode Island

SKILLET POTATO CAKE

1 pound potatoes, cooked	¼ cup grated Parmesan cheese
2 tablespoons chopped chives	
	½ teaspoon salt
½ teaspoon salt	½ teaspoon seasoned salt
2 tablespoons butter	⅛ teaspoon pepper
3 eggs, beaten	2 tablespoons butter
¼ cup light cream	

Cool potatoes completely. Peel and shred into bowl. Add chives and ½ teaspoon salt; mix well. Heat 2 tablespoons butter in 10-inch nonstick skillet over medium heat. Add potatoes; shape into 8-inch patty. Reduce heat to low. Pour mixture of eggs, cream, cheese and seasonings over potato patty. Cook for 15 minutes or until brown. Invert patty onto plate. Heat remaining 2 tablespoons butter in skillet. Place patty, brown side up, in skillet. Cook for 10 minutes or until brown. Remove to serving platter; cut into wedges. Garnish with parsley and serve with small sausages. Leftovers are easily reheated.
Yield: 4 to 6 servings.
Note: In German this is called *Kartoffelpfannkuchen* which literally means "Potato Pancake."

Susan Foster, Xi Alpha
Grand Rapids, Michigan

TEXAS CREAM OF POTATO SOUP

3 cups chopped peeled potatoes	Chopped chives
1 cup sliced carrots	¼ teaspoon parsley flakes
8 ounces bacon	¼ teaspoon celery salt
1 cup chopped onion	¼ teaspoon garlic salt
1 cup chopped celery	1½ teaspoons salt
2 cups light cream	¼ teaspoon pepper
1 cup shredded American cheese	2 tablespoons cornstarch
	2 cups milk

Cook potatoes and carrots in boiling water to cover in saucepan; drain. Cook bacon in skillet until crisp; drain and crumble, reserving drippings. Sauté onion and celery in bacon drippings. Combine potatoes, carrots, bacon, sautéed vegetables and next 8 ingredients in saucepan. Mix cornstarch with a small amount of the milk in bowl. Stir cornstarch and remaining milk into soup; mix well. Simmer for 30 minutes. Yield: 6 servings.

Carol Sassin, Xi Psi Beta
Beeville, Texas

GRANNY'S SAUERKRAUT AND TOMATOES

1 15-ounce can sauerkraut	1 15-ounce can tomatoes
	1¼ cups sugar

Drain sauerkraut; rinse in colander. Place in saucepan. Add chopped tomatoes and sugar. Simmer, covered, over low heat for 1½ hours, stirring occasionally. Remove to serving dish with slotted spoon. Yield: 6 servings.

Norma Wright, Gamma Theta
Baltimore, Maryland

SPINACH-BROCCOLI CASSEROLE

2 10-ounce packages frozen chopped spinach	1 10-ounce can cream of celery soup
2 10-ounce packages frozen chopped broccoli	Salt and pepper to taste
½ cup chopped onion	Bread crumbs

Cook broccoli and spinach according to package directions, adding onion; drain well. Combine with soup and salt and pepper in bowl; mix well. Spoon into 1½-quart casserole. Top with bread crumbs. Bake at 350 degrees for 20 minutes. Yield: 8 servings.

Ila Jeane Lepp, Xi Mu Chi
Orland, California

BAKED BUTTERNUT SQUASH

3 medium butternut squash	Butter
Salt and pepper to taste	Parmesan cheese
	Paprika

Cut each squash in half; scoop out and discard seed. Parboil squash in boiling salted water in saucepan for 15 minutes; drain. Place in baking dish. Sprinkle with salt and pepper; dot generously with butter. Sprinkle with cheese and paprika. Bake at 375 degrees for 20 minutes. Yield: 6 servings.

Bettie Plummer, Laureate Pi
Independence, Missouri

PARTY SQUASH CASSEROLE

3 pounds yellow squash, sliced	1 cup sour cream
1 pound onions, chopped	½ 10-ounce can cream of chicken soup
1 cup water	¼ cup butter, softened
12 ounces sharp cheese, shredded	½ cup cracker crumbs

Cook squash and onions in water in saucepan until tender; drain well. Add cheese. Cook until melted. Add sour cream, soup and butter; mix well. Pour into greased 2-quart casserole. Sprinkle with cracker crumbs. Bake at 350 degrees for 20 to 30 minutes or until bubbly. Serve hot with roast, ham or meat loaf. Yield: 6 to 8 servings.

Wanda McMahon, Preceptor Epsilon Alpha
Winter Haven, Florida

SPINACH CASSEROLE

¼ cup melted margarine	⅛ teaspoon pepper
2 tablespoons all-purpose flour	2 10-ounce packages frozen chopped spinach, cooked
¾ cup milk	¾ cup cracker crumbs
1 tablespoon minced onion	½ cup shredded Cheddar cheese
2 hard-boiled eggs, chopped	¼ cup melted margarine
½ teaspoon salt	

Blend ¼ cup margarine and flour in saucepan. Stir in milk and minced onion. Cook over low heat until thickened, stirring constantly. Add eggs, salt, pepper and well-drained spinach; mix well. Combine cracker crumbs, cheese and ¼ cup melted margarine in bowl; mix until crumbly. Mix half the crumb mixture into spinach mixture. Pour into greased baking dish; top with remaining crumb mixture. Bake at 350 degrees for 25 minutes. Yield: 6 to 8 servings.

Nancy Burkhardt, Xi Gamma Gamma
Richmond, Indiana

GUATEMALA SQUASH

3 ounces cream cheese, softened	½ teaspoon cinnamon
2 cups cooked squash	½ teaspoon salt
⅔ cup packed brown sugar	1 tablespoon bread crumbs
1 egg, beaten	⅓ cup raisins
1 tablespoon butter, softened	¼ cup slivered almonds
	6 or 7 almond halves

Beat cream cheese in bowl until smooth. Add squash, brown sugar, egg, butter, cinnamon, salt and bread crumbs; mix well. Stir in raisins and almonds. Spoon into greased 1-quart baking dish. Top with almond halves. Bake at 350 degrees for 40 minutes. Serve with poultry or baked ham. Yield: 6 servings.

June C. Hackett, Laureate Omicron
Sunbury, Pennsylvania

SQUASH CASSEROLE

2 pounds yellow squash, sliced
1 medium onion, chopped
1 green pepper, chopped
1 carrot, grated
½ cup melted butter
1 10-ounce can cream of chicken soup
1 cup sour cream
1 package herb-seasoned stuffing mix

Simmer squash, onion and green pepper in a small amount of water until tender; drain. Add carrot, butter, soup, sour cream and half the stuffing mix; mix well. Pour into greased 2-quart baking dish. Top with remaining stuffing mix. Bake at 350 degrees for 35 minutes. Yield: 8 servings.

Carole Chorlton, Preceptor Alpha Xi
Jacksonville, Florida

PEAR AND SWEET POTATO CASSEROLE

1 16-ounce can pear halves
3 cups mashed cooked sweet potatoes
3 tablespoons butter, softened
3 tablespoons brown sugar
¼ teaspoon salt
¼ teaspoon nutmeg
2 tablespoons honey
1 tablespoon butter, softened
1 teaspoon grated orange rind
1 16-ounce can whole cranberry sauce

Drain pears, reserving juice. Combine 2 tablespoons juice, sweet potatoes, 3 tablespoons butter, brown sugar, salt and nutmeg in mixer bowl; beat until fluffy. Spoon into greased shallow 1½-quart casserole. Arrange pear halves, cut side up, on top. Bring honey, 1 tablespoon butter and orange rind to a boil in small saucepan, stirring occasionally. Drizzle half the mixture over pears. Bake, uncovered, at 350 degrees for 30 minutes. Drizzle remaining honey mixture over pears. Bake for 15 minutes longer. Fill pear halves with cranberry sauce before serving. Yield: 6 servings.

Mrs. Robert L. Scofield, Laureate Eta
Clarksville, Tennessee

SWEET POTATO CASSEROLE

3 cups mashed cooked sweet potatoes
½ cup sugar
2 eggs, beaten
¼ cup melted margarine
½ cup milk
1½ teaspoons vanilla extract
½ teaspoon salt
½ cup packed brown sugar
⅓ cup all-purpose flour
1 cup chopped pecans
2⅔ tablespoons melted margarine

Combine first 7 ingredients in bowl; mix well. Spoon into 1½-quart baking dish. Combine brown sugar, flour, pecans and 2⅔ tablespoons melted margarine in small bowl; mix well. Spread over sweet potato mixture. Bake at 350 degrees for 35 minutes. Yield: 8 servings.

Lucy S. Sox, Xi Alpha Gamma
Beaufort, South Carolina

SWEET POTATO FLUFF

3 cups mashed cooked sweet potatoes
½ cup sugar
2 eggs, beaten
6 tablespoons melted butter
1½ teaspoons vanilla extract
½ cup all-purpose flour
1 cup chopped pecans
½ cup packed brown sugar
3 tablespoons butter, softened

Combine sweet potatoes, sugar, eggs, melted butter and vanilla in bowl; mix well. Spoon into 8-inch baking dish. Combine remaining ingredients in small bowl; mix well. Sprinkle over sweet potato mixture. Bake at 350 degrees for 35 minutes. Yield: 10 to 16 servings.

Carol Jarman, Beta Sigma
New Bern, North Carolina

SWEET POTATO SOUFFLÉ

3 cups mashed cooked sweet potatoes
2 eggs, beaten
½ cup milk
1 cup sugar
1 teaspoon lemon extract
2 tablespoons butter, softened
1 cup packed brown sugar
½ cup melted butter
½ cup all-purpose flour
1 cup chopped pecans

Combine sweet potatoes, eggs, milk, sugar, flavoring and softened butter in bowl; mix well. Pour into greased baking dish. Mix brown sugar and remaining ingredients in bowl until crumbly. Sprinkle over sweet potato mixture. Bake at 350 degrees for 30 minutes. Yield: 8 to 10 servings.

Dottie Fortson, Gamma Theta
Baltimore, Maryland

CANDIED YAMS

2 29-ounce cans yams
1 cup packed brown sugar
1 teaspoon cinnamon
¼ cup butter
3 tablespoons cornstarch
Pineapple slices
1 cup miniature marshmallows

Drain yams, reserving juice. Combine reserved juice, brown sugar, cinnamon and butter in saucepan. Cook until brown sugar dissolves, stirring constantly. Blend cornstarch with enough water to make paste. Stir into brown sugar mixture. Cook until thickened, stirring constantly. Line casserole with pineapple slices; add yams. Pour sauce over yams. Bake at 325 degrees for 1 hour. Top with marshmallows. Broil until light brown. Yield: 8 to 12 servings.

Shirley Jones, Preceptor Iota Theta
Clayton, California

Sherried sweet potatoes are easy and delicious. Add ⅛ cup each butter and packed brown sugar to 6 mashed cooked sweet potatoes. Beat until light and fluffy. Beat in 2 tablespoons Sherry. Serve hot.

MICROWAVE CRANBERRY YAMS

½ cup all-purpose flour	1 teaspoon cinnamon
½ cup packed brown sugar	2 17-ounce cans yams, drained, sliced
½ cup oats	2 cups cranberries
⅓ cup margarine, softened	1½ cups miniature marshmallows

Combine flour, brown sugar, oats, margarine and cinnamon in small bowl; mix until crumbly. Toss 1 cup mixture with yams and cranberries in bowl. Pour into 1½-quart glass casserole; top with remaining crumb mixture. Microwave, covered, on High for 8 to 9 minutes. Top with marshmallows. Microwave, uncovered, for 2 to 3 minutes or until marshmallows are melted.
Yield: 6 to 8 servings.

Pat McMillan, Psi
Little Rock, Arkansas

HOLIDAY YAMS

1 16-ounce can sliced peaches	1 cup whole cranberry sauce
1 tablespoon cornstarch	2 tablespoons butter
⅓ cup packed brown sugar	2 pounds yams, cooked, peeled
½ teaspoon cinnamon	

Drain peaches, reserving juice. Dissolve cornstarch in ¼ cup reserved juice. Combine remaining peach juice, brown sugar, cinnamon, cranberry sauce and butter in skillet. Cook until well blended. Stir in cornstarch mixture. Cook until thickened, stirring constantly. Cut yams into halves; place in cranberry mixture. Cook for 10 minutes. Add peaches. Cook for 5 minutes longer.
Yield: 8 servings.

Jackie Vogler, Xi Sigma Pi
Hilltop Lakes, Texas

ORANGE JUICE YAMS

4 medium yams	2 tablespoons butter, softened
¾ cup orange juice	
⅓ cup sugar	3 tablespoons all-purpose flour
⅓ cup packed brown sugar	

Cook yams in boiling water until almost tender; peel and slice. Place in casserole. Combine orange juice, sugar, brown sugar, butter and flour in saucepan. Cook over medium heat until thickened, stirring constantly. Pour over yams. Bake at 350 degrees for 30 minutes.
Yield: 4 to 6 servings.

Joann Kikel, Xi Gamma Epsilon
Corvallis, Oregon

YAM SOUFFLÉ

1 29-ounce can sweet potatoes	¾ cup crushed pecans
2 eggs, beaten	1 tablespoon baking powder
¾ cup sugar	½ teaspoon nutmeg
¾ cup milk	½ teaspoon cinnamon

Drain sweet potatoes; mash in bowl. Add remaining ingredients; mix well. Pour into soufflé dish. Bake at 350 degrees for 50 to 60 minutes or until set.
Yield: 6 servings.

Frieda Allen, Preceptor Lambda
Parkersburg, West Virginia

YAM CRUNCH

1½ cups packed light brown sugar	¼ teaspoon salt
	1 29-ounce can yams, mashed
1½ cups crushed cornflakes	2 eggs, beaten
1¼ cups all-purpose flour	¼ cup milk
	¼ cup sugar
1 cup chopped pecans	½ teaspoon cinnamon
1½ tablespoons margarine, softened	⅛ teaspoon ginger
	⅛ teaspoon salt

Combine first 6 ingredients in bowl; mix until crumbly. Reserve a small amount for topping. Press remaining mixture over bottom and sides of 7x11-inch casserole. Combine yams and remaining ingredients in bowl; mix well. Pour into prepared casserole. Sprinkle with reserved mixture. Bake at 350 degrees for 40 minutes. Cool for 10 minutes before serving. Yield: 8 servings.

Janice Goodrich, Alpha Epsilon Xi
Yoakum, Texas

ZUCCHINI CASSEROLE

2 pounds zucchini, grated	8 ounces cheddar cheese, shredded
1 cup buttermilk baking mix	½ teaspoon salt
4 eggs, beaten	Pepper to taste
¼ cup oil	

Combine all ingredients in bowl; mix well. Pour into greased 7x11-inch casserole. Bake at 350 degrees for 30 to 40 minutes or until firm. Yield: 8 servings.

Janice Goodrich, Alpha Epsilon Xi
Yoakum, Texas

SWISS-STYLE VEGETABLE BAKE

1 20-ounce package frozen cauliflower	2 cups shredded Swiss cheese
1 10-ounce package frozen chopped broccoli	1 10-ounce can cream of celery soup
1 17-ounce can cream-style corn	1½ cups soft rye bread crumbs
1 17-ounce can whole kernel corn, drained	3 tablespoons melted butter

Cook each frozen vegetable according to package directions; drain. Mix with canned vegetables, cheese and soup in large bowl. Pour into greased 3-quart casserole. Mix crumbs and butter in bowl; sprinkle over vegetable mixture. Bake at 375 degrees for 40 minutes or until bubbly. Yield: 12 servings.

Jean Weller, Xi Alpha Pi
McConnellsburg, Pennsylvania

VEGETABLE MEDLEY CASSEROLE

6 to 7 ounces process cheese spread	1 10-ounce package frozen corn, thawed
2 to 4 tablespoons milk	2 20-ounce packages frozen mixed vegetables
1 10-ounce can cream of celery soup	¼ cup melted margarine
3 ounces cream cheese	1 8-ounce package herb-seasoned stuffing mix
¼ cup margarine	

Combine process cheese and milk in saucepan. Heat over low heat until well blended, stirring constantly. Add soup, cream cheese and ¼ cup margarine. Heat until well blended, stirring constantly. Mix vegetables in large bowl. Add cheese mixture; mix well. Pour into 3-quart casserole. Bake at 350 degrees for 40 minutes. Mix melted margarine with stuffing mix. Spread over vegetables. Bake for 20 minutes longer. Yield: 12 to 14 servings.

Velda M. Kloke, Xi Gamma Zeta
Harvard, Nebraska

VEGETABLE STRUDEL

3 cups chopped broccoli	2½ teaspoons minced parsley
3 cups chopped cauliflower	½ teaspoon crumbled dried basil
2½ cups chopped carrots	1 teaspoon minced tarragon
1 large onion, coarsely chopped	1 pound Swiss cheese, shredded
2 cloves of garlic, finely chopped	14 sheets phyllo
2 tablespoons butter	6 tablespoons melted butter
3 eggs	Sesame seed
1 teaspoon salt	
Freshly ground pepper to taste	

Steam broccoli, cauliflower and carrots over boiling water until tender-crisp. Cool slightly. Cook onion and garlic in 2 tablespoons butter in covered skillet for 10 minutes or until golden, stirring occasionally. Combine eggs and seasonings in large bowl; mix well. Add cheese, steamed vegetables, onion and garlic; mix gently. Layer phyllo sheets 1 at a time on work surface, brushing each with melted butter. Keep unused phyllo covered with plastic wrap. Spread vegetable mixture over phyllo, leaving 3-inch border. Fold in ends of phyllo; fold sides to center, overlapping slightly. Brush with butter and seal. Brush top with remaining butter; sprinkle with sesame seed. Bake at 375 degrees for 20 to 30 minutes or until golden. Serve immediately. Yield: 6 to 8 servings.

Daryl Rodway, Iota Alpha
Hammond, Louisiana

Interesting toppings make vegetables attractive and delicious. Top with croutons, cheese triangles, chopped nuts, sliced olives, French-fried onion rings, pimento strips or mixture of Parmesan cheese or herbs, butter and bread crumbs.

CHEESE GRITS CASSEROLE

1 cup grits	2 eggs, beaten
4 cups water	1 teaspoon seasoned salt
1½ teaspoons salt	1 teaspoon Worcestershire sauce
1 8-ounce roll smoky cheese	¾ cup butter
6 ounces sharp Cheddar cheese, shredded	

Cook grits with water and salt according to package directions. Add cheeses; stir until melted. Mix in remaining ingredients. Pour into 2-quart casserole. Bake at 350 degrees for 45 minutes. Yield: 6 servings.

Nancy Roberson, Xi Theta Omicron
Holden, Missouri

FETTUCINI WITH SPINACH

1 10-ounce package frozen spinach, thawed, drained	½ teaspoon white pepper
	1 12-ounce can evaporated milk
1 teaspoon chopped garlic	12 ounces fettucini, cooked
¼ cup melted butter	16 ounces cream-style cottage cheese
2 tablespoons olive oil	
1 teaspoon salt	

Sauté spinach and garlic in mixture of butter and olive oil with salt and white pepper in large skillet for 2 to 3 minutes. Add evaporated milk, fettucini and cottage cheese; mix well. Heat to serving temperature, stirring occasionally. Spoon into serving dish.
Yield: 4 to 6 servings.

Charlene Field, Iota Alpha
Hammond, Louisiana

BROWN RICE

1½ cups long grain rice	½ cup margarine
1 clove of garlic, finely chopped	2 10-ounce cans beef consommé

Sauté rice and garlic in margarine in heavy skillet over medium heat until light brown, stirring occasionally. Pour into greased 2-quart casserole. Add consommé to skillet, stirring to deglaze. Pour into casserole. Bake, covered, at 350 degrees for 1 hour, stirring occasionally. Serve with beef dishes. Yield: 6 to 8 servings.

Wanda E. Dudley, Preceptor Pi
Albuquerque, New Mexico

COMPANY RICE

1½ tablespoons instant bouillon	¼ cup wild rice
	½ cup rice
1½ cups boiling water	

Dissolve bouillon in boiling water in saucepan. Rinse wild rice; add to saucepan. Simmer, covered, for 15 minutes. Add rice. Cook, covered, for 14 minutes. Very good served with fish. Yield: 4 servings.
Note: May add sautéed onion or other seasonings.

Geraldine Reed, Preceptor Upsilon
Omaha, Nebraska

FRIED RICE

6 to 8 slices bacon,
  chopped
4 green onions, chopped
2 cloves of garlic, minced
2 carrots, chopped

1 large zucchini, chopped
3 cups cooked rice
2 eggs, scrambled
2 tablespoons soy sauce

Stir-fry bacon in wok for 5 to 10 minutes or until crisp; remove bacon. Add green onions and garlic. Stir-fry for 1 minute. Add carrots. Stir-fry for 4 minutes. Add zucchini. Stir-fry for 3 to 4 minutes or until vegetables are tender. Add rice, bacon, eggs and soy sauce. Stir-fry for 1 minute. Spoon into serving dish. Yield: 4 servings.

Cathy Vins, Xi Alpha
Honolulu, Hawaii

MUSHROOM WILD RICE

½ cup wild rice
1 6-ounce can broiled-
  in-butter sliced
  mushrooms

½ teaspoon salt
1⅓ cups minute rice
3 tablespoons butter

Cook wild rice using package directions. Drain mushrooms, reserving liquid. Add enough water to reserved liquid to measure 1⅓ cups. Add salt. Cook minute rice according to package directions, using mushroom liquid. Combine all ingredients in saucepan. Heat to serving temperature over low heat. Spoon into serving dish. Yield: 6 servings.

Bettie Plummer, Laureate Pi
Independence, Missouri

CREAM OF WILD RICE SOUP

1 package long grain
  and wild rice mix
1 cup chopped onion
1½ tablespoons butter
1½ tablespoons
  all-purpose flour
1 teaspoon salt

¼ teaspoon mace
Freshly ground
  pepper to taste
3 cans chicken broth
2 cups half and half
½ cup dry white wine

Cook rice mix according to package directions. Sauté onion in butter in large saucepan for 8 minutes or until tender. Stir in flour, salt, mace and pepper; mix well. Add rice, chicken broth, half and half and wine. Heat just to boiling point, stirring constantly. Remove from heat. Ladle 1½ cups at a time into blender container. Process until smooth. Return to saucepan. Heat to serving temperature, stirring occasionally. Ladle into soup bowls. Garnish with sour cream and chopped parsley. Yield: 2½ quarts.

Cheryl Huntoon, Preceptor Theta
Sparks, Nevada

To serve rice during the holidays, mold into ring. Pack mixture of 6 cups hot cooked rice, ¼ cup chopped parsley and 3 tablespoons butter into 5½-cup ring mold. Let stand for 1 minute. Loosen edges; unmold onto serving plate.

GOURMET RICE DRESSING

1 cup rice
1 cup chopped onion
1 cup chopped celery
1 cup chopped celery
  leaves
1 4-ounce can sliced
  mushrooms, drained

3 tablespoons butter
2 cups boiling chicken
  broth
¾ teaspoon poultry
  seasoning
½ cup toasted sliced
  almonds

Sauté rice, onion, celery, celery leaves and mushrooms in butter in skillet until vegetables are tender and rice is golden. Stir in chicken broth and poultry seasoning. Spoon into buttered shallow 2-quart baking dish. Bake, covered, at 350 degrees for 30 to 35 minutes or until rice is tender and liquid is absorbed. Fluff with fork. Sprinkle with almonds. Yield: 8 servings.

Photograph for this recipe on page 2.

SOUTHERN CORN BREAD DRESSING

1 cup melted butter
1 large onion, chopped
½ stalk celery, sliced
6 cups mixed crumbled
  corn bread and dry
  bread
1 teaspoon salt

Pepper to taste
1½ teaspoons poultry
  seasoning
3 eggs, beaten
1½ cups hot broth
3 tablespoons minced
  parsley

Combine first 4 ingredients and seasonings in bowl; mix well. Add eggs and broth; mix well. Add parsley. Spoon into baking pan. Bake at 350 degrees for 45 minutes. Yield: 8 to 10 servings.
Note: May add drained cooked sausage.

Jackie Vogler, Xi Sigma Pi
Hilltop Lakes, Texas

STUFFING BALL DRESSING

½ cup chopped onion
1 cup chopped celery
1 16-ounce can cream-
  style corn
¾ cup water

¼ cup margarine
1 8-ounce package herb-
  flavored stuffing mix
3 egg yolks
Melted margarine

Combine onion, celery, corn, water and ¼ cup margarine in saucepan. Bring to a boil. Pour over stuffing mix in bowl; mix well. Stir in egg yolks. Shape into 16 to 18 balls with ice cream scoop. Place in 9x13-inch baking dish. Drizzle with melted margarine. Bake at 350 degrees for 20 minutes. Yield: 6 to 8 servings.

Connie Cross, Xi Alpha Nu
St. Cloud, Minnesota

Prepare stuffing just before roasting the chicken, turkey, or duckling. Prepare ¾ to 1 cup stuffing per pound of poultry. Pack lightly into poultry to allow for expansion during cooking. Bake extra stuffing in covered greased casserole during last 30 to 45 minutes roasting time.

TURKEY STUFFING

1 cup finely chopped onion	½ teaspoon pepper
¾ cup finely chopped celery	1 tablespoon poultry seasoning
¾ cup butter	1 28-ounce jar mincemeat
12 cups dry bread cubes	¾ cup water
1 tablespoon salt	

Sauté onion and celery in butter in large skillet until tender. Add bread cubes, seasonings and mincemeat; mix well. Add water; toss gently until moistened. Stuff 12 to 15-pound turkey loosely just before roasting. Bake remaining stuffing in casserole at 325 degrees for 30 minutes. Yield: 12 servings.

Glee Tappan, Preceptor Beta Alpha
Portland, Oregon

CRANBERRY SAUCE

3 cups cranberries	2 oranges
1½ cups sugar	

Process cranberries in food processor. Combine with sugar in bowl; mix well. Cut oranges into halves; scoop out and chop pulp, reserving orange rind shells. Add chopped orange pulp to cranberries; mix well. Spoon into orange rind shells. Yield: 4 servings.

Brenda Pringle, Xi Alpha Nu
Florence, South Carolina

CRANBERRY SHERBET

4 cups fresh cranberries	2 cups sugar
2 cups water	2 tablespoons dry lemon gelatin
Juice of 2 lemons	

Bring cranberries and water to a boil in saucepan. Boil for 8 minutes. Put through sieve. Add lemon juice, sugar and dry gelatin; mix well. Pour into shallow dish. Freeze, covered, until almost firm. Place in bowl; whip until light but not melted. Pour into shallow dish. Freeze until firm. Cut into squares. Serve as accompaniment with turkey, ham or roast beef. Yield: 12 servings.

Dolores R. Seward, Xi Epsilon Alpha
Muskogee, Oklahoma

HOT FRUIT CURRY

2 16-ounce cans fruit for salad, drained	1 16-ounce can sliced peaches, drained
1 banana, sliced	½ cup melted margarine
1 6-ounce bottle of maraschino cherries, drained	½ cup packed brown sugar
	1 teaspoon curry powder
	2 teaspoons cinnamon
1 cup slivered almonds	

Combine all ingredients in bowl; mix well. Pour into 9x12-inch glass casserole. Bake at 350 degrees for 30 minutes or until bubbly. Serve hot. Yield: 8 servings.

Diann Walters, Delta Kappa
Ellisville, Mississippi

SCALLOPED PINEAPPLE

1 16-ounce can crushed pineapple	½ cup milk
½ cup melted butter	½ cup sugar
3 eggs, beaten	6 slices bread, crusts trimmed, cubed

Combine all ingredients in bowl; mix well. Pour into greased 8-inch baking dish. Bake at 350 degrees for 35 minutes. Delicious with baked ham.
Yield: 8 to 10 servings.

Janice Mell, dec'd, Preceptor Phi
York, Pennsylvania

PINEAPPLE PUDDING

½ cup butter, softened	1 20-ounce can crushed pineapple, drained
1 cup sugar	
4 eggs, beaten	5 slices bread, cubed

Cream butter and sugar in bowl until light and fluffy. Add eggs; mix well. Stir in pineapple and bread cubes. Pour into greased 2-quart casserole. Bake, covered, at 350 degrees for 30 minutes. Bake, uncovered, for 30 minutes longer. Serve with ham. Yield: 6 servings.

Diana Bal, Xi Delta Xi
Rochester, New York

SECRET SAUCE

1 16-ounce package brown sugar	1 cup ginger ale
	1 cup pineapple juice
1 cup orange juice	3 tablespoons cornstarch

Combine first 4 ingredients in saucepan. Cook until brown sugar dissolves, stirring frequently. Blend cornstarch with enough water to make paste. Stir into juice mixture. Cook until thickened and clear, stirring constantly. Serve with ham. Yield: 4 cups.

Shirley Jones, Preceptor Iota Theta
Clayton, California

TERIYAKI SAUCE

½ cup soy sauce	1 clove of garlic, minced
½ cup water	2 teaspoons sugar
¼ cup minced onion	½ teaspoon ginger

Combine all ingredients in bowl; mix well. Use as marinade for beef or chicken. Yield: 1 cup.

Kim Churas, Xi Alpha
Providence, Rhode Island

Begin with basic white sauce made with 2 tablespoons each flour and butter and 1 cup milk blended together and cooked until thickened. Stir in one of the following: 1 cup shredded cheese and ¼ teaspoon dry mustard; ¼ cup sautéed minced onion, 2 teaspoon curry powder and 1 teaspoon lemon juice; 2 sliced hard-boiled eggs and ½ teaspoon dry mustard; ¼ cup each mayonnaise and bottled chili sauce.

Holiday Breads

ANGEL BISCUITS

*5 cups sifted self-rising
  flour*
3 tablespoons sugar
1 cup shortening
1 package dry yeast
*5 tablespoons lukewarm
  water*
1 teaspoon soda
*2 cups buttermilk, at
  room temperature*
Melted margarine

Sift flour and sugar into bowl. Cut in shortening until crumbly. Dissolve yeast in warm water. Mix with soda and buttermilk. Add to flour mixture; beat until smooth. Roll on floured surface; cut with biscuit cutter. Brush with margarine; fold as for Parker House rolls. Place on greased baking sheet. Brush with margarine. Bake at 375 degrees until golden brown. Yield: 5 dozen.
Note: May store dough in refrigerator for several days.

*Mrs. Robert L. Scofield, Laureate Eta
Clarksville, Tennessee*

MAKE-AHEAD ANGEL BISCUITS

1 package dry yeast
2 tablespoons warm water
5 cups all-purpose flour
1 teaspoon soda
1 teaspoon baking powder
¼ cup sugar
1 teaspoon salt
1 cup shortening
2 cups buttermilk

Dissolve yeast in warm water. Sift flour, soda, baking powder, sugar and salt into bowl. Cut in shortening until crumbly. Stir in buttermilk and yeast just until mois- tened. Knead on floured surface for 1 to 2 minutes. Roll to desired thickness; cut with biscuit cutter. Place on baking sheet. Bake at 400 degrees until golden brown. Yield: 5 dozen.
Note: May store dough in airtight container in refrigerator for up to 10 days. May freeze unbaked biscuits until needed.

*Ann Kesley, Epsilon Kappa
Nashville, Tennessee*

BUTTERSCOTCH-PECAN BISCUITS

⅓ cup melted butter
*¾ cup packed brown
  sugar*
2 tablespoons cream
1 cup pecans
2 cups all-purpose flour
2 tablespoons sugar
*1 tablespoon baking
  powder*
1 teaspoon salt
⅓ cup shortening
¾ cup milk

Combine butter, brown sugar and cream in bowl; mix well. Place 2 teaspoons mixture in 18 muffin cups. Sprinkle pecans over mix. Mix flour, sugar, baking powder and salt in bowl. Cut in shortening until crumbly. Stir in milk. Knead gently on floured surface. Place dough in muffin cups. Bake at 425 degrees for 15 minutes or until golden. Invert onto serving plate immediately.
Yield: 1½ dozen.

*Jeanette Bush, Zeta Omega
Stillwater, Oklahoma*

WINE BISCUITS

1 cup sugar	4 teaspoons baking
1 cup oil	powder
1 cup red wine	1/8 teaspoon salt
4 cups all-purpose flour	1 egg, beaten

Combine sugar, oil and wine in bowl. Add flour, baking powder and salt; mix well. Knead on floured surface until smooth. Shape into biscuits. Place on baking sheet. Brush with egg. Bake at 375 degrees for 20 minutes. Yield: 2 dozen.

Beth O'Neil, Xi Alpha
Providence, Rhode Island

BREAD STICKS

1/4 cup butter, softened	1 cup all-purpose flour
1 cup Parmesan cheese	1 egg yolk
1/2 cup sour cream	1 tablespoon water
1/2 teaspoon Italian	Caraway seed
seasoning	

Cream butter in mixer bowl until light. Add cheese; beat until fluffy. Add sour cream gradually, beating well after each addition. Stir in mixture of Italian seasoning and flour. Roll 1/2 at a time into rectangle on lightly floured surface. Cut into 1/2x6-inch strips. Brush with egg yolk beaten with water. Sprinkle with caraway seed. Twist each strip 2 or 3 times. Place on buttered baking sheet. Bake at 350 degrees for 12 to 15 minutes or until light brown. Yield: 10 to 12 servings.
Note; May substitute poppy seed or coarse salt for caraway seed.

Patricia Simon, Beta Lambda
Evanston, Wyoming

CHRISTMAS COFFEE CAKE

1 cup butter, softened	1 teaspoon cinnamon
1 1/4 cups sugar	1 cup raisins
2 eggs	1/4 cup all-purpose flour
1 cup sour cream	4 teaspoons cinnamon
1 teaspoon vanilla extract	1 cup packed brown sugar
2 cups all-purpose flour	3 tablespoons melted
1/2 teaspoon soda	butter
1/2 teaspoon salt	Chopped nuts
1 teaspoon baking powder	

Cream softened butter and sugar in bowl until light and fluffy. Add eggs, sour cream and vanilla; mix well. Sift 2 cups flour, soda, salt, baking powder and cinnamon together. Add to sour cream mixture; mix well. Stir in raisins. Pour into greased and floured 9x13-inch baking pan. Top with mixture of remaining ingredients. Bake at 350 degrees for 35 minutes. Yield: 12 to 16 servings.

Barbara Ball, Xi Alpha Kappa
Grand Junction, Colorado

PLUCK-IT COFFEE CAKE

3 cans refrigerator	1 cup melted margarine
biscuits	1 cup chopped pecans
1 1/2 cups packed brown	2 teaspoons cinnamon
sugar	

Cut biscuits into quarters or smaller pieces. Mix remaining ingredients in bowl. Alternate layers of biscuit pieces and brown sugar mixture 1/3 at a time in greased bundt pan. Bake at 325 degrees for 45 minutes. Invert onto serving plate. Yield: 20 to 24 servings.

Paula Middleton, Xi Mu Eta
Houston, Texas

MOTHER CHEEK'S CORN BREAD

2 1/2 cups freshly ground	1 tablespoon baking
cornmeal	powder
2 eggs, beaten	1 teaspoon soda
2 tablespoons oil	1 1/2 teaspoons salt
1 1/2 cups buttermilk	2 tablespoons oil
1 tablespoon sugar	1 tablespoon (about)
2 tablespoons self-rising	all-purpose flour
flour	

Combine cornmeal, eggs, 2 tablespoons oil, buttermilk, sugar, self-rising flour, baking powder, soda and salt in bowl; mix well. Heat 2 tablespoons oil in large cast-iron skillet in 350-degree oven. Sprinkle all-purpose flour in skillet. Add batter. Bake for 20 minutes or until golden brown; do not overbake. Yield: 8 servings.

Diane Walters, Delta Kappa
Ellisville, Missouri

CORNMEAL CRISPS

2 cups yellow cornmeal	5 dashes of cayenne
1/2 teaspoon seasoned salt	pepper
1/2 teaspoon pepper	2 1/2 cups boiling water
4 teaspoons butter	

Combine first 5 ingredients in bowl. Add boiling water; mix until smooth. Preheat cast-iron corn stick pans. Add batter by tablespoonfuls. Bake at 375 degrees for 20 minutes. Reduce temperature to 250 degrees. Bake for 15 minutes longer. Yield: 3 to 4 dozen.

Jackie Vogler, Xi Sigma Pi
Hilltop Lakes, Texas

AMISH APPLE FRITTERS

1 cup all-purpose flour	1 egg, beaten
1 1/2 teaspoons baking	1/2 cup milk
powder	3 apples
1/2 teaspoon salt	Oil for deep frying
2 tablespoons sugar	

Combine first 4 ingredients in bowl. Add egg and milk; mix until smooth. Peel and core apples; slice thinly. Dip apples into batter. Deep-fry in hot oil until golden brown. Drain on paper towels. Garnish with sprinkle of confectioners' sugar. Serve with spiced cider. Yield: 3 dozen.

Colleen Scott, Iota Alpha
Independence, Louisiana

SQUASH HUSH PUPPIES

6 tablespoons all-purpose
  flour
1 tablespoon sugar
¼ cup (or more) cornmeal
Salt and pepper to taste

1 egg, beaten
2 cups grated squash
1 small onion, grated
Oil for deep frying

Combine flour, sugar, cornmeal, salt and pepper in bowl. Add egg, squash and onion; mix well. Shape into 1½-inch balls. Deep-fry in hot oil until golden brown. Drain on paper towel. Yield: 6 servings.

Linda Manning, Epsilon Kappa
Nashville, Tennessee

SPUDNUTS

1 package dry yeast
½ cup warm water
¾ cup sugar
1½ teaspoons salt
1⅓ cups instant
  potato flakes
½ cup shortening
2 cups milk, scalded

2 eggs, beaten
5½ to 6 cups all-purpose
  flour
Oil for deep frying
1¾ cups confectioners'
  sugar
¼ teaspoon vanilla extract
¼ cup (about) milk

Dissolve yeast in warm water. Let stand for several minutes. Combine sugar, salt, instant potatoes and shortening in large bowl. Add hot milk; mix well. Cool to lukewarm. Add eggs, yeast and 1 cup flour; mix well. Add enough remaining flour to make soft dough. Let rise for 2 hours. Roll on floured surface; cut with doughnut cutter. Let rise until doubled in bulk. Deep-fry in hot oil until brown, turning once. Drain well. Blend confectioners' sugar, vanilla and enough milk to make of desired consistency in bowl. Drizzle over spudnuts.
Yield: 30 to 35 spudnuts.

Teresa Curto, Rho
Ely, Nevada

APPLE-NUT BREAD

½ cup shortening
1 cup sugar
2 eggs, well beaten
2 cups all-purpose flour
1 teaspoon baking
  powder
1 teaspoon soda
¼ teaspoon salt

1½ tablespoons
  sour cream
1 cup finely chopped
  red apple
1 teaspoon vanilla extract
1½ cups finely chopped
  walnuts
Cinnamon to taste

Cream shortening, 1 cup sugar and eggs in mixer bowl until light and fluffy. Add mixture of dry ingredients alternately with sour cream, mixing well after each addition. Fold in apple, vanilla and 1¼ cups walnuts. Spoon into greased and floured loaf pan. Sprinkle with mixture of remaining ¼ cup walnuts, cinnamon and additional sugar. Bake at 375 degrees for 1 hour or until loaf tests done. Remove to wire rack to cool.
Yield: 15 to 20 servings.
Note: May sprinkle greased loaf pan with wheat germ. May bake in 3 small loaf pans or three 8-ounce cans.

Adeline Hamilton, Laureate Beta
Rapid City, South Dakota

APPLE BUTTER BREAD

½ cup butter, softened
1 cup packed brown sugar
1 egg
2 cups all-purpose flour
2½ teaspoons cinnamon
2 teaspoons nutmeg

2 teaspoons allspice
1 teaspoon cloves
2 teaspoons soda
¾ cup buttermilk
1 cup apple butter
½ cup chopped nuts

Cream butter and brown sugar in mixer bowl until light and fluffy. Blend in egg. Combine flour and spices in bowl. Add to creamed mixture alternately with mixture of soda and buttermilk, beginning and ending with flour mixture and mixing well after each addition. Stir in apple butter and nuts. Pour into greased 5x9-inch loaf pan. Bake at 350 degrees for 1 hour and 5 minutes. Cool in pan for 5 minutes. Serve warm or cool with whipped cream cheese or butter. Yield: 16 to 18 servings.

Janet Niehouse, Sigma Omicron
Fulton, Missouri

BANANA BREAD

3 large bananas, mashed
1 egg
¾ cup sugar
2 tablespoons melted
  butter

2 cups sifted all-purpose
  flour
1 teaspoon soda
1 teaspoon salt

Combine bananas, egg and sugar in bowl; mix well. Stir in butter. Add sifted dry ingredients; mix well. Pour into greased loaf pan. Bake at 350 degrees for 1 hour. Yield: 10 servings.

Beverly Davis, Epsilon Kappa
Nashville, Tennessee

BANANA-NUT-CHOCOLATE CHIP BREAD

½ cup butter, softened
1 cup sugar
2 eggs
3 small bananas, mashed
1 teaspoon soda

2 cups sifted all-purpose
  flour
½ cup chopped nuts
¼ cup chocolate chips

Cream butter and sugar in mixer bowl until light and fluffy. Blend in eggs and bananas. Add soda and flour; mix well. Stir in nuts and chocolate chips. Spoon into greased loaf pan. Bake at 350 degrees for 45 to 60 minutes or until loaf tests done. Remove to wire rack to cool.
Yield: 12 servings.

Marlene Null, Eta Nu
Charles City, Iowa

Vary homemade doughnuts (such as Spudnuts on this page or Fastnachts on page 33) by adding 1½ squares melted chocolate, ½ cup chopped nuts or substituting 5 cups whole wheat flour for all-purpose flour in batter. Coat with mixture of 1 cup sugar and ¾ teaspoon nutmeg or ½ cup honey and ⅔ cup confectioners' sugar. Serve plain hot doughnuts with syrup made from simmering 12 ounces maple-flavored syrup and 2 tablespoons red cinnamon candies.

BANANA-NUT BREAD

½ cup shortening	2 cups all-purpose flour
1 cup sugar	1 teaspoon soda
2 eggs	¼ teaspoon salt
3 or 4 ripe bananas, mashed	1 cup chopped pecans

Cream shortening and sugar in mixer bowl until light and fluffy. Blend in eggs and bananas. Add dry ingredients; mix well. Stir in pecans. Spoon into greased loaf pan. Bake at 300 degrees for 1 hour or until light brown. Remove to wire rack to cool. Yield: 12 servings.

Tricia Nipper, Epsilon Kappa
Nashville, Tennessee

BANANA-WALNUT BREAD

⅓ cup shortening	1¼ teaspoons baking
½ cup sugar	powder
2 eggs	¼ teaspoon soda
2 small ripe bananas, mashed	½ teaspoon salt
1⅓ cups all-purpose flour	Chopped walnuts

Cream shortening and sugar in mixer bowl until light and fluffy. Blend in eggs and bananas. Add mixture of dry ingredients and walnuts; mix just until moistened. Spoon into greased loaf pan. Bake at 350 degrees for 45 minutes or until loaf tests done. Remove to wire rack to cool. Yield: 12 servings.

Christine Davis, Xi Epsilon Alpha
Oktaha, Oklahoma

CHOCOLATE CHIP BREAD

½ cup shortening	½ teaspoon allspice
1 cup sugar	1 teaspoon cinnamon
2 eggs	1 cup applesauce
1¾ cups all-purpose flour	½ cup chopped nuts
1 teaspoon soda	½ cup raisins
¼ teaspoon salt	1 cup chocolate chips
¼ teaspoon cloves	

Cream shortening and sugar in mixer bowl until light and fluffy. Blend in eggs. Add mixture of dry ingredients alternately with applesauce, mixing well after each addition. Stir in nuts, raisins and ½ cup chocolate chips. Pour into greased and floured loaf pan. Sprinkle with remaining ½ cup chocolate chips. Bake at 325 degrees for 1 hour and 15 minutes. Remove to wire rack to cool. Let stand, wrapped in plastic wrap, overnight before serving. Yield: 12 servings.

Marcia Nestler, Xi Zeta Mu
Eldridge, Iowa

CRANBERRY BREAD

2 cups all-purpose flour	2 tablespoons shortening
1½ teaspoons baking powder	Grated orange rind to taste
1 cup sugar	¾ cup orange juice
½ teaspoon soda	1 egg, beaten
½ teaspoon salt	1 cup chopped cranberries

Combine dry ingredients in bowl. Add shortening, orange rind, orange juice, egg and cranberries; mix well. Spoon into greased and floured loaf pan. Bake at 350 degrees for 1 hour. Cool in pan for 10 minutes. Remove to wire rack to cool completely. Yield: 12 servings.

Sharon Pilkington, Xi Epsilon Psi
Ann Arbor, Michigan

CRANBERRY-WALNUT BREAD

2 cups all-purpose flour	2 tablespoons melted
1¼ teaspoons baking powder	butter
	½ cup orange juice
1 cup sugar	2 tablespoons hot water
½ teaspoon soda	1 cup whole cranberries
½ teaspoon salt	½ cup walnuts
1 egg	

Combine dry ingredients in bowl. Add egg, butter, orange juice and hot water; mix well. Stir in cranberries and walnuts. Pour into greased loaf pan. Bake at 350 degrees for 1 hour and 10 minutes. Remove to wire rack to cool. Yield: 12 servings.

Alma Bakko, Xi Upsilon Delta
Borrego Springs, Colorado

NORMA'S DATE-NUT BREAD

1½ cups chopped dates	2¾ cups all-purpose flour
1½ cups boiling water	1 teaspoon soda
2 tablespoons shortening	1 teaspoon cream of tartar
1½ cups sugar	1 cup chopped nuts
1 teaspoon salt	1 teaspoon vanilla extract
1 egg, beaten	

Combine dates and boiling water in bowl. Stir in shortening, sugar and salt. Let stand until cool. Mix in egg. Beat in sifted flour, soda and cream of tartar. Stir in nuts and vanilla. Pour into greased loaf pan. Bake at 350 degrees for 45 minutes or until loaf tests done. Serve with butter or cream cheese. Yield: 12 servings.

Note: May bake in 2 small loaf pans or 5 miniature loaf pans; reduce baking time accordingly.

Norma McConnell, Laureate Gamma Phi
Arvada, Colorado

DATE BREAD

1 cup chopped dates	1 cup sugar
1 cup boiling water	1 tablespoon butter
1 teaspoon soda	1 egg
1½ cups all-purpose flour	

Combine dates, boiling water and soda in bowl. Let stand until cool. Add remaining ingredients; mix well. Spoon into greased loaf pan. Bake at 350 degrees for 40 minutes. Remove to wire rack to cool. Yield: 12 servings.
Note: May add nuts if desired.

Mary B. Meddles, Preceptor Delta Tau
Richwood, Ohio

ORANGE-DATE-NUT BREAD

1 medium orange	2 cups sifted all-purpose
2/3 cup chopped dates	flour
1/2 cup English walnuts	1 1/2 teaspoons baking
2 tablespoons butter	powder
1/2 cup hot water	1/2 teaspoon soda
1 egg	1/4 teaspoon salt
3/4 cup sugar	

Grind orange, dates and walnuts. Combine butter with hot water in bowl; stir until melted. Stir in ground mixture and egg. Add sifted dry ingredients; mix well. Spoon into greased loaf pan. Bake at 350 degrees for 1 hour and 15 minutes. Serve with honey or cream cheese. Yield: 20 servings.

Margaret A. Bohls, Preceptor Beta Lambda
Arvada, Colorado

DATE-NUT BREAD

1 cup chopped dates	2 eggs
2 teaspoons soda	4 cups all-purpose flour
2 cups boiling water	1 teaspoon salt
2 tablespoons butter,	2 teaspoons vanilla extract
softened	1 cup chopped nuts
2 cups sugar	

Combine dates, soda and boiling water in bowl. Let stand until cool. Cream butter in mixer bowl. Add sugar gradually, beating until light and fluffy. Add eggs 1 at a time, mixing well after each addition. Add date mixture. Stir in flour, salt, vanilla and nuts gradually. Fill 5 or 6 greased and floured 16-ounce cans 1/2 full. Bake at 350 degrees for 50 minutes. Remove to wire rack to cool.
Yield: 5 to 6 loaves.
Note: May bake in 4 miniature loaf pans if crustier bread is desired.

Dolores Brown, Xi Alpha Gamma
Sheldon, South Carolina

NOT SO LIGHT BEER BREAD

3 cups self-rising flour	1 12-ounce can beer
1/2 cup sugar	Butter

Combine flour and sugar in bowl. Add beer; mix well. Spoon into 2 greased loaf pans. Bake at 350 degrees for 30 minutes. Brush tops with butter. Bake for 15 minutes longer. Serve with jam or cheese. Yield: 2 loaves.
Note: Do not use light beer.

Roberta DeNegre, Preceptor Gamma Upsilon
Blue Springs, Missouri

LEMON BREAD

3/4 cup margarine,	1 teaspoon salt
softened	1/2 cup milk
1 1/4 cups sugar	1/3 cup lemon juice
3 eggs	3/4 cup pecans
2 1/2 cups all-purpose flour	2 teaspoons grated
2 teaspoons baking	lemon rind
powder	

Cream margarine and sugar in mixer bowl until light and fluffy. Blend in eggs. Add dry ingredients alternately with milk and lemon juice, mixing well after each addition. Stir in nuts and lemon rind. Pour into greased and floured loaf pan. Bake at 350 degrees for 1 hour and 10 minutes. Cool in pan for 5 minutes. Remove to wire rack to cool completely. Yield: 12 servings.

Mary Anne Johnson, Beta Lambda
Evanston, Kentucky

PINEAPPLE-PECAN LOAF

3/4 cup packed brown	1 teaspoon baking powder
sugar	1/2 teaspoon salt
1/4 cup shortening	1/3 cup frozen orange
1 egg	juice concentrate
2 cups sifted all-purpose	1 cup crushed pineapple
flour	1/2 cup chopped nuts

Cream brown sugar and shortening in bowl until light and fluffy. Add egg; mix well. Add sifted dry ingredients alternately with orange juice concentrate, mixing well after each addition. Stir in pineapple and nuts. Spoon into greased loaf pan. Bake at 350 degrees for 50 to 60 minutes or until loaf tests done. Remove to wire rack to cool. Serve with honey butter. Yield: 12 servings.

Kari Schultz, Theta
Lenexa, Kansas

POPPY SEED BREAD

3 eggs	1 1/2 teaspoons butter
1 1/2 cups oil	flavoring
2 1/2 cups sugar	1 1/2 teaspoons vanilla
3 cups all-purpose flour	extract
1 1/2 teaspoons baking	1/4 cup orange juice
powder	3/4 cup sugar
1 1/2 teaspoons salt	1/2 teaspoon almond
1 1/2 cups milk	flavoring
1 1/2 teaspoons poppy seed	1/2 teaspoon butter
1 1/2 teaspoons almond	flavoring
flavoring	1/2 teaspoon vanilla extract

Beat eggs, oil and 2 1/2 cups sugar in mixer bowl until thick and lemon-colored. Sift flour, baking powder and salt together. Add to egg mixture alternately with milk, mixing well after each addition. Stir in poppy seed and 1 1/2 teaspoons each flavoring. Pour into 2 lightly greased and floured loaf pans. Bake at 350 degrees for 1 hour. Remove to wire rack. Cool for 15 to 20 minutes. Combine remaining ingredients in bowl; mix well. Spoon over loaves. Yield: 2 loaves.

Toni Larson, Beta Lambda
Evanston, Wyoming

Serve breads with flavored softened butters for the holidays. Combine 1 stick butter and 1 cup confectioners' sugar with one of the following: 1 teaspoon vanilla extract, 1 tablespoon Grand Marnier or Brandy, 10 ounces thawed frozen strawberries, 1/2 cup chopped nuts, 1/4 cup honey, or 1/2 teaspoon cinnamon plus 1/4 teaspoon cloves.

DENYS' PUMPKIN BREAD

1½ cups all-purpose flour	½ teaspoon nutmeg
1½ cups sugar	½ teaspoon cloves
1 teaspoon soda	½ cup oil
¼ teaspoon baking	1 cup pumpkin
powder	2 eggs
¾ teaspoon salt	½ cup water
½ teaspoon cinnamon	

Combine dry ingredients in bowl. Add oil, pumpkin, eggs and water; mix well. Spoon into greased loaf pan. Bake at 325 degrees for 1½ hours. Remove to wire rack to cool. Yield: 12 servings.

Denys D. Dallapé, Beta Alpha Pi
Garden Grove, California

CHRISTMAS PUMPKIN BREAD

3⅓ cups all-purpose flour	1 16-ounce can pumpkin
3 cups sugar	1 cup oil
1 tablespoon soda	4 eggs
1½ tablespoons salt	⅔ cup water
1½ teaspoons cinnamon	½ cup nuts
1 teaspoon nutmeg	

Combine flour, sugar, soda, salt and spices in bowl. Add pumpkin, oil, eggs and water; mix until smooth. Stir in nuts. Spoon into 3 greased and floured 1-pound coffee cans. Bake at 350 degrees for 1 hour and 15 minutes. Remove to wire rack to cool. Yield: 3 small loaves.

Wanda Rapp, Laureate Beta Nu
El Campo, Texas

PUMPKIN SPICE BREAD

1¾ cups all-purpose flour	⅛ teaspoon cloves
1½ cups sugar	½ cup melted margarine
1 teaspoon soda	1 egg, beaten
½ teaspoon salt	1 cup pumpkin
1 teaspoon cinnamon	⅓ cup water
½ teaspoon nutmeg	

Sift dry ingredients together into bowl. Make well in center. Pour cooled margarine into well; stir until mixed. Combine egg, pumpkin and water in bowl; mix slightly. Add to flour mixture; mix just until moistened. Spoon into greased and floured loaf pan. Bake at 350 degrees for 1 hour and 10 minutes. Serve with whipped topping or ice cream. Yield: 12 servings.

Carol Jarman, Beta Sigma
New Bern, North Carolina

JAN'S PUMPKIN BREAD

⅔ cup shortening	2 teaspoons soda
2⅔ cups sugar	1½ teaspoons salt
4 eggs	1 teaspoon cinnamon
1 16-ounce can pumpkin	1 teaspoon cloves
⅔ cup water	⅔ cup nuts
3⅓ cups all-purpose flour	⅔ cup raisins
½ teaspoon baking	
powder	

Cream shortening and sugar in mixer bowl until light and fluffy. Blend in eggs, pumpkin and water. Add flour, baking powder, soda, salt and spices; mix well. Stir in nuts and raisins. Spoon into 2 greased loaf pans. Bake at 350 degrees for 1 hour and 5 minutes to 1 hour and 15 minutes or until bread tests done. Yield: 24 servings.

Jan Treaster, Xi Epsilon Psi
Ann Arbor, Michigan

THANKSGIVING PUMPKIN BREAD

2 cups canned pumpkin	3 cups sugar
1 cup oil	2 teaspoons soda
⅔ cup water	1½ teaspoons salt
4 eggs	2 teaspoons cinnamon
3½ cups all-purpose flour	1 teaspoon nutmeg

Combine pumpkin, oil, water and eggs in mixer bowl; beat until smooth. Add sifted dry ingredients; mix well. Spoon into 2 greased loaf pans. Bake at 350 degrees for 1 hour and 15 minutes or until toothpick inserted in center comes out clean. Cool in pans on wire rack. Serve with butter or cream cheese. Yield: 2 loaves.

Candy DeStefano, Xi Kappa Beta
Wintersville, Ohio

PUMPKIN-RAISIN BREAD

⅔ cups shortening	1½ teaspoons baking
2⅔ cups sugar	powder
4 eggs	1½ teaspoons salt
1 16-ounce can pumpkin	1 teaspoon cinnamon
⅔ cup water	1 teaspoon cloves
3⅓ cups all-purpose flour	⅔ cup chopped nuts
2 teaspoons soda	⅔ cup raisins

Cream shortening and sugar in mixer bowl until light and fluffy. Blend in eggs, pumpkin and water. Add dry ingredients; mix well. Stir in nuts and raisins. Spoon into 2 greased 5x9-inch loaf pans. Bake at 350 degrees for 1 hour and 5 minutes to 1 hour and 10 minutes or until loaves test done. Remove to wire rack to cool.
Yield: 2 loaves.

Marilyn Borras, Xi Epsilon Alpha
Stafford, Virginia

RHUBARB BREAD

2 cups chopped rhubarb	1 teaspoon cinnamon
1½ cups sugar	1 teaspoon salt
2 cups all-purpose flour	1 cup milk
4 teaspoons baking	2 eggs
powder	3 tablespoons oil
1 cup sugar	1 cup nuts

Combine rhubarb and 1½ cups sugar in bowl. Let stand for 30 minutes. Sift flour, baking powder, 1 cup sugar, cinnamon and salt into bowl. Add milk, eggs and oil; mix well. Stir in rhubarb mixture and nuts. Spoon into large square baking pan. Bake at 375 degrees for 1 hour. Serve topped with whipped cream. Yield: 12 servings.

Donna Price, Preceptor Laureate Nu
Olympia, Washington

STRAWBERRY-NUT BREAD

1 cup margarine, softened	½ teaspoon soda
1½ cups sugar	1 teaspoon salt
1 teaspoon vanilla extract	¾ teaspoon cream of tartar
¼ teaspoon lemon extract	1 cup strawberry jam
4 eggs	½ cup sour cream
3 cups all-purpose flour	½ cup chopped walnuts

Cream margarine, sugar and flavorings in mixer bowl until light and fluffy. Add eggs 1 at a time, mixing well after each addition. Sift flour, soda, salt and cream of tartar together. Mix jam and sour cream in small bowl. Add dry ingredients to batter alternately with jam mixture, mixing well after each addition. Stir in walnuts. Spoon into 3 waxed paper-lined 4x8-inch loaf pans. Bake at 350 degrees for 50 minutes. Remove to wire rack to cool.
Yield: 3 loaves.

Garlene Knight, Preceptor Beta Epsilon
Cedar Rapids, Iowa

PRIZE-WINNING STRAWBERRY BREAD

2 10-ounce packages frozen strawberries	1 cup oil
3 cups all-purpose flour	4 eggs
2 cups sugar	8 ounces cream cheese, softened
1 teaspoon soda	½ cup confectioners' sugar
½ teaspoon salt	⅓ cup whipped butter
1 teaspoon cinnamon	

Drain strawberries, reserving ⅓ cup juice. Mix flour, sugar, soda, salt and cinnamon in bowl. Add oil, eggs and strawberries; mix well. Tint with red food coloring if desired. Spoon into 2 greased 5x9-inch loaf pans. Bake at 325 degrees for 30 to 40 minutes or until loaves test done. Remove to wire rack to cool. Slice as desired. Blend reserved strawberry juice, cream cheese, confectioners' sugar and whipped butter in bowl until smooth. Spoon into serving dish. Serve with bread.
Yield: 2 loaves.

Pam Lewis, Delta Kappa
Ellisville, Mississippi

STRAWBERRY-PECAN BREAD

1 cup butter, softened	½ cup sour cream
1½ cups sugar	½ teaspoon soda
1 teaspoon salt	3 cups all-purpose flour
1 teaspoon vanilla extract	½ cup chopped pecans
1 teaspoon lemon juice	1 cup strawberry preserves
4 eggs	

Cream butter, sugar, salt, vanilla and lemon juice in mixer bowl until light and fluffy. Add eggs 1 at a time, mixing well after each addition. Blend in mixture of sour cream and soda. Add flour; mix well. Fold in pecans and preserves. Pour into 2 greased loaf pans. Bake at 350 degrees for 40 to 60 minutes or until loaves test done.
Yield: 24 servings.
Note: May bake in 6 miniature loaf pans.

Glenda Ruyle, Xi Epsilon Omicron
Claremore, Oklahoma

BLUEBERRY MUFFINS

3½ cups sifted all-purpose flour	5 eggs, slightly beaten
¾ cup sugar	½ cup milk
2 tablespoons baking powder	10 tablespoons unsalted butter, melted, cooled
Pinch of salt	4 to 5 cups blueberries

Preheat oven to 425 degrees. Combine flour, sugar, baking powder and salt in bowl. Add eggs, milk and butter; mix just until moistened. Fold in blueberries gently. Spoon into paper-lined muffin cups. Sprinkle with additional sugar. Reduce oven temperature to 400 degrees. Place muffins on middle shelf. Bake for 25 minutes or until golden brown. Remove to wire rack to cool.
Yield: 15 to 16 muffins.

Sarah Thacker, Epsilon Kappa
Nashville, Tennessee

CRANBERRY MUFFINS

1¾ cups all-purpose flour	¾ cup milk
½ cup sugar	⅓ cup oil
2½ teaspoons baking powder	1 cup coarsely chopped cranberries
¾ teaspoon salt	¼ cup sugar
1 egg, beaten	

Mix dry ingredients in bowl. Make well in center. Beat egg with milk and oil in bowl. Pour into well; stir just until moistened. Batter will be lumpy. Fold in cranberries mixed with ¼ cup sugar. Spoon into greased muffin cups. Bake at 400 degrees for 20 to 25 minutes or until golden. Yield: 10 to 12 muffins.

Jan Treaster, Xi Epsilon Psi
Ann Arbor, Michigan

LUNCHEON MUFFINS

1¾ cups all-purpose flour	2 eggs, beaten
¼ cup sugar	⅔ cup tomato soup
3½ teaspoons baking powder	½ cup milk
½ teaspoon dry mustard	⅓ cup oil
1 teaspoon seasoned salt	3 tablespoons chopped onion

Sift dry ingredients together into bowl; make well in center. Combine eggs, soup, milk, oil and onion in bowl; mix well. Pour into well in dry ingredients; stir until moistened. Fill greased muffin cups ⅔ full. Bake at 375 degrees for 20 to 25 minutes or until brown.
Yield: 12 servings.

Barbara Ball, Xi Alpha Kappa
Grand Junction, Colorado

Make bakery-type muffins for the holidays. Fill very large muffin cups or 7-ounce custard cups ⅔ full. Top with crumb mixture of 1 cup brown sugar, 2 tablespoons each flour and butter, and ½ cup chopped nuts. Bake until muffins test done. Or, dip hot muffins into melted butter then sugar.

CHEDDAR BRAN MUFFINS

1¼ cups buttermilk
1 cup whole bran
¼ cup shortening
⅓ cup sugar
1 egg
1½ cups sifted all-purpose
    flour
1½ teaspoons baking
    powder
½ teaspoon salt
¼ teaspoon soda
1 cup shredded sharp
    Cheddar cheese

Pour buttermilk over bran in small bowl; let stand until bran is softened. Cream shortening and sugar in bowl until fluffy. Beat in egg. Sift flour, baking powder, salt and soda. Add to creamed mixture alternately with bran mixture. Stir in shredded cheese. Fill greased muffin cups ⅔ full. Bake at 400 degrees for 30 minutes or until golden brown. Serve immediately.

Frances Brown, Xi Delta Gamma
Raytown, Missouri

RAISIN BRAN MUFFINS

5 cups all-purpose flour
5 teaspoons soda
2 teaspoons salt
1 tablespoon pumpkin
    pie spice
½ cup margarine
½ cup shortening
2½ cups (about) sugar
4 eggs, beaten
1 quart buttermilk
2 tablespoons vanilla
    extract
1 15-ounce package
    raisin bran cereal
1 cup chopped nuts

Mix flour, soda, salt and pumpkin pie spice in large bowl. Cut in margarine and shortening until crumbly. Add sugar, eggs, buttermilk and vanilla; mix well. Stir in cereal and nuts. Store, covered, in refrigerator for up to 6 weeks. Fill greased muffin cups ⅔ full. Bake at 400 degrees for 15 to 20 minutes or until brown.
Yield: 6 dozen.

Janean Baker, Preceptor Beta Delta
Orange Park, Florida

FRENCH BREAKFAST PUFFS

½ cup sugar
⅓ cup shortening
1 egg
1½ cups sifted
    all-purpose flour
1½ teaspoons baking
    powder
½ teaspoon salt
¼ teaspoon ground
    nutmeg
½ cup milk
½ cup sugar
1 teaspoon cinnamon
6 tablespoons melted
    butter

Cream ½ cup sugar, shortening and egg in mixer bowl. Sift flour, baking powder, salt and nutmeg. Add to creamed mixture alternately with milk, beating well after each addition. Fill 12 greased muffin cups ⅔ full. Bake at 350 degrees for 20 minutes or until golden. Combine ½ cup sugar and cinnamon; blend well. Remove muffins from cups. Dip into melted butter; dip into cinnamon-sugar. Serve immediately. Yield: 1 dozen.

Carol Boyer, Theta Alpha
Seymour, Indiana

ONE-BOWL FRENCH BREAD

1 package dry yeast
2 tablespoons sugar
1 tablespoon salt
2½ cups warm water
6 cups all-purpose flour
1 egg white, beaten

Dissolve yeast, sugar and salt in water in large bowl. Mix in 3 to 4 cups flour. Add remaining flour, kneading on floured surface until smooth and elastic. Place in greased bowl, turning to grease surface. Let rise, covered, in warm place for 1½ hours. Shape into 2 loaves. Place on greased baking sheet. Slash tops diagonally at 1-inch intervals. Brush with egg white. Let rise until doubled in bulk. Bake at 450 degrees for 15 minutes. Reduce temperature to 300 degrees. Bake for 10 minutes longer.
Yield: 2 loaves.

Becky Larson, Iota Phi
Mallard, Iowa

NUT SWIRL RING

2 packages dry yeast
¼ cup warm water
¾ cup milk, scalded
⅓ cup melted butter
¼ cup sugar
1 egg, beaten
1 tablespoon grated
    lemon rind
1 teaspoon vanilla extract
½ teaspoon salt
3½ to 4 cups (or more)
    all-purpose flour
½ cup chopped dried
    apricots
⅔ cup raisins
2 cups chopped walnuts
½ cup packed brown
    sugar
2 teaspoons grated
    orange rind
1 teaspoon grated
    lemon rind
1½ teaspoons cinnamon
¼ teaspoon nutmeg
¼ cup melted butter
1 egg
1 tablespoon milk

Dissolve yeast in water in large bowl. Cool scalded milk to lukewarm. Add milk, ⅓ cup melted butter, sugar, 1 egg, lemon rind, vanilla and salt to yeast. Stir in 3½ cups flour gradually. Knead on surface sprinkled with ½ cup flour until smooth and elastic, adding additional flour if necessary. Place in greased bowl, turning to grease surface. Let rise, covered, for 1 hour or until doubled in bulk. Soak apricots and raisins in a small amount of warm water; drain. Add to mixture of walnuts, brown sugar, rinds, spices and ¼ cup melted butter; mix well. Roll dough to 16x21-inch rectangle. Cut off and reserve 3x21-inch strip. Spread rectangle with walnut mixture to within 1 inch of edge. Roll as for jelly roll. Shape into ring around empty 4-inch diameter can on greased baking sheet; seal ends together. Let rise, covered, for 1 hour or until doubled in bulk. Roll reserved dough ⅛ inch thick on floured surface; cut out flowers and leaves. Moisten decorative cut outs with water; attach to ring. Brush ring with egg beaten with 1 tablespoon milk. Bake in preheated 375-degree oven for 35 minutes or until golden brown. Cover with foil if necessary to prevent over-browning. Cool on baking sheet for 10 minutes. Remove to wire rack. Serve warm. May be frozen.

Phyllis Mason, Lambda Nu
Pattonsburg, Missouri

PASKA

1 cup milk	5 eggs
¼ cup 105 to 115-degree water	4½ cups all-purpose flour
2 packages dry yeast	1 cup seedless raisins
½ cup sugar	1 egg
½ cup butter	1 tablespoon water

Bring milk to the simmering point in saucepan. Cool to lukewarm. Place ¼ cup warm water in large bowl rinsed with hot water. Sprinkle yeast into water; stir until dissolved. Add lukewarm milk, sugar, butter, 5 eggs and 3 cups flour. Beat at medium speed until smooth. Stir in remaining 1½ cups flour with wooden spoon. Beat vigorously for 2 minutes or until dough leaves side of bowl. Mix in raisins. Place in greased bowl, turning to grease surface. Let rise, covered, in warm place for 1 hour or until doubled in bulk. Grease and flour 9-inch springform pan. Attach strip of greased foil to extend 2 inches above rim of pan. Spoon dough into prepared pan. Let rise for 1 hour. Preheat oven to 350 degrees. Brush top of bread with 1 egg beaten with 1 tablespoon water. Bake for 1 hour or until toothpick inserted in center comes out clean. Cool in pan for 15 minutes. Remove side of pan. Place on serving plate. Serve warm or toasted. Yield: 16 servings.

Paulette Klaja, Xi Delta Lambda
Pittsburg, Pennsylvania

POTATO BREAD

1 cup Potato Starter	1½ cups warm water
¼ cup sugar	6 cups unbleached or
½ cup oil	bread flour
1 teaspoon salt	Butter, melted

Combine first 5 ingredients in bowl. Add flour; mix well. Dough will be stiff. Place in large greased bowl; brush with oil. Cover lightly with plastic wrap. Let rise at room temperature overnight. Punch dough down; divide into 3 portions. Knead each portion on lightly floured surface until smooth and elastic. Shape into loaf; place in loaf pan sprayed with nonstick cooking spray. Brush with oil. Let rise, lightly covered with plastic wrap, for 6 to 11 hours or until doubled in bulk. Bake on bottom rack of oven at 350 degrees for 30 to 35 minutes or until golden. Brush tops with butter. Cool on wire rack. Yield: 3 loaves.

POTATO STARTER

1 package dry yeast	2 teaspoons salt
2 cups warm water	3 tablespoons instant
½ cup instant potato	potato flakes
flakes	¾ cup sugar
½ cup sugar	1 cup warm water

Dissolve yeast in ½ cup warm water in bowl. Stir in 1½ cups warm water, ½ cup potato flakes, ½ cup sugar and 2 teaspoons salt. Let stand, lightly covered, at room temperature for 24 hours. Store in refrigerator. Remove from refrigerator every 3 to 5 days. Add 3 tablespoons potato flakes, ¾ cup sugar and 1 cup warm water; mix well. Let stand at room temperature. Remove 1 cup Starter to use, give away or discard. Refrigerate remaining starter.

Deanne Walters, Delta Kappa
Ellisville, Mississippi

PAM'S CINNAMON ROLLS

2 packages dry yeast	Margarine, softened
2½ cups warm water	Brown sugar
1 2-layer package yellow cake mix	Cinnamon
	Nuts
4½ cups all-purpose flour	Raisins

Dissolve yeast in warm water in bowl. Add cake mix and flour; mix well. Knead on floured surface until smooth and elastic. Place in greased bowl, turning to grease surface. Let rise, covered, until doubled in bulk. Roll to ¼-inch thickness on floured surface. Spread with margarine. Sprinkle with brown sugar, cinnamon, nuts and raisins. Roll as for jelly roll; cut into ½-inch slices. Arrange in 2 greased 9x13-inch baking pans. Let rise until doubled in bulk. Bake at 350 degrees for 15 to 20 minutes or until golden brown. Garnish with confectioners' sugar glaze if desired. Yield: 3 to 4 dozen.

Fran Ebert, Epsilon Mu
Topeka, Kansas

JUST RIGHT ROLLS

1 package dry yeast	1 egg
1 cup warm water	1 teaspoon salt
¼ cup sugar	2½ cups all-purpose flour
¼ cup margarine	

Dissolve yeast in warm water in mixer bowl. Add sugar, margarine, egg, salt and 1½ cups flour; beat until smooth. Let rise, covered, in warm place for 1 hour. Stir in remaining 1 cup flour. Spoon into greased muffin cups. Let rise for 1 hour. Bake at 375 degrees until golden brown. Yield: 1 dozen.

Paula Middleton, Xi Mu Eta
Houston, Texas

REFRIGERATOR ROLLS

⅓ cup shortening	1 teaspoon sugar
⅓ to ½ cup sugar	¼ cup lukewarm water
1 tablespoon salt	2 eggs
2 cups boiling water	7 cups all-purpose flour
2 cakes yeast	

Combine shortening, ⅓ to ½ cup sugar, salt and boiling water in bowl; mix well. Cool to lukewarm. Dissolve yeast and 1 teaspoon sugar in lukewarm water. Add yeast and eggs to shortening mixture; mix well. Add 4 cups flour; beat until smooth. Stir in remaining flour. Store, covered, in refrigerator. Shape as desired. Place in greased baking pan. Let rise, covered, in warm place for 1 hour. Bake at 400 degrees for 20 to 25 minutes or until light brown. Yield: 3 dozen.

Linda Hawkins, Preceptor Delta
Cookeville, Tennessee

CHEESE-ONION TWISTS

2 teaspoons minced onion	2 tablespoons water
1 tablespoon butter, softened	½ cup buttermilk baking mix
2 tablespoons shredded Cheddar cheese	Melted butter
	Dillweed

Combine onion, 1 tablespoon butter and cheese in bowl; mix well. Mix water with baking mix in bowl; shape into ball. Knead 5 times on floured surface. Roll into ¼-inch thick rectangle. Spread onion mixture over ⅔ of dough, leaving 1 long edge uncovered. Fold dough into thirds lengthwise, folding uncovered edge over first. Press edges to seal. Cut lengthwise into 6 strips. Place on ungreased baking sheet, twisting each strip twice. Brush with butter. Sprinkle with dillweed. Bake at 325 degrees for 10 minutes. Yield: 6 twists.

Mary C. Shapard, Epsilon Psi
Shelbyville, Tennessee

SPOON ROLLS

1 package dry yeast	¼ cup sugar
2 cups lukewarm water	¾ cup melted shortening
4 cups self-rising flour	1 egg, well beaten

Dissolve yeast in lukewarm water in bowl. Add remaining ingredients; mix well. Spoon into buttered muffin cups. Bake at 450 degrees for 20 minutes. Yield: 2 dozen. Note: May store batter in covered container in refrigerator for several days.

Beverly Davis, Epsilon Kappa
Nashville, Tennessee

HERBED CHEESE ROLLS

8 to 12 sourdough rolls	½ to 1 teaspoon lemon-pepper seasoning
½ cup butter, softened	
½ teaspoon basil	8 ounces Cheddar cheese, sliced
½ teaspoon oregano	
2 cloves of garlic, minced	

Slice rolls horizontally to form pockets. Spread cut sides with mixture of butter, basil, oregano, garlic and lemon-pepper. Place slice cheese in each roll. Wrap each roll in foil. Bake at 350 degrees for 15 to 20 minutes. Yield: 8 to 12 servings.

Wendy T. Kircher, Zeta Eta
Bellevue, Washington

HOT HERB BREAD

1 loaf French bread	1 tablespoon chopped chives
½ cup margarine, softened	
½ teaspoon dillweed	2 tablespoons chopped parsley

Slice loaf diagonally to but not through bottom. Combine margarine and herbs in bowl; mix well. Spread bread slices with herb mixture. Wrap loaf in foil. Bake at 400 degrees for 15 minutes. Yield: 6 to 8 servings.

Jackie Vogler, Xi Sigma Pi
Hilltop Lakes, Texas

UNFORGETTABLE ROLLS

½ cup chopped pecans	1 package butterscotch pudding and pie filling mix
24 frozen dinner rolls	
½ cup packed brown sugar	½ cup melted butter
1 tablespoon cinnamon	

Sprinkle pecans in greased 9x13-inch baking pan. Arrange frozen rolls in prepared pan. Mix brown sugar, cinnamon and pudding mix in bowl. Sprinkle over rolls. Drizzle with butter. Let rise, covered, in warm place overnight. Bake at 350 degrees for 20 minutes. Invert onto serving plate immediately. Yield: 8 servings.

Judy Swope, Alpha Tau
Kansas City, Missouri

ZESTY FRENCH BREAD

1 8-ounce bottle of zesty Italian salad dressing	1 loaf French bread

Shake salad dressing until well mixed. Split bread lengthwise. Brush cut surfaces with salad dressing, reassemble loaf. Brush top of loaf with salad dressing. Place on baking sheet. Bake at 400 degrees until heated through. Yield: 6 servings.

Brenda Pringle, Xi Alpha Nu
Florence, South Carolina

SOUR CREAM HOT CAKES

2 eggs, beaten	¼ teaspoon soda
2 tablespoons all-purpose flour	Dash of salt
	1 cup sour cream
2 tablespoons sugar	

Combine eggs, flour, sugar, soda, salt and sour cream in bowl; mix well. Spoon onto hot griddle. Bake until brown on both sides. Yield: 4 servings.

Linda L. Schlegel, Delta Delta Xi
Richmond, California

RICE WAFFLES

1 cup all-purpose flour	1½ cups buttermilk
2 teaspoons baking powder	⅓ cup melted shortening
	1 cup cooked rice
½ teaspoon salt	½ cup butter
1 tablespoon sugar	1 cup maple syrup
3 eggs, separated	

Sift flour, baking powder, salt and sugar into large bowl. Beat egg yolks in bowl until thick. Add buttermilk and shortening; mix well. Add flour mixture; mix well. Fold in rice. Beat egg whites until stiff peaks form. Fold gently into rice mixture. Bake in hot waffle iron until golden. Beat butter at high speed in medium bowl. Add syrup gradually, beating until mixture is light and fluffy. Serve with waffles. Store remaining maple butter in refrigerator.

Nancy Black, Xi Iota Sigma
La Canada, California

Holiday Desserts

ALMOND SHEET DESSERT

½ gallon vanilla ice cream, softened	1 cup butter, softened
½ cup Bourbon	2 tablespoons almond extract
Several macaroons, crumbled	2 cups graham cracker crumbs
1 16-ounce package confectioners' sugar	1 2-ounce package shaved almonds, toasted

Mix softened ice cream, Bourbon and macaroons in bowl. Freeze until serving time. Cream confectioners' sugar and butter in bowl. Add almond extract, 1 cup graham cracker crumbs and almonds; mix well. Roll on cookie sheet to ½-inch thickness. Chill until serving time. Cut into 2-inch squares. Top each square with scoop of ice cream; sprinkle with remaining graham cracker crumbs.

Rene Francis, Epsilon Psi
Shelbyville, Tennessee

APPLE KUCHEN

½ cup margarine, softened	½ cup sugar
1 2-layer package yellow cake mix	1 20-ounce can pie-sliced apples, drained
½ cup flaked coconut	1 cup sour cream
1 teaspoon cinnamon	2 egg yolks

Cut margarine into cake mix in bowl until crumbly. Mix in coconut. Pat into ungreased 9x13-inch baking pan, forming slight edge. Bake at 350 degrees for 10 minutes. Combine cinnamon and sugar. Arrange apples on warm crust. Sprinkle with cinnamon-sugar. Blend sour cream and egg yolks; drizzle over apples. Bake for 25 minutes or until edges are light brown; do not overbake. Serve warm. Yield: 12 servings.

Pat Hamlin, Chi Phi
Lompoc, California

BANANAS FOSTER

¼ cup butter	4 large bananas
⅓ cup packed brown sugar	2 tablespoons 151-proof rum
½ teaspoon cinnamon	Vanilla ice cream

Melt butter in saucepan. Add brown sugar and cinnamon. Bring to a boil, stirring constantly. Reduce heat. Cut bananas into thick slices. Add to brown sugar mixture. Simmer for several minutes. Heat rum until warm. Pour over bananas; ignite. Serve over vanilla ice cream. Yield: 4 servings.

Michel Elsbernd, Preceptor Beta Delta
Calmar, Iowa

BANANA SPLIT CAKE

2 cups graham cracker crumbs	5 bananas, sliced
½ cup melted margarine	16 ounces whipped topping
8 ounces cream cheese, softened	1 4-ounce jar maraschino cherries
2 eggs	1 6-ounce package butter brickle chips
2 cups confectioners' sugar	
1 13½-ounce can crushed pineapple	

Combine graham cracker crumbs and margarine in bowl. Pat into 9x13-inch dish. Freeze for 15 minutes. Combine cream cheese and eggs in bowl. Beat until blended. Add confectioners' sugar; mix well. Spread over graham cracker layer. Layer pineapple, bananas, whipped topping, cherries and brickle chips on top. Chill for 1½ hours. Yield: 12 to 16 servings.

B.J. Tueller, Beta Lambda
Evanston, Wyoming

ORIGINAL BANANA SPLIT DESSERT

1 cup chocolate chips	1 recipe graham cracker crust
½ cup margarine	
2 cups packed confectioners' sugar	3 large bananas, sliced
1½ cups evaporated milk	½ gallon Neopolitan ice cream
1 teaspoon vanilla extract	

Combine chocolate chips, margarine, confectioners' sugar, evaporated milk and vanilla in double boiler pan. Cook over hot water until chocolate melts. Cook for 8 minutes longer, stirring constantly. Cool. Pat graham cracker crust into 9x13-inch dish. Arrange bananas on top. Slice ice cream. Place on top of bananas. Pour chocolate sauce over top. Freeze until serving time. Cut into squares. Yield: 10 to 12 servings.

Julie Bargman, Iota Phi
Radman, Iowa

BANANA SPLIT DESSERT

2 cups graham cracker crumbs	1 15-ounce can crushed pineapple
½ cup sugar	16 ounces whipped topping
½ cup melted butter	
2 egg whites	½ cup chopped pecans
1 teaspoon vanilla extract	1 4-ounce jar maraschino cherries, drained
2 cups confectioners' sugar	½ cup (about) chocolate syrup
½ cup melted butter	
3 bananas, sliced	

Combine first 3 ingredients in bowl; mix well. Press into 9x13-inch dish. Combine egg whites, vanilla, confectioners' sugar and ½ cup melted butter in mixer bowl. Beat for 10 minutes. Pour into prepared dish. Layer sliced bananas, pineapple and whipped topping over mixture. Sprinkle with pecans and cherries. Drizzle chocolate syrup over top. Chill until serving time. Yield: 12 servings.

Lisa Gilmore, Epsilon Chi
Lafayette, Tennessee

BANANA SPLIT CAKE DESSERT

2½ cups graham cracker crumbs	1 teaspoon vanilla extract
½ cup melted margarine	5 or 6 bananas, sliced
2 tablespoons sugar	2 20-ounce cans crushed pineapple, drained
3 eggs	16 ounces whipped topping
3 cups confectioners' sugar	Finely chopped nuts
1 cup margarine, softened	Coconut

Combine first 3 ingredients in bowl; mix well. Pat into 9x13-inch dish. Cream eggs, confectioners' sugar, softened margarine and vanilla in mixer bowl for 15 minutes. Spread in prepared dish. Layer banana slices, well-drained pineapple and whipped topping over creamed mixture. Sprinkle with chopped nuts and coconut. Garnish with maraschino cherries. Refrigerate overnight. Yield: 12 to 15 servings.

Bev Smith, Preceptor Alpha Kappa
Fresno, California

BLUEBERRY SUPREME

1 12-ounce package vanilla wafers, crushed	2 eggs
½ cup butter, softened	1 22-ounce can blueberry pie filling
1 cup sifted confectioners' sugar	1 cup whipped cream
	½ cup chopped pecans

Sprinkle half the vanilla wafer crumbs in 9-inch square dish. Cream butter and confectioners' sugar in mixer bowl until light and fluffy. Add eggs 1 at a time, beating well after each addition. Spread in prepared dish. Layer blueberry pie filling, whipped cream, pecans and remaining vanilla wafer crumbs on top. Chill until serving time. Yield: 6 servings.

Veda Dabney, Beta Lambda
Evanston, Wyoming

CHERRY ANGEL DESSERT

1 angel food cake	1 cup sour cream
1 20-ounce can cherry pie filling	1 4-ounce package vanilla instant pudding mix
1½ cups milk	

Cut enough cake into ½-inch cubes to measure 8 cups. Place half the cake cubes in deep 8x8-inch pan. Reserve ⅓ cup pie filling. Spoon remaining pie filling over cake in pan. Add remaining cake cubes. Combine milk, sour cream and pudding mix in bowl; blend well. Spoon over cake. Chill for 5 hours or longer. Cut into squares. Garnish with remaining pie filling. Yield: 9 servings.

Marian Giffen, Preceptor Alpha Zeta
Arlington, Texas

LICKIN' GOOD CHERRY DESSERT

1 cup all-purpose flour	½ teaspoon baking
½ cup margarine,	powder
softened	1 teaspoon vanilla extract
2 tablespoons	2½ cups pitted sour
confectioners' sugar	cherries
2 eggs, beaten	Pinch of salt
1 cup sugar	¼ cup all-purpose flour
½ cup coconut	½ cup chopped nuts

Combine 1 cup flour, margarine and confectioners' sugar in bowl; mix well. Pat into 8x8-inch square baking dish. Bake at 350 degrees for 15 minutes or until light brown. Beat eggs and sugar in bowl until thick. Add remaining ingredients; mix well. Pour over baked layer. Bake for 30 minutes longer. Serve with whipped topping or ice cream. Yield: 8 to 12 servings.

Norma McConnell, Laureate Gamma Phi
Arvada, Colorado

BAKED CHEESECAKE

16 ounces cream cheese,	6 tablespoons all-purpose
softened	flour, sifted
2 cups small curd	2 tablespoons lemon
cottage cheese	juice
1½ cups sugar	1 teaspoon vanilla extract
4 eggs	½ cup melted butter
6 tablespoons cornstarch	2 cups sour cream

Beat cream cheese and cottage cheese in mixer bowl until fluffy. Mix in sugar gradually. Add lightly beaten eggs 1 at a time, mixing well after each addition. Add cornstarch, flour, lemon juice and vanilla; blend well. Add cooled butter and sour cream; beat until very smooth. Pour into buttered 9-inch springform pan. Bake at 325 degrees for 1 hour and 10 minutes. Turn off oven. Let stand in closed oven for 2 hours. Refrigerate until serving time. Place on serving plate; remove side of pan. May top with favorite fresh fruit. Yield: 10 to 12 servings.

Judy Y. Rich, Epsilon Chi
Lafayette, Tennessee

CHOCOLATE CHEESECAKE

1 cup chocolate wafer	12 ounces semisweet
crumbs	chocolate chips, melted
2 tablespoons melted	4 eggs
butter	2 teaspoons vanilla extract
24 ounces cream cheese,	
softened	
1 14-ounce can	
sweetened condensed	
milk	

Mix chocolate wafer crumbs with melted butter. Press into 9-inch springform pan. Beat cream cheese in mixer bowl until fluffy. Add condensed milk; beat until smooth. Add melted chocolate, eggs and vanilla; beat until smooth. Pour into prepared pan. Bake at 300 degrees for 1 hour and 5 minutes or until cheesecake springs back when touched lightly. Cool to room temperature. Chill until serving time. Place on serving plate; remove side of pan. Yield: 10 to 12 servings.

Lisa Seckora, Xi Zeta
The Dalles, Oregon

CREAM CHEESECAKE

1¼ cups graham cracker	1½ cups sugar
crumbs	5 eggs
2 tablespoons melted	24 ounces sour cream
butter	1½ teaspoons vanilla
2 tablespoons sugar	extract
24 ounces cream cheese,	
softened	

Sprinkle greased 9-inch springform pan with 2 table-spoons cracker crumbs. Mix remaining crumbs with butter and 2 tablespoons sugar in bowl. Press over bottom of prepared pan. Beat cream cheese in mixer bowl until fluffy. Add 1½ cups sugar gradually, beating until light. Beat in eggs 1 at a time. Fold in sour cream and vanilla. Pour into pan. Bake at 375 degrees for 45 minutes. Turn off oven. Let cheesecake stand in closed oven for 1 hour. Place on serving plate. Remove side of pan. Chill overnight. Yield: 12 to 16 servings.

Marilyn Kelly, Xi Gamma Upsilon
Dunedin, Florida

DREAM WHIP CHEESECAKE

2 cups graham cracker	2 envelopes whipped
crumbs	topping mix
2 tablespoons sugar	1 cup cold milk
1 tablespoon all-purpose	1 teaspoon vanilla extract
flour	1 20-ounce can cherry
¼ cup melted butter	pie filling
16 ounces cream cheese,	
softened	

Combine first 4 ingredients in bowl; mix well. Press into buttered loaf pan. Chill until firm. Beat cream cheese in bowl until fluffy. Set aside. Combine whipped topping mix, milk and vanilla in mixer bowl. Beat until soft peaks form. Fold in cream cheese. Pour into prepared pan. Chill until set. Spoon pie filling over top. Chill for 4 hours to overnight. Yield: 8 servings.

Helen M. Harris, Xi Epsilon Alpha
Woodbridge, Virginia

LEMON CHEESECAKE SQUARES

1 2-layer package lemon cake mix	2 eggs
½ cup butter, softened	½ cup sugar
1 egg	2 teaspoons lemon juice
16 ounces cream cheese, softened	½ teaspoon vanilla extract
	Confectioners' sugar

Combine cake mix, butter and 1 egg in bowl. Beat with mixer until crumbly. Press over bottom of greased and floured 9x13-inch baking pan. Bake at 350 degrees for 8 minutes. Beat cream cheese in mixer bowl until fluffy. Add 2 eggs, sugar, lemon juice and vanilla; mix well. Pour over hot crust. Bake for 25 minutes or until edges are light brown. Sprinkle with confectioners' sugar. Store in refrigerator. Yield: 16 servings.

Note: Do not use cake mix with pudding.

Sharon H. Childs, Xi Kappa Theta
DuQuoin, Illinois

SIMPLE CHEESECAKE

30 graham crackers, crushed	1 3-ounce package lemon gelatin
½ cup melted margarine	1 cup boiling water
1 cup sugar	Juice of 1 lemon
8 ounces cream cheese, softened	1 12-ounce can evaporated milk, chilled

Mix crumbs and melted margarine in bowl; press into two 9-inch pie plates. Cream sugar and cream cheese in bowl until light and fluffy. Dissolve gelatin in boiling water in bowl. Add lemon juice. Cool. Fold into cream cheese mixture. Beat evaporated milk in chilled mixer bowl until soft peaks form. Fold into gelatin mixture. Spoon into prepared pie plates. Chill until firm. Top with favorite pie filling or fresh strawberries. Yield: 16 servings.

Velda Kloke, Xi Gamma Zeta
Harvard, Nebraska

CHOCOLATE PUDDING DELIGHT

1½ cups graham cracker crumbs	¼ cup sugar
¼ cup sugar	2 tablespoons milk
½ cup melted butter or margarine	8 ounces whipped topping
8 ounces cream cheese, softened	2 4-ounce packages chocolate instant pudding mix
	2½ cups milk

Combine graham cracker crumbs, ¼ cup sugar and butter in bowl; mix well. Press into bottom of 9x13-inch dish. Combine cream cheese, ¼ cup sugar and 2 tablespoons milk in bowl. Beat until creamy. Fold in half the whipped topping. Spread over crumb layer. Prepare pudding mix according to package directions, using 2½ cups milk. Spread over cream cheese layer. Chill for several hours. Spread remaining whipped topping over pudding. Garnish with grated chocolate or chopped nuts. Yield: 12 to 15 servings.

Sue Lynch, Xi Chi
Waterbury, Connecticut

CHOCOLATE DELIGHT

1 cup all-purpose flour	1 cup whipped topping
½ cup melted margarine	2 4-ounce packages chocolate instant pudding mix
½ cup chopped pecans	
8 ounces cream cheese, softened	3½ cups milk
1 cup confectioners' sugar	

Combine first 3 ingredients in bowl; mix well. Press into 9x13-inch baking pan. Bake at 350 degrees for 15 minutes. Cool. Blend cream cheese and confectioners' sugar in bowl. Add whipped topping; mix well. Spread over baked layer. Chill in refrigerator. Mix pudding mix and milk in bowl. Pour over cream cheese layer. Chill until set. Garnish with additional whipped topping and chopped pecans. Chill. Yield: 12 to 15 servings.

Claudia Holland, Xi Gamma Kappa
Havelock, North Carolina

QUICK AND EASY CHOCOLATE ECLAIRS

½ cup water	Christmas sprinkles
¼ cup butter	1 4-ounce package vanilla instant pudding mix
½ cup self-rising flour	
2 eggs	
1 can chocolate fudge frosting	

Bring water and butter to a boil in saucepan. Stir in flour. Cook over low heat for 1 minute or until mixture forms ball, stirring constantly; remove from heat. Add eggs; beat until smooth. Drop by scant ¼ cupfuls 3 inches apart onto ungreased baking sheet. Bake in preheated 400-degree oven for 35 minutes or until golden. Cool. Cut off tops; remove soft dough. Frost tops; decorate with sprinkles. Prepare pudding using package directions. Fill puffs with pudding. Replace tops. Yield: 6 servings.

Sheri Schlemper, Omicron Phi
Union, Missouri

ECLAIR CAKE DESSERT

1 cup water	8 ounces cream cheese, softened
½ cup margarine	
1 cup flour	12 to 16 ounces whipped topping
4 eggs	
2 4-ounce packages vanilla instant pudding mix	1 8-ounce can chocolate syrup

Bring water and margarine to a boil in saucepan. Add flour; stir until mixture forms ball. Remove from heat. Let stand for 2 minutes. Add eggs 1 at a time, mixing well after each addition. Spread on 10x15-inch baking sheet sprayed with cooking spray; shape rim. Bake at 375 degrees for 1 hour. Cool for 15 minutes. Prepare pudding mix according to package directions, using ½ cup less milk. Blend in cream cheese. Pour over crust. Spread with whipped topping. Drizzle with chocolate syrup. Chill. Yield: 15 to 20 servings.

Marilyn Borras, Xi Epsilon Alpha
Stafford, Virginia

CHOCOLATE ECLAIR DESSERT

1 pound honey graham crackers	1½ cups confectioners' sugar
2 4-ounce packages French vanilla instant pudding mix	3 tablespoons milk
	1 tablespoon vanilla extract
2½ cups milk	2 envelopes premelted chocolate
4½ ounces whipped topping	
3 tablespoons butter, softened	2 teaspoons light corn syrup

Line buttered 9x13-inch dish with graham crackers. Prepare pudding mix according to package directions, using 2½ cups milk. Fold in whipped topping. Layer pudding and remaining graham crackers ½ at a time in prepared dish. Blend butter, confectioners' sugar, milk and vanilla in bowl. Add chocolate and corn syrup; mix until of spreading consistency, adding a small amount of water if necessary. Spread over graham crackers. Chill for 12 hours. Yield: 12 servings.

Teresa Puccio, Xi Eta Pi
North East, Pennsylvania

FROSTED CHOCOLATE ECLAIR RING

1 cup water	8 ounces whipped topping
½ cup margarine	
1 cup all-purpose flour	2 squares semisweet chocolate
4 eggs	
2 small packages French vanilla instant pudding mix	2 tablespoons margarine
	1 cup confectioners' sugar
	1 tablespoon milk
2½ cups milk	1 teaspoon vanilla extract

Bring water and ½ cup margarine to a boil in saucepan; remove from heat. Stir in flour. Add eggs 1 at a time, mixing well after each addition. Spread into ring on greased pizza pan. Bake at 375 degrees for 40 to 45 minutes or until light brown. Slice horizontally into 2 layers. Beat pudding mix with 2½ cups milk in bowl. Fold in whipped topping. Spread between layers. Place on serving plate. Melt chocolate and 2 tablespoons margarine in double boiler pan. Add confectioners' sugar and remaining ingredients; mix well. Drizzle over ring. Yield: 12 servings.

Sharon H. Childs, Xi Kappa Theta
DuQuoin, Illinois

CHOCOLATE ICEBOX DESSERT

½ cup butter or margarine, softened	5 graham crackers, crushed
1 cup sifted confectioners' sugar	¼ cup wheat germ
	½ cup finely chopped nuts
2 egg yolks	
2 squares unsweetened chocolate, melted	1 to 2 cups whipped topping
3 egg whites, stiffly beaten	Grated chocolate

Cream butter and confectioners' sugar in mixer bowl until light and fluffy. Add egg yolks. Beat until light and fluffy. Fold in stiffly beaten egg whites gently. Sprinkle mixture of graham cracker crumbs and wheat germ in lightly greased 8-inch square dish. Spoon chocolate mixture over crumbs. Sprinkle with nuts. Spread whipped topping over all. Garnish with grated chocolate. Chill in refrigerator. Yield: 10 to 14 servings.

Note: Tint whipped topping pink or green if desired.

Adeline Hamilton, Laureate Beta
Rapid City, South Dakota

FRUIT-FILLED CHOCOLATE TACOS

¼ cup all-purpose flour	1 egg white
¼ cup sugar	⅛ teaspoon salt
1 tablespoon cocoa	½ cup sliced strawberries
2 tablespoons skim milk	½ cup sliced mango
2 tablespoons oil	1 kiwifruit, peeled, sliced
1 teaspoon vanilla extract	1 starfruit, sliced

Combine first 8 ingredients in mixer bowl. Beat at medium speed until smooth. Chill, covered, for 2 hours. Pour 3 tablespoons batter into hot 8-inch skillet with nonstick coating. Tilt to coat bottom of pan. Bake for 2 minutes or until surface appears dry; turn. Bake for 1 minute longer. Place wire rack over large deep bowl. Drape tortilla darker side up over 1 to 2 bars of wire rack to form shell. Cool for 15 to 20 minutes. Fill with strawberries, mango and kiwifruit. Garnish with starfruit. Yield: 6 servings.

Note: Store unfilled tortilla shells in airtight container until ready to serve.

Katheryn Ray, Xi Epsilon Sigma
Oscoda, Michigan

MISSISSIPPI MUD

1 cup melted margarine	½ cup margarine, softened
⅓ cup cocoa	
4 eggs	⅓ cup cocoa
2 cups sugar	1 16-ounce package confectioners' sugar
1½ cups chopped nuts	
1 cup flaked coconut	½ cup evaporated milk
1 12-ounce jar marshmallow creme	1 teaspoon vanilla extract

Combine first 6 ingredients in bowl; mix well. Pour into ungreased 9x13-inch baking pan. Bake at 350 degrees for 30 minutes or until toothpick inserted near center comes out clean. Spread marshmallow creme over hot baked layer. Cool. Combine softened margarine and cocoa in mixer bowl; blend well. Add confectioners' sugar, evaporated milk and vanilla; beat until of spreading consistency. Spread over marshmallow layer. Garnish with nuts. Yield: 3 dozen.

Jan Angotti, Preceptor Nu
Walla Walla, Washington

CRISPY HOLIDAY NESTS

1 7-ounce jar marshmallow creme	Confectioners' sugar Holiday M & M's
¼ cup peanut butter	chocolate peanut
2 tablespoons melted butter	candies
1 5-ounce can chow mein noodles	

Combine marshmallow creme, peanut butter and butter in bowl; mix well. Stir in noodles. Shape by ⅓ cupfuls into nests on greased cookie sheet. Let stand until firm. Dust bottoms of nests with confectioners' sugar. Fill with candies. Yield: 10 to 12 nests.

Stacey Freese, Alpha
Plymouth, Nebraska

CROWN JEWEL DESSERT

1 3-ounce package cherry gelatin	1 3-ounce package lemon gelatin
1 3-ounce package lime gelatin	¼ cup sugar
1 3-ounce package orange gelatin	1 cup boiling water
3 cups boiling water	½ cup pineapple juice
1½ cups cold water	2 envelopes whipped topping mix

Prepare cherry, lime and orange gelatins separately according to package directions, using 1 cup boiling water and ½ cup cold water for each. Pour into separate 8x8-inch pans. Chill for 3 hours or until firm. Cut into ½-inch cubes. Dissolve lemon gelatin and sugar in 1 cup boiling water in bowl. Add pineapple juice. Chill until slightly thickened. Prepare whipped topping mix using package directions. Fold into lemon gelatin. Reserve several gelatin cubes for garnish. Fold remaining cubes into lemon gelatin. Spoon into 9-inch springform pan. Chill for 5 hours to overnight. Run spatula around inside edge of pan. Place on serving plate; remove side of pan. Garnish with reserved gelatin cubes. Yield: 16 servings.

Barbara Mills, Xi Chi
Stephens City, Virginia

DATE LOAF

1 16-ounce package graham crackers, crushed	16 ounces marshmallows, chopped
1 16-ounce package pitted dates, chopped	1 cup chopped pecans 1 cup cream

Combine cracker crumbs, dates, marshmallows and pecans in bowl; mix well. Stir in cream. Shape into roll. Wrap in dampened cloth and waxed paper. Store in refrigerator or freezer. Slice as desired. Yield: 20 servings.

Norma Jean McPherson, Laureate Iota
Midwest City, Oklahoma

DATE ROLL

2 cups sugar	1 cup chopped dates
1 cup milk	1 cup chopped pecans
⅓ cup light corn syrup	

Combine sugar, milk, corn syrup and dates in saucepan. Cook to 234 to 240 degrees on candy thermometer, softball stage. Add pecans. Cool to lukewarm; do not stir. Beat until mixture thickens and loses its luster. Pour onto cold damp cloth; shape into roll. Chill until firm but slightly warm. Slice as desired. Yield: 2 pounds.

Margaret Bell, Xi Psi
Oklahoma City, Oklahoma

FOUR-FRUIT FREEZE

1 cup crushed pineapple	½ cup chopped pecans
½ cup chopped maraschino cherries	1 cup maraschino cherries 1 gallon pineapple
½ cup mandarin oranges	sherbet, softened
½ cup fruit cocktail	

Drain fruit. Combine with remaining ingredients in bowl; mix well. Spoon into freezer container. Freeze until firm. Yield: 24 servings.

BEST OREO ICE CREAM DESSERT

16 ounces Oreo cookies	16 ounces whipped topping
½ gallon vanilla ice cream, softened	

Crush cookies in food processor. Combine cookie crumbs, ice cream and whipped topping in large bowl; mix well. Spread in 9x13-inch cake pan. Freeze until firm. Yield: 12 to 15 servings.

Linda Manning, Epsilon Kappa
Nashville, Tennessee

BUSTER BAR

¼ cup melted margarine	1½ cups evaporated milk
½ 16-ounce package Oreo cookies, crumbled	⅔ cup milk chocolate chips
½ gallon vanilla ice cream, softened	½ cup butter 2 teaspoons vanilla extract
2 cups confectioners' sugar	

Combine melted margarine and cookie crumbs in 9x13-inch baking dish. Bake at 350 degrees for 5 minutes. Cool. Spread ice cream over cookie layer. Freeze until firm. Combine confectioners' sugar, evaporated milk, milk chocolate chips and butter in saucepan. Bring to a boil. Cook for 8 minutes. Cool. Pour over ice cream layer. Freeze until serving time. Yield: 12 servings.

Betty Spurgeon, Preceptor Beta Beta
Columbus, Indiana

BUSTER BAR DESSERT

1 16-ounce package
   Oreo cookies, crushed
½ cup melted margarine
½ gallon vanilla ice
   cream, softened
1 16-ounce jar salted
   Spanish peanuts
2 cups confectioners'
   sugar
⅔ cup chocolate chips
½ cup margarine
1 13-ounce can
   evaporated milk

Combine Oreo crumbs and melted margarine in 9x13-inch dish; press evenly over bottom. Spoon ice cream over crumbs. Sprinkle with peanuts. Freeze until firm. Combine confectioners' sugar, chocolate chips, ½ cup margarine and evaporated milk in saucepan. Bring to a boil over low heat. Simmer for 10 minutes. Cool completely. Pour over frozen layer. Freeze until firm. Let stand at room temperature for several minutes before serving.
Yield: 10 to 12 servings.

Julie Bargman, Iota Phi
Rodman, Iowa

FROZEN GREEN CHRISTMAS DESSERT

1 quart vanilla ice cream
1 pint lime sherbet
¼ cup Crème de Menthe
2 cups whipped topping

Combine ice cream, sherbet and Crème de Menthe in bowl. Beat until smooth. Fold in whipped topping. Freeze until firm. Garnish with shaved chocolate.
Yield: 12 to 15 servings.
Note: May freeze in 9x11-inch dish lined with Oreos or in two 9-inch chocolate cookie pie shells.

Reva J. Falk, Preceptor Alpha Epsilon
Tuscon, Arizona

FROZEN FRUIT DREAM CUPS

½ cup sugar
8 ounces cream cheese,
   softened
1 teaspoon Brandy extract
1 teaspoon lemon juice
8 ounces whipped topping

Cream sugar and cream cheese in bowl. Add flavoring, lemon juice and food coloring if desired; blend well. Fold in whipped topping. Spoon into 8 portions on waxed paper-lined sheet. Shape as desired into shells. Freeze until firm. Fill with assorted fresh fruit or canned cherry pie filling. Yield: 8 servings.

Carol Brakeall, Eta Alpha
Shawnee, Kansas

EASY CHOCOLATE ICE CREAM

1 15-ounce can
   sweetened condensed
   milk
9 ounces whipped topping
1 gallon chocolate milk

Combine all ingredients in ice cream freezer container. Freeze using manufacturer's directions.
Yield: 1½ gallons.
Note: May use whole milk instead of chocolate milk and add fruits of choice.

Beverly Davis, Epsilon Kappa
Nashville, Tennessee

CAMERON'S FROZEN DESSERT

1 cup butter, melted
2 cups crushed pretzels
6 tablespoons sugar
1 14-ounce can
   sweetened condensed
   milk
1 20-ounce can cherry
   pie filling
12 ounces whipped
   topping
1 20-ounce can crushed
   pineapple, drained

Combine first 3 ingredients in bowl; mix well. Press into 9x13-inch baking dish. Bake at 350 degrees for 5 minutes. Combine condensed milk, pie filling, whipped topping and pineapple in bowl; mix well. Pour into pretzel crust. Freeze until firm. Cut into squares. Yield: 12 servings.

Cameron Stimson, Xi Theta
Mayfield, Kentucky

DELICIOUS ICE CREAM

1 pint half and half
1 pint whipping cream
1 4-ounce package
   vanilla ice cream mix
1 14-ounce can
   sweetened condensed
   milk
1 3-ounce package
   vanilla instant
   pudding mix
Lemon flavoring to taste
Chopped bananas to taste
Milk

Combine half and half and whipping cream in bowl; mix well. Stir in ice cream mix gradually. Blend in condensed milk. Stir in pudding mix gradually. Pour into 4-quart ice cream freezer container. Add flavoring and bananas. Add milk to fill line. Freeze according to manufacturer's directions. Spoon into parfait glasses. Serve with orange or lemon thins or homemade cookies. Yield: 20 servings.

Brenda Pringle, Xi Alpha Nu
Florence, South Carolina

CHOCOLATE-PEPPERMINT FREEZER DESSERT

¼ cup melted butter
2 cups vanilla wafer
   crumbs
½ cup butter, softened
1½ cups confectioners'
   sugar
3 ounces sweet chocolate,
   melted
3 eggs, slightly beaten
1½ cups whipping cream
3 tablespoons sugar
1 8-ounce package
   miniature marshmallows
½ cup crushed hard
   peppermint candy

Combine melted butter and vanilla wafer crumbs in bowl; mix well. Press into 7x11-inch dish. Cream softened butter and confectioners' sugar in mixer bowl. Add chocolate and eggs. Beat until light and fluffy. Pour into prepared dish. Chill until set. Whip cream until foamy. Add sugar gradually, whipping until soft peaks form. Fold in marshmallows. Spoon over chocolate layer. Sprinkle crushed candy on top. Freeze until firm. Cut into squares. Yield: 12 servings.

Marjorie Lessman, Xi Alpha Kappa
Dalton, Nebraska

CRANBERRY ICE

1 16-ounce can jellied cranberry sauce	¾ cup ginger ale

Mash cranberry sauce in bowl. Blend in ginger ale. Freeze until slushy. Beat until fluffy; do not thaw. Freeze until serving time. Yield: 4 to 6 servings.

Jackie Vogler, Xi Sigma Pi
Hilltop Lakes, Texas

MEXICAN ICE

½ gallon vanilla ice cream	4 teaspoons coarsely ground orange rind
½ gallon pineapple-orange sherbet	4 teaspoons grated lemon rind
½ cup Grand Marnier	1 8-ounce bar German's chocolate, grated
½ cup Triple Sec	

Combine ice cream, sherbet, liqueurs, and orange and lemon rind in bowl. Beat until smooth. Spoon into mold. Freeze until firm. Unmold onto serving plate. Sprinkle with chocolate. Yield: 30 servings.

Note: Ice may be served in stemmed goblets, orange shells or chocolate shells.

Greer Neal, Preceptor Alpha Gamma
Scottsdale, Arizona

FROZEN RAINBOW DESSERT

1 angel food cake	½ gallon vanilla ice cream
1 3-ounce package strawberry gelatin	1 16-ounce can blueberries, drained
1 3-ounce package lime gelatin	1 or 2 8-ounce cans mandarin oranges, drained
1 3-ounce package orange gelatin	
1 10-ounce package frozen strawberries, thawed	

Tear cake into bite-sized pieces. Combine each package gelatin with ⅓ of the cake in separate bowls; toss to coat. Combine strawberries and strawberry-flavored cake in tube pan. Spoon ⅓ of the ice cream over cake. Repeat layers with lime-flavored cake and blueberries and orange-flavored cake and oranges and remaining ice cream, ending with ice cream layer. Freeze for 24 hours. Dip tube pan into warm water; loosen with knife. Unmold onto serving plate. Freeze, wrapped, until serving time. Cut into slices. Yield: 16 to 20 servings.

Chris Schroder, Preceptor Epsilon Alpha
Webster, Florida

FROZEN RASPBERRY MOUSSE

1 egg white	1 8-ounce carton raspberry yogurt
¼ cup sugar	
1 cup whipping cream	1 12-ounce can peaches, drained
2 10-ounce packages frozen raspberries, thawed	1 tablespoon water
	1 tablespoon cornstarch

Beat egg white with sugar in mixer bowl until stiff peaks form. Whip whipping cream in bowl until soft peaks form. Purée raspberries. Fold half the purée gently into whipped cream. Fold in yogurt and egg white gently. Pour into serving dish. Freeze until firm. Purée peaches. Combine peach purée and remaining raspberry purée in saucepan. Stir in mixture of water and cornstarch. Cook until thickened, stirring constantly. Remove mousse from freezer 30 minutes before serving. Serve with sauce. Yield: 8 servings.

Patricia Ullrich, Xi Tau
Milfono, Michigan

SILVER TORTE

2 cups sifted all-purpose flour	2 cups sugar
1 cup butter or margarine	Juice and grated rind of 1½ lemons
2 tablespoons sugar	1 cup whipping cream, whipped
1 tablespoon unflavored gelatin	1 cup grated coconut
¾ cup cold water	1 tablespoon grated orange rind
8 eggs, separated	

Combine flour, butter and sugar in bowl; mix until crumbly. Pat into 9x13-inch baking dish. Bake at 350 degrees for 25 to 30 minutes or until golden. Cool completely. Soften gelatin in cold water in bowl; set aside. Beat egg whites until soft peaks form. Add 1 cup sugar gradually, beating until very stiff peaks form; set aside. Combine egg yolks and remaining 1 cup sugar in saucepan; mix well. Add lemon juice, rind and softened gelatin. Cook over low heat until mixture thickens and coats spoon, stirring constantly. Fold hot mixture gently into egg whites. Pour into cooled crust. Chill until set. Spread whipped cream on top. Sprinkle with mixture of coconut and orange rind. Chill for 8 hours or longer. Yield: 12 servings.

Lori McCarley, Pi
Newark, Delaware

FROSTY STRAWBERRY SQUARES

1 cup all-purpose flour	¾ cup sugar
¼ cup packed brown sugar	1 10-ounce package frozen strawberries, thawed
½ cup chopped walnuts	
½ cup butter or margarine	1 cup whipping cream, whipped
2 egg whites	

Combine first 4 ingredients in 9x13-inch baking pan; mix well. Bake at 350 degrees for 20 minutes, stirring frequently. Cool completely. Combine egg whites and sugar in mixer bowl. Beat at high speed for 10 minutes. Add strawberries and juice. Beat for 2 minutes longer. Fold in whipped cream. Pour over crumbs. Freeze for 8 hours or longer. Cut into squares. Yield: 20 servings.

Terrie Richard, Xi Eta Tau
Neosho, Missouri

FRUIT COMPOTE

1 6-ounce can frozen lemonade concentrate, thawed	1 16-ounce package frozen strawberries, thawed
1 6-ounce can frozen orange juice concentrate, thawed	3 bananas, chopped
	1 4-ounce bottle of maraschino cherries
1 20-ounce can pineapple tidbits	1 cup sugar
	2½ cups water

Combine all ingredients in large bowl; mix well. Spoon into small plastic glasses. Freeze until firm. Thaw slightly before serving. Serve slushy. Yield: 16 servings.

Dorothy A. Kramer, Laureate Theta
Omaha, Nebraska

SPARKLING FRUIT BOWL

1 ice bowl	Assorted fruits
Assorted sherbets	

Pour water into large plastic bowl. Place smaller bowl inside; add enough weight to hold smaller bowl in place. Freeze until firm. Remove ice bowl; place on tray. Arrange fresh or silk leaves around bowl. Fill bowl with scoops of assorted sherbet. Top with fresh or frozen fruit. Serve immediately.

Mitzi Smirl, Delta Lambda
Bedford, Texas

FESTIVE FRUIT WREATH

¼ cup butter or margarine	½ cup chopped red candied cherries
40 marshmallows	
1 teaspoon vanilla extract	½ cup chopped green candied cherries
5 cups crisp rice cereal	
½ cup chopped dates	½ cup broken walnuts

Melt butter in saucepan. Add marshmallows. Cook over low heat until marshmallows melt, stirring constantly. Remove form heat. Blend in vanilla. Stir in cereal, dates, cherries and walnuts. Shape into 8-inch wreath on waxed paper-lined surface. Cool. Decorate with candy, confectioners' sugar or icing. Yield: 32 servings.

Dolores Snyder, Xi Alpha Pi
Hagerstown, Maryland

GALA FRUIT WEATH

2 16-ounce cans pear halves	Red food coloring
2 16-ounce cans peach halves	3 to 8 ounces cream cheese, softened
1 16-ounce can sliced pineapple	Candied ginger, minced
	8 ounces (or more) cream cheese, softened
1 16-ounce can peeled apricot halves	Walnut halves
	Fresh kumquats

Drain and chill canned fruit. Pat pears dry with paper towel. Mix several drops of red food coloring with a small amount of water. Pat pears lightly with paper towel dipped in coloring to give light blush. Let stand until dry.

Mix 3 to 8 ounces cream cheese with candied ginger to taste; shape into small balls. Place 1 cream cheese ball in each of half the pear halves. Assemble with remaining pear halves to resemble whole pears. Pipe additional cream cheese around pears with pastry tube. Shape 8 ounces or more cream cheese into small balls; press between walnut halves. Place 1 in each peach half. Reserve remaining cream cheese and walnut balls. Place Fluffy Mayonnaise in center of large round lettuce-lined tray. Arrange Cinnamon Apple Cups in groups of 2 or 3 around mayonnaise. Add pears, peaches, Frosted Grapes and remaining fruit in decorative fashion. Garnish with holly leaves and remaining cream cheese and walnut balls.

FLUFFY MAYONNAISE

½ cup whipping cream	1 cup mayonnaise

Whip whipping cream in bowl until soft peaks form. Fold in mayonnaise until well blended. Spoon into serving dish. Yield: 2 cups.

CINNAMON APPLE CUPS

2 3-ounce packages lemon gelatin	2 cups applesauce
	1 tablespoon lemon juice
½ cup red cinnamon candies	Dash of salt
	3 ounces cream cheese
2 cups boiling water	½ cup broken walnuts

Dissolve gelatin and candies in boiling water in bowl. Add applesauce, lemon juice and salt; mix well. Chill until partially set. Shape cream cheese into tiny balls. Stir cream cheese balls and walnuts into gelatin mixture. Spoon into ⅓-cup molds. Chill until firm. Unmold onto plate. Yield: 15 servings.

FROSTED GRAPES

2 pounds red and green grapes	1 egg white
	1 to 2 cups sugar

Snip grapes into small cluster. Brush with slightly beaten egg white; sprinkle with sugar. Let stand until dry. Yield: 2 pounds.

Bettie Plummer, Laureate Pi
Independence, Missouri

FRUIT PUDDING REFRESHER

1 20-ounce can pineapple chunks	1 16-ounce can fruit cocktail
2 bananas, sliced	1 4-ounce package lemon instant pudding mix
1 cup flaked coconut	
1 11-ounce can mandarin oranges, drained	

Combine pineapple with juice, bananas, coconut, mandarin oranges and fruit cocktail with juice in serving bowl. Stir in pudding mix. Let stand for 5 minutes. Yield: 8 to 10 servings.

Mary Anne Johnson, Beta Lambda
Evanston, Wyoming

GRANDMA GULYBAN'S HUNGARIAN SHEET CAKE DESSERT

1 pound margarine, softened	1 cup sour cream
6½ cups (about) all-purpose flour	4 egg yolks
	1 12-ounce jar apricot preserves
1 cup sugar	4 egg whites, beaten
1 teaspoon soda	2 cups chopped walnuts
½ teaspoon salt	1 12-ounce jar pineapple preserves
Grated rind of 1 lemon	
1 teaspoon vanilla extract	

Cut margarine into 6 cups flour in large bowl until crumbly. Add sugar, soda, salt, lemon rind and vanilla. Add sour cream and egg yolks; mix well to form dough. Add ½ cup flour if necessary to make of handling consistency. Divide into 4 portions. Roll 1 portion into 10x15-inch rectangle on floured surface. Place on greased baking sheet. Spread with apricot preserves. Divide 1 portion dough into several pieces; shape each into long thin rope. Arrange diagonally lattice-fashion over preserves. Brush with beaten egg whites; sprinkle with half the walnuts. Repeat process with remaining dough, pineapple preserves and remaining walnuts. Pierce with fork in several places to prevent bubbling. Bake at 350 degrees for 1 hour. Cut into squares. Yield: 3 dozen.

Mary Ann Madar, Laureate Alpha Delta
Elizabeth Township, Pennsylvania

LEMON CRACKER TORTE

40 Waverly wafers, crushed	1 cup sugar
½ cup melted butter or margarine	1 20-ounce can lemon pie filling
4 egg whites	2 cups whipping cream, whipped

Combine wafer crumbs and butter in bowl; mix well. Press into 9x13-inch baking pan. Beat egg whites until stiff peaks form. Add sugar gradually, beating until very stiff peaks form. Spoon into prepared pan. Bake at 350 degrees for 15 to 20 minutes. Cool. Spread lemon pie filling on baked layer. Top with whipped cream. Chill in refrigerator. Yield: 12 servings.

Gail Engel, Xi Beta Zeta
Brookfield, Wisconsin

HOMEMADE SWEETENED CONDENSED MILK

½ cup hot water	1 cup sugar
2 tablespoons butter or margarine	2 cups dry milk powder

Combine water, butter and sugar in blender container. Process until well mixed. Add milk powder gradually, processing after each addition. Use in any recipe calling for sweetened condensed milk. Store any remaining mixture in closed jar in refrigerator. Yield: 2 cups.

Alice Mikelson, Preceptor Gamma Delta
Port Orchard, Washington

CHOCOLATE MOUSSE EXTRAORDINAIRE

4½ ounces semisweet chocolate chips	3 egg yolks
2 tablespoons Kahlua	9 tablespoons sugar
3 tablespoons orange juice	¾ cup whipping cream

Combine chocolate chips, Kahlua and orange juice in saucepan. Cook over low heat until chocolate melts, stirring constantly. Cool slightly. Combine egg yolks and sugar in food processor container. Process until smooth. Add chocolate mixture. Pulse until mixed. Add whipping cream through feed tube gradually, processing constantly. Pour into serving dishes. Chill until serving time. Garnish with whipped cream and chocolate curls or fresh mint leaves. Yield: 6 to 8 servings.

Carolyn Wyckoff, Preceptor Lambda Xi
Arvada, Colorado

ST. TROPEZ HOLIDAY MOUSSE

1 20-ounce can juice-pack crushed pineapple	1 teaspoon grated lemon rind
1 6-ounce package strawberry gelatin	3 tablespoons fresh lemon juice
1 16-ounce can whole cranberry sauce	¼ teaspoon nutmeg
	2 cups sour cream
	½ cup chopped pecans

Drain pineapple, reserving juice. Add enough water to juice to measure 2 cups. Combine reserved juice and gelatin in saucepan. Bring to a boil, stirring until gelatin dissolves; remove from heat. Add cranberry sauce, lemon rind, lemon juice and nutmeg. Chill until partially set. Add sour cream; blend well. Fold in pineapple and pecans. Pour into 2-quart mold. Chill until firm. Unmold onto serving plate. Yield: 12 servings.

Joan Craig Bown, Xi Kappa Beta
Wellsburg, West Virginia

NUT ROLL

7 eggs, separated	1 teaspoon baking powder
¾ cup sugar	Confectioners' sugar
1½ cups ground nuts	2 cups whipped cream

Brush 10x15-inch jelly roll pan with oil. Line with waxed paper; brush with oil. Beat egg whites in mixer bowl until stiff peaks form. Beat egg yolks and sugar in mixer bowl until thick. Add nuts and baking powder; mix well. Fold in egg whites gently. Spread in prepared pan. Bake at 350 degrees for 15 to 20 minutes or until golden brown; do not overbake. Cool in pan. Cover with damp towel. Chill in refrigerator. Dust top of cake with confectioners' sugar. Invert onto waxed paper. Peel off waxed paper on bottom of cake. Spread stiffly whipped cream on cake. Roll as for jelly roll. Sprinkle with confectioners' sugar. Place on serving plate. Chill until serving time. Cut into slices. Yield: 8 servings.

Carol Jarman, Beta Sigma
New Bern, North Carolina

PINEAPPLE DESSERT FOR TWENTY

1 20-ounce can crushed
  pineapple
1 envelope unflavored
  gelatin
1 large angel food cake
8 ounces miniature
  marshmallows

1 4-ounce jar maraschino
  cherries
1 4-ounce can flaked
  coconut
4 cups whipping cream
¼ teaspoon vanilla extract

Pour pineapple and juice into double boiler. Heat just until warm. Sprinkle gelatin over pineapple. Heat until gelatin dissolves. Break cake into small pieces. Combine cake, marshmallows, cherries and coconut in bowl. Whip cream and vanilla in bowl until soft peaks form. Fold into cake mixture gently. Fold in pineapple gently. Spoon into 9x14-inch dish. Garnish with nuts.
Yield: 10 to 12 servings.

Veda Daleney, Beta Lambda
Evanston, Wyoming

PINEAPPLE DESSERT FOR DIETERS

1 16-ounce can crushed
  pineapple, drained
12 ounces small curd
  cottage cheese

9 ounces whipped topping
1 3-ounce package
  flavored gelatin

Combine all ingredients in bowl; mix well. Chill until serving time. Yield: 12 to 15 servings.

Wanda Odom, Preceptor Epsilon Upsilon
Denison, Texas

PINEAPPLE DELIGHT

1 cup half and half
1 12-ounce package
  miniature marshmallows
8 ounces cream cheese,
  softened

1 20-ounce can pineapple
  chunks, drained
1 4-ounce jar maraschino
  cherries, cut into halves

Combine half and half and marshmallows in bowl; mix well. Chill for several hours, stirring occasionally. Cut cream cheese into pieces. Add to marshmallow mixture; mix well. Stir in pineapple. Chill overnight. Fold in cherries just before serving. Yield: 8 to 10 servings.

Nancy Burkhardt, Xi Gamma Gamma
Richmond, Indiana

PINEAPPLE DUMP CAKE DESSERT

2 cups crushed pineapple
1½ cups coconut
1 cup chopped pecans

1 2-layer package
  yellow cake mix
2 sticks margarine, sliced

Layer pineapple, coconut and pecans in greased 9x13-inch cake pan. Spread dry cake mix over top. Dot with margarine slices. Bake at 350 degrees for 25 minutes. Yield: 12 servings.

Marlene Baucum, Preceptor Omega
Phoenix, Arizona

PINEAPPLE ICEBOX CAKE

1 16-ounce can crushed
  pineapple
1 3-ounce package
  lemon gelatin
1 cup boiling water
12 large marshmallows

½ cup sugar
½ cup water
12 ounces whipped
  topping
½ cup crushed pecans
Vanilla wafers

Drain pineapple, reserving 1 cup juice. Dissolve gelatin in 1 cup boiling water in bowl. Stir in reserved pineapple juice. Chill until partially set. Melt marshmallows with sugar and ½ cup water in saucepan; mix well. Cool. Stir into partially congealed mixture. Add whipped topping, pineapple and pecans; mix well. Arrange single layer of vanilla wafers in 9x13-inch dish. Top with half the pineapple mixture. Repeat layers. Sprinkle with crushed vanilla wafers. Chill for 24 hours. Yield: 8 servings.

Mae Warren, Preceptor Nu
Oxford, Alabama

PINEAPPLE SURPRISE

½ cup pineapple juice
1 3-ounce package
  lemon gelatin
1 cup shortening
1½ cups sugar
4 eggs, separated

1 cup canned crushed
  pineapple, drained
1 cup ground pecans
2 cups vanilla
  wafer crumbs

Bring pineapple juice to a boil in saucepan. Add gelatin; stir until dissolved. Cool. Cream shortening and sugar in mixer bowl until light and fluffy. Beat in egg yolks. Add gelatin, pineapple and pecans; mix well. Beat egg whites in mixer bowl until stiff peaks form. Fold into pineapple mixture. Sprinkle half the crumbs in 7x11-inch dish. Add pineapple mixture. Sprinkle with remaining crumbs; pat in gently. Chill for 24 hours. Serve with hot coffee or tea. Yield: 12 servings.

Barbara P. Fowler, Laureate Theta
Richland, Washington

NOODLE PUDDING

3 eggs
1 cup cream-style
  cottage cheese
¼ cup packed brown sugar
⅛ teaspoon nutmeg
½ teaspoon cinnamon

½ cup golden raisins
1 16-ounce can crushed
  pineapple
1 8-ounce package
  medium noodles,
  cooked

Beat eggs, cottage cheese, brown sugar and spices in bowl until blended. Fold in fruit with juice and noodles. Spoon into 9x13-inch baking dish. Bake at 375 degrees for 50 minutes. Yield: 8 servings.
Note: May be served as side dish with meat or poultry.

Dora Sheerer, Eta Mu
Woodstock, Georgia

PINEAPPLE CUSTARD

3 eggs
1 15-ounce can crushed
   pineapple

¾ cup sugar
2 tablespoons cornstarch

Beat eggs in bowl. Add pineapple and mixture of sugar and cornstarch; mix well. Pour into 1½-quart casserole. Bake at 325 degrees for 45 to 60 minutes or until set. Yield: 6 to 8 servings.

Barbara Ball, Xi Alpha Kappa
Grand Junction, Colorado

PINEAPPLE DELIGHT PUDDING

2 cups drained juice-
   pack crushed pineapple
2 cups low-fat yogurt

1 3-ounce package
   sugar-free vanilla
   instant pudding mix

Combine all ingredients in bowl; mix well. Spoon into serving dishes. Chill until serving time. Yield: 4 servings.

Carol Payne, Xi Alpha
Providence, Rhode Island

STRAWBERRY PUDDING

8 ounces cream cheese,
   softened
12 ounces whipped
   topping
1 14-ounce can
   sweetened condensed
   milk

1 quart fresh strawberries,
   sliced
1 jar strawberry glaze
1 12-ounce package
   vanilla wafers, crushed

Combine cream cheese, whipped topping and condensed milk in bowl; mix well. Combine strawberries and glaze in bowl; mix gently. Layer vanilla wafer crumbs, cream cheese mixture and strawberries ½ at a time in glass bowl. Chill until serving time. Yield: 8 servings.

Frances Reynolds, Delta Kappa
Ellisville, Missouri

DATE PUDDING

3 egg whites
1 tablespoon baking
   powder

1 cup sugar
1 cup chopped pecans
2 cups chopped dates

Beat egg whites in mixer bowl until stiff peaks form. Fold in baking powder, sugar, pecans and dates gently. Pour into greased 9-inch round cake pan. Bake at 325 degrees for 40 minutes. Cool. Serve with whipped cream. Yield: 8 servings.

Note: This was my great-grandmother's recipe used only at Thanksgiving and Christmas.

Catherine Martin, Preceptor Alpha Eta
Stuttgart, Arizona

SWEDISH RICE PUDDING

1 cup rice
4 cups milk
3 eggs, separated
2 tablespoons milk
1 cup sugar

1 teaspoon vanilla extract
1 almond
¼ cup confectioners'
   sugar

Combine rice with cold water to cover in 3-quart saucepan. Bring to a boil; drain. Add 4 cups milk. Cook over low heat for 30 to 45 minutes or just until rice is tender. Combine egg yolks and 2 tablespoons milk; mix well. Stir sugar and egg yolk mixture into rice. Add vanilla. Bring to a boil. Cook for 1 minute, stirring constantly. Add almond. Pour into 1-quart casserole. Beat egg whites until stiff peaks form. Beat in confectioners' sugar. Spread over pudding, sealing to edge. Bake at 350 degrees for 10 to 12 minutes or until light brown. Serve hot or cold. Yield: 8 servings.

Note: The person who finds the almond in his serving has good luck during the next year.

Mary E. Larson, Preceptor Sigma
Pecatonica, Illinois

UPDATED STEAMED PUDDING

1 cup boiling water
1 cup Grape Nuts cereal
½ cup butter or margarine
1 cup sugar
2 eggs
1 teaspoon vanilla extract

1¼ cups all-purpose flour
1 teaspoon baking powder
1 teaspoon soda
1 teaspoon cinnamon
½ teaspoon salt

Pour boiling water over Grape Nuts and butter in bowl. Let stand for 5 minutes or until softened. Add sugar, eggs and vanilla; mix well. Add sifted dry ingredients; mix well. Pour into greased 8x8-inch baking pan. Bake at 350 degrees for 35 minutes or until pudding springs back when touched lightly. Cut into squares. Yield: 6 servings.

VANILLA SAUCE

1½ cups sugar
1 tablespoon cornstarch
Dash of salt

1½ cups water
¼ cup butter
1 teaspoon vanilla extract

Mix sugar, cornstarch and salt in saucepan. Stir in water gradually. Cook over medium heat until sugar dissolves completely, stirring constantly. Bring to a boil; do not stir. Boil for several minutes; remove from heat. Sauce will be thin. Stir in butter until melted. Add vanilla. Serve warm sauce over pudding. Yield: 2 cups.

Barbara Ball, Xi Alpha Kappa
Grand Junction, Colorado

Hard sauce is traditionally served with baked or steamed puddings. Basic sauce combines 1 cup confectioners' sugar, 5 tablespoons butter and ¼ cup cream. Add one of the following: 1 tablespoon coffee, 2 tablespoons wine, ⅔ cup crushed strawberries, raspberries, apricots or bananas, or 1 tablespoon vanilla, rum, whiskey or Brandy. Chill in refrigerator to blend flavors.

PUMPKIN CAKE DESSERT

1 29-ounce can pumpkin
1½ cups sugar
4 eggs
1 large can Milnot
2 teaspoons pumpkin
  pie spice
1 teaspoon nutmeg
1 2-layer package
  yellow cake mix
1 cup melted margarine
1 cup chopped pecans

Combine first 6 ingredients in bowl; mix well. Pour into 9x13-inch baking pan. Sprinkle dry cake mix over top. Drizzle margarine over cake mix. Top with pecans. Bake at 325 degrees for 1½ hours. Serve hot with ice cream. Yield: 12 to 16 servings.

Sandra Sharp, Gamma Epsilon
Clarksville, Arkansas

PUMPKIN CRUNCH

1 cup evaporated milk
3 eggs, beaten
1 16-ounce can pumpkin
1 teaspoon pumpkin
  pie spice
1 cup sugar
1 2-layer package
  yellow cake mix
1 cup chopped pecans
1 cup melted margarine

Combine first 5 ingredients in bowl; mix well. Pour into well-greased 9x13-inch baking pan. Sprinkle with dry cake mix and pecans. Drizzle margarine over top. Bake at 350 degrees for 1 hour. Cover loosely with foil. Bake for 30 minutes longer. Cool. Chill until serving time. May serve from pan or invert onto large tray so that cake mix layer becomes crust. Garnish with whipped topping. Cut into squares. Store in refrigerator. Yield: 12 servings.

Pam Closson, Upsilon
Claremore, Oklahoma

PUMPKIN PIE DESSERT

4 eggs, slightly beaten
1 29-ounce can pumpkin
1½ cups sugar
1 teaspoon ginger
½ teaspoon cloves
2 teaspoons cinnamon
½ teaspoon allspice
2 teaspoons vanilla extract
1½ 13-ounce cans
  evaporated milk
1 2-layer package
  yellow cake mix
1 cup melted butter
  or margarine
1 cup chopped nuts

Combine eggs, pumpkin, sugar, spices, vanilla and evaporated milk in bowl; mix well. Pour into 9x13-inch baking dish. Sprinkle with cake mix. Drizzle with butter. Sprinkle nuts on top. Bake at 375 degrees for 45 minutes or until set. Cool. Cut into squares. Serve with whipped cream. Yield: 24 servings.

Leigh Hawkins, Xi Upsilon Delta
Borrego Springs, California

PUMPKIN UPSIDE-DOWN DESSERT

3 eggs
2 16-ounce cans
  pumpkin
1¼ cups sugar
1 12-ounce can
  evaporated milk
2 teaspoons cinnamon
1 teaspoon nutmeg
½ teaspoon ginger
1 2-layer package
  yellow cake mix
¾ cup melted margarine
1 cup pecans

Beat eggs lightly in medium bowl. Add pumpkin, sugar, evaporated milk and spices; mix well. Pour into ungreased 9x13-inch baking dish. Sprinkle dry cake mix evenly over pumpkin mixture. Drizzle with butter. Bake at 350 degrees for 30 minutes. Sprinkle with pecans. Bake for 30 minutes longer or until golden brown. Cool in pan on wire rack. Serve with whipped cream if desired. Yield: 16 servings.

Jean Zeller, Laureate Theta
New Albany, Indiana

LAYERED PUNCH BOWL CAKE

1 2-layer package
  yellow cake mix
2 4-ounce packages
  vanilla instant
  pudding mix
1 20-ounce can cherry
  pie filling
1 16-ounce can fruit
  cocktail, drained
1 16-ounce can
  pineapple chunks,
  drained
1½ cups chopped nuts
12 ounces shredded
  coconut
16 ounces whipped
  topping

Prepare and bake cake mix according to package directions for 8 or 9-inch layers. Cool. Prepare pudding mix according to package directions. Chill in refrigerator. Place 1 cake layer in 6-quart punch bowl. Add layers of half the pudding, pie filling, fruit cocktail, pineapple, nuts, coconut and whipped topping. Add second cake layer and remaining ingredients in same order. Garnish with cherries and additional nuts or coconut. Chill until serving time. Serve by spooning through all layers. Yield: 35 servings.

Mary Jo Bent, Laureate Lambda
Kansas City, Missouri

Chocolate makes wonderful garnishes for cakes. Shave thin slices from sweet cooking chocolate with vegetable peeler for curls. Dip clean rose leaves in melted chocolate chips, chill and remove leaves for chocolate leaves. Pipe melted chocolate chips into decorative designs onto waxed paper with plain tip for chocolate doodles.

PUNCH BOWL CAKE

1 2-layer package yellow cake mix	1 16-ounce can crushed pineapple, drained
1 3-ounce package chocolate instant pudding mix	7 ounces whipped topping
3 cups milk	1 8-ounce jar maraschino cherries, drained
1 16-ounce can cherry pie filling	1 cup chopped pecans
	½ cup flaked coconut

Prepare and bake cake mix using package directions. Cool. Prepare pudding mix according to package directions, using 3 cups milk. Chill in refrigerator. Crumble cake into punch bowl. Layer pie filling, pineapple and pudding over cake. Spread whipped topping in ring around edge of pudding. Place cherries in center. Sprinkle with pecans and coconut.
Yield: 10 to 15 servings.

Annette Lauer, Xi Alpha Epsilon
Greensboro, North Carolina

FRUITY PUNCH BOWL CAKE

4 cups white cake cubes	1 cup mandarin orange segments
16 ounces whipped topping	2 6-ounce packages vanilla instant pudding mix
1 cup sliced bananas	
1 cup seedless grapes	6 cups milk
1 cup drained crushed pineapple	½ cup sliced kiwifruit
1 cup sliced strawberries	Red maraschino cherries

Layer half the cake, ⅓ of the whipped topping and half the bananas, grapes, pineapple, strawberries and mandarin oranges in punch bowl. Combine pudding mix and milk in bowl; mix until thickened. Spoon half the pudding over fruit. Repeat layers. Spread remaining whipped topping over pudding. Decorate with kiwifruit and cherries. Chill for several hours or until serving time.
Yield: 12 servings.

Dorothy Hartigan, Xi Sigma Pi
Hilltop Lakes, Texas

RASPBERRY-NUT DESSERT

1¼ cups all-purpose flour	1 10-ounce package frozen raspberries, thawed
¼ teaspoon soda	
¼ teaspoon salt	
½ cup margarine	2 tablespoons cornstarch
⅓ cup sugar	½ cup chopped nuts
2 egg yolks	2 egg whites, stiffly beaten
1 teaspoon vanilla extract	¼ cup chopped nuts
¼ cup sugar	1 tablespoon sugar

Combine first 3 ingredients in bowl. Add margarine, ⅓ cup sugar, egg yolks and vanilla; mix well. Press into 9x9-inch baking pan. Combine ¼ cup sugar, raspberries and cornstarch in saucepan. Cook over low heat until thickened, stirring constantly. Pour into prepared pan. Sprinkle with ½ cup nuts. Spread egg whites over top.

Sprinkle with remaining ¼ cup nuts and 1 tablespoon sugar. Bake at 350 degrees for 25 to 30 mintues.
Yield: 6 servings.

Adeline Hamilton, Laureate Beta
Rapid City, South Dakota

RHUBARB CRUNCH

1 cup oats	3 cups rhubarb
1 cup all-purpose flour	½ cup sugar
1 cup packed brown sugar	1 teaspoon cinnamon
½ cup butter	1 tablespoon water

Combine oats, flour and brown sugar in bowl. Cut in butter until crumbly. Pat half the mixture into greased 8x8-nch baking pan. Add mixture of rhubarb, sugar, cinnamon and water. Top with remaining oats mixture. Bake at 350 degrees for 45 minutes. Yield: 8 servings.

Mary Suiter, Xi Beta Theta
Northfork, West Virginia

RASPBERRY KUCHEN

3 ounces cream cheese, softened	⅓ cup milk
¼ cup butter or margarine, softened	½ cup seedless raspberry preserves
2 cups buttermilk baking mix	1 cup confectioners' sugar
	1 to 2 tablespoons milk

Blend cream cheese and butter in bowl. Add baking mix; mix until crumbly. Add ⅓ cup milk; mix well. Knead 8 to 10 times in bowl. Roll into 8x12-inch rectangle on greased baking sheet. Spread preserves in 3-inch strip down center of rectangle. Cut 1-inch wide strips from edge to preserves. Fold alternately over preserves. Bake at 425 degrees for 15 minutes or until golden brown. Blend confectioners' sugar with 1 to 2 tablespoons milk. Drizzle over coffee cake. Serve warm. Yield: 4 servings.

RHUBARB KUCHEN

1 cup sifted all-purpose flour	5 cups sliced rhubarb
1 tablespoon sugar	1 3-ounce package strawberry gelatin
1½ teaspoons baking powder	⅓ cup sugar
⅛ teaspoon salt	3 tablespoons all-purpose flour
2 tablespoons butter	⅔ cup sugar
1 egg	⅓ cup all-purpose flour
2 tablespoons milk	3 tablespoons butter

Mix first 4 ingredients in bowl. Cut in 2 tablespoons butter until crumbly. Add mixture of egg and milk; stir just until moistened. Pat over bottom and 1 inch up sides of 9x9-inch baking pan. Mix rhubarb, gelatin, ⅓ cup sugar and 3 tablespoons flour. Place in prepared pan. Mix ⅔ cup sugar and ⅓ cup flour in bowl. Cut in 3 tablespoons butter until crumbly. Sprinkle over rhubarb. Bake at 375 degrees for 45 minutes or until rhubarb is tender and topping is light brown. Serve hot or cold with ice cream. Yield: 9 to 12 servings.

Patsy Phillips, Preceptor Omega
Pasco, Washington

RICE KRISPIES-FUDGE TREAT

¼ cup melted margarine
4 cups miniature
  marshmallows
¼ cup peanut butter

5 cups crisp rice cereal
1 box Salada 4-minute
  fudge mix

Combine margarine and marshmallows in saucepan. Cook over low heat until marshmallows melt, stirring constantly. Stir in peanut butter. Remove from heat. Stir in cereal until coated. Press into buttered 10x15-inch pan. Chill for 20 minutes. Prepare fudge using package directions. Cut cereal layer crosswise into 2 layers. Spread fudge on 1 layer. Top with remaining layer; press gently. Chill until firm. Cut into squares.
Yield: 25 squares.

Chris Richardson, Xi Zeta Eta
Pasadena, Texas

SIRNAYA PASKHA

3 pounds pot cheese
1 cup ground almonds
1 cup sugar
4 egg yolks

1 cup whipping cream
1 tablespoon Cognac
8 ounces unsalted butter

Force cheese through sieve or ricer. Add almonds, sugar, egg yolks, whipping cream and Cognac; mix well. Melt butter in saucepan over very low heat. Cool to lukewarm. Add to cheese mixture; mix well. Line clean clay flowerpot with drainage opening with moistened cheesecloth. Press cheese mixture into prepared flowerpot; fold cheesecloth over top. Place small plate on top; add weight. Place pot in deep dish. Refrigerate for 8 hours to overnight. Turn cheese onto serving plate; remove cheesecloth. Decorate with colored candies.

Anne Beirth, Laureate Rho
Norristown, Pennsylvania

FROZEN GRAND MARNIER SOUFFLÉ

1 cup sugar
⅓ cup water
2 tablespoons grated
  orange rind

6 egg yolks
¼ cup Grand Marnier
2 cups whipping cream
1 9-inch sponge cake

Combine sugar, water and orange rind in saucepan. Cook to 220 degrees on candy thermometer. Beat egg yolks in mixer bowl until thick and lemon-colored. Add sugar syrup gradually, beating until thick. Cool. Add Grand Marnier; beat well. Whip cream in bowl until soft peaks form. Fold into egg yolk mixture gently. Cut cake into 1-inch cubes. Fit 4-cup soufflé dish with 3-inch waxed paper collar. Brush waxed paper with oil. Layer custard and cake ½ at a time in soufflé dish. Freeze for 6 hours. Remove waxed paper. Serve with whipped cream flavored with Grand Marnier. Yield: 6 to 8 servings.

Hazel Jackson, Preceptor Kappa Nu
San Bruno, California

LEMON SOUFFLÉ SURPRISE

1 3-ounce package
  lemon gelatin
2 tablespoons water
⅓ cup concentrated
  lemon juice

¾ cup sugar
4 egg whites
¾ cup whipping cream,
  whipped

Soften gelatin in water. Heat lemon juice and sugar in saucepan over low heat until sugar dissolves, stirring constantly. Add softened gelatin. Heat until dissolved, stirring constantly. Cool for 20 minutes. Beat egg whites in mixer bowl until stiff peaks form. Fold in gelatin mixture. Fold in stiffly whipped cream. Pour into soufflé dish fitted with waxed paper collar. Chill for 1 hour or until set. Yield: 4 to 6 servings.

Dorothy Sewell, Laureate Beta Iota
Bedford, Texas

STRAWBERRY ANGEL DESSERT

1 angel food cake
1 cup milk
1 16-ounce package
  miniature
  marshmallows

2 10-ounce packages
  frozen strawberries,
  thawed
16 ounces whipped
  topping

Crumble cake into 9x13-inch cake pan. Heat milk and marshmallows in saucepan over low heat until marshmallows melt, stirring constantly. Pour over cake. Let stand until completely cool and firm. Pour strawberries over cake layer. Top with whipped topping.
Yield: 12 to 15 servings.
Note: May substitute white cake for angel food.

Chris Richardson, Xi Zeta Eta
Pasadena, Texas

STRAWBERRY GOODIES

1 6-ounce package wild
  strawberry gelatin
1 cup chopped nuts

1 cup grated coconut
¾ cup sweetened
  condensed milk

Combine all ingredients in bowl; mix well. Chill for 30 minutes. Shape into balls. Store in refrigerator.
Yield: 4 dozen.

Sue Mock, Xi Alpha
Providence, Rhode Island

Fresh strawberries dipped in chocolate or fondant are delicious confections. Melt 6 ounces semisweet chocolate in double boiler. Dip 2 cups whole fresh strawberries with stems into chocolate. Let stand on waxed paper. Or, prepare package fluffy white frosting using package directions and dip strawberries as above. Serve both confections within several hours.

MILE-HIGH STRAWBERRY DESSERT

2 egg whites	*1 cup sugar*
1 10-ounce package	*1 cup whipping cream,*
frozen strawberries,	*whipped*
partially thawed	*1 teaspoon vanilla extract*
1 teaspoon lemon juice	*Vanilla wafers, crushed*

Combine first 4 ingredients in mixer bowl. Beat at high speed for 15 minutes or until stiff peaks form. Fold in whipped cream flavored with vanilla. Spoon into 9x12-inch dish lined with vanilla wafer crumbs. Freeze until firm. Cut into squares. Garnish with additional whipped cream and whole strawberry. Yield: 12 servings.

Mary Elizabeth Reinhart, Laureate Eta
Fox Point, Wisconsin

STRAWBERRY MERINGUES

6 egg whites, at	*½ cup cornstarch*
room temperature	*1 20-ounce can*
¼ teaspoon cream of tartar	*strawberry pie filling*
1½ cups sugar	*8 to 12 ounces whipped*
1 cup coconut	*topping*

Beat egg whites in mixer bowl until foamy. Add cream of tartar and sugar 1 tablespoon at a time, beating constantly until stiff peaks form. Fold in mixture of coconut and cornstarch. Grease and flour baking sheet; make outlines of 2-inch circles with cookie cutter on prepared sheet. Spoon meringue onto marked circles; spread to fill outlines. Bake in preheated 300-degree oven for 30 minutes. Turn off oven; leave door ajar. Let stand in oven for 5 minutes or longer. Press centers of warm meringues lightly with thumb to make depression. Cool completely. Fill each meringue with 1 tablespoonful pie filling and 1 tablespoonful whipped topping. Top half the meringues with remaining meringues. Garnish each with fresh strawberry. Chill for 3 hours or until serving time. Arrange on crystal plate. Yield: 30 servings.

Sharon Lee Neal, Delta Mu
Indianapolis, Indiana

TALLY TORTE

5 eggs	*⅓ cup cornstarch*
1 cup sugar	*⅓ cup sugar*
1 cup all-purpose flour	*1 cup butter*
1 teaspoon baking powder	*1 cup confectioners'*
½ cup grated unsweetened	*sugar*
chocolate	*1 cup whipping cream,*
1 teaspoon vanilla extract	*whipped*
2 cups milk	

Beat eggs in mixer bowl for 5 minutes. Add 1 cup sugar. Beat for 5 minutes. Sift flour 4 times. Add flour and baking powder to creamed mixture. Beat for 5 minutes. Stir in chocolate and vanilla. Pour into 2 greased 9-inch cake pans. Bake at 350 degrees until layers test done. Cool in pans for several minutes. Invert onto wire rack to cool completely. Combine milk, cornstarch and ⅓ cup sugar in double boiler. Cook until thickened, stirring constantly. Cool. Cream butter and confectioners' sugar in bowl until light and fluffy. Add to cooked mixture; beat well. Split cake layers. Alternate cake layers and filling on cake plate. Top with whipped cream. Chill in refrigerator. Garnish with shaved chocolate. Yield: 8 servings.

Gail Engel, Xi Beta Zeta
Brookfield, Wisconsin

SAUCY WINTER CRÊPES

3 eggs	*½ teaspoon salt*
⅔ cup milk	*1 16-ounce can whole*
⅔ cup water	*cranberry sauce*
1 cup all-purpose flour	*½ cup CocoRibe coconut*
3 tablespoons oil	*rum liqueur*
2 teaspoons sugar	

Combine eggs, milk, water, flour, oil, sugar and salt in blender container; process until smooth. Pour 3 tablespoons into hot oiled 6-inch crêpe pan or skillet, tilting pan to coat well. Bake until light brown. Remove to aluminum foil. Repeat process with remainig batter. Heat cranberry sauce and ¼ cup liqueur in chafing dish. Fold each crêpe into quarters; place in chafing dish. Baste with sauce. Heat remaining ¼ cup liqueur in small saucepan. Ignite. Pour over crêpes. Serve when flames subside. Yield: 18 crêpes.

Photograph for this recipe on page 1.

WAFFLE-IRON TURTLES

4 1-ounce squares	*4 eggs*
unsweetened	*1½ cups sugar*
chocolate	*2 cups all-purpose flour*
1 cup butter	

Melt chocolate with butter in double boiler; mix well. Beat eggs in mixer bowl. Add sugar; beat until thick and lemon-colored. Add chocolate mixture and flour; mix well. Drop by teaspoonfuls onto hot waffle iron. Bake on medium for 1 to 1½ minutes. Remove to paper towel to cool. Frost with chocolate frosting if desired. Yiedl: 5 dozen.

Barbara Ball, Xi Alpha Kappa
Grand Junction, Colorado

Cakes

APPLE POUND CAKE

2 cups sugar
3 eggs, beaten
1¼ cups oil
1 tablespoon vanilla
  extract
3 cups all-purpose flour

1 teaspoon baking powder
1 teaspoon salt
3 cups chopped apples
1 cup chopped pecans
1 cup coconut

Beat sugar, eggs, oil and vanilla in mixer bowl until thick and lemon-colored. Add sifted flour, baking powder and salt; mix well. Mix apples, pecans and coconut in small bowl. Stir into batter. Pour into greased bundt pan. Bake at 325 degrees for 1 hour and 20 minutes. Remove to wire rack to cool. Garnish with confectioners' sugar, if desired. Serve with whipped topping or ice cream.
Yield: 16 servings.
Note: May bake in 2 loaf pans.

Carol Jarman, Beta Sigma
New Bern, North Carolina

GLAZED FRESH APPLE CAKE

2 eggs
1¼ cups oil
2 teaspoons vanilla extract
3 cups all-purpose flour
2 cups sugar
1 teaspoon soda
1 teaspoon salt

3 cups finely chopped
  peeled apples
1 cup chopped pecans
¼ cup margarine
1 cup packed brown sugar
¼ cup milk

Beat eggs in mixer bowl. Add oil and vanilla. Beat until thick. Sift flour, sugar, soda and salt together. Add to egg mixture; mix well. Stir in apples and pecans; mixture will be thick. Spoon into greased and floured tube pan. Bake at 350 degrees for 1 hour. Invert onto serving plate. Bring remaining ingredients to a boil in saucepan. Cook for 3 minutes. Cool slightly. Drizzle over cake.
Yield: 16 servings.

Betty Jo Hunter, Laureate Pi
Huntington, West Virginia

APPLE PIE CAKE

1 cup sugar
1 egg
¼ cup shortening
1 teaspoon vanilla extract
1 teaspoon soda
2½ teaspoons hot water

1 cup all-purpose flour
¼ teaspoon nutmeg
1 teaspoon cinnamon
½ cup chopped nuts
2 cups chopped apples

Combine sugar, egg, shortening and vanilla in mixer bowl. Add soda dissolved in hot water. Beat until smooth. Add sifted flour, nutmeg and cinnamon; mix well. Stir in nuts and apples. Pour into greased 9-inch round cake pan. Bake at 325 degrees for 45 minutes or until cake tests done. Cut into wedges. Serve with whipped cream or ice cream. Yield: 6 to 8 servings.

Wanda E. Dudley, Preceptor Pi
Albuquerque, New Mexico

APPLE HILL CAKE

2 cups sugar	*2 teaspoons soda*
½ cup oil	*1 teaspoon salt*
2 eggs	*2 teaspoons cinnamon*
4 cups chopped peeled	*1 teaspoon nutmeg*
apples	*1 cup chopped pecans*
2 cups all-purpose flour	*½ cup raisins*

Combine sugar, oil, eggs and apples in mixer bowl. Beat until well mixed. Add sifted dry ingredients; mix well. Stir in pecans and raisins. Spoon into bundt pan sprayed with nonstick cooking spray. Bake at 350 degrees for 1 hour or until cake tests done. Remove to wire rack to cool. Serve hot Nutmeg Sauce over slices of cake.
Yield: 16 servings.

NUTMEG SAUCE

1 cup sugar	*¼ cup butter*
2 tablespoons cornstarch	*2 teaspoons nutmeg*
2 cups boiling water	

Mix sugar and cornstarch in saucepan. Stir in boiling water. Cook for 1 minute, stirring constantly. Stir in butter and nutmeg.
Note: May substitute 2 teaspoons vanilla or 2 teaspoons lemon juice and 1 tablespoon grated lemon rind for nutmeg if preferred.

Edith Alexander, Preceptor Beta Gamma
Salida, Colorado

FRESH APPLE-RAISIN CAKE

2 cups sugar	*2 teaspoons cinnamon*
2 eggs, well beaten	*2 teaspoons vanilla extract*
½ cup oil	*4 cups sliced peeled*
2½ cups all-purpose flour	*apples*
1 teaspoon salt	*1 cup nuts*
2 teaspoons soda	*1 cup raisins*

Beat sugar, eggs and oil in mixer bowl until thick and lemon-colored. Add dry ingredients and vanilla; mix well. Batter will be thick. Fold in apples, nuts and raisins. Spoon into greased and floured 12-cup bundt pan. Bake at 325 degrees for 1 hour. Cool in pan on wire rack. Invert onto serving plate. Garnish with confectioners' sugar or serve with whipped topping. Yield: 16 to 20 servings.

Laura Alverson, Preceptor Laureate Nu
Olympia, Washington

JEWISH APPLE CAKE

3 cups all-purpose flour	*⅓ cup orange juice*
2 cups sugar	*2½ teaspoons vanilla*
1 tablespoon baking	*extract*
powder	*¾ cup sugar*
1 cup oil	*2 teaspoons cinnamon*
4 eggs, well beaten	*5 large apples, sliced*

Combine flour, 2 cups sugar and baking powder in mixer bowl. Add oil, eggs, orange juice and vanilla. Beat for 10 minutes. Batter will be very thick. Mix ¾ cup sugar and

cinnamon in bowl. Layer cake batter and apples and cinnamon mixture ⅓ at a time in greased and floured tube pan. Bake at 350 degrees for 1 hour and 15 minutes or until toothpick inserted near center comes out clean. Cool in pan for 1 hour. Remove to serving plate. Garnish with confectioners' sugar if desired.
Yield: 15 to 20 servings.

Teresa C. Schafer, Xi Alpha Pi
Williamsport, Maryland

FRESH APPLE CAKE

½ cup shortening	*1 cup golden raisins*
1 cup sugar	*½ cup chopped walnuts*
2 eggs	*½ cup margarine,*
1½ cups all-purpose flour	*softened*
1 teaspoon salt	*2 cups confectioners'*
1 teaspoon cinnamon	*sugar*
¾ teaspoon cloves	*2 eggs*
½ cup cold coffee	*1 teaspoon vanilla extract*
2 cups chopped apples	

Cream shortening and sugar in mixer bowl until light and fluffy. Blend in 2 eggs. Add dry ingredients alternately with coffee, mixing well after each addition. Fold in apples, raisins and walnuts. Spoon into greased and floured 6-cup tube pan. Bake at 350 degrees for 1 hour. Cool on wire rack. Combine remaining ingredients in mixer bowl. Beat until light and smooth. Place cake on serving plate. Spoon sauce into center. Yield: 12 servings.

Gloria Hayungs
Granvilla, Illinois

BLUE RIBBON APPLESAUCE CAKE

¾ cup raisins	*2 eggs, beaten*
½ cup boiling water	*1½ cups applesauce*
½ cup shortening	*2½ cups sifted all-purpose*
1½ cups packed brown	*flour*
sugar	*¾ cup chopped walnuts*
1 teaspoon salt	*2 teaspoons soda*
½ teaspoon cinnamon	*2 cups confectioners'*
½ teaspoon cloves	*sugar*
½ teaspoon allspice	*Milk*

Combine raisins and boiling water in bowl; set aside. Cream shortening, brown sugar, salt, spices and eggs in mixer bowl until light and fluffy, scraping bowl frequently. Mix in applesauce, flour and walnuts. Stir soda into raisins; do not drain. Add to batter; mix well. Pour into greased and floured tube pan. Bake at 350 degrees for 40 to 45 minutes or until cake tests done. Cool in pan for 10 minutes. Remove to wire rack to cool completely. Combine confectioners' sugar with enough milk to make of glaze consistency. Drizzle over cake.
Yield: 16 servings.

Margaret Bell, Xi Psi
Oklahoma City, Oklahoma

HOT APPLESAUCE CAKE

1 cup butter, softened	*2 teaspoons cinnamon*
2 cups sugar	*1 teaspoon cloves*
2 eggs, well beaten	*2 cups raisins*
2½ cups all-purpose flour	*2 cups nuts*
2 teaspoons soda	*2 cups hot applesauce*
1 teaspoon salt	

Cream butter in mixer bowl until light. Add sugar gradually, mixing until fluffy. Blend in eggs. Add sifted dry ingredients; mix well. Stir in raisins, nuts and hot applesauce. Spoon into 2 greased and floured 8-inch cake pans. Bake at 350 degrees for 1 hour or until toothpick inserted in center comes out clean. Remove to wire rack to cool. Spread Caramel Frosting between layers and over top and side of cake. Yield: 16 servings.

CARAMEL FROSTING

½ cup butter	*2 cups (about)*
1 cup packed brown sugar	*confectioners' sugar*
¼ cup milk	*1 cup coconut*

Melt butter in saucepan. Stir in brown sugar. Cook over low heat for 2 minutes, stirring constantly. Stir in milk. Bring to a boil; remove from heat. Cool. Add enough confectioners' sugar to make of desired consistency; mix until smooth. Stir in coconut.

Margaret Hill
Ottawa, Illinois

MOM'S APPLESAUCE CAKE

2 cups applesauce	*1 teaspoon soda*
1½ cups sugar	*1 teaspoon cinnamon*
½ cup butter, softened	*2 cups all-purpose flour*
2 tablespoons cocoa	

Combine applesauce, sugar, butter, cocoa, soda and cinnamon in bowl. Add flour; mix to form a thick batter. Pour into greased 9x13-inch cake pan. Bake at 350 degrees for 35 minutes. Cut into squares. Pour hot Lemon Sauce over squares to serve. Yield: 15 servings.

LEMON SAUCE

½ cup butter	*1 cup boiling water*
1½ cups sugar	*1 teaspoon lemon extract*
1 tablespoon cornstarch	

Melt butter in saucepan. Stir in sugar and cornstarch. Add boiling water; mix well. Bring to a boil. Cook until thickened, stirring constantly. Stir in lemon flavoring.

Beverly J. Beaver, Xi Beta Xi
Huntingdon, Pennsylvania

WEST VIRGINIA APPLESAUCE CAKE

3 cups applesauce	*1 16-ounce package*
1 cup margarine	*raisins*
4 teaspoons soda	*½ cup walnuts*
4 cups all-purpose flour	*2 teaspoons cloves*
2 cups sugar	*1 teaspoon cinnamon*
1 cup cherry preserves	*1 teaspoon nutmeg*

Combine applesauce, margarine and soda in saucepan. Heat until margarine is melted. Cool. Combine remaining ingredients in large bowl. Add applesauce mixture; mix well. Pour into greased and floured tube pan. Bake at 300 degrees for 3 hours. Remove to wire rack to cool. Serve with whipped topping or ice cream. Yield: 15 servings.

Mary J. Moreland, Delta Tau
Stephens City, Virginia

BETTER THAN SEX CAKE

1 2-layer package yellow	*3 cups milk*
cake mix	*1 cup whipping cream*
1 20-ounce can juice-	*¼ cup confectioners'*
pack crushed pineapple	*sugar*
¾ cup sugar	*1 teaspoon vanilla extract*
2 4-ounce packages	*¾ cup toasted coconut*
vanilla instant	
pudding mix	

Prepare and bake cake mix according to package directions for 9x13-inch cake pan. Combine pineapple with juice and sugar in medium saucepan. Cook over medium heat for 20 minutes or until thick and syrupy, stirring occasionally. Pierce top of cake with fork at 1-inch intervals. Pour pineapple mixture over cake. Cool completely. Beat pudding mix with milk in bowl until smooth. Spread over cooled cake. Whip cream in mixer bowl until slightly thickened. Add confectioners' sugar and vanilla. Whip until soft peaks form. Spread over top of cake. Chill for 24 hours. Sprinkle with coconut just before serving. Yield: 16 servings.

Marjorie A. Green, Preceptor Alpha
Abilene, Kansas

JOANNE'S BETTER THAN SEX CAKE

1 2-layer package yellow	*1 cup coconut*
cake mix	*12 ounces whipped*
1 cup sugar	*topping*
1 20-ounce can crushed	*½ cup coconut*
pineapple	*½ cup chopped pecans*
¾ cup chopped pecans	
1 6-ounce package	
vanilla instant	
pudding mix	

Prepare and bake cake mix according to package directions for 9x13-inch cake pan. Combine sugar and pineapple in saucepan. Bring to a boil. Cook until of desired consistency. Punch pencil-sized holes in hot cake. Pour pineapple mixture over cake. Cool. Sprinkle with ¾ cup pecans. Prepare pudding mix according to package directions. Stir in 1 cup coconut. Spread on cake. Top with whipped topping. Sprinkle with remaining coconut and pecans. Store in refrigerator. Yield: 12 to 16 servings.

Joanne Wilkerson, Preceptor Alpha Rho
Pasadena, Texas

CARROT CAKE

2 cups all-purpose flour	1½ teaspoons vanilla
2½ cups sugar	extract
2 teaspoons soda	2 cups grated carrots
2 teaspoons cinnamon	1 cup chopped dates
½ teaspoon salt	1 7-ounce can crushed
1 cup oil	pineapple
3 eggs	1 cup chopped nuts

Combine first 5 dry ingredients in mixer bowl. Add oil, eggs and vanilla; mix well. Stir in carrots, dates, pineapple and nuts. Pour into greased and floured 10-inch tube pan. Bake at 350 degrees for 1 hour to 1 hour and 15 minutes. Cool in pan on wire rack. Frost with Lemony Cream Cheese Frosting. Garnish with maraschino cherries. Yield: 15 servings.

LEMONY CREAM CHEESE FROSTING

½ cup margarine,	1 teaspoon lemon extract
softened	1 16-ounce package
8 ounces cream cheese,	confectioners' sugar
softened	

Cream margarine, cream cheese and lemon extract in mixer bowl until light and fluffy. Add confectioners' sugar gradually; beat until smooth after each addition.

Marilyn Borras, Xi Epsilon Alpha
Stafford, Virginia

OLD SOUTH CARROT CAKE

4 eggs	¼ teaspoon salt
1 cup oil	1 teaspoon cinnamon
2 cups all-purpose flour	1 teaspoon nutmeg
2 cups sugar	1 teaspoon cloves
1 teaspoon soda	2 cups grated carrots

Beat eggs and oil in mixer bowl until thick and lemon-colored. Add mixture of dry ingredients; mix well. Stir in carrots. Pour batter into 3 greased and floured 9-inch cake pans. Bake at 375 degrees for 25 minutes or until cake tests done. Remove to wire rack to cool. Spread Deluxe Cream Cheese Frosting between layers and over top and side of cake. Yield: 16 servings.

DELUXE CREAM CHEESE FROSTING

½ cup butter, softened	1 16-ounce package
8 ounces cream cheese,	confectioners' sugar
softened	1 cup chopped pecans
2 teaspoons vanilla extract	1 cup coconut

Cream butter and cream cheese in mixer bowl until light and fluffy. Add vanilla and confectioners' sugar; mix until smooth. Stir in pecans and coconut.

Vickie Landers, Xi Xi Rho
Fort Worth, Texas

Vary Lemony Cream Cheese Frosting (above) by adding ½ 8-ounce can drained crushed pineapple, 1 cup coconut, ¼ cup whole cranberry sauce or 2 tablespoons maple syrup.

CHERRY CAKE

2 cups all-purpose flour	2 eggs
¾ cup sugar	2 teaspoons vanilla extract
1 teaspoon soda	1 21-ounce can cherry
½ teaspoon cinnamon	pie filling
¾ cup oil	6 ounces chocolate chips

Combine flour, sugar, soda and cinnamon in bowl. Add oil, eggs, vanilla and pie filling; mix well. Stir in chocolate chips. Pour into 2 greased and floured cake pans. Bake at 350 degrees for 35 to 40 minutes or until cake tests done. Remove to wire rack to cool. Frost with whipped cream or whipped topping. Yield: 8 servings. Note: May bake in loaf pan.

Dot McCurley, Preceptor Beta Tau
Panama City, Florida

BLACK BOTTOM CUPCAKES

1½ cups flour	1 teaspoon vanilla extract
1 cup sugar	8 ounces cream cheese,
¼ cup cocoa	softened
1 teaspoon salt	1 egg
½ teaspoon soda	⅓ cup sugar
⅓ cup oil	⅛ teaspoon salt
1 cup water	6 ounces chocolate chips
1 teaspoon vinegar	

Combine first 5 dry ingredients in bowl. Add oil, water, vinegar and vanilla; mix well. Fill greased muffin cups ⅓ full. Beat cream cheese, egg, ⅓ cup sugar and ⅛ teaspoon salt in bowl until well blended. Stir in chocolate chips. Place 1 heaping teaspoonful in each muffin cup. Bake at 350 degrees for 30 to 35 minutes or until cupcakes test done. Cool on wire rack. Yield: 1½ dozen.

Betty I. Storsberg, Preceptor Psi
Whitesboro, New York

CHERRY-CHOCOLATE CAKE

1 2-layer package	1 cup sugar
chocolate cake mix	5 tablespoons butter
3 eggs	⅓ cup milk
1 21-ounce can cherry	6 ounces semisweet
pie filling	chocolate chips

Combine cake mix, eggs and pie filling in bowl; mix well. Pour into greased and floured 9x13-inch cake pan. Bake at 350 degrees for 35 to 40 minutes or until cake tests done. Cool. Combine sugar, butter and milk in saucepan. Bring to a boil, stirring constantly. Cook for 1 minute; remove from heat. Stir in chocolate chips until melted. Spread over cake. Yield: 12 servings.

Georgia M. Cuneo, Laureate Alpha
Winston-Salem, North Carolina

CHO-CHERRY CAKE

2 cups all-purpose flour	2 eggs
¾ cup sugar	2 teaspoons vanilla extract
2 teaspoons soda	1 21-ounce can cherry
⅛ teaspoon salt	pie filling
1 teaspoon cinnamon	12 ounces chocolate chips
¾ cup (scant) oil	1 cup chopped nuts

Mix first 5 ingredients in bowl. Stir in oil, eggs and vanilla. Add pie filling, chocolate chips and nuts; stir until moistened. Spoon into greased and floured bundt pan. Bake at 350 degrees for 45 to 55 minutes or until cake tests done. Cool in pan for 15 minutes. Remove to wire rack to cool completely. Yield: 12 to 18 servings.

Faye Dabney, Laureate Iota
Colorado Springs, Colorado

CHOCOLATE MINT CAKE

½ cup butter, softened	*½ teaspoon salt*
1¼ cups sugar	*½ cup sifted unsweetened*
2 eggs	*cocoa*
1½ cups sifted all-purpose	*1 cup hot water*
flour	*2 cups heavy cream*
¼ teaspoon baking	*1 tablespoon sugar*
powder	*1 tablespoon peppermint*
1 teaspoon soda	*extract*

Beat butter, 1¼ cups sugar and eggs in mixer bowl until light and smooth. Sift next 4 ingredients together. Add to batter alternately with mixture of cocoa and water, mixing well at low speed after each addition. Pour into 3 greased and floured 8-inch cake pans. Bake at 350 degrees for 25 to 30 minutes or until cake tests done. Remove to wire rack to cool. Combine remaining ingredients in bowl. Whip until soft peaks form. Tint with green food coloring if desired. Spread between layers. Frost with Whipped Chocolate Frosting.
Yield: 16 servings.

WHIPPED CHOCOLATE FROSTING

2 squares unsweetened	*2 tablespoons hot water*
chocolate	*1 egg*
2 cups sifted	*¼ cup butter, softened*
confectioners' sugar	*½ teaspoon vanilla extract*

Melt chocolate in double boiler. Combine with confectioners' sugar and hot water in bowl. Beat until smooth. Add egg, butter and vanilla. Beat until thick. Place bowl in larger bowl of ice water. Beat with wooden spoon until frosting is of desired consistency.

Linda Barron, Alpha Iota
Independence, California

CRAZY CHOCOLATE CAKE

1 21-ounce can cherry	*3 eggs*
pie filling	*1½ cups sugar*
1 2-layer package	*6 tablespoons milk*
chocolate cake mix	*6 tablespoons butter*
with pudding	*6 ounces chocolate chips*

Process pie filling in blender or food processor until smooth. Add cake mix and eggs; process until well mixed. Pour into greased and floured 9x13-inch cake pan. Bake at 350 degrees for 25 to 30 minutes or until cake tests done. Bring sugar, milk and butter to a boil in saucepan. Cook for 1 minute. Stir in chocolate chips. Spread on warm cake. Yield: 15 to 20 servings.

Shirley Carnine, Xi Tau
New Haven, Connecticut

CHOCOLATE POUND CAKE

1 cup butter, softened	*½ teaspoon baking*
½ cup shortening	*powder*
3 cups sugar	*½ teaspoon cinnamon*
5 eggs	*½ teaspoon salt*
3 cups sifted all-purpose	*1¼ cups milk*
flour	*1 teaspoon vanilla extract*
½ cup cocoa	

Cream butter and shortening in mixer bowl until light. Add sugar gradually, mixing until fluffy. Blend in eggs 1 at a time, beating well after each addition. Add sifted dry ingredients alternately with milk and vanilla; mix well. Spoon into greased tube pan. Bake at 325 degrees for 1 hour and 45 minutes. Remove to wire rack to cool. Frost with Chocolate Frosting. Yield: 16 servings.

CHOCOLATE FROSTING

1 cup butter	*1 16-ounce package*
2 1-ounce squares	*confectioners' sugar*
chocolate	*1 cup nuts*
1 egg, beaten	*1 teaspoon vanilla extract*
1 teaspoon lemon juice	

Melt butter and chocolate squares in double boiler. Add remaining ingredients. Beat with mixer until smooth. Spread on cake.
Note: May add ½ teaspoon cinnamon and 1 teaspoon almond extract if desired.

Ann Kesley, Epsilon Kappa
Nashville, Tennessee

HERSHEY'S FUDGE CAKE

½ cup butter, softened	*1 16-ounce can Hershey's*
1 cup sugar	*chocolate syrup*
4 eggs	*1 teaspoon vanilla extract*
1 cup all-purpose flour	*½ cup butter, softened*
1 teaspoon baking	*1 cup sugar*
powder	*⅓ cup cream*
¼ teaspoon salt	*½ cup chocolate chips*

Cream ½ cup butter and 1 cup sugar in mixer bowl until light and fluffy. Blend in eggs 1 at a time, beating well after each addition. Sift flour, baking powder and salt together. Add to creamed mixture alternately with chocolate syrup, mixing well after each addition. Mix in vanilla. Pour into greased and floured 9x13-inch cake pan. Bake at 350 degrees for 30 minutes. Bring ½ cup butter, 1 cup sugar and cream to a boil in saucepan. Cook for 1 minute. Stir in chocolate chips until melted. Pour over hot cake. Let stand for 10 minutes before serving.
Yield: 18 servings.

Lucy S. Sox, Xi Alpha Gamma
Beaufort, South Carolina

RING OF COCONUT FUDGE CAKE

¼ cup sugar	3 cups all-purpose flour
1 teaspoon vanilla extract	¾ cup cocoa
8 ounces cream cheese, softened	2 teaspoons baking powder
1 egg	2 teaspoons soda
½ cup coconut	1½ teaspoons salt
1 cup chocolate chips	1 teaspoon vanilla extract
2 cups sugar	1 cup hot coffee
1 cup oil	1 cup buttermilk
2 eggs	½ cup chopped nuts

Cream ¼ cup sugar, 1 teaspoon vanilla and cream cheese in mixer bowl until light and fluffy. Blend in 1 egg. Stir in coconut and chocolate chips. Set aside. Beat 2 cups sugar, oil and 2 eggs at high speed in mixer bowl for 1 minute. Add dry ingredients alternately with 1 teaspoon vanilla, coffee and buttermilk, mixing well after each addition. Stir in nuts. Pour half the batter into greased and floured bundt pan. Spoon chocolate chip mixture evenly over batter. Top with remaining batter. Bake at 350 degrees for 1 hour and 10 minutes to 1 hour and 15 minutes or until cake tests done. Cool in pan for 15 minutes; do not invert pan. Invert cake onto serving plate to cool completely. Yield: 16 servings.

Juanita Mills, Preceptor Lambda
Washington, West Virginia

SALLY'S CHOCOLATE ICING

½ cup margarine	1 teaspoon vanilla extract
3½ tablespoons cocoa	2 cups confectioners' sugar
⅓ cup milk	

Combine margarine, cocoa and milk in saucepan. Bring to a boil over low heat, stirring constantly. Boil for 1 minute, stirring constantly; remove from heat. Add vanilla and confectioners' sugar; beat with electric mixer until smooth. Pour over cake or brownies.
Yield: Enough frosting for 2-layer cake.
Note: Unused icing may be refrigerated for up to 2 weeks. Bring to room temperature and add 3 tablespoons milk or enough to make of spreading consistency.

Rebecca Council, Epsilon, Chi
Wallace, North Carolina

DEONA'S TURTLE CAKE

1 2-layer package German chocolate cake mix	1 8-ounce package caramels
3 eggs	1 cup chopped pecans
½ cup oil	½ cup margarine
1 cup water	¼ cup cocoa
½ cup margarine, softened	6 tablespoons milk
½ 14-ounce can sweetened condensed milk	1 16-ounce package confectioners' sugar
	1 teaspoon vanilla extract
	1 cup chopped pecans

Combine cake mix, eggs, oil, water and ½ cup margarine in bowl; mix well. Pour half the batter into buttered and floured 9x13-inch cake pan. Bake at 325 degrees for 20 minutes. Heat sweetened condensed milk and caramels in double boiler until caramels melt; blend well. Stir in 1 cup pecans. Pour over baked layer. Top with remaining cake batter. Bake for 25 to 30 minutes or until cake tests done. Bring ½ cup margarine, ¼ cup cocoa and milk to a boil in saucepan. Add confectioners' sugar, vanilla and 1 cup pecans. Spread over cooled cake. Yield: 16 servings.

Deona Constant, Preceptor Theta Epsilon
Conroe, Texas

TURTLE CAKE

½ cup margarine	½ cup buttermilk
½ cup shortening	1 14-ounce package caramels
¼ cup cocoa	½ cup evaporated milk
1 cup water	¾ cup butter
2 cups all-purpose flour	1 cup chocolate chips
2 cups sugar	2 cups chopped nuts
2 eggs, slightly beaten	
1 teaspoon soda	

Bring ½ cup margarine, shortening, ¼ cup cocoa and water to a boil in saucepan. Add to mixture of flour and sugar in bowl; mix well. Add eggs and soda dissolved in buttermilk. Pour half the batter into ungreased 9x13-inch cake pan. Bake at 350 degrees for 15 to 20 minutes. Combine caramels, evaporated milk and butter in saucepan. Heat until caramels are melted; mix well. Pour over baked layer. Sprinkle with chocolate chips and nuts. Pour remaining batter over top. Bake for 20 to 30 minutes longer. Cool. Frost with Cocoa Frosting.
Yield: 16 servings.

COCOA FROSTING

¼ cup margarine	1 16-ounce package confectioners' sugar
⅓ cup milk	
¼ cup cocoa	

Bring margarine, milk and cocoa to a boil in saucepan; remove from heat. Add confectioners' sugar. Beat until smooth.

Chris Richardson, Xi Zeta Eta
Pasadena, Texas

NANCY'S TURTLE CAKE

1 2-layer package double chocolate cake mix	1 12-ounce package caramels
1 14-ounce can sweetened condensed milk	1 16-ounce package chocolate chips
	1 cup chopped nuts

Prepare cake mix according to package directions. Pour half the batter into greased and floured 9x13-inch cake pan. Bake at 350 degrees for 15 minutes. Heat condensed milk and caramels in double boiler until caramels melt; blend well. Pour over baked layer. Mix chocolate chips and nuts. Sprinkle ⅔ of the mixture over caramel layer. Top with remaining cake batter and nut mixture. Bake for 20 minutes longer. Serve with whipped cream or ice cream. Yield: 12 to 15 servings.

Nancy Packard, Chi Alpha
Nokomis, Florida

PENNY'S TURTLE CAKE

1 2-layer package German chocolate cake mix	½ cup evaporated milk
	¾ cup butter
	1 cup miniature chocolate chips
1 14-ounce package caramels	2 cups chopped pecans

Prepare cake mix according to package directions. Pour half the batter into greased 9x13-inch cake pan. Bake at 350 degrees for 20 minutes. Melt caramels with evaporated milk and butter in saucepan over low heat, stirring constantly. Pour over baked layer. Sprinkle with chocolate chips and 1 cup pecans. Top with remaining cake batter. Sprinkle remaining 1 cup pecans over top. Bake for 25 to 30 minutes longer. Serve with whipped cream or ice cream. Yield: 18 servings.

Penny C. Vennare, Xi Delta Lambda
Pittsburgh, Pennsylvania

COCONUT CAKE

1 2-layer package yellow cake mix	16 ounces sour cream
	1 cup coconut
1 cup sugar	

Prepare and bake cake mix according to package directions for 2 layers. Remove to wire rack to cool. Combine sugar, sour cream and coconut in bowl; mix well. Spread between layers and over top and side of cake. Yield: 16 servings.

Eloise W. Evans, Preceptor Upsilon
Omaha, Nebraska

COCONUT-SOUR CREAM LAYER CAKE

1 2-layer package butter-flavored cake mix	1 12-ounce package frozen coconut, thawed
16 ounces sour cream	1½ cups whipped topping
2 cups sugar	

Prepare and bake cake mix according to package directions in 2 greased and floured 8-inch cake pans. Remove to wire rack to cool. Combine sour cream, sugar and coconut in bowl; mix well. Reserve 1 cup coconut mixture. Split cake layers into halves horizontally. Spread coconut mixture between layers. Mix reserved coconut mixture into whipped topping. Spread over top and side of cake. Store in airtight container in refrigerator for 3 days before serving. Yield: 10 servings.

Patricia Burakowski, Eta Kappa
St. Marys, Georgia

CRANBERRY CAKE

1 cup sugar	1 cup milk
2 cups all-purpose flour	2 cups fresh cranberries
2 teaspoons baking powder	½ cup butter
	1 cup sugar
2 tablespoons melted shortening	¾ cup cream

Sift 1 cup sugar, flour and baking powder together into bowl. Add melted shortening and milk; mix well. Stir in cranberries. Pour into greased and floured 9x13-inch cake pan. Bake at 350 degrees for 20 to 25 minutes or until cake tests done. Melt butter in saucepan. Stir in 1 cup sugar and cream. Bring to a boil. Simmer for 10 minutes. Serve sauce hot over warm cake. Yield: 15 servings.

Sharon H. Mashek, Xi Delta Omega
Spillville, Iowa

CRANBERRY SWIRL CAKE

½ cup butter, softened	1 teaspoon almond extract
1 cup sugar	1 8-ounce can whole cranberry sauce
2 eggs	
2 cups all-purpose flour	1 cup chopped walnuts
1 teaspoon baking powder	1 cup confectioners' sugar
1 teaspoon soda	4 teaspoons warm water
½ teaspoon salt	½ teaspoon almond extract
8 ounces sour cream	

Cream butter in mixer bowl until light. Add sugar gradually, mixing until fluffy. Blend in eggs. Sift flour, baking powder, soda and salt together. Add to creamed mixture alternately with sour cream, mixing well after each addition. Stir in 1 teaspoon almond extract. Spread ⅓ of the batter in greased 10-inch tube pan. Spoon ⅓ of the cranberry sauce over batter. Swirl cranberry sauce into batter with spoon. Repeat layers twice, using all ingredients. Sprinkle with walnuts. Bake at 350 degrees for 50 to 55 minutes or until knife inserted near center comes out clean. Cool in pan for 10 minutes. Remove to wire rack. Drizzle mixture of remaining ingredients over cake.

Jackie Vogler, Xi Sigma Pi
Hilltop Lakes, Texas

CRÈME DE MENTHE CAKE

1 2-layer package white cake mix	2 tablespoons Crème de Menthe
2 tablespoons Crème de Menthe	9 ounces whipped topping
1 cup fudge ice cream topping	

Prepare cake mix according to package directions, adding 2 tablespoons Crème de Menthe. Bake as directed in 9x13-inch cake pan. Cool. Spread with ice cream topping. Frost with mixture of 2 tablespoons Crème de Menthe and whipped topping. Store in refrigerator. Yield: 16 servings.

Stacey Freese, Alpha
Plymouth, Nebraska

Butter Cream Frosting is easy to make and to customize for any cake. Beat 1 pound confectioners' sugar, 6 tablespoons softened butter, ¼ cup milk and 1½ teaspoons vanilla extract until smooth. Vary with one of the following: use ¼ cup lemon juice for milk and vanilla; add ½ cup cocoa and ⅓ cup coffee for milk; use 2 egg yolks and 1 teaspoon orange rind for half the milk.

MINTED ANGEL CAKE

1 angel food cake mix	2 cups whipping cream,
2¼ cups miniature	whipped
marshmallows	1 square chocolate, melted
½ cup milk	¼ teaspoon shortening,
¼ cup green Crème	melted
de Menthe	Chopped pistachio nuts

Prepare and bake angel food cake according to package directions. Cool; remove from pan. Split into 3 layers. Heat marshmallows and milk in saucepan over low heat until melted. Cool. Blend in Crème de Menthe and 6 drops of green food coloring. Fold in whipped cream. Spread between layers and over top and side of cake. Drizzle mixture of melted chocolate and shortening over top. Garnish with pistachio nuts. Yield: 12 servings.

Nancy Burns, Preceptor Alpha Gamma
Scottsdale, Arizona

CURRANT CAKE

1½ cups corn oil	2 eggs
margarine	Milk
3¼ cups self-rising flour	Light brown sugar
1 cup sugar	¾ cup chopped pecans
1¾ cups black currants	

Cut margarine into flour in bowl until crumbly. Mix in sugar and currants. Add eggs beaten with enough milk to make of desired consistency; mix well. Spoon into tube pan lined with greased waxed paper. Sprinkle with brown sugar. Bake on upper rack at 400 degrees for 15 minutes. Sprinkle with pecans. Reduce oven temperature to 325 degrees. Bake for 1 hour and 45 minutes longer. Remove to serving plate. Yield: 16 servings.

Jane Koehn, Laureate Alpha Zeta
Jacksonville, Florida

GLAZED CALICO CAKE

2 cups all-purpose flour	2 cups finely shredded
1 cup sugar	carrots
1 teaspoon soda	1 cup flaked coconut
½ teaspoon salt	1 8-ounce can crushed
1½ teaspoons cinnamon	pineapple, drained
⅛ teaspoon cloves	¼ cup butter
3 eggs	¼ cup buttermilk
¾ cup buttermilk	2 tablespoons corn syrup
½ cup oil	½ cup sugar
1½ teaspoons vanilla	¼ teaspoon soda
extract	½ teaspoon vanilla extract
1 cup chopped walnuts	

Combine first 6 dry ingredients in bowl. Beat eggs in bowl. Stir in ¾ cup buttermilk, oil and 1½ teaspoons vanilla. Add to flour mixture; mix well. Stir in walnuts, carrots, coconut and pineapple. Pour into greased and floured 9-cup fluted tube pan. Bake at 350 degrees for 45 to 50 minutes or until cake tests done. Cool in pan for 10 minutes. Melt butter in saucepan over medium heat. Stir in ¼ cup buttermilk, corn syrup, ½ cup sugar and ¼ teaspoon soda. Bring to a boil, stirring constantly. Cook for

5 minutes over very low heat. Stir in ½ teaspoon vanilla. Remove cake to serving plate. Pierce cake with fork. Drizzle glaze over warm cake. Yield: 16 servings.

Judy Titus, Xi Upsilon
Anchor Point, Alaska

JEWEL CAKE

1 10¾-ounce bakery loaf	½ pint whipping cream
pound cake	Sugar to taste
⅓ cup mint jelly	Vanilla, almond or rum
⅓ cup strawberry	extract to taste
preserves	

Slice cake horizontally into thirds. Spread mint jelly on bottom slice and strawberry preserves on center slice. Reassemble cake on serving platter. Whip cream with sugar and flavoring to taste in mixer bowl until soft peaks form. Spread over top and sides of cake. Freeze until firm. Let stand at room temperature for 1 hour before serving. Yield: 8 servings.

Note: Garnish with holly spray of horizontally-sliced spearmint candy leaves and cinnamon candy berries.

Jackie Vogler, Xi Sigma Pi
Hilltop Lakes, Texas

GLAZED LEMON CAKE

1 2-layer package lemon	1 cup plus 2 tablespoons
cake mix	water
1 4-ounce package	2 cups confectioners'
lemon instant	sugar
pudding mix	1 6-ounce can frozen
4 eggs	lemonade concentrate
⅓ cup oil	

Combine cake mix, pudding mix, eggs, oil and water in mixer bowl; mix well. Pour into greased and floured 9x13-inch cake pan. Bake at 350 degrees until cake tests done. Blend confectioners' sugar and lemonade in bowl. Pierce cake with large fork. Pour lemonade mixture over cake. Bake for 5 minutes longer. Cool on wire rack. Yield: 12 servings.

Ann Corrigan, Preceptor Gamma Epsilon
Blue Springs, Missouri

LEMON CAKE

1 2-layer package lemon	1 cup water
cake mix	1½ cups confectioners'
¾ cup corn oil	sugar
3 eggs	Lemon juice

Combine cake mix, oil, eggs and water in mixer bowl. Beat until smooth. Pour into greased and floured 8x11-inch cake pan. Bake at 350 degrees for 30 to 35 minutes or until cake tests done. Pierce warm cake with fork. Combine confectioners' sugar with enough lemon juice to make thin glaze. Drizzle over warm cake. Serve warm. Yield: 12 servings.

Faye Dabney, Laureate Iota
Colorado Springs, Colorado

MOCHA MYSTERY CAKE

1 2-layer package yellow cake mix	½ cup sugar
½ cup packed brown sugar	¼ cup cocoa
	1 cup cold strong coffee

Prepare cake mix according to package directions. Pour into greased 9x13-inch baking pan. Combine sugars and cocoa in bowl. Sprinkle over batter. Pour coffee over top. Bake at 350 degrees for 40 minutes. Serve warm with whipped cream. Yield: 18 to 20 servings.

Note: May substitute white, chocolate or spice cake mix for yellow cake mix.

Veda Dabney, Beta Lambda
Evanston, Wyoming

OATMEAL CHOCOLATE CHIP CAKE

1¾ cups boiling water	1 teaspoon soda
1 cup oats	1 teaspoon salt
1 cup packed brown sugar	1 tablespoon cocoa
½ cup margarine	12 ounces semisweet
2 extra large eggs	chocolate chips
1¾ cups all-purpose flour	¾ cup chopped nuts

Pour boiling water over oats in bowl. Let stand for 10 minutes. Add brown sugar and margarine; stir until margarine melts. Add eggs; mix well. Add mixture of flour, soda, salt and cocoa; mix well. Stir in half the chocolate chips. Pour into greased and floured 9x13-inch cake pan. Sprinkle remaining chocolate chips and nuts on top. Bake at 350 degrees for 35 to 40 minutes or until cake tests done. Cool. Yield: 12 servings.

Teresa Curto, Rho
Ely, Neveda

OLD-FASHIONED GERMAN CAKE

1 cup butter, softened	2 teaspoons baking
1½ cups sugar	powder
4 eggs	¼ cup Brandy
3 tablespoons cream	2 teaspoons lemon juice
2 cups all-purpose flour	

Cream butter and sugar in mixer bowl until light and fluffy. Add eggs 1 at a time, beating well after each addition. Mix in cream. Add flour and baking powder alternately with Brandy and lemon juice, mixing well after each addition. Pour into greased 12-cup bundt pan. Bake at 350 degrees for 1 hour. Invert onto serving plate to cool. Garnish with sprinkle of confectioners' sugar. Yield: 16 servings.

Note: May omit confectioners' sugar garnish and glaze warm cake if desired.

Janice Cygan, Xi Delta Zeta
Webster, New York

OOOEY GOOEY CAKE

1 2-layer package yellow cake mix	8 ounces cream cheese, softened
3 eggs	1 16-ounce package
½ cup melted margarine	confectioners' sugar
3 eggs	½ cup chopped pecans

Combine cake mix, 3 eggs and margarine in bowl; mix well. Batter will be thick. Spread in greased and floured 10x15-inch cake pan. Combine 3 eggs, cream cheese and 4 cups confectioners' sugar in bowl; blend well. Stir in pecans. Pour over batter; swirl to marbleize. Bake at 325 degrees for 30 to 35 minutes. Sprinkle warm cake with remaining confectioners' sugar. Cool. Yield: 25 servings.

Roberta DeNegre, Preceptor Gamma Upsilon
Blue Springs, Missouri

PINEAPPLE CAKE

2 cups all-purpose flour	1 20-ounce can crushed
2 cups sugar	pineapple
2 eggs	1½ cups chopped nuts
2 teaspoons soda	

Combine first 5 ingredients and ½ cup nuts in bowl; mix well. Pour into greased 9x13-inch cake pan. Bake at 350 degrees for 45 to 55 minutes or until golden brown. Spread hot cake with Cream Cheese Frosting. Sprinkle with 1 cup nuts. Yield: 12 to 18 servings.

CREAM CHEESE FROSTING

8 ounces cream cheese, softened	½ cup margarine, softened
1 cup confectioners' sugar	2 teaspoons vanilla extract

Combine all ingredients in mixer bowl. Beat until fluffy.

Stella Jenks, Preceptor Zeta Lambda
Santa Rosa, California

PINEAPPLE-COCONUT CAKE

1 20-ounce can crushed pineapple	8 ounces cream cheese, softened
1 2-layer package yellow cake mix	1 cup milk
2 eggs	10 ounces whipped topping
1 4-ounce package vanilla instant pudding mix	Coconut
	Chopped nuts

Drain pineapple, reserving juice. Add enough water to reserved juice to measure 1½ cups. Combine with cake mix and eggs in bowl; mix well. Pour into greased and floured 10x15-inch cake pan. Bake at 350 degrees for 16 minutes. Cool. Combine pudding mix, cream cheese and milk in bowl; mix well. Stir in pineapple. Layer pineapple mixture and whipped topping over cooled cake, sealing to edge of pan. Sprinkle with coconut and nuts. Refrigerate for several hours to overnight. Yiedl: 12 to 16 servings.

Rosemary Battaglia, Xi Chi
Waterbury, Connecticut

PINEAPPLE UPSIDE-DOWN CAKE

⅓ cup margarine	¾ cup pineapple juice
½ cup packed brown sugar	1½ teaspoons vanilla extract
1 20-ounce can sliced pineapple, drained	1½ cups sifted all-purpose flour
3 eggs, beaten	1½ teaspoons baking powder
1½ cups sugar	

Melt margarine in 10-inch cast-iron skillet. Stir in brown sugar until melted; spread evenly in skillet. Arrange pineapple slices in skillet. Combine eggs, sugar, pineapple juice and vanilla in bowl; mix with wooden spoon. Sift in flour and baking powder; mix well. Pour into prepared skillet. Bake at 350 degrees for 30 to 40 minutes or until brown. Invert onto serving plate. Serve warm with ice cream or whipped cream. Yield: 8 servings.

Gail E. Frics, Preceptor Upsilon
Omaha, Nebraska

MEXICAN PECAN CAKE

2 cups all-purpose flour	8 ounces cream cheese, softened
2 cups sugar	
1 cup chopped pecans	2 cups confectioners' sugar
2 teaspoons soda	
2 eggs	1 tablespoon vanilla extract
½ cup margarine, softened	

Combine flour, sugar, pecans and soda in bowl. Add eggs; mix well. Spoon into greased and floured 9x12-inch cake pan. Bake at 350 degrees for 45 minutes or until cake tests done. Combine margarine and remaining ingredients in mixer bowl. Mix until smooth. Spread on hot cake. Yield: 30 servings.

Lydia Shaffer, Alpha Zeta
Thermopolis, Wyoming

PISTACHIO CAKE ROLL

1 quart pistachio ice cream	4 eggs
½ cup CocoRibe coconut rum liqueur	1 cup sugar
	1 teaspoon vanilla extract
1 cup all-purpose flour	Confectioners' sugar
1 teaspoon baking powder	Candied cherries
¼ teaspoon salt	Angelica

Mix ice cream and liqueur in bowl; return to freezer. Sift flour, baking powder and salt together. Beat eggs in mixer bowl until foamy. Add sugar and vanilla gradually, beating constantly. Beat for 5 minutes or until thick and lemon- colored. Fold in dry ingredients. Spread evenly in waxed paper-lined 10x15-inch baking pan. Bake at 375 degrees for 15 minutes or until cake tests done. Invert on towel sprinkled with confectioners' sugar; remove waxed paper. Roll cake in towel as for jelly roll. Cool on wire rack. Soften ice cream just to spreading consistency. Unroll cake. Spread with ice cream; reroll. Wrap in foil. Freeze for 12 hours to overnight. Sprinkle with confectioner' sugar; decorate with cherries and angelica. Yield: 10 servings.

Photograph for this recipe on page 1.

PISTACHIO CAKE

1 2-layer package yellow cake mix	1 cup sour cream
	1 4-ounce package pistachio instant pudding mix
1 4-ounce package pistachio instant pudding mix	
	16 ounces whipped topping
4 eggs	
6 tablespoons oil	

Combine cake mix and 1 package pudding mix in bowl; make well in center. Break eggs into well. Beat until smooth. Add oil and sour cream. Beat for 4 minutes. Spoon into greased tube pan. Bake at 350 degrees for 1 hour or until cake tests done. Remove to wire rack to cool. Prepare 1 package pudding mix according to package directions. Fold in whipped topping. Spread over top and side of cake. Yield: 16 servings.

Helen M. Harris, Xi Epsilon Alpha
Woodbridge, Virginia

DR. BYRD CAKE

3 cups all-purpose flour	1½ cups oil
2 cups sugar	1½ teaspoons vanilla extract
1 teaspoon soda	
1 teaspoon salt	2 cups chopped bananas
1 teaspoon cinnamon	1 8-ounce can crushed pineapple
3 eggs	

Sift dry ingredients into bowl; make well in center. Add eggs, oil, vanilla, bananas and pineapple with juice into well. Stir until well mixed. Pour into greased tube pan. Bake at 350 degrees for 1 hour and 10 minutes. Cool in pan on wire rack. Loosen side with spatula. Invert onto serving plate. Yield: 16 servings.

Jean Weller, Xi Alpha Pi
McConnellsburg, Pennsylvania

POOR MAN'S CAKES

2 cups packed brown sugar	3 cups all-purpose flour
	4 teaspoons soda
2 tablespoons lard	½ teaspoon salt
2 cups hot water	1 teaspoon cinnamon
1 cup raisins	1 teaspoon cloves
1 cup chopped dates	½ teaspoon ginger

Bring brown sugar, lard, water, raisins and dates to a boil in saucepan. Cook for 5 minutes. Cool. Add remaining ingredients; mix well. Pour into greased and floured loaf pans. Bake at 350 degrees for 30 minutes or until cake tests done. Yield: 2 loaves.

Andrea Ryan, Zeta Alpha
Williamsport, Pennsylvania

PRUNE CAKE

½ cup shortening	½ teaspoon salt
1½ cups sugar	¾ teaspoon nutmeg
3 eggs	1 teaspoon cinnamon
2¼ cups all-purpose flour	1 cup sour milk
1 teaspoon baking powder	1 cup chopped drained canned prunes
1 teaspoon soda	

Cream shortening and sugar in bowl until light and fluffy. Beat eggs in small bowl until thick and lemon-colored. Add to creamed mixture; beat well. Add mixture of flour, baking powder, soda, salt, nutmeg and cinnamon alternately with milk, mixing well after each addition. Fold in prunes. Pour into 2 greased and floured 9-inch cake pans. Bake at 350 degrees for 15 to 20 minutes or until layers test done. Cool on wire rack.
Yield: 12 to 16 servings.

Mary Meddles, Preceptor Delta Tau
Richwood, Ohio

POPPY SEED CAKE

1 2-layer package white cake mix	¼ cup poppy seed
1 4-ounce package vanilla instant pudding mix	5 eggs
	½ cup oil
	1 cup water
	1 teaspoon almond extract

Combine cake mix, pudding mix and poppy seed in mixer bowl. Add eggs, oil, water and flavoring. Beat for 5 minutes. Pour into greased and floured 10x15-inch baking pan. Bake at 350 degrees for 25 minutes. Cool in pan on wire rack. Spread with Cream Cheese Frosting.
Yield: 24 servings.
Note: May omit frosting and garnish with sprinkle of confectioners' sugar. Do not use cake mix with pudding.

CREAM CHEESE FROSTING

½ cup butter, softened	1½ cups confectioners' sugar
3 ounces cream cheese, softened	⅛ teaspoon salt
1 teaspoon vanilla extract	

Cream butter and cream cheese in mixer bowl until fluffy. Add remaining ingredients. Beat until smooth.

Marjorie K. E. Lessman, Xi Alpha Kappa
Dalton, Nebraska

POTATO CAKE

2 cups sugar	1 teaspoon allspice
1 cup shortening	¼ teaspoon cinnamon
4 eggs	¼ teaspoon nutmeg
3 tablespoons grated white chocolate	2 teaspoons baking powder
1 cup chopped walnuts	2 cups all-purpose flour
1 cup warm mashed potatoes	¼ teaspoon salt

Cream first 3 ingredients in mixer bowl until light and fluffy. Add chocolate, walnuts, mashed potatoes, spices, baking powder, flour and salt; mix well. Pour into greased and floured tube pan. Bake at 350 degrees for 45 minutes. Cool in pan for 10 minutes. Remove to wire rack to cool completely. Frost with confectioners' sugar frosting. Yield: 16 servings.

Elfreda Schlenz, Preceptor Pi
Fresno, California

PRALINE CARAMEL ICING

2 cups sugar	½ cup buttermilk
1 cup butter	½ teaspoon soda
2 tablespoons (scant) light corn syrup	½ teaspoon vanilla extract

Combine sugar, butter, corn syrup, buttermilk and soda in saucepan. Cook over low heat to 234 to 240 degrees on candy thermometer, soft-ball stage; remove from heat. Stir in vanilla. Cool slightly. Spread between layers and over top and side of cake.
Yield: Enough frosting for 2-layer cake.
Note: This recipe is 100 years old. It is especially good on yellow cake or pound cake. Ingredients can be increased by ⅓ for 3-layer cake.

Blanche Thompson, Alpha Chi Mu
Azle, Texas

PUMPKIN POUND CAKES

3 cups sugar	½ teaspoon salt
4 eggs	2 cups pumpkin
3 cups all-purpose flour	1 teaspoon cinnamon
¾ cup oil	1 teaspoon nutmeg
½ cup water	1 pound golden raisins
1 tablespoon soda	2 cups chopped pecans

Combine first 10 ingredients in bowl; mix well. Stir in raisins and pecans. Fill 4 greased and floured 1-pound coffee cans ½ full. Bake at 350 degrees for 1 hour. Cool in cans on wire rack. Place plastic lids on cans. Store in refrigerator or freezer. Remove from cans. Serve sliced with whipped cream or ice cream and garnished with maraschino cherries. Yield: 4 cakes.

Marie Duke, Laureate Tau
Clovis, New Mexico

PUMPKIN PRALINE CAKE

1 2-layer package yellow cake mix	1 teaspoon cinnamon
½ 16-ounce can pumpkin	½ teaspoon allspice
	¼ teaspoon nutmeg
½ cup oil	4 eggs
¾ cup packed light brown sugar	½ cup chopped nuts
	⅓ cup packed dark brown sugar
¼ cup water	⅓ cup butter, softened

Combine cake mix, pumpkin, oil, light brown sugar, water and spices in mixer bowl. Beat at medium speed for 1 minute. Add eggs 1 at a time. Beat for 1 minute after each addition. Mix nuts, dark brown sugar and butter in small bowl. Layer half the cake batter, all the nut mixture and remaining batter in greased bundt pan. Bake at 350 degrees for 1 hour. Remove to wire rack to cool.
Yield: 16 servings.

Wilma Hayes, Preceptor Zeta Chi
Baytown, Texas

PUMPKIN CAKE

2 cups sugar	2 cups self-rising flour
1 cup oil	2 teaspoons cinnamon
4 eggs, beaten	½ teaspoon salt
1 cup canned pumpkin	

Combine sugar, oil and eggs in mixer bowl; mix well. Blend in pumpkin. Add dry ingredients. Beat at medium speed for 3 minutes. Pour into greased and floured 9x13-inch cake pan. Bake at 350 degrees for 40 to 45 minutes or until cake tests done. Cool on wire rack. Frost with Cream Cheese-Pecan Frosting. Garnish with coconut and pecans. Yield: 16 servings.

CREAM CHEESE-PECAN FROSTING

½ cup butter, softened	1 16-ounce package
8 ounces cream cheese,	confectioners' sugar
softened	Milk
½ teaspoon vanilla extract	1 cup chopped pecans

Cream butter and cream cheese in mixer bowl until light and fluffy. Add vanilla and confectioners' sugar. Beat until smooth. Blend in a small amount of milk if necessary to make of desired consistency. Stir in pecans.

Linda Hawkins, Preceptor Delta
Cookeville, Tennessee

CREAM-FILLED PUMPKIN ROLL

3 eggs	½ teaspoon nutmeg
1 cup sugar	1 cup finely chopped
1 teaspoon lemon juice	walnuts
⅔ cup pumpkin	8 ounces cream cheese,
¾ cup all-purpose flour	softened
½ teaspoon salt	1 cup confectioners' sugar
2 teaspoons cinnamon	½ teaspoon vanilla extract
1 teaspoon ginger	

Beat eggs at high speed in mixer bowl. Add sugar gradually, beating constantly. Stir in lemon juice and pumpkin. Fold in mixture of flour, salt and spices. Pour into greased 15x17-inch baking pan. Sprinkle with walnuts. Bake at 375 degrees for 15 minutes. Invert onto towel sprinkled with confectioners' sugar. Roll up in towel as for jelly roll. Cool. Beat cream cheese, confectioners' sugar and vanilla in mixer bowl until light. Unroll cake. Spread with cream cheese mixture; reroll to enclose filling. Place on serving plate. Sprinkle with additional confectioners' sugar. Yield: 12 to 16 servings.

Bev Smith, Preceptor Alpha Kappa
Fresno, California

PUMPKIN CAKE ROLL

3 eggs	1 teaspoon ginger
1 cup sugar	½ teaspoon nutmeg
⅔ cup pumpkin	1 cup finely chopped nuts
1 teaspoon lemon juice	¼ cup butter, softened
¾ cup all-purpose flour	6 ounces cream cheese,
1 teaspoon baking	softened
powder	1 cup confectioners' sugar
½ teaspoon salt	½ teaspoon vanilla extract
2 teaspoons cinnamon	

Beat eggs in mixer bowl for 5 minutes. Add sugar, pumpkin and lemon juice gradually, beating until smooth. Fold in flour, baking powder, salt and spices. Spoon into greased and floured 10x14-inch baking pan. Sprinkle with nuts. Bake at 375 degrees for 15 minutes. Invert onto towel sprinkled with confectioners' sugar. Roll in towel from narrow end as for jelly roll. Cool. Cream remaining ingredients in mixer bowl until light and fluffy. Unroll cake. Spread with creamed mixture; reroll to enclose filling. Wrap in foil. Chill until serving time. Cut into slices. Yield: 8 to 10 servings.

Ann Campbell, Xi Beta Psi
Topeka, Kansas

PUMPKIN ROLL

3 eggs	½ teaspoon salt
1 cup sugar	1 cup nuts
⅔ cup pumpkin	4 teaspoons butter,
1 tablespoon lemon juice	softened
¾ cup all-purpose flour	8 ounces cream cheese,
1 teaspoon baking powder	softened
2 teaspoons cinnamon	1 cup confectioners' sugar
1 teaspoon ginger	½ teaspoon vanilla extract
½ teaspoon nutmeg	

Beat eggs at high speed in mixer bowl for 5 minutes or until thick and lemon-colored. Add sugar, pumpkin and lemon juice gradually, beating constantly at medium speed. Sift flour, baking powder, cinnamon, ginger, nutmeg and salt together 3 times. Stir into pumpkin mixture by hand. Pour into greased and floured 10x14-inch baking pan. Sprinkle with nuts. Bake at 375 degrees for 15 minutes. Invert onto towel sprinkled with confectioners' sugar. Roll up in towel as for jelly roll. Cool. Cream butter and cream cheese in mixer bowl until light. Blend in confectioners' sugar and vanilla. Unroll cake. Spread with cream cheese mixture; reroll. Wrap in foil. Freeze until firm. Let stand at room temperature for 15 to 20 minutes before serving. Cut into slices.
Yield: 12 to 13 servings.

Mary Louise Irby, Laureate Beta Omicron
Harlingen, Texas

PUMPKIN SPICE ROLL

3 eggs	1 cup finely chopped nuts
1 cup sugar	8 ounces cream cheese,
⅔ cup canned pumpkin	softened
1 teaspoon lemon juice	¼ cup butter, softened
¾ cup all-purpose flour	1 cup confectioners' sugar
1 teaspoon baking powder	1 teaspoon vanilla extract
2 teaspoons pumpkin pie	
spice	

Beat 3 eggs in mixer bowl until thick and lemon-colored. Add sugar gradually, beating until smooth. Add pumpkin and lemon juice; mix well. Fold in flour, baking powder and pumpkin pie spice. Spoon into greased 10x15-inch baking pan. Sprinkle with nuts. Bake at 375 degrees for 15 minutes. Invert onto towel sprinkled generously with confectioners' sugar. Roll up in towel as for jelly roll. Cool. Beat cream cheese with remaining ingredients in mixer bowl. Unroll cake. Spread with cream cheese mixture; reroll to enclose filling. Chill until serving time. Cut into ½-inch slices. Yield: 12 servings.

Mary M. Dalton, Xi Kappa Beta
Steubenville, Ohio

RHUBARB CAKE

1½ cups packed brown sugar	1 teaspoon soda
½ cup shortening	1 cup buttermilk
1 egg	2 cups chopped rhubarb
1 teaspoon vanilla extract	¼ cup packed brown sugar
2 cups all-purpose flour	1 teaspoon cinnamon

Cream 1½ cups brown sugar, shortening, egg and vanilla in bowl. Add flour and soda alternately with buttermilk, mixing well after each addition. Mix in rhubarb. Pour into greased and floured 9x13-inch baking pan. Sprinkle with mixture of ¼ cup brown sugar and cinnamon. Bake at 350 degrees for 45 minutes or until cake tests done. Cool in pan on wire rack. Yield: 16 servings.

Mary L. Suiter, Xi Beta Theta
Northfolk, West Virginia

RUM CAKE

1 cup chopped pecans	½ cup oil
1 2-layer package yellow cake mix	½ cup cold water
	½ cup dark rum
1 4-ounce package vanilla instant pudding mix	½ cup butter
	¼ cup water
	1 cup sugar
4 eggs	½ cup dark rum

Sprinkle pecans in bottom of greased and floured 12-cup bundt pan. Mix cake mix and pudding mix in mixer bowl. Add eggs, oil, ½ cup cold water and ½ cup rum; mix until smooth. Pour into prepared pan. Bake at 325 degrees for 1 hour. Remove to wire rack to cool. Invert onto serving plate. Melt butter in saucepan. Stir in ¼ cup water and sugar. Bring to a boil. Cook for 5 minutes, stirring constantly; remove from heat. Stir in ½ cup rum. Drizzle over top and side of cake. Yield: 16 servings.

Dorothy Hall, Preceptor Alpha Lambda
Newport News, Virginia

BASIC 7-UP CAKE

1 2-layer package yellow cake mix	4 eggs
	¾ cup oil
1 4-ounce package vanilla instant pudding mix	1 10-ounce bottle of 7-Up

Combine cake mix, pudding mix, eggs and oil in mixer bowl; mix well. Mix in 7-Up. Pour into greased and floured 9x13-inch cake pan. Bake at 350 degrees for 40 minutes. Pour Pineapple Frosting over cake. Yield: 16 servings.

PINEAPPLE FROSTING

½ cup margarine	2 eggs, beaten
1½ cups sugar	1 cup undrained crushed pineapple
1 tablespoon all-purpose flour	

Melt margarine in saucepan. Stir in mixture of sugar and flour. Add eggs and pineapple; mix well. Cook over low heat until thickened, stirring constantly.

Marilyn Borras, Xi Epsilon Alpha
Stafford, Virginia

LEMON 7-UP CAKE

1 2-layer package lemon cake mix	¾ cup oil
	4 eggs
1 4-ounce package lemon instant pudding mix	1 10-ounce bottle of 7-Up

Combine cake mix, pudding mix, oil, eggs and half the 7-Up in mixer bowl; mix well. Add remaining 7-Up. Beat until smooth. Pour into 2 greased and floured 8-inch cake pans. Bake at 350 degrees for 35 minutes or until cake tests done. Remove to wire rack. Spread Pineapple-Coconut Frosting between layers and over top and side of cake. Serve warm or cool. Yield: 10 servings.

PINEAPPLE-COCONUT FROSTING

2 eggs	1½ cups sugar
1 tablespoon all-purpose flour	1 16-ounce can crushed pineapple
½ cup margarine, softened	1 8-ounce package coconut

Combine eggs, flour, margarine, sugar and pineapple in saucepan; mix well. Cook over medium heat for 12 minutes, stirring occasionally. Stir in coconut.

Mary Woolard, Beta Sigma
New Bern, North Carolina

JEANNE'S STRAWBERRY CAKE

1 2-layer package yellow cake mix	7 ounces cream cheese, softened
	Milk
1 4-ounce package vanilla instant pudding mix	1 quart fresh strawberries, cut into quarters
1¾ cups milk	1 can cherry frosting

Prepare and bake cake mix in 3 greased and floured 8-inch cake pans according to package directions. Remove to wire rack to cool. Prepare pudding mix with 1¾ cups milk in bowl; mix well. Blend cream cheese with enough milk to make of spreading consistency. Spread ⅓ of the cream cheese mixture on 1 cake layer. Layer ⅓ of the pudding and ⅓ of the strawberries over cream cheese. Repeat with remaining 2 layers. Stack layers on serving plate. Frost side with cherry frosting. Chill until serving time. Yield: 16 servings.

Jeanne Davis, Preceptor Alpha Alpha
Tempe, Arizona

STRAWBERRY CAKE

1 2-layer package white cake mix	1 cup chopped pecans
1 cup oil	½ cup margarine, softened
1 3-ounce package strawberry gelatin	1 16-ounce package confectioners' sugar
4 eggs	½ cup drained strawberries
½ cup milk	½ cup coconut
1 cup frozen strawberries, thawed	½ cup chopped pecans
1 cup coconut	

Combine cake mix, oil, gelatin, eggs and milk in mixer bowl. Beat at medium speed until smooth. Mix in 1 cup strawberries, 1 cup coconut and 1 cup pecans. Spoon into 3 greased and floured layer cake pans. Bake at 350 degrees for 30 minutes. Remove to wire rack to cool. Cream margarine, confectioners' sugar and ½ cup strawberries in mixer bowl until fluffy. Mix in ½ cup coconut and ½ cup pecans. Spread between layers and over top and side of cake. Yield: 16 servings.

Margaret E. Niemyer, Preceptor Xi
Aberdeen, South Dakota

STRAWBERRY-NUT POUND CAKE

1 cup shortening	1 teaspoon soda
2 cups sugar	½ teaspoon salt
4 eggs	⅓ cup chopped strawberries
⅔ cup buttermilk	½ cup chopped pecans
1 teaspoon butter flavoring	1 cup sugar
1 teaspoon vanilla extract	½ cup strawberry juice
½ teaspoon strawberry extract	¼ cup chopped strawberries
1½ teaspoons red food coloring	½ teaspoon vanilla extract
3 cups sifted all-purpose flour	½ teaspoon butter flavoring
½ teaspoon baking powder	½ teaspoon strawberry extract

Cream shortening and 2 cups sugar in mixer bowl until light and fluffy. Add eggs 1 at a time, beating well after each addition. Mix buttermilk, 1 teaspoon butter flavoring, 1 teaspoon vanilla, ½ teaspoon strawberry extract and red food coloring. Sift flour, baking powder, soda and salt together. Add to batter alternately with buttermilk mixture, mixing well after each addition. Fold in ⅓ cup strawberries and pecans. Pour into greased and floured 10-inch tube pan. Bake at 350 degrees for 1 hour and 20 minutes or until toothpick inserted near center comes out clean. Invert onto serving plate. Combine remaining ingredients in small saucepan. Bring to a boil, stirring constantly. Cook for 1 minute. Brush over top and side of hot cake. Yield: 16 servings.

Wilma Hayes, Preceptor Zeta Chi
Baytown, Texas

SOUR CREAM CAKE

½ cup butter, softened	1 teaspoon baking powder
1 cup sugar	1 teaspoon soda
2 eggs	1 cup sour cream
2 cups sifted cake flour	½ teaspoon vanilla extract

Cream butter and sugar in mixer bowl until light. Blend in eggs. Add dry ingredients alternately with sour cream, mixing well after each addition. Stir in vanilla. Pour into greased 8-inch square cake pan. Bake at 350 degrees for 40 minutes. Cool. Yield: 12 servings.

Becky Espar, Alpha
Columbus, Georgia

TORNADO CAKE

1½ cups sugar	¼ cup packed brown sugar
2 eggs	½ cup butter
2 cups fruit cocktail	¾ cup sugar
2 cups all-purpose flour	½ cup evaporated milk
2 teaspoons soda	1 cup flaked coconut
1 cup chopped nuts	

Combine first 5 ingredients in bowl; mix well. Pour into lightly greased and floured 9 x 13-inch cake pan. Sprinkle with mixture of nuts and brown sugar. Bake at 325 degrees for 40 minutes. Bring remaining ingredients to a boil in saucepan. Boil for 2 minutes. Add coconut. Spoon over hot cake. Cool. Yield: 25 to 30 servings.

Pam Lewis, Delta Kappa
Ellisville, Mississippi

VANILLA WAFER CAKE

1 cup margarine, softened	½ cup milk
2 cups sugar	1 7-ounce package coconut
6 eggs	1 cup chopped nuts
1 12-ounce package vanilla wafers, crushed	

Cream margarine and sugar in mixer bowl until light and fluffy. Blend in eggs 1 at a time. Add cookie crumbs and milk; mix well. Stir in coconut and nuts. Pour into greased and floured tube pan. Bake at 300 degrees for 1½ hours. Reduce temperature to 250 degrees. Bake for 30 minutes longer. Cool on wire rack. Yield: 16 servings.

Chris Richardson, Xi Zeta Eta
Pasadena, Texas

Broiled toppings make icing cakes baked in 9 x 13-inch pans easy. Spread one of the following mixtures over hot cake and broil for 2 minutes or until bubbly: 2 tablespoons melted butter, ¼ cup honey and ¾ cup chopped nuts; 1 cup each packed brown sugar, coconut and chopped nuts plus ⅓ cup evaporated milk; ¼ cup melted butter, ⅔ cup packed brown sugar, 3 tablespoons cream and 1 cup each coconut and brickle chips; ½ cup each orange juice concentrate, chopped nuts and melted butter plus 1 cup each packed brown sugar and flaked coconut.

Cookies

ANGEL COOKIES

½ cup butterscotch chips
2 tablespoons margarine
1 teaspoon vanilla extract
2 cups confectioners' sugar
2 eggs, beaten

½ teaspoon salt
4 cups miniature
  marshmallows
1 cup chopped nuts
Coconut

Melt butterscotch chips with margarine in double boiler; blend well. Mix with vanilla, confectioners' sugar, eggs and salt in bowl. Stir in marshmallows and nuts. Drop by teaspoonfuls into coconut, coating well; place on waxed paper. Let stand until set. Yield: 5 dozen.

Shirley Fitch, Xi Upsilon
Flagstaff, Arizona

ANISE COOKIE CUT-OUTS

3 cups shortening
6 cups sugar
8 eggs, beaten
18 cups all-purpose flour
2 teaspoons salt

6 tablespoons baking
  powder
3 cups milk
1 cup warm water
4 teaspoons pure anise oil

Cream shortening and sugar in large bowl until light and fluffy. Add eggs; mix well. Add mixture of flour, salt and baking powder alternately with milk and water, mixing well after each addition. Add anise oil; mix well. Chill, covered, for several hours. Roll very thinly on floured surface; cut into desired shapes. Place on greased cookie sheet. Bake at 375 degrees for 10 to 12 minutes or until golden. Cool on wire rack. Frost cooled cookies if desired. Yield: 33 dozen.

Elaine Montrois, Xi Delta
Rochester, New York

ADDICTIVE APRICOT BARS

½ cup unsalted butter,
  softened
⅓ cup packed brown sugar
1¼ cups all-purpose flour
¾ cup apricot preserves
¼ cup butter, softened
½ cup packed brown sugar

½ teaspoon almond extract
¾ cup all-purpose flour
⅛ teaspoon salt
¾ cup confectioners' sugar
1 tablespoon milk
1 tablespoon almond
  extract

Mix ½ cup unsalted butter, ⅓ cup brown sugar and 1¼ cups flour in bowl until crumbly. Press into greased 9x9-inch baking dish. Bake at 350 degrees for 15 to 20 minutes until light brown. Cool. Spread preserves over crust, leaving ½-inch border. Cream ¼ cup butter, ½ cup brown sugar and ½ teaspoon almond flavoring in bowl until light and fluffy. Add ¾ cup flour and salt; mix until crumbly. Sprinkle over preserves. Bake at 350 degrees for 20 to 25 minutes or until light brown. Cool. Beat confectioners' sugar, milk and 1 tablespoon almond extract in small bowl until smooth. Drizzle over cooled baked layer. Cut into squares. Yield: 3 dozen.

Sissy Smith, Epsilon Psi
Shelbyville, Tennessee

BLONDIES

⅔ cup oil	2½ teaspoons baking
1 16-ounce package	powder
dark brown sugar	12 ounces semisweet
3 eggs	chocolate chips
2¾ cups all-purpose	1 cup coarsely chopped
flour	nuts
½ teaspoon salt	

Beat oil, brown sugar and eggs in mixer bowl until thick and smooth. Add mixture of flour, salt and baking powder; mix well. Stir in chocolate chips and nuts. Spoon into buttered 9x13-inch baking dish. Bake at 325 degrees for 25 minutes for moist Blondies and 30 minutes for cake-like Blondies. Cool in pan on wire rack until almost cool. Cut into bars. Yield: 3 dozen.
Note: May substitute peanut butter chips for chocolate chips. Bars freeze well.

Stella Jenks, Preceptor Zeta Lambda
Santa Rosa, California

BROWNIES

½ cup margarine,	1 teaspoon vanilla extract
softened	⅓ cup cocoa
1 cup sugar	½ cup all-purpose flour
2 eggs, beaten	

Cream margarine and sugar in bowl until light and fluffy. Add eggs and vanilla; mix well. Add mixture of cocoa and flour; mix well. Pour into greased 8x8-inch baking dish. Bake at 325 degrees for 25 minutes; do not overbake. Cool. Cut into squares. Yield: 1½ dozen.

Wanda Odom, Preceptor Epsilon Upsilon
Denison, Texas

EASY BROWNIES

1 cup melted margarine	1 teaspoon vanilla extract
1 teaspoon hot water	2¼ cups sifted self-rising
2 cups sugar	flour
4 eggs, beaten	5 tablespoons cocoa

Combine first 5 ingredients in bowl; mix until creamy. Sift in flour and cocoa; mix until smooth. Pour in foil-lined 9x13-inch baking pan. Bake at 350 degrees for 35 to 45 minutes or until brownies pull from side of pan. Remove from pan by lifting out foil. Cool on wire rack. Cut into squares. May be frosted. Yield: 3 dozen.

Rebecca Council, Epsilon Chi
Wallace, North Carolina

CARAMEL CHOCOLATE SQUARES

1 14-ounce package	1 2-layer package
caramels	German chocolate
1 6-ounce can	cake mix
evaporated milk	1 cup chopped nuts
¾ cup melted margarine	1 cup chocolate chips

Melt caramels in ⅓ cup evaporated milk in double boiler; blend well. Combine remaining evaporated milk, margarine and cake mix in bowl; mix well. Mix in nuts. Press half the mixture into greased and floured 9x13-inch baking pan. Bake at 350 degrees for 6 minutes. Sprinkle with chocolate chips. Spoon caramel mixture over chips. Crumble remaining cake mix mixture over top. Bake for 15 to 20 minutes longer. Cool. Cut into squares. Garnish each with spoonful of whipped cream. Yield: 2 dozen.

Pam Feldhaus, Epsilon Psi
Shelbyville, Tennessee

GRANDMA O'LEARY'S DATE BARS

1 16-ounce package dates	1 cup packed brown
½ cup milk	sugar
⅓ cup sugar	3 cup quick-cooking oats
1 cup melted butter	1 teaspoon soda
1 cup all-purpose flour	1 teaspoon (scant) salt

Combine dates, milk and sugar in saucepan. Cook until dates are very tender but not dry, adding additional milk if necessary to make of desired consistency. Combine butter, flour, brown sugar, oats, soda and salt in bowl; mix well. Spread half the oats mixture in 9x13-inch baking pan. Spread date filling over oats. Top with remaining oats mixture. Bake at 350 degrees for 30 minutes. Cool. Cut into bars. Yield: 2 dozen.

Dena Olson, Preceptor Sigma
Mountain Home, Idaho

SCOTCH FRUIT BARS

⅔ cup shortening	1 teaspoon baking powder
2 cups packed brown	½ teaspoon salt
sugar	1½ to 2 cups chopped
2 eggs, beaten	candied or dried fruit
1 teaspoon vanilla extract	½ cup chopped nuts
2 cups sifted all-purpose	Confectioners' sugar
flour	

Cream shortening and brown sugar in bowl until light and fluffy. Add eggs and vanilla; mix well. Add mixture of flour, baking powder and salt; mix well. Stir in fruit and nuts. Pour into greased 7x11-inch baking pan. Bake at 350 degrees for 30 minutes or until golden brown. Blend desired amount of confectioners' sugar with enough warm water to make of desired consistency. Spread over warm baked layer. Cool. Cut into bars. Yield: 1½ dozen.

Billy Jane Gabel, Xi Mu Eta
Houston, Texas

Bar cookies are magic—just bake and cut for dozens of cookies from one pan. Use the following pan sizes and cuts as a guide. For 9x13-inch pan: make 2 lengthwise x 7 crosswise cuts for 2 dozen; 5 lengthwise x 5 crosswise cuts for 3 dozen; 7 lengthwise x 5 crosswise cuts for 4 dozen. For 10x15-inch pan: make 3 lengthwise x 8 crosswise cuts for 3 dozen; 3 lengthwise x 11 crosswise cuts for 4 dozen; 3 lengthwise x 14 crosswise cuts for 5 dozen; 7 lengthwise x 6 crosswise cuts for 6 dozen.

GRAHAM CRACKER COOKIES

Graham crackers	1 cup packed brown sugar
1 cup margarine, softened	1 cup chopped pecans

Arrange whole graham crackers in 10x15-inch baking pan. Bring margarine and brown sugar to a full rolling boil in saucepan. Add pecans; mix wll. Pour over graham crackers. Bake at 350 degrees for 7 to 8 minutes. Cool. Break into pieces. May be stored, wrapped, in freezer. Yield: 1 dozen.

Wanda Odom, Preceptor Epsilon Upsilon
Denison, Texas

SHAUN'S MICROWAVE BARS

2 cups Cheerios cereal	8 ounces semisweet
1 14-ounce can	chocolate chips
sweetened condensed	6 ounces butterscotch
milk	chips
1½ cups coconut	

Combine all ingredients in bowl; mix well. Spoon into greased 8x8-inch glass dish. Microwave on High for 5 minutes or until chocolate chips are soft but not melted. Stir until cereal is well coated. Microwave for 5 to 10 minutes or just until mixture begins to pull from sides of dish. Cool in pan on wire rack. Cut into squares. Yield: 2 dozen.
Note: May substitute Kix cereal for Cheerios and/or peanut butter chips for butterscotch chips. May add 1 to 2 cups miniature marshmallows.

D. Shaun Shipman, Iota Gamma
Oakland, California

NEIMAN-MARCUS BARS

½ cup melted butter	8 ounces cream cheese,
1 2-layer package	softened
yellow cake mix	1 16-ounce package
1 egg, beaten	confectioners's sugar
1 cup chopped pecans	½ teaspoon lemon extract
2 eggs	

Combine butter, cake mix, 1 egg and pecans in bowl; mix until crumbly. Press into greased 9x13-inch pan. Combine 2 eggs, cream cheese, confectioners' sugar and lemon flavoring in bowl; mix until creamy. Pour over cake mix layer. Bake at 350 degrees for 40 minutes. Cool. Cut into bars. Yield: 2 dozen.

Diana Bal, Xi Delta Xi
Rochester, New York

PINEAPPLE BARS

1 cup butter, softened	½ cup butter, softened
1 teaspoon vanilla extract	8 ounces cream cheese,
2 eggs	softened
2 cups all-purpose flour	2 cups confectioners'
1 tablespoon soda	sugar
1 16-ounce can crushed	1 teaspoon vanilla extract
pineapple	Chopped nuts
1 cup chopped nuts	

Cream 1 cup butter, 1 teaspoon vanilla and eggs in bowl. Add mixture of flour and soda. Mix in pineapple and 1 cup nuts. Pour into greased and floured 15x18-inch baking pan. Bake at 375 degrees for 35 minutes. Cool. Cream ½ cup butter, cream cheese, confectioners' sugar and 1 teaspoon vanilla in bowl. Frost cooled baked layer. Sprinkle with additional nuts. Cut into 2-inch squares. Yield: 5 to 5½ dozen.

Donna Chiarello, Xi Kappa Beta
Follansbee, West Virginia

ALICE'S PUMPKIN BARS

2 cups mashed cooked	½ teaspoon salt
pumpkin	3 ounces cream cheese,
2 cups sugar	softened
1 cup oil	6 tablespoons butter,
4 eggs, beaten	softened
2 cups flour	1¾ cups confectioners'
2 teaspoons baking	sugar
powder	1 tablespoon cream
2 teaspoons cinnamon	1 teaspoon vanilla extract
1 teaspoon soda	

Combine pumpkin, sugar, oil and eggs in large bowl; mix well. Stir in mixture of flour, baking powder, cinnamon, soda and salt; mix well. Spread in 7x11-inch baking pan. Bake at 350 degrees for 25 minutes. Cool. Beat cream cheese, butter and confectioners' sugar in bowl until light and fluffy. Add cream and vanilla; mix well. Frost cooled baked layer. Cut into bars. Yield: 2 dozen.

Mary Ann Mader, Laureate Alpha Delta
Elizabeth Township, Pennsylvania

SAUCEPAN OATMEAL COOKIES

2 cups sugar	2 cups quick-cooking oats
¼ cup cocoa	¼ cup peanut butter
½ cup milk	1 tablespoon light
½ cup butter or margarine	corn syrup

Combine sugar and cocoa in saucepan. Stir in milk. Add butter. Bring to a boil. Cook for 3 minutes. Stir in oatmeal and peanut butter. Return to a boil. Remove from heat. Drop by teaspoonfuls onto waxed paper. Cool. Yield: 3 dozen.
Note: Our chapter uses this and other cookie favorites at a chapter Christmas cookie exchange. Each person brings enough cookies of one kind to give one dozen cookies to each member. Cookies should be packaged with one dozen to a bag tied with a pretty ribbon.

Preceptor Zeta Chi
Baytown, Texas

Vary Saucepan Oatmeal Cookies by adding one of the following: ¼ teaspoon cinnamon; ½ cup chopped nuts; ½ cup coconut; 1 package vanilla instant pudding mix for cocoa; rice cereal for oats; additional peanut butter up to 1 cup.

SAUCEPAN RAISIN BARS

1 cup raisins	1 teaspoon cinnamon
1 cup sugar	1/4 teaspoon each cloves,
1 cup water	nutmeg and salt
1/2 cup oil	2 cups all-purpose flour
1 teaspoon vanilla extract	1 teaspoon soda

Combine raisins, sugar, water, oil, vanilla and seasonings in saucepan. Cook for 3 minutes. Cool. Add flour and soda; mix well. Spread on buttered cookie sheet. Cool. Frost with confectioners' sugar frosting if desired. Cut into bars. Yield: 2 dozen.
Note: May add candied fruit and dates if desired.

Lorraine Kirkpatrick, Xi Eta Kappa
Barstow, California

SOUR CREAM RAISIN BARS

4 egg yolks	1 cup packed brown sugar
1 1/2 cups sugar	1 3/4 cups quick-cooking
2 cups sour cream	oats
2 cups raisins	1 3/4 cups all-purpose flour
3 tablespoons cornstarch	1 teaspoon soda
1 cup margarine, softened	

Bring mixture of egg yolks and next 4 ingredients to a boil in saucepan over low heat, stirring constantly. Cook for 15 minutes or until thick, stirring constantly. Cool. Cream margarine and brown sugar in bowl until light and fluffy. Add mixture of oats, flour and soda; mix until crumbly. Press half the mixture into greased 9x13-inch baking pan. Bake at 350 degrees for 15 minutes. Spread raisin mixture over baked layer. Sprinkle remaining oats mixture on top. Bake at 350 degrees for 20 minutes. Cool. Cut into squares. Yield: 2 1/2 dozen.

Darlene Burchinal, Preceptor Beta
Bismarck, North Dakota

BUTTER THUMB COOKIES

1 cup butter, softened	2 teaspoons vanilla extract
1/3 cup sugar	2 cups all-purpose flour

Cream butter, sugar and vanilla in mixer bowl until light and fluffy. Blend in flour. Chill in refrigerator. Divide into 4 portions. Roll each portion into rope on floured surface. Slice diagonally into 2-inch lengths. Roll in additional sugar. Place on cookie sheet. Cut 3 diagonal slashes in top of each cookie. Bake at 375 degrees for 10 to 12 minutes or until golden brown. Cool on wire rack.
Yield: 2 dozen.
Note: May double or triple recipe.

Lisa Fay, Alpha Omicron
Williston, North Dakota

Butter cookies may be formed into a variety of shapes: shape into balls, indent with thumb and fill with preserves; or roll into thin 7-inch ropes, twist 2 ropes together, shape into wreaths and seal ends.

CHOCOLATE THUMBPRINT COOKIES

1/2 cup butter, softened	2 tablespoons sugar
2/3 cup sugar	1/2 cup confectioners' sugar
1 egg, separated	1 tablespoon butter,
2 tablespoons milk	softened
1 teaspoon vanilla extract	2 tablespoons milk
1 cup all-purpose flour	1/4 teaspoon vanilla extract
1/4 cup cocoa	Candied cherries, walnut
1/4 teaspoon salt	or pecan halves,
1 cup finely chopped nuts	chocolate kisses

Cream 1/2 cup butter, 2/3 cup sugar, egg yolk, 2 tablespoons milk and 1 teaspoon vanilla in bowl until light and fluffy. Add mixture of flour, cocoa and salt; blend well. Chill for 1 hour. Shape into 1-inch balls. Dip into beaten egg white. Coat with mixture of chopped nuts and 2 tablespoons sugar. Place on lightly greased cookie sheet. Make indentation in center of each. Bake at 350 degrees for 10 minutes or until set. Combine confectioners' sugar, 1 tablespoon butter, 2 tablespoons milk and 1/4 teaspoon vanilla in bowl; mix well. Spoon 1/4 teaspoon into each hot cookie. Place cherry, nut half or chocolate kiss in center. Cool on wire rack. Yield: 2 dozen.

Photograph for this recipe on Cover.

CHERUB PUFFS

2 egg whites, at room	1/2 cup sugar
temperature	6 ounces chocolate chips
1/2 teaspoon white vinegar	1/2 cup finely chopped
1/2 teaspoon vanilla extract	pecans
1/8 teaspoon salt	

Combine egg whites, vinegar, vanilla and salt in bowl. Beat with small wire whisk until soft peaks form. Add sugar gradually, beating until very stiff. Fold in chocolate chips and nuts. Drop by teaspoonfuls onto foil-lined cookie sheet. Bake at 350 degrees for 5 minutes. Turn off oven. Let cookies stand in closed oven for 2 to 3 hours or until cool. Yield: 2 to 3 dozen.

Lucile Davis, Preceptor Nu
Anniston, Alabama

CHOCOLATE CHIP COOKIES

1 cup margarine, softened	2 eggs
1 cup sugar	2 1/4 cups all-purpose flour
1/2 cup packed brown	1 teaspoon soda
sugar	1 teaspoon salt
1 teaspoon vanilla extract	12 ounces chocolate chips

Cream margarine, sugars and vanilla in bowl until light and fluffy. Add eggs; mix well. Add mixture of flour, soda and salt; mix well. Stir in chocolate chips. Drop by teaspoonfuls onto greased cookie sheet. Bake at 350 degrees for 10 minutes or until light brown. Cool on wire rack. Yield: 5 dozen.

Andrea Ryan, Zeta Alpha
Williamsport, Pennsylvania

CHOCOLATE SNOWBALLS

1¼ cups butter, softened　　*½ cup cocoa*
⅔ cup sugar　　*⅛ teaspoon salt*
1 teaspoon vanilla extract　　*2 cups chopped nuts*
2 cups all-purpose flour　　*Confectioners' sugar*

Cream butter, sugar and vanilla in bowl until light and fluffy. Sift in flour, cocoa and salt; mix well. Stir in nuts. Chill, covered, overnight. Shape into small balls. Place ½ inch apart on ungreased cookie sheet. Bake at 350 degrees for 20 minutes. Cool on wire rack. Roll cooled cookies in confectioners' sugar. Yield: 3 dozen.

Dolores Brown, Xi Alpha Gamma
Sheldon, South Carolina

FILLED CHOCOLATE BARS

½ cup butter　　*1 cup confectioners' sugar*
2 ounces unsweetened　　*1 tablespoon milk*
　baking chocolate　　*2 tablespoons butter,*
2 eggs, beaten　　　*softened*
1 cup sugar　　*½ teaspoon vanilla extract*
½ cup all-purpose flour　　*¼ cup sugar*
¼ teaspoon salt　　*2 tablespoons water*
1 teaspoon vanilla extract　　*½ cup chocolate*
1 cup finely chopped nuts　　*Mini Chips*

Melt ½ cup butter in saucepan. Remove from heat. Add baking chocolate; stir until melted. Combine eggs, 1 cup sugar, flour and salt in bowl; beat well. Add melted chocolate and 1 teaspoon vanilla; blend well. Stir in nuts. Spread batter in greased waxed paper-lined 10x15-inch baking pan. Bake at 400 degrees for 10 minutes. Cool. Cut in half crosswise. Invert onto cutting board. Combine confectioners' sugar, milk, 2 tablespoons butter and ½ teaspoon vanilla in bowl. Beat until smooth. Spread on 1 layer. Place on serving plate. Top with remaining layer. Bring ¼ cup sugar and water to a boil in saucepan; remove from heat. Stir in chocolate chips until melted. Spread over top layer. Cut into bars. Garnish with almonds or walnuts. Yield: 2 dozen.

Photograph for this recipe on Cover.

CHRISTMAS COOKIE VARIETY

BASIC COOKIE DOUGH

1 cup butter, softened　　*2½ cups all-purpose flour*
1½ cups confectioners'　　*1 teaspoon soda*
　sugar　　*1 teaspoon cream of tartar*
1 egg　　*¼ teaspoon salt*
1 teaspoon vanilla extract

Cream butter and confectioners' sugar in mixer bowl until light and fluffy. Blend in egg and vanilla. Add flour, soda, cream of tartar and salt; mix well. Add ingredients and shape according to variety selected. Bake at 400 degrees for 8 to 10 minutes or until brown. Remove to wire rack to cool.
Note: Three recipes Basic Cookie Dough will make all 5 varieties.

VARIETY 1

Mix ½ recipe Basic Cookie Dough with ½ cup chopped pecans and ¼ cup chopped maraschino cherries. Chill in refrigerator. Shape into small finger-sized rolls. Sprinkle hot cookies with sugar.

VARIETY 2

Drop ½ recipe Basic Cookie Dough by ½ teaspoonfuls onto cookie sheet. Top each with piece of candied fruit or nut half.

VARIETY 3

Mix ½ recipe Basic Cookie Dough with ¾ cup ground walnuts. Chill in refrigerator. Shape into marble-sized balls. Roll hot cookies in confectioners' sugar.

VARIETY 4

Chill ½ recipe Basic Cookie Dough. Shape into walnut-sized balls. Roll in mixture of 2 tablespoons sugar and ½ teaspoon cinnamon.

VARIETY 5

Mix 1 recipe Basic Cookie Dough with ¼ cup molasses, 2 teaspoons cinnamon, ½ teaspoon ginger and ½ teaspoon nutmeg. Roll ¼ inch thick on floured surface. Cut with cookie cutters. Bake for 6 minutes.

Frances E. Adam, Xi Alpha Theta
Chestertown, Maryland

GRANDMA'S CHRISTMAS NUT COOKIES

1½ cups melted　　*1 cup chopped walnuts*
　shortening　　*5 cups all-purpose flour*
1 cup sugar　　*1 teaspoon cinnamon*
1 cup packed brown sugar　　*1 teaspoon soda*
3 eggs, beaten　　*1 teaspoon salt*

Beat shortening and sugars in bowl until light and fluffy. Add eggs 1 at a time, beating well after each addition. Stir in walnuts. Add mixture of flour, cinnamon, soda and salt; mix well. Shape into logs. Chill, wrapped in plastic wrap, overnight. Slice thinly; arrange on greased cookie sheet. Bake at 350 degrees for 10 to 12 minutes or until golden. Cool on wire rack. Yield: 6 dozen.

Kandee Graham, Preceptor Beta Kappa
Hershey, Pennsylvania

COCONUT ORANGE BALLS

1　12-ounce box vanilla　　*1 cup sifted confectioners'*
　wafers, crushed　　　*sugar*
1　6-ounce can frozen　　*¾ cup chopped nuts*
　orange juice　　*2　7-ounce cans flaked*
　concentrate, thawed　　　*coconut*
½ cup melted butter

Combine wafer crumbs, orange juice concentrate, butter, confectioners' sugar and nuts in bowl; mix well. Shape into ¾-inch balls. Roll in coconut. Store, covered, in refrigerator. Yield: 4 dozen.

Georgia M. Cuneo, Laureate Alpha
Winston-Salem, North Carolina

CHRISTMAS ROCKS

2 pounds dates	2 teaspoons soda
3 slices candied	2 teaspoons cinnamon
pineapple	2 teaspoons salt
1½ pounds candied	1 pound walnuts
cherries	1 pound pecans
1 pound raisins	1 pound butter, softened
1 pound Brazil nuts	3 cups packed brown
½ pound cashews	sugar
½ pound almonds	4 eggs
5 cups all-purpose flour	½ cup cream

Chop fruit, Brazil nuts, cashews and almonds. Sift flour, soda, cinnamon and salt into bowl. Coat mixture of all nuts and fruit with 1 cup flour mixture in bowl; toss to coat. Cream butter and brown sugar in large mixer bowl until light and fluffy. Blend in eggs 1 at a time. Add remaining flour mixture alternately with cream, mixing well after each addition. Fold in fruit and nuts. Drop by spoonfuls onto greased cookie sheet. Bake at 275 degrees for 25 to 30 minutes or until brown. Cool on wire rack. Yield: 12 dozen.

Helen Williams, Preceptor Kappa Psi
Sebastopol, California

CRANBERRY CHEWS

4 eggs, beaten	½ teaspoon salt
2 cups sugar	1 16-ounce can jellied
Juice of 1 lemon	cranberry sauce
½ teaspoon lemon extract	1½ cups chopped pecans
½ teaspoon almond	3 cups confectioners'
extract	sugar
3 cups all-purpose flour	6 to 8 tablespoons milk
1 tablespoon baking	¼ cup butter, softened
powder	1 teaspoon vanilla extract

Beat eggs and sugar in mixer bowl until thick and smooth. Blend in lemon juice, lemon extract and almond extract. Add sifted flour, baking powder and salt; mix well. Chop cranberry sauce into ¼-inch cubes. Fold cranberry cubes and pecans into batter. Spread in 2 greased 10x15-inch baking pans. Bake at 350 degrees for 30 minutes. Combine confectioners' sugar and remaining ingredients in bowl; mix until smooth and creamy. Spread on warm cranberry layer. Cut into squares while warm. Yield: 6 to 7 dozen.

Violet R. Nolfi, Xi Upsilon Delta
Borrego Springs, California

CRY BABIES

1 cup butter, softened	1 teaspoon baking powder
1 cup sugar	1 teaspoon cinnamon
1 cup molasses	1 teaspoon ginger
2 eggs	¼ teaspoon salt
2 teaspoons soda	1 teaspoon vinegar
1 cup hot coffee	1 cup raisins
4½ cups all-purpose flour	1 cup chopped nuts

Cream butter and sugar in bowl until light and fluffy. Add molasses and eggs; mix well. Dissolve soda in coffee. Add alternately with mixture of flour, baking powder, cinnamon, ginger and salt, mixing well after each addition. Stir in vinegar, raisins and nuts. Drop by teaspoonfuls onto greased baking sheet. Bake at 350 degrees for 15 to 20 minutes or until cookie springs back when lightly touched. Cool on wire rack. Frost warm cookies with confectioners' sugar glaze. Serve with chilled canned peaches. Yield: 6 to 8 dozen.

Note: These cookies were family favorites as I was growing up in the 40's.

Jean Kuhn, Xi Iota
Wyoming, Michigan

DATE PINWHEELS

2½ cups chopped dates	1 cup sugar
1 cup water	3 eggs, beaten
1 cup sugar	4 cups all-purpose flour
1 cup chopped nuts	1 teaspoon soda
1 cup shortening	¾ teaspoon salt
1 cup packed brown sugar	

Bring dates, water and 1 cup sugar to a boil in saucepan. Simmer until tender, stirring occasionally. Stir in nuts. Cool. Cream shortening, brown sugar and 1 cup sugar in bowl until light and fluffy. Add eggs; mix well. Add mixture of flour, soda and salt; mix well. Divide into 4 portions. Roll each into 9x11-inch rectangle on floured surface. Spread with cooled date mixture. Roll as for jelly roll. Cut into 1-inch slices. Place on ungreased cookie sheet. Bake at 350 degrees for 10 to 12 minutes or until golden. Cool on cookie sheet for 1 minute. Remove to wire rack to cool completely. Yield: 12 dozen.

Willie Cook, Preceptor Beta Gamma
Augusta, Kansas

MELTING MOMENTS COOKIES

1 cup butter, softened	2 tablespoons butter,
5 tablespoons	softened
confectioners' sugar	1 cup sifted confectioners'
1 teaspoon vanilla extract	sugar
1 cup all-purpose flour	1 teaspoon almond extract
¾ cup cornstarch	Juice of ½ lemon
½ teaspoon salt	

Cream 1 cup butter and 5 tablespoons confectioners' sugar in bowl until light and fluffy. Add vanilla; mix well. Add mixture of flour, cornstarch and salt; mix well. Shape into small balls. Place on greased cookie sheet. Make indentation in each cookie with moistened finger. Bake at 350 degrees for 12 to 15 minutes. Cool on wire rack. Cream 2 tablespoons butter and 1 cup confectioners' sugar in bowl until light and fluffy. Add almond flavoring and enough lemon juice to make of spreading consistency. Frost cooled cookies. Yield: 2½ dozen.

Mary Louise Irby, Laureate Beta Omicron
Harlingen, Texas

CHRISTMAS FRUIT COOKIES

1 pound butter, softened	8 ounces Brazil nuts
1 cup sugar	4 ounces red candied
1 cup packed brown sugar	cherries
4 eggs	4 ounces green candied
1 teaspoon vanilla extract	cherries
4 cups all-purpose flour	6 ounces candied
1 teaspoon soda	pineapple
Dash of salt	8 ounces dates
8 ounces pecans	1 cup all-purpose flour

Cream butter, sugar and brown sugar in bowl until creamy. Add eggs and vanilla; beat until light and fluffy. Add next 3 sifted dry ingredients; mix well. Dough will be stiff. Mix whole nuts and fruits with 1 cup flour. Stir into dough. Shape into ten 1½-inch diameter logs; wrap in plastic wrap. Store in freezer for up to 1 year. Slice with serrated knife. Place on lightly greased cookie sheet. Bake at 350 degrees for 18 to 20 minutes or until golden. Cool on wire rack. Yield: 3 dozen per roll.

Jackie Vogler, Xi Sigma Phi
Hilltop Lakes, Texas

FRUITCAKE COOKIES

¼ cup margarine,	½ teaspoon cloves
softened	1 pound pecans, chopped
1 cup packed brown sugar	1 pound raisins
2 eggs, beaten	1 pound candied cherries,
⅓ cup dark rum	chopped
1½ teaspoons soda	½ pound candied green
1½ tablespoons milk	pineapple, chopped
2 cups all-purpose flour	½ pound candied yellow
½ teaspoon cinnamon	pineapple, chopped
½ teaspoon nutmeg	

Cream margarine and brown sugar in large bowl until light and fluffy. Add eggs and rum; mix well. Add mixture of soda and milk; mix well. Add mixture of flour, cinnamon, nutmeg and cloves; mix well. Stir in pecans, raisins and candied fruit. Drop by teaspoonfuls onto greased cookie sheet. Bake at 325 degrees for 12 minutes. Cool on wire rack. Yield: 12 dozen.

Joanne Wilkerson, Preceptor Alpha Rho
Pasadena, Texas

BOURBON FRUITCAKE COOKIES

1½ cups raisins	1½ teaspoons soda
¼ cup Bourbon	1½ teaspoons cinnamon
¼ cup melted butter	½ teaspoon nutmeg
½ cup packed brown	½ teaspoon cloves
sugar	1 pound mixed candied
2 eggs, beaten	fruit
1½ cups all-purpose flour	2 cups pecan halves

Soak raisins in Bourbon in bowl for 1 hour. Beat butter, brown sugar and eggs in bowl with fork until light and fluffy. Add mixture of flour, soda, cinnamon, nutmeg and cloves; mix well. Add raisins and Bourbon; mix well.

Stir in candied fruit and pecans. Chill, covered, overnight. Shape into walnut-sized balls; place on greased cookie sheet. Bake at 325 degrees for 12 minutes. Cool on wire rack. Yield: 4 dozen.

Jacqueline Neil, Xi Gamma Alpha
Dubuque, Iowa

EVELYN'S HOLIDAY HORNS

1 cup butter	½ cup packed brown
2 cups all-purpose flour	sugar
1 egg yolk, slightly beaten	¼ cup sugar
¾ cup sour cream	1 teaspoon cinnamon
½ cup chopped walnuts	

Cut butter into flour in bowl with pastry cutter. Add egg yolk and sour cream; mix well. Shape into ball; wrap in lightly floured waxed paper. Chill for several hours to overnight. Mix remaining ingredients in bowl or food processor. Divide chilled dough into 4 portions. Roll each into very thin circle on floured surface. Sprinkle with ¼ of the walnut filling. Cut into 16 wedges. Roll up from wide end. Place on lightly greased cookie sheet. Bake at 375 degrees for 20 to 25 minutes or until brown. Cool on wire rack. Yield: 5 dozen.

Patricia V. West, Epsilon Rho
Colorado Springs, Colorado

GINGERBREAD PEOPLE

¼ cup butter or	1 teaspoon soda
margarine, softened	¼ teaspoon cloves
½ cup packed light	½ teaspoon cinnamon
brown sugar	2 teaspoons ginger
½ cup light molasses	½ teaspoon salt
3½ cups all-purpose	¼ cup water
flour, sifted	¼ cup raisins

Cream first 3 ingredients in bowl until light and fluffy. Sift flour, soda, spices and salt together. Add to creamed mixture alternately with water, mixing well after each addition. Roll on floured surface. Cut with cookie cutter. Place on greased cookie sheet. Bake at 350 degrees for 8 minutes. Cool on pan for 4 minutes. Remove to wire rack to cool completely. Decorate with Royal Icing and raisins for eyes and buttons.
Yield: 8 to 12 cookies.

ROYAL ICING

1¼ cups confectioners'	⅛ teaspoon cream of tartar
sugar	Food coloring
1 egg white, beaten	

Combine confectioners' sugar, egg white and cream of tartar in bowl; mix well. Tint with food coloring of choice. Add enough water 1 drop at a time to make of spreading consistency, mixing well after each addition.

GINGER COOKIES (LEBKUCHEN)

½ cup butter, softened	1½ teaspoons cinnamon
½ cup sugar	1 teaspoon ginger
1 egg	½ teaspoon cloves
½ cup molasses	½ teaspoon nutmeg
2¼ cups all-purpose flour	1 egg white
1 teaspoon baking powder	⅛ teaspoon cream of tartar
½ teaspoon soda	1 cup plus 2 tablespoons
½ teaspoon salt	confectioners' sugar

Cream butter and ½ cup sugar in bowl until light and fluffy. Add egg and molasses; mix well. Sift dry ingredients together. Add to creamed mixture; mix well. Chill, covered, for 2 hours. Roll ¼ inch thick on floured surface; cut as desired. Place on lightly greased cookie sheet. Bake at 375 degrees for 8 to 10 minutes or until golden. Cool on wire rack. Beat egg white in bowl until foamy. Add cream of tartar. Beat until soft peaks form. Add confectioners' sugar gradually, beating constantly. Spread, drizzle or pipe onto cookies. Yield: 3 to 5 dozen.

Lotte Wacht, Xi Gamma Upsilon
Sycamore, Illinois

SWEDISH GINGER COOKIES

¾ cup butter, softened	½ teaspoon salt
1 cup sugar	½ teaspoon cinnamon
1 egg	¼ teaspoon cloves
¼ cup sorghum molasses	¼ teaspoon ginger
2 cups all-purpose flour	Extra-fine granulated
2 teaspoons soda	sugar

Cream butter and 1 cup sugar in mixer bowl until light and fluffy. Blend in egg and molasses. Add mixture of flour, soda, salt and spices; mix well. Shape into walnut-sized balls. Roll in extra-fine sugar, coating well. Place on ungreased cookie sheet. Bake at 375 degrees for 9 to 12 minutes or until crisp. Yield: 4 dozen.

Shirley Thillen, Preceptor Sigma
Rockford, Illinois

MERINGUE FRUIT DROPS

3 egg whites	1 cup sugar
½ teaspoon salt	1 cup coconut
1 teaspoon vanilla extract	1 cup chopped nuts
½ teaspoon almond	1 cup chopped dates
extract	

Beat egg whites with salt in mixer bowl until stiff peaks form. Fold in remaining ingredients. Drop by spoonfuls onto buttered cookie sheet. Bake at 300 degrees for 20 minutes; do not overbake. Cool. Serve immediately or store in airtight container.

Jackie Vogler, Xi Sigma Phi
Hilltop Lakes, Texas

MACAROONS

4 egg whites	4 cups crushed cornflakes
1 cup sugar	12 ounces chocolate chips
½ teaspoon salt	

Beat egg whites in mixer bowl until soft peaks form. Add sugar and salt gradually, beating until stiff peaks form. Fold in cornflakes and chocolate chips. Drop by spoonfuls onto nonstick cookie sheet. Bake at 350 degrees for 12 to 15 minutes or just until cookies begin to brown. Cool on wire rack. Yield: 6 dozen.

Carol Ann Chapman, Delta Chi
Waukesha, Wisconsin

MINCEMEAT SURPRISE COOKIES

1 cup shortening	1⅔ cups sifted all-purpose
1 teaspoon salt	flour
1 teaspoon vanilla extract	¾ teaspoon soda
1 cup packed brown sugar	2 cups oats
2 eggs, well beaten	2 cups mincemeat

Cream shortening with salt and vanilla in bowl until light. Add brown sugar. Cream until fluffy. Blend in eggs. Add sifted flour and soda; mix well. Stir in oats. Roll ⅛ inch thick on floured surface. Cut with 2½-inch cookie cutter. Place 1 teaspoon mincemeat on each of half the cookies. Top with remaining cookies. Seal edges with fork. Place on lightly greased cookie sheet. Bake at 350 degrees for 10 to 15 minutes or until brown. Cool on wire rack. Yield: 2 to 3 dozen.

Rosalind Ratchford, Preceptor Beta Eta
Ellenton, Florida

MRS. MILBRIET'S MOLASSES COOKIES

2 eggs	¼ teaspoon ginger
1 cup sugar	¼ teaspoon cloves
1 cup (scant) lard	4 cups all-purpose flour
1 cup molasses	2 teaspoons soda
¼ teaspoon cinnamon	½ cup hot water

Beat eggs and sugar in mixer bowl until thick. Add molasses, cinnamon, ginger and cloves; mix well. Add flour and mixture of soda and hot water; mix well. Chill overnight. Roll ¼ inch thick on floured surface. Cut in large circles. Place on cookie sheet. Bake at 350 degrees for 10 to 12 minutes or until brown. Remove to wire rack to cool. Frost with white frosting. Yield: 6 dozen.

Note: This recipe is from a 1918 newspaper.

Nancy Creamer, Xi Beta Lambda
Oshkosh, Wisconsin

Trim a kitchen tree to decorate the most important room of the house. Make a "gingerbread" house tree stand from cardboard box large enough for base of small tree to fit inside. Decorate with white caulk piped on with narrow tip for windows, doors and to attach candies. Decorate tree with gingerbread cookies, small wooden alphabet blocks, and cranberry and popcorn chains. For other kitchen trees, decorate with small utensils such as measuring spoons or cookie cutters, tiny bags of spices, macaroni chains, Cinnamon Ornaments (page 54), or Play Clay ornaments (page 54).

MOSAIC COOKIES

1 cup chocolate chips
2 tablespoons butter
1 egg, beaten
1 cup confectioners' sugar

1 cup chopped nuts
4 cups miniature colored
    marshmallows
Graham cracker crumbs

Melt chocolate chips and butter in saucepan; blend well. Mix in egg and confectioners' sugar. Add nuts and marshmallows; mix until well coated. Shape into two 1½-inch diameter rolls. Roll in cracker crumbs to coat. Store, wrapped in foil, in refrigerator. Slice as needed.
Yield: 3 dozen.

Barbara Ball, Xi Alpha Kappa
Grand Junction, Colorado

NOEL WREATHS

1 cup maragarine,
    softened
½ cup sugar
1 egg
1 teaspoon vanilla extract
2½ cups all-purpose flour
¼ cup light corn syrup

1 cup finely chopped
    walnuts
¼ teaspoon maple
    flavoring
Red and green candied
    cherries

Cream margarine and sugar in mixer bowl until light and fluffy. Blend in egg and vanilla. Add flour gradually, mixing well after each addition. Reserve ¼ cup dough. Spoon remaining dough into cookie press fitted with star tip. Press into 4-inch lengths on ungreased cookie sheet; join ends to form wreaths. Mix reserved dough with corn syrup, walnuts and flavoring in small bowl. Spoon about 1 teaspoonful into center of each wreath. Decorate with bows cut from candied cherries. Bake at 350 degrees for 15 minutes. Cool on wire rack. Yield: 4 dozen.

Carey Anne Grey-Tingler, Alpha Alpha
Glasgow, Montana

TRAILSIDE OATMEAL TREATS

½ cup butter, softened
½ cup chunky peanut
    butter
1 cup sugar
1 cup packed brown sugar
2 eggs
¼ cup milk
1 teaspoon vanilla extract

1¾ cups all-purpose flour
1 teaspoon soda
½ teaspoon salt
2½ cups oats
½ cup semisweet
    chocolate chips
½ cup raisins

Cream butter, peanut butter, sugar and brown sugar in mixer bowl until light and fluffy. Beat in eggs, milk and vanilla. Stir in mixture of flour, soda and salt. Mix in oats, chocolate chips and raisins. Drop by rounded tablespoonfuls 3 inches apart onto ungreased cookie sheet. Bake at 350 degrees for 15 minutes. Cool on wire rack.

Linda Gizienski, Xi Alpha
Providence, Rhode Island

OATMEAL COOKIES

1 cup butter-flavored
    shortening
1 cup sugar
1 cup packed brown sugar
2 eggs
2 teaspoons vanilla extract
1½ cups all-purpose flour

1 teaspoon soda
1 teaspoon salt
3 cups quick-cooking oats
1 cup drained plumped
    raisins
1 cup chopped pecans

Cream shortening and sugars in bowl until light and fluffy. Add eggs and vanilla; mix well. Add mixture of flour, soda and salt; mix well. Mix in oats, raisins and pecans. Shape into 4 or 5 logs; wrap each in waxed paper. Refrigerate overnight. Slice ¼ inch thick; place on baking sheet. Bake at 325 degrees for 12 to 15 minutes. Cool on wire rack. Pack in holiday canisters for gifts.

Dolores R. Seward, Xi Epsilon Alpha
Muskogee, Oklahoma

PEANUT BUTTER COOKIES

1 cup shortening
1 cup sugar
1 cup packed brown sugar
2 eggs
1 teaspoon vanilla extract

1 cup crunchy peanut
    butter
2 cups all-purpose flour
2 teaspoons soda

Cream shortening, sugar and brown sugar in mixer bowl until light and fluffy. Blend in eggs, vanilla and peanut butter. Add flour and soda; mix well. Drop by teaspoonfuls onto ungreased cookie sheet. Bake at 350 degrees for 10 minutes. Cool on wire rack. Yield: 5 dozen.

Joyce Stimmel, Preceptor Delta

PINKSTERS

⅔ cup shortening
½ cup packed brown
    sugar
1 egg, well beaten
1 egg yolk, well beaten
2 cups sifted all-purpose
    flour

½ teaspoon salt
1 egg white, slightly
    beaten
1½ cups chopped pecans
1   12-ounce jar seedless
    raspberry jam

Cream shortening and brown sugar in mixer bowl until light and fluffy. Blend in egg and egg yolk. Mix in flour and salt. Shape into small balls. Dip into egg white; roll in pecans. Place on greased baking sheet. Make depression with finger in center of each ball. Bake at 400 degrees for 5 minutes. Press down centers again. Bake for 15 minutes longer. Cool slightly. Spoon jam into centers. Remove to wire rack to cool completely.
Yield: 2 to 3 dozen.

Kimberly L. Birch, Eta Nu
Charles City, Iowa

To make extra easy peanut butter cookies, simply mix 1 cup each sugar and peanut butter and 1 egg in bowl. Drop by spoonfuls onto cookie sheet; flatten with fork. Bake at 325 degrees for 10 minutes.

Quick and easy holiday cookies are a cinch with purchased refrigerator sugar cookie dough. Roll dough on floured surface. Cut into large cookies. Cut into stars, frost and stack 2 together to make 10-point star. Or, for ribbon cookies, stack layers of 3 different flavors in loaf pan; unmold and slice into ¼-inch slices. Bake as directed.

RAISIN BALLS

¼ cup chopped raisins	⅛ teaspoon cinnamon
2 teaspoons coconut	⅔ cup nonfat dry milk
3 tablespoons peanut	powder
butter	¼ cup water
2 teaspoons honey	2 2½ x 2½-inch graham
1 teaspoon lemon juice	crackers, crushed

Combine raisins and coconut in bowl. Add peanut butter, honey, lemon juice and cinnamon; mix well. Add dry milk powder; knead until well mixed. Mix in water gradually. Chill, covered, for 30 minutes. Shape into 18 balls. Roll in cracker crumbs; place on waxed paper. Chill for 1 hour. Yield: 1½ dozen.

Lorraine Kirkpatrick, Xi Eta Kappa
Barstow, California

DENNY'S SUGAR COOKIES

1 cup butter, softened	1 cup sugar
1 cup oil	1½ cups all-purpose flour
2 eggs	1 teaspoon cream of tartar
1 teaspoon vanilla extract	1 teaspoon soda
1 cup confectioners'	Tinted sugar
sugar	

Blend butter, oil, eggs and vanilla in mixer bowl. Stir in confectioners' sugar, sugar and half the flour. Mix in cream of tartar and soda. Add remaining flour; mix well. Chill, covered, for 2 hours or longer. Shape into small balls. Place on ungreased cookie sheet. Flatten with bottom of glass buttered and dipped into tinted sugar. Bake at 350 degrees for 10 minutes. Cool on wire rack. Yield: 6 dozen.

Marlene Hunt, Eta Nu
Charles City, Iowa

SORGHUM SUGAR COOKIES

1½ cups shortening,	4 teaspoons soda
melted	2 teaspoons cinnamon
2 cups sugar	1 teaspoon ginger
½ cup sorghum	1 teaspoon cloves
2 eggs	1 teaspoon salt
4 cups all-purpose flour	

Combine shortening, sugar, sorghum and eggs in large bowl; mix well. Add mixture of flour, soda, cinnamon, ginger, cloves and salt; mix well. Shape into 1-inch balls. Roll in additional sugar. Place 2 inches apart on greased cookie sheet. Flatten with bottom of glass dipped into sugar. Bake at 275 degrees for 8 to 10 minutes or until golden. Cool on wire rack. Yield: 8 dozen.

Jimmie V. Rush, Preceptor Beta Gamma
Augusta, Kansas

Store soft cookies and crisp cookies separately. Store soft cookies in airtight container. If cookies become dry, add moisture by placing apple slice in container for 1 day. Store crisp cookies in container with loose fitting cover. Freshen in 300-degree oven for 5 minutes before serving if necessary.

SWEDISH DROP SUGAR COOKIES

1 cup butter-flavored	1 teaspoon vanilla extract
shortening	1½ teaspoons almond
1½ cups packed brown	extract
sugar	1 teaspoon cream of tartar
1 teaspoon salt	1¾ cups all-purpose flour
1 egg, beaten	

Cream shortening, sugar and salt in bowl until light and fluffy. Add egg and flavorings; mix well. Add mixture of cream of tartar and flour; mix well. Drop by scant tablespoonfuls 2 inches apart onto ungreased cookie sheet. Bake at 350 degrees for 10 minutes or until golden brown. Cool on cookie sheet for 1 minute. Cool on wire rack. Store in airtight container. Yield: 3½ dozen.

Terry Ann Walker
Pittsburg, Kansas

TWO-TONE WALNUT JUMBLES

¼ cup shortening	1 teaspoon salt
¼ cup butter, softened	2¾ cups sifted all-purpose
1 cup packed brown sugar	flour
½ cup sugar	1 cup sour cream
1 teaspoon vanilla extract	½ cup semisweet
2 eggs	chocolate chips, melted
1 cup chopped walnuts	½ cup chopped walnuts
½ teaspoon soda	

Cream first 5 ingredients in mixer bowl until light. Beat in eggs. Stir in 1 cup walnuts. Sift soda and salt with flour. Stir into creamed mixture alternately with sour cream. Drop half the batter by small spoonfuls 2 inches apart onto greased cookie sheet. Stir chocolate into remaining batter. Drop by small spoonfuls next to and touching each plain cookie. Sprinkle with remaining walnuts. Bake at 375 degrees for 15 minutes. Remove to wire rack to cool. Yield: 2 dozen.

Dorothy Hartigan, Xi Sigma Pi
Hilltop Lakes, Texas

WHOOPIE PIES

6 tablespoons shortening	1½ teaspoons soda
1 cup sugar	¼ cup all-purpose flour
1 cup milk	1 cup milk
1 egg	¾ cup shortening
1 teaspoon vanilla extract	1 cup sugar
2½ cups all-purpose flour	1 teaspoon vanilla extract
5 tablespoons cocoa	

Cream 6 tablespoons shortening and 1 cup sugar in mixer bowl until light. Blend in 1 cup milk, egg and 1 teaspoon vanilla. Sift in 2½ cups flour, cocoa and soda; mix well. Drop by tablespoonfuls onto ungreased cookie sheet. Bake at 425 degrees for 8 minutes or until brown. Cool on wire rack. Blend ¼ cup flour and 1 cup milk in saucepan. Cook until thickened, stirring constantly. Cool. Cream ¾ cup shortening and 1 cup sugar in mixer bowl until light. Beat in cooled mixture and 1 teaspoon vanilla. Spread between cookies. Yield: 1½ dozen.

Linda Gizienski, Xi Alpha
Providence, Rhode Island

Pies

ANGEL PIES

1 15-ounce can sweetened condensed milk	2 tablespoons lemon juice
1 14-ounce can crushed pineapple, partially drained	16 ounces whipped topping
	2 9-inch graham cracker pie shells
	Coconut

Combine condensed milk, pineapple, lemon juice and whipped topping in bowl; mix well. Spoon into pie shells. Chill for 12 hours or longer. Sprinkle with coconut. Yield: 12 servings.

Veda Dabney, Beta Lambda
Evanston, Wyoming

APRICOT FLUFF PIE

1 tablespoon unflavored gelatin	1 egg white
1½ cups apricot juice	½ cup whipping cream, whipped
½ cup sugar	1 baked 8-inch pie shell
3 tablespoons lemon juice	

Soften gelatin in apricot juice in top of double boiler. Stir in sugar. Cook over boiling water until gelatin is dissolved. Stir in lemon juice. Cool to lukewarm. Stir in unbeaten egg white. Chill until partially set. Whip until light and fluffy. Fold in whipped cream. Spoon into pie shell. Chill until set. Yield: 8 servings.

Edith Savage, Laureate Delta
Sudbury, Ontario, Canada

CHEESE-CRUST APPLE PIE

1 recipe Cheese Pie Pastry	2 tablespoons all-purpose flour
1 tablespoon melted shortening	1 teaspoon cinnamon
5 or 6 large tart apples, peeled, sliced	1 teaspoon nutmeg
¾ cup sugar	2 tablespoons (or more) butter

Divide pastry into 2 portions. Roll on floured surface. Fit half the pastry into 9-inch pie plate. Brush with melted shortening. Alternate layers of apples and mixture of sugar, flour and spices in pie shell. Dot with butter. Top with remaining pastry; seal edge and cut steam vents. Bake in preheated 450-degree oven for 10 minutes. Reduce temperature to 350 degrees. Bake for 30 minutes longer or until golden brown. Cool. Yield: 6 to 8 servings.

CHEESE PIE PASTRY

½ cup shortening	1 cup shredded Cheddar cheese
2 cups sifted all-purpose flour	6 to 8 tablespoons cold water
¾ teaspoon salt	

Cut shortening into mixture of flour and salt in bowl until crumbly. Add cheese; mix lightly with fork. Add enough cold water to bind mixture. Shape into ball.

Mrs. Robert L. Scofield, Laureate Eta
Clarksville, Tennessee

COCONUT-APPLE PIE

1 recipe 2-crust pie pastry	½ cup butter
8 to 10 Jonathan apples, peeled, thinly sliced	½ cup sugar
	3 tablespoons corn syrup
Sugar, flour, cinnamon and nutmeg to taste	¼ cup water
	1 teaspoon coconut flavoring
1 8-ounce package frozen coconut, thawed	1 teaspoon vanilla extract

Roll pastry into 1 large circle on floured surface. Place in 9-inch deep-dish pie plate with excess pastry extending over edge. Place 1 layer apples in prepared pie plate. Sprinkle with sugar, flour, cinnamon, nutmeg and generous amount of coconut. Repeat layers until all ingredients are used. Fold pastry over top of pie leaving opening in center. Bake at 375 degrees for 40 minutes. Melt butter with ½ cup sugar in saucepan over medium heat. Stir in corn syrup and water. Cook for 20 minutes or to desired consistency; remove from heat. Stir in flavorings. Place pie on baking sheet. Pour butter sauce over and into pie. Bake for 10 minutes longer or until golden brown. Yield: 8 servings.

Sharon Tabor, Xi Beta Phi
Marion, Illinois

BAKED ALASKA SPUMONI PIE

1 stick pie crust mix	1 pint chocolate ice cream
1 pint strawberry ice cream	2 egg whites
1 pint pistachio ice cream	¼ cup sugar

Prepare and bake pie crust in 9-inch pie plate according to package directions. Cool. Layer scoops of ice cream in pie shell. Freeze until firm. Beat egg whites in bowl until soft peaks form. Add sugar gradually, beating until stiff peaks form. Spread over ice cream, sealing to crust. Bake at 500 degrees for 3 to 5 minutes or until light brown. Serve immediately. Yield: 6 servings.

Rosilyn Henline, Xi Kappa Beta
Follanshee, West Virginia

BANANA CREAM PIE

3 tablespoons flour	1 cup cream
1 tablespoon cornstarch	2 egg yolks, beaten
½ cup sugar	1 teaspoon vanilla extract
¼ teaspoon salt	1 baked pie shell
1 cup milk	Sliced bananas

Mix dry ingredients in saucepan. Stir milk into cream in bowl. Stir in egg yolks. Add to dry ingredients. Cook until thickened, stirring constantly. Add vanilla. Cool. Pour into pie shell. Top with bananas.
Yield: 6 to 8 servings.

Geraldine Kauffman, Xi Eta Lambda
Lena, Illinois

BLUEBERRY CREAM PIES

1¼ cups confectioners' sugar	½ cup chopped nuts
8 ounces cream cheese, softened	1 20-ounce can blueberry pie filling
2 baked pie shells	9 ounces whipped topping

Cream confectioners' sugar and cream cheese in mixer bowl until light and fluffy. Spread evenly in pie shells. Sprinkle with nuts. Spoon pie filling over nuts. Top with whipped topping. Chill for 2 hours. Yield: 12 servings.

Brenda Steakley, Epsilon Kappa
Nashville, Tennessee

BLACKBERRY PIE

1 15-ounce can sweetened condensed milk	2 cups fresh blackberries
	1 baked pie shell
	8 ounces whipped topping
¼ cup lemon juice	

Combine condensed milk and lemon juice in bowl; mix well. Fold in blackberries. Spoon into pie shell. Top with whipped topping. Chill until serving time.
Yield: 8 servings.

Pam Feldhaus, Epsilon Psi
Shelbyville, Tennessee

MOM SEE'S CARAMEL PIES

6 eggs, separated	1 cup sour plum or currant jelly
2 cups packed brown sugar	
	2 teaspoons vanilla extract
½ cup butter, softened	Pinch of salt
1 teaspoon flour	2 unbaked pie shells
2 cups milk	

Beat egg yolks in mixer bowl. Cream brown sugar and butter in mixer bowl until light and fluffy. Blend in egg yolks. Add flour, milk, jelly, vanilla and salt. Beat until smooth. Beat egg whites in mixer bowl until stiff peaks form. Fold gently into filling. Spoon into pie shells. Bake at 350 degrees for 45 minutes or until knife inserted in center comes out clean. Yield: 12 servings.

Martha W. Clark, Member at Large
San Diego, California

CHERRY CHEESE PIE

½ cup (about) sugar	1 9-inch graham cracker pie shell
8 ounces cream cheese, softened	
	1 cup cherry pie filling
2 cups whipped topping	

Cream sugar and cream cheese in mixer bowl until light and fluffy. Mix in whipped topping. Spoon into pie shell. Top with pie filling. Chill. Yield: 8 servings.

Dawn Martin, Beta Omicron
Red Lodge, Montana

CHERRY CREAM PIE

½ cup finely chopped almonds	1 teaspoon vanilla extract
	½ teaspoon almond extract
1 unbaked 9-inch pie shell	½ cup whipping cream, whipped
1 14-ounce can sweetened condensed milk	
	1 21-ounce can cherry pie filling
⅓ cup lemon juice	

Press almonds into unbaked pie shell. Bake at 450 degrees for 12 to 15 minutes or until brown. Cool. Combine condensed milk, lemon juice, vanilla extract and almond extract in bowl. Stir until mixture thickens. Fold in whipped cream. Spoon into cooled shell. Top with cherry pie filling. Chill. Sprinkle with additional chopped almonds, if desired. Yield: 6 to 8 servings.

Diana Amon, Iota Gamma
Lewis, Kansas

CHOCOLATE PIE

2 cups half and half	*3 eggs, beaten*
2 tablespoons (heaping)	*2 1-ounce squares*
all-purpose flour	*chocolate, grated*
1 cup sugar	*1 teaspoon vanilla extract*
Pinch of salt	*1 baked pie shell*

Heat half and half in double boiler. Stir in mixture of flour, sugar and salt. Cook until thickened, stirring constantly. Stir a small amount of hot mixture into beaten eggs; stir eggs into hot mixture. Add chocolate. Cook, until thickened, stirring constantly; remove from heat. Beat until smooth. Chill slightly. Stir in vanilla. Spoon into pie shell. Chill until serving time. Garnish with whipped cream. Yield: 6 servings.

Marjorie Fletcher, Xi Upsilon Delta
Borrego Springs, California

CHART HOUSE MUD PIE

½ package chocolate	*1 gallon coffee ice*
wafers, crushed	*cream, softened*
¼ cup melted butter	*1½ cups fudge sauce*

Combine chocolate wafer crumbs and butter in bowl; mix well. Press over bottom and side of 9-inch pie plate. Spoon ice cream into prepared plate. Freeze until firm. Spoon chilled fudge sauce over top. Freeze for 10 hours. Serve on chilled dessert plates. Garnish with whipped cream and slivered almonds. Yield: 8 servings.

Sarah Thacker, Epsilon Kappa
Nashville, Tennessee

EASY FUDGE PIE

¼ cup cocoa	*2 eggs*
1 cup sugar	*½ cup melted butter*
¼ cup all-purpose flour	*1 unbaked pie shell*
Dash of salt	

Combine cocoa, sugar, flour and salt in bowl. Add eggs and butter; mix well. Pour into pie shell. Bake at 350 degrees for 35 to 40 minutes or until set.
Yield: 6 to 8 servings.

Brenda Steakley, Epsilon Kappa
Nashville, Tennessee

For perfect meringue, beat 4 egg whites at room temperature and ¼ teaspoon salt until soft peaks form. Add sugar gradually, beating until very stiff. Spread to edge of pie. Bake at 400 degrees until golden.

CHRISTMAS CHIFFON PIE

3 tablespoons margarine,	*½ cup lime juice*
softened	*1 tablespoon grated*
½ cup sugar	*lime rind*
1 egg, beaten	*⅛ teaspoon salt*
¼ cup milk	*3 tablespoons sugar*
1¾ cups all-purpose flour	*¼ cup dry lime gelatin*
1 teaspoon baking powder	*½ cup boiling water*
½ teaspoon salt	*¼ teaspoon cream of tartar*
½ teaspoon ginger	*3 tablespoons sugar*
3 eggs, separated	

Cream first 3 ingredients in mixer bowl until smooth. Beat in milk. Sift flour, baking powder, ½ teaspoon salt and ginger together into creamed mixture; mix well. Chill for 1 hour. Roll ⅔ of the pastry ⅛ inch thick on floured surface. Fit into 9½-inch pie plate. Trim and flute edge. Place second pie plate in shell. Bake at 400 degrees for 12 minutes or until brown. Remove second pie plate. Cool. Roll remaining pastry ¼-inch thick on floured surface; cut 6 bells with cookie cutter. Place on cookie sheet. Bake at 400 degrees for 12 minutes or until golden. Cool. Garnish with red sugar. Combine egg yolks, lime juice, rind, salt and 3 tablespoons sugar in double boiler. Cook until thickened, stirring constantly. Dissolve gelatin in boiling water. Add to cooked mixture. Chill until partially set. Beat until smooth. Beat egg whites with cream of tartar until frothy. Add 3 tablespoons sugar gradually, beating until stiff. Fold in lime mixture. Pour into pie shell. Chill for 2 hours or until set. Place cookies on pie. Yield: 6 servings.

Bettie Lou Plummer, Laureate Pi
Independence, Missouri

FRENCH COCONUT PIE

1¼ cups sugar	*3 eggs*
1 tablespoon all-purpose	*1 teaspoon vanilla extract*
flour	*¼ cup buttermilk*
¼ cup margarine,	*1 3½-ounce can coconut*
softened	*1 unbaked 9-inch pie shell*

Cream sugar, flour and margarine in bowl. Add eggs and vanilla; mix well. Add buttermilk; mix well. Stir in coconut. Pour into pie shell. Bake at 400 degrees for 10 minutes. Reduce temperature to 300 degrees. Bake for 45 to 50 minutes longer or until golden. Yield: 8 servings.

Jean K. Hunter, Xi Lambda Delta
Dunedin, Florida

OLD-FASHIONED COCONUT PIE

1 3½-ounce can	*1 cup sugar*
shredded coconut	*3 eggs, slightly beaten*
½ cup milk	*1 10-inch unbaked*
¼ cup butter, softened	*pie shell*

Mix coconut and milk in bowl; set aside. Cream butter and sugar in bowl until light. Mix in eggs and coconut mixture. Pour into pie shell. Bake at 350 degrees for 40 minutes or until set. Yield: 6 servings.

Diane Ashworth, Beta Sigma
New Bern, North Carolina

CRANBERRY-CHEESE PIE

1 15-ounce can sweetened condensed milk	½ teaspoon vanilla extract
	1 16-ounce can whole cranberry sauce
⅓ cup lemon juice	1 9-inch vanilla wafer pie shell
8 ounces cream cheese, softened	Whipped cream

Combine first 4 ingredients in blender container. Process until smooth. Reserve several whole cranberries from cranberry sauce. Fold remaining cranberry sauce into cream cheese mixture. Spoon into pie shell. Freeze until firm. Remove from freezer 10 minutes before serving. Spoon whipped cream into circle on top of pie. Garnish with reserved cranberries. Yield: 8 servings.

Eloise Hood, Preceptor Epsilon
Winter Haven, Florida

CREAM AND CHEESE PIES

3 cups cake flour	1½ cups sugar
¾ cup sugar	6 cups milk
1 tablespoon baking powder	9 eggs, separated
¾ cup margarine	1 tablespoon vanilla extract
3 eggs	2 tablespoons sugar
½ cup cornstarch	2 pounds ricotta cheese
¼ cup all-purpose flour	

Combine first 3 ingredients in bowl. Cut in margarine until crumbly. Add eggs; mix with hands until mixture forms ball. Divide into 3 portions. Roll 2 portions on lightly floured surface; fit into one 8-inch pie plate and one 10-inch pie plate. Mix cornstarch, ¼ cup flour and 1½ cups sugar in double boiler. Add a small amount of milk; mix to form paste. Stir in remaining milk gradually. Add beaten egg yolks. Cook until thickened, stirring frequently. Remove from heat. Add vanilla. Cool. Beat egg whites with 2 tablespoons sugar until stiff peaks form. Fold in ricotta cheese gently. Divide cooked mixture between pie plates. Top with ricotta mixture. Roll remaining dough; cut into strips. Arrange over ricotta mixture; flute and seal edges. Bake at 350 degrees for 1 hour. Cool. Yield: 18 servings.

Linda Hargraves, Xi Tau
East Haven, Connecticut

FRUIT FLUFF PIE

1 cup fine cornflake crumbs	½ cup cold water
1 tablespoon brown sugar substitute	1 cup drained canned fruit, chilled
3 tablespoons melted margarine	1½ tablespoons sugar substitute
1½ teaspoons sugar-free lemon gelatin	½ teaspoon cinnamon
1 cup boiling water	⅛ teaspoon allspice
	⅛ teaspoon nutmeg

Mix cornflake crumbs, brown sugar substitute and margarine in bowl. Press into 9-inch pie plate. Bake at 375 degrees for 8 minutes. Cool. Dissolve gelatin in 1 cup boiling water in mixer bowl. Stir in cold water. Chill until partially set. Mix fruit, 1½ tablespoons sugar substitute and spices in bowl. Whip gelatin at high speed until fluffy. Fold in fruit. Tint with food coloring if desired. Spoon into pie shell. Chill for 3 hours or until firm. Yield: 8 servings.

Amy Wykes
Kansas City, Missouri

HOLIDAY PIE

3 eggs	¼ cup butter, softened, creamed
1½ cups sugar	1 teaspoon vanilla extract
1½ teaspoons (heaping) cornstarch	1 cup chopped pecans
1 teaspoon cinnamon	1 cup raisins
⅛ teaspoon nutmeg	1 unbaked 9-inch deep-dish pie shell
Pinch of salt	
1 tablespoon vinegar	

Beat eggs in mixer bowl. Add next 10 ingredients in order listed, mixing well after each addition. Pour into pie shell. Bake at 350 degrees for 45 minutes to 1 hour or until set and golden brown. Cool on wire rack. Yield: 8 servings.

Cameron Stimson, Xi Theta
Mayfield, Kentucky

ICE CREAM PIE

1 Crispy Chocolate Pie Shell	Chocolate syrup
½ gallon mint chocolate chip ice cream, softened	Whipped topping

Fill pie shell with ice cream. Freeze until firm. Store, wrapped in plastic wrap, in freezer. Thaw for 20 minutes before serving. Drizzle chocolate syrup over top. Top with whipped topping. Yield: 6 to 8 servings.

CRISPY CHOCOLATE PIE SHELL

6 ounces semisweet chocolate chips	¼ cup margarine
	2 cups crisp rice cereal

Melt chocolate chips and margarine in double boiler; mix well. Stir in cereal. Press into buttered 10-inch pie shell. Chill until firm.

Lou Alexander, Xi Xi Rho
Arlington, Texas

CANDY CRUST ICE CREAM PIE

⅔ cup semisweet chocolate chips	2 3½-ounce cans flaked coconut
¼ cup butter	1 quart cherry-vanilla ice cream
¼ cup milk	

Heat chocolate, butter and milk in small saucepan over low heat, stirring until chocolate is melted. Remove from heat. Stir in coconut. Press over bottom and side of buttered 9-inch pie plate. Chill until firm. Fill pie shell with ice cream. Freeze until firm. Let stand in refrigerator 20 minutes before serving time. Garnish with whipped cream. Yield: 6 servings.

KAHLUA PIE

1½ quarts vanilla ice
    cream, softened
¼ cup Kahlua
1 9-inch graham cracker
    pie shell
1 4 to 5-ounce jar hot
    fudge topping
8 ounces whipped topping
½ cup chopped nuts

Blend ice cream and Kahlua in bowl. Spoon into pie shell. Freeze for 1 hour or longer. Heat hot fudge topping in saucepan just until warm. Spread over ice cream. Freeze for 1 hour or longer. Top with whipped topping and nuts. Freeze for 3 hours or longer. Yield: 8 servings.
Note: May substitute ¼ cup Crème de Cacao or 1½ tablespoons instant coffee crystals for Kahlua, chocolate crumb pie shell for graham cracker shell and shaved chocolate for nuts.

Betty Thompson, Preceptor Beta Eta
Bradenton, Florida

FOUR-LAYER LEMON PIE

½ cup melted margarine
1 cup all-purpose flour
1 cup chopped pecans
8 ounces cream cheese,
    softened
1 cup confectioners' sugar
16 ounces whipped
    topping
2 4-ounce packages
    lemon instant
    pudding mix
3 cups milk

Combine first 3 ingredients in bowl; mix well. Press into deep 2-quart baking dish. Bake at 350 degrees until light brown. Cool completely. Blend cream cheese, confectioners' sugar and 1 cup whipped topping in bowl. Spread over crust. Mix pudding mix with milk in bowl until thick. Pour over cream cheese layer. Top with remaining whipped topping. Chill until serving time.
Yield: 6 to 8 servings.

Dot McCurley, Preceptor Beta Tau
Panama City, Florida

FROZEN KEY LIME PIE

4 eggs, separated
1 14-ounce can
    sweetened condensed
    milk
½ cup key lime juice
½ teaspoon cream of tartar
1 graham cracker pie shell
¼ cup sugar

Beat egg yolks in mixer bowl at high speed until thick and light. Add condensed milk. Beat at low speed until blended. Add half the lime juice, cream of tartar and remaining lime juice, beating constantly at low speed. Pour into pie shell. Bake at 325 degrees for 10 to 15 minutes or until set. Freeze for 3 hours. Heat egg whites and sugar in double boiler to 110 degrees on candy thermometer, stirring frequently. Beat at high speed of electric mixer until stiff peaks form. Spread over pie. Freeze until serving time. Yield: 8 to 10 servings.

Elizabeth Brennan, Preceptor Delta Mu
Titusville, Florida

KEY LIME PIE

4 egg yolks
1 15-ounce can
    sweetened condensed
    milk
1 cup lime juice
6 egg whites
½ teaspoon cream of tartar
¾ cup sugar
1 baked 10-inch pie shell

Beat egg yolks in bowl until thick. Add condensed milk gradually, beating until smooth. Mix in lime juice. Beat egg whites with cream of tartar in bowl until soft peaks form. Add sugar gradually, beating until stiff peaks form. Fold 6 tablespoons egg white mixture into lime mixture. Spoon lime mixture into pie shell. Spread remaining meringue over top, sealing to crust. Bake at 330 degrees until golden. Yield: 8 to 10 servings.

Paula Middleton, Xi Mu Eta
Houston, Texas

MILLIONAIRE PIE

8 ounces cream cheese,
    softened
¼ cup milk
1 20-ounce can crushed
    pineapple
1 cup chopped pecans
1 4-ounce package
    vanilla instant
    pudding mix
8 ounces whipped topping
1 baked 9-inch deep-
    dish pie shell

Beat cream cheese and milk in mixer bowl until smooth. Add pineapple with juice, pecans and dry pudding mix; mix well. Fold in whipped topping. Pour into pie shell. Chill until serving time. Yield: 8 servings.

Joanna Akers, Chi
Laramie, Wyoming

PINEAPPLE PIES

2½ cups undrained
    crushed pineapple
3 tablespoons
    all-purpose flour
½ cup sugar
4 egg whites
¼ cup sugar
2 baked pie shells

Combine pineapple, flour and ½ cup sugar in saucepan; mix well. Cook until thickened, stirring constantly. Cool. Beat egg whites with ¼ cup sugar in bowl until stiff peaks form. Fold in pineapple mixture. Spoon into pie shells. Garnish with whipped topping. Yield: 2 pies.

Margaret Fitzpatrick, Preceptor Beta Beta
Jacksonville, Illinois

FRESH PEACH PIE PRALINE

4 cups sliced peaches
¾ cup sugar
2 tablespoons cornstarch
2 teaspoons lemon juice
¼ teaspoon almond extract
¼ cup self-rising flour
⅓ cup packed brown sugar
½ cup chopped pecans
3 tablespoons butter
1 unbaked 9-inch pie shell

Combine first 5 ingredients in bowl; mix lightly. Mix flour, brown sugar and pecans in bowl. Add butter. Mix with fork until crumbly. Layer ⅓ of the pecan mixture, all the peaches and remaining pecan mixture in pie shell. Bake at 350 degrees for 45 minutes. Yield: 6 to 8 servings.

Diann Walters, Delta Kappa
Ellisville, Mississippi

CHOCOLATE-TOPPED PEANUT BUTTER PIE

3 ounces cream cheese, softened	1 Peanut Butter Pie Shell
¾ cup confectioners' sugar	½ cup chocolate chips
	2 tablespoons margarine
½ cup peanut butter	2 tablespoons milk
8 ounces whipped topping	1 teaspoon confectioners' sugar

Blend cream cheese, ¾ cup confectioners' sugar and peanut butter in bowl. Fold in whipped topping. Pour into pie shell. Chill until firm. Melt chocolate chips and 2 tablespoons margarine with milk and 1 teaspoon confectioners' sugar in saucepan over low heat, stirring constantly. Spread over peanut butter mixture. Chill until serving time. Yield: 12 servings.

PEANUT BUTTER PIE SHELL

3 cups miniature marshmallows	¼ cup margarine
½ cup peanut butter	4 cups cornflakes

Melt marshmallows, peanut butter and margarine in saucepan over low heat, stirring constantly. Stir in cornflakes. Press into 10-inch pie plate. Chill until firm.

Paula Disterhaupt, Preceptor Alpha Pi
Glenwood, Iowa

EASY PEANUT BUTTER PIE

2 eggs	½ cup peanut butter
1 cup corn syrup	1 teaspoon vanilla extract
1 cup sugar	1 unbaked 9-inch pie shell

Beat eggs in mixer bowl until light. Add corn syrup, sugar, peanut butter and vanilla; beat until blended. Pour into pie shell. Bake at 350 degrees for 50 to 60 minutes or until set. Cool. Yield: 6 servings.

Jane Niehouse, Sigma Omicron
Fulton, Missouri

PEANUT BUTTER PIE

¾ cup peanut butter	2 egg whites
1 cup confectioners' sugar	¼ cup sugar
1 baked pie shell	
1 8-ounce package vanilla pudding and pie filling mix	

Mix peanut butter and confectioners' sugar in bowl until crumbly. Sprinkle ¾ of the mixture in pie shell. Prepare and cook pie filling mix according to package directions. Cool. Spoon into prepared pie shell. Beat egg whites in mixer bowl until soft peaks form. Add sugar gradually, beating until stiff peaks form. Spread over pie, sealing to crust. Sprinkle with remaining crumb mixture. Bake at 425 degrees until light brown. Yield: 6 servings.

Norma Jean Engler, Laureate Alpha Beta
Princeton, Indiana

FLUFFY PEANUT BUTTER PIE

8 ounces cream cheese, softened	½ cup milk
	8 ounces whipped topping
½ cup creamy peanut butter	1 9-inch graham cracker pie shell
1 cup confectioners' sugar	

Whip cream cheese in mixer bowl until light. Blend in peanut butter and confectioners' sugar. Add milk gradually, beating constantly. Fold in whipped topping. Spoon into pie shell. Garnish with chopped peanuts. Freeze until firm. Yield: 6 to 8 servings.

Viola Dorrian, Omega
Kansas City, Missouri

CALLIE'S PECAN PIE

1½ cups pecan halves	2 tablespoons flour
1 unbaked 9-inch pie shell	1 teaspoon vanilla extract
3 eggs, beaten	⅛ teaspoon salt
2 tablespoons melted butter	½ cup sugar
	1½ cups light corn syrup

Sprinkle pecans in pie shell. Combine remaining ingredients in bowl; mix well. Pour into prepared pie shell. Bake in preheated 425-degree oven for 10 minutes. Reduce temperature to 325 degrees. Bake for 40 minutes longer. Yield: 6 servings.

Dolores R. Seward, Xi Epsilon Alpha
Muskogee, Oklahoma

MYSTERY PECAN PIES

8 ounces cream cheese, softened	Pecans
⅓ cup sugar	3 eggs, slightly beaten
1 egg	¼ cup sugar
1 teaspoon vanilla extract	1 cup corn syrup
¼ teaspoon salt	1 teaspoon vanilla extract
2 unbaked 8-inch pie shells	

Combine first 5 ingredients in bowl; beat until smooth. Spread in pie shells. Sprinkle with pecans. Combine 3 eggs and remaining ingredients in bowl; mix well. Pour over pecans. Bake at 375 degrees for 35 to 40 minutes or until center is firm. Yield: 2 pies.

Janice Venrick, Preceptor Beta Psi
Akron, Colorado

PECAN PIE

2 eggs, well beaten	¼ teaspoon cloves
1 cup sugar	1 cup chopped pecans
1 tablespoon vinegar	¼ cup raisins
2 tablespoons melted butter	¼ cup golden raisins
½ teaspoon cinnamon	1 unbaked pie shell

Combine first 6 ingredients in bowl; mix well. Stir in pecans and raisins. Spoon into pie shell. Bake at 325 degrees for 35 minutes. Yield: 6 to 8 servings.

Carol Jarman, Beta Sigma
New Bern, North Carolina

PUMPKIN PIE

2 eggs, beaten
½ cup cooked pumpkin
¾ cup sugar
1 teaspoon cinnamon
½ teaspoon allspice

¼ teaspoon nutmeg
¼ teaspoon salt
1 teaspoon vanilla extract
1 cup milk
1 unbaked 8-inch pie shell

Combine eggs, pumpkin, sugar, seasonings and milk in bowl; mix well. Pour into pie shell. Bake in preheated 400-degree oven for 10 minutes. Reduce temperature to 350 degrees. Bake for 1 hour longer. Yield: 6 servings.

Nell Walker, Beta Sigma Phi
Oaklandon, Indiana

PUMPKIN PIES

⅔ cup shortening
2 cups sifted all-purpose
 flour
1 teaspoon salt
5 to 6 tablespoons
 cold water
1 cup sugar
½ teaspoon salt

1½ teaspoons cinnamon
½ teaspoon each cloves,
 nutmeg, ginger and
 allspice
2 eggs, beaten
1 16-ounce can pumpkin
1 12-ounce can
 evaporated milk

Cut shortening into mixture of flour and 1 teaspoon salt in bowl. Add enough cold water to form dough. Roll into 2 thin circles on floured surface. Fit each into 8-inch pie plate; trim and flute edges. Combine sugar, ½ teaspoon salt and spices in bowl. Add eggs, pumpkin and evaporated milk; mix well. Pour into pie shells. Bake at 450 degrees for 10 minutes. Reduce temperature to 350 degrees. Bake for 30 to 35 minutes longer or until knife inserted near center comes out clean. Cool on wire rack. Serve with whipped cream. Yield: 12 servings.

Carolyn J. McClung, Alpha Chi
Fort Bragg, North Carolina

OLD-FASHIONED PUMPKIN PIE

2 eggs
1 16-ounce can pumpkin
1⅔ cups evaporated milk
¾ cup sugar
½ teaspoon salt

1 teaspoon cinnamon
½ teaspoon ginger
¼ teaspoon cloves
1 unbaked 9-inch pie shell

Beat eggs in bowl with rotary beater. Add pumpkin, evaporated milk, sugar, salt and spices; mix well. Spoon into pie shell. Bake at 350 degrees for 45 minutes or until knife inserted in center come out clean. Cool. Yield: 6 to 8 servings.

Ann Corrigan, Preceptor Gamma Epsilon
Blue Springs, Missouri

PUMPKIN-PECAN PIE

3 eggs
1 cup canned pumpkin
1 cup sugar
½ cup corn syrup
1 teaspoon vanilla extract

½ teaspoon cinnamon
¼ teaspoon salt
1½ cups chopped pecans
1 unbaked pie shell
½ cup pecan halves

Beat eggs in bowl. Add pumpkin, sugar, corn syrup, vanilla, cinnamon and salt; mix well. Stir in chopped pecans. Pour into pie shell. Arrange pecan halves over top. Bake at 350 degrees for 50 minutes. Serve with whipped cream or ice cream. Yield: 8 servings.

Pat Roether, Xi Eta
Ogden, Utah

RAISIN CHESS PIE

1 cup shortening
1 cup sugar
¼ teaspoon salt
3 eggs

1 cup chopped pecans
1 cup raisins
½ teaspoon vanilla extract
1 unbaked 9-inch pie shell

Cream shortening and sugar in bowl until light and fluffy. Add salt. Add eggs 1 at a time, beating well after each addition. Stir in pecans, raisins and vanilla. Pour into pie shell. Bake at 350 degrees for 40 minutes or until set. Yield: 6 to 8 servings.

Marlene Barcum, Preceptor Omega
Phoenix, Arizona

RICOTTA PIES

3 pounds ricotta cheese
3 eggs, beaten
1 teaspoon vanilla extract
1 teaspoon lemon extract

1½ cups sugar
1 recipe Sweet Pie Pastry
Dash of cinnamon

Combine ricotta cheese, eggs, flavorings and sugar in bowl; mix well. Spoon into 2 pastry-lined lightly greased 9-inch pie plates. Cut remaining pie pastry into strips. Place over filling; sprinkle with cinnamon. Bake in preheated 385-degree oven for 15 minutes. Reduce temperature to 350 degrees. Bake for 30 to 40 minutes or until brown. Yield: 2 pies.

SWEET PIE PASTRY

2½ cups all-purpose flour
1 cup sugar
1 teaspoon baking powder

½ cup oil
1 teaspoon vanilla extract
3 eggs, beaten

Combine first 3 ingredients in bowl; mix well. Stir in oil and vanilla. Add eggs gradually, mixing well after each addition. Roll on floured surface. Yield: 2 pie shells.

Arlene Burroughs, Xi Chi
Waterbury, Connecticut

STRAWBERRY PIE

½ cup butter
1 cup all-purpose flour
⅓ cup chopped nuts
¾ cup sugar
2 tablespoons cornstarch

1 12-ounce can 7-Up
1 3-ounce package
 strawberry gelatin
2 cups sliced strawberries

Combine butter, flour and nuts in bowl; mix well. Press into pie plate. Bake at 400 degrees for 10 to 15 minutes or until brown. Cool. Mix sugar and cornstarch in saucepan. Stir in 7-Up. Cook until thickened, stirring constantly. Stir in gelatin until dissolved. Cool. Mix in strawberries gently. Spoon into pie shell. Chill. Garnish with whipped topping before serving. Yield: 6 servings.

Beth Rush, Xi Kappa
Rawlins, Wyoming

SWEET POTATO CUSTARD PIE

1 small sweet potato, peeled	1 tablespoon lemon extract
½ cup margarine	3 eggs
1½ cups sugar	1 5⅓-ounce can evaporated milk
1 tablespoon sifted self-rising flour	1 unbaked 10-inch pie shell
1 tablespoon vanilla extract	

Cook sweet potato in boiling water in saucepan until tender; drain. Mash with margarine in bowl. Add sugar, flour and flavorings; beat well. Add eggs 1 at a time, beating well after each addition. Add evaporated milk; beat well. Pour into pie shell. Bake at 350 degrees for 45 minutes or until set. Yield: 8 servings.

Diann Walters, Delta Kappa
Ellisville, Missouri

RASPBERRY VELVET PIE

1 10-ounce package frozen raspberries	¼ pound marshmallows
1 3-ounce package raspberry gelatin	1 cup whipping cream, whipped
1 cup boiling water	Vanilla wafers

Drain raspberries, reserving syrup. Add enough water to reserved syrup to measure 1 cup liquid. Dissolve gelatin in 1 cup boiling water. Stir in marshmallows until partially melted. Add raspberry liquid. Chill until partially congealed. Beat until fluffy. Fold in raspberries and whipped cream. Line 9-inch pie plate with vanilla wafers. Fill with raspberry mixture. Chill until set. Serve with additional whipped cream. Yield: 6 servings.

Audrey L. Maclean, Xi Alpha
Moncton, New Brunswick, Canada

RHUBARB CUSTARD PIE

3 eggs	¾ teaspoon nutmeg
3 tablespoons milk	4 cups diced rhubarb
2 cups sugar	1 unbaked pie shell
¼ cup flour	Butter

Beat eggs lightly in bowl. Beat in milk, sugar, flour and nutmeg. Stir in rhubarb. Pour into pie shell. Dot with butter. Bake at 425 degrees for 1 hour or until set. Yield: 6 to 8 servings.

Jackie Stahlecker, Xi Tau
Havre, Montana

RHUBARB PIE DELIGHT

2 cups finely chopped rhubarb	1 3-ounce package whipped topping mix
1 cup sugar	¼ teaspoon salt
¼ cup water	1 teaspoon vanilla extract
1 3-ounce package strawberry gelatin	1 baked 9-inch pie shell

Combine rhubarb, sugar and water in saucepan. Simmer until tender. Add gelatin; stir until dissolved. Cool until syrupy. Prepare whipped topping mix according to package directions, adding salt and vanilla. Fold into rhubarb mixture. Pour into pie shell. Chill for 2 hours or until set. Yield: 6 to 8 servings.

Nancy Tosetti, Omicron
Nokomis, Illinois

AMISH VANILLA PIE

½ cup packed brown sugar	1 unbaked 9-inch pie shell
1 tablespoon all-purpose flour	1 cup all-purpose flour
1 egg, beaten	½ cup packed brown sugar
¼ cup dark corn syrup	¼ cup melted butter
1½ teaspoons vanilla extract	½ teaspoon cream of tartar
1 cup water	½ teaspoon soda
	⅛ teaspoon salt

Combine ½ cup brown sugar, 1 tablespoon flour, egg, corn syrup and vanilla in 2-quart saucepan. Stir in water. Cook over medium heat until mixture comes to a boil and thickens, stirring constantly. Cool. Pour into pie shell. Combine 1 cup flour and remaining ingredients in bowl; mix until crumbly. Sprinkle over pie. Bake at 350 degrees for 40 minutes or until golden brown. Yield: 8 servings.

Beverly J. Beaver, Xi Beta Xi
Huntingdon, Pennsylvania

WALNUT-COFFEE PIE

½ cup packed brown sugar	½ cup strong coffee
½ cup butter, softened	1 cup chopped walnuts
1 cup sugar	1 teaspoon vanilla extract
3 eggs	1 unbaked 9-inch pie shell
¼ teaspoon salt	½ cup chopped walnuts
¼ cup heavy cream	

Cream brown sugar and butter in mixer bowl until light. Add sugar; mix well. Add eggs one at a time, beating well after each addition. Combine with salt, cream and coffee in double boiler. Cook over boiling water for 5 minutes, stirring constantly. Remove from heat. Stir in 1 cup walnuts and vanilla. Pour into pie shell. Bake at 350 degrees for 1 hour. Sprinkle remaining walnuts on top. Bake for 5 minutes longer. Yield: 6 to 8 servings.

Phyllis Umstead, Xi Beta Psi
Harrisburg, Pennsylvania

APRICOT TART

2 17-ounce cans apricot halves, drained	¾ cup sugar
3 egg yolks	¼ cup all-purpose flour
⅓ cup sour cream	1 unbaked 9-inch tart shell

Drain apricots on paper towels. Beat egg yolks, sour cream, sugar and flour in bowl until blended. Arrange apricots in tart shell. Pour sour cream mixture over top. Bake at 350 degrees for 45 minutes or until golden brown. Serve at room temperature. Yield: 8 servings.

Christella Snyder, Xi Delta Omicron
Savannah, Georgia

VICTORIA'S CHEESE TARTS

Vanilla wafers	1 teaspoon lemon juice
¾ cup sugar	1 teaspoon vanilla extract
16 ounces cream cheese,	1 20-ounce can cherry
softened	pie filling
2 eggs	

Place vanilla wafer in each miniature muffin cup. Place muffin cups on baking sheet. Cream sugar and cream cheese in mixer bowl until light. Blend in eggs, lemon juice and vanilla. Spoon into prepared muffin cups. Bake at 350 degrees for 15 to 20 minutes or until set. Cool slightly. Top with pie filling. Yield: 40 servings.

Mary Ann Madar, Laureate Alpha Delta
Elizabeth Township, Pennsylvania

FRUIT PIZZA

1 roll refrigerator sugar	3 strawberries, sliced
cookie dough	1 banana, sliced
8 ounces cream cheese,	1 8-ounce can pineapple,
softened	drained
⅓ cup sugar	Blueberries
½ teaspoon vanilla extract	1 kiwifruit
Coconut	¼ cup orange marmalade,
1 cup chopped pecans	melted

Press cookie dough into greased pizza pan. Bake according to package directions. Cool. Blend cream cheese, sugar and vanilla in bowl. Spread over cookie crust. Sprinkle with coconut and pecans. Arrange fruit in order given in concentric circles from outer edge, ending with kiwifruit in center. Brush with warm marmalade. Chill until serving time. Cut into wedges. Yield: 10 servings.

Patricia Burakowski, Eta Kappa
St. Marys, Georgia

TAFFY TARTS

2 sticks pie crust mix	Pinch of salt
½ cup packed brown	1 teaspoon vanilla extract
sugar	½ cup chopped nuts
2 eggs	

Prepare pie crust mix according to package directions. Press into miniature muffin cups. Combine brown sugar, eggs, salt and vanilla in bowl; mix well. Stir in nuts. Fill prepared muffin cups ½ full. Bake at 400 degrees for 15 minutes. Reduce temperature to 350 degrees. Bake until golden brown.

Betty I. Storsberg, Preceptor Psi
Whitesboro, New York

TEA TASSIES

½ cup margarine,	¾ cup packed brown
softened	sugar
3 ounces cream cheese,	1 tablespoon butter
softened	1 teaspoon vanilla extract
1 cup all-purpose flour	⅔ cup chopped pecans
1 egg	

Cream margarine and cream cheese in mixer bowl until light. Mix in flour. Chill in refrigerator. Press into miniature muffin cups. Combine remaining ingredients in bowl; mix well. Spoon into tassie shells. Bake at 325 degrees for 25 minutes.

Wanda Odom, Preceptor Epsilon Upsilon
Denison, Texas

PIE CRUSTS

1½ cups (heaping)	½ cup oil
all-purpose flour	3 tablespoons plus 1
Pinch of salt	teaspoon ice water

Combine flour, salt and oil in bowl. Add ice water; mix well. Divide into 2 portions. Place each portion in center of pie plate. Press evenly over bottom and side of pie plates. Prick with fork. Bake at 350 degrees until brown. Fill as desired. Yield: 2 pie shells.
Note: May store wrapped pastry dough in refrigerator for up to 12 days.

Lottie M. Stout, Laureate Alpha
Lynchburg, Virginia

DEEP-DISH PIE CRUST

2½ cups flour	1 cup shortening
2 tablespoons sugar	1 egg yolk
1 teaspoon baking powder	⅔ cup milk
1 teaspoon salt	1 egg white

Combine flour, sugar, baking powder and salt in bowl. Cut in shortening until crumbly. Add mixture of egg yolk and milk; mix well. Chill in refrigerator. Divide into 2 portions. Roll into rectangles to fit 9x13-inch baking dish on floured surface. Fill with cobbler filling as desired. Brush top pastry with beaten egg white. Sprinkle with additional sugar. Bake according to cobbler directions. Yield: 12 servings.

Christine Davis, Xi Epsilon Alpha
Oktaha, Oklahoma

OLD-FASHIONED PIE CRUSTS

5 cups sifted	1 pound shortening
all-purpose flour	1 egg
1 tablespoon baking powder	1½ teaspoons white
2 teaspoons salt	vinegar
1 teaspoon brown sugar	

Combine first 4 ingredients in bowl. Cut in shortening until crumbly. Set aside. Break egg into measuring cup; add enough cold water to measure ¾ cup. Beat until foamy; add vinegar. Mix well. Add to flour mixture; mix until dough forms. Shape into 6 balls. Chill, wrapped, for 1 hour to several days. Yield: 6 crusts.

Betty Reinaking, Kappa Phi
Dunsmuir, California

No-roll nut crusts are easy and add texture to pies. Press finely chopped nuts into purchased pie shell before baking. Or, mix either 1 cup flour, ½ cup butter and ¼ cup each confectioners' sugar and chopped nuts or 1½ cups ground nuts, 3 tablespoons sugar and 2 tablespoons butter in pie plate. Press mixtures over surface. Bake at 400 degrees for 8 to 10 minutes or until golden.

Index

Microwave recipe page numbers are preceded by an M.

Menu Recipe Index

The British Museum
Occasional Paper
Number 111

Selection of Materials for the Storage or Display of Museum Objects

D. Thickett and L.R. Lee

British Museum
Occasional Papers

Publishers

The British Museum
Great Russell Street
London WC1B 3DG

Production Editor

Josephine Turquet

Distributors

British Museum Press
46 Bloomsbury Street
London WC1B 3QQ

Selection of Materials for the Storage or Display
of Museum Objects
D. Thickett and L.R. Lee
Occasional Paper No. 111, first published 1996,
new and completely revised edition 2004

ISBN 0 86159 117 8
ISSNISSN 0142 4815
© The Trustees of the British Museum 2004

Front cover: Silver tigress from the Hoxne hoard, Romano-British,
probably intended as one of a pair of handles for a large silver
amphora or vase. Buried in the 5th century AD, excavated in 1992
and conserved at the British Museum.

For a complete catalogue giving information on the full range
of available Occasional Papers please see the Occasional Papers
website: www/the britishmuseum.ac.uk/occasionalpapers
or write to:
Oxbow Books
Park End Place
Oxford OX1 1HN
UK
Tel: (+44) (0) 1865 241249
Fax (+44) (0) 1865 794449
e mail oxbow@oxbowbooks.com
website www.oxbowbooks.com
or
The David Brown Book Co
PO Box 511
Oakville
CT 06779
USA
Tel: (+1) 860 945 9329; Toll free 1 800 791 9354
Fax: (+1) 860 945 9468
e mail david.brown.bk.co@snet.net

Printed and bound in the UK by Kingswood Steele

List of Plates, Figures and Tables

Figures

Tables

Introduction

For the past 30 years, conservation scientists at the British Museum have been world leaders in research into the sources and effects of emissions from display and storage systems in museums. A valuable object may be housed in an enclosure such as a cupboard or showcase, as its physical security is often considered to be improved; it is protected from theft and dust, and allows for environmental conditioning if required. However, this may inadvertently put an object at risk, due to emissions of harmful gases discharged by the associated storage and display materials.

In 1972, an accelerated corrosion test was designed to find materials which would be safe for long term use and would not cause degradation of enclosed artefacts. All materials used in the storage and display of artefacts at the British Museum now have to pass one or more tests before they can be used, which has made a dramatic impact on the stability of the collection.

This Occasional Paper has been compiled as a result of continual enquiries received by the British Museum from a wide range of professionals: designers, architects, conservators, collectors, curators, and showcase manufacturers, and indeed anyone involved in the task of creating a safe environment for precious objects. It is not the intention to cover all aspects of storage or display; the aim of this publication is to explain the background to why materials need to be tested for use with artefacts. It is also a comprehensive test manual, including full test methods for evaluating storage and display materials, with the relative merits and drawbacks of each test discussed. Practical implementation of results is considered and methods to mitigate the effects of unsuitable materials are suggested.

The authors would like to acknowledge the support of their colleagues in the Conservation Research Group in the preparation of this document.

1.
Why is Testing Necessary?

Accelerated corrosion in a museum environment

As early as the 1st century AD, Pliny wrote of the corrosive effects of timber on lead (Rackham 1968). One of the first investigations into damage of objects caused by unsuitable storage materials was described by Byne in 1899, when he attributed the degradation of shells to the vapours emitted by their wooden storage cabinets (Byne 1899). The cause was later identified as acetic acid (ethanoic acid) (Nicholls 1934).

Rathgen wrote in his book *The Preservation of Antiquities* in 1905 of the various changes undergone by antiquities in earth and air (Rathgen 1905). However, very little was detailed on the changes to artefacts in air. For example, although Rathgen reported that 'sulphuretted hydrogen' (hydrogen sulphide) caused the formation of metal sulphides, he appeared to be unaware that materials used within a museum could be a source of such gases, and thus promote degradation of the objects housed there; he also stated 'when placed in museums, silver objects remain unaltered and no further chemical change takes place'. It is also of interest that he mentioned that objects of lead are always white; we now know that although stable burial patinas on lead can appear almost white, lead often appears white due to active corrosion. Dr Alexander Scott was seconded to the British Museum to examine the degradation of objects which had been stored during the first World War, and was founder of the British Museum Research Laboratory. In his first report, in 1921, he reported two types of degradation caused by pollutant gases (Scott 1921). He stated that lead white would be blackened in the presence of sulphuretted hydrogen, and suggested that it was 'unwise to store medals and small objects of lead in cabinets of oak... probably due to traces of volatile acids given off from the oak'. In his later paper to the Royal Society of Arts he confirmed this statement, reporting that traces of acetic acid cause lead to 'rapidly become brittle and almost shapeless masses of basic lead carbonate' (Scott 1922). The primary work by Scott was continued by Plenderleith, when he was Assistant Keeper in the British Museum Laboratory and a handbook was produced outlining causes of deterioration, and methods of conservation (Plenderleith 1934). He discussed storage conditions but only with reference to relative humidity and temperature. However, in the section on lead, he reiterated Scott's warning against the use of wooden storage for lead due to its potential to emit volatile acids.

By the early 1970s, in depth investigations were underway at the British Museum to determine methods to avoid the problem of corrosion of artefacts on display and in storage and a standard testing method for detecting potentially harmful materials was reported (Werner 1972,

Oddy 1973, Blackshaw *et al.* 1974, Oddy 1975). Development of these studies to investigate the sources of emissions, and resulting damage to artefacts, has been continued at the British Museum, at various other museums and at research institutes and there is now a more comprehensive understanding of the reasons for decay (Blackshaw and Daniels 1978, Blackshaw and Daniels 1979, Blackshaw 1982, Padfield 1982, Graedel and McGill 1986, Werner 1986, Brimblecombe 1990). More recently methods have been developed to quantify the amounts of many of the important corrosive pollutants in common museum atmospheres such as display cases and storage boxes (Gibson *et al* 1997, Grzywacz and Tennant 1994, Watts). This provides an alternative route to assessing environments, and has lead significant advances in understanding the relative risk posed by these pollutants. However, testing to exclude corrosive materials still provides the best safeguard against corrosion problems associated with materials.

Effects of pollutants

Air is composed mainly of nitrogen and oxygen, but also contains a complex mixture of many different gases present at much lower concentrations, for example ozone, sulphur dioxide and oxides of nitrogen. These low background concentrations can cause slow deterioration of objects; outdoor stone sculpture will form a sulphate crust and bronze statues become covered with a patina of corrosion products, particularly in an industrial or maritime area.

However, these 'outdoor' pollutants are generally present at much lower levels inside a building (Graedel and McGill 1986), and the indoor environment often possesses its own characteristic range of pollutants. For example it may contain higher levels of organic acids, particularly formic (methanoic acid) and acetic acid. This is because they are emitted by materials such as timber and timber-composites. The problems arise when such materials are used in confined spaces, where any emissions become trapped and their concentration increases.

If enclosed with inappropriate materials, metal artefacts can corrode, inorganic objects can suffer adverse reactions such as the formation of mixed salts and organic materials can become brittle. In this section, effects of various pollutant gases on each of these types of object will be explored in turn. At this point it is worth mentioning the deleterious effects of particulate matter; this absorbs moisture and pollutant gases, and therefore a layer of dust on an object can exacerbate any of the following effects. The importance of clean storage and display areas cannot be over-emphasised.

If silver is placed on open display, it will become dull and eventually acquire a tarnished appearance. This is due to reaction with low background levels of sulphide and other gases, for example hydrogen sulphide and carbonyl sulphide or hydrogen chloride. However, if enclosed on display or in storage with inappropriate materials such as woollen felt, silver can tarnish rapidly. Although silver sulphide is the major corrosion product found on much tarnished silver, other compounds such as sulphates, nitrates, hydroxides and chlorides have been identified (Rice *et al.* 1980, Lee 1996). The silver sulphate may have formed due to oxidation of atmospheric carbonyl sulphide (Wayne 1985). Disruptive effects of sulphide gases on silver chloride patinas have also been found (Shashoua and Green 1990). Objects made of alloys of silver with metals other than gold are generally less resistant to corrosion than pure silver.

Silver artefacts can be polished to remove disfiguring silver tarnish, although excessive polishing is undesirable as a small amount of the silver is removed. Repeated polishing can lead to loss of detail where the surface is decorated, or complete loss of the surface where an object is silver plated. However, in some situations, cleaning is extremely difficult as with silver leaf on manuscripts and scrolls (**Pl. 1**). Silver based photographic media can also be irreversibly damaged by sulphide gases resulting in darkening and loss of contrast of the image. It is also reported that formaldehyde (methanal) will discolour photographs (Weyde 1972).

High purity gold is considered to be resistant to most pollutant gases. However, where gold exists in combination with other metals, for example as silver gilt or as a low purity alloy, the effects of pollutants on the associated metals must be considered.

Polished copper is susceptible to attack by sulphides, organic acids, chlorides and formaldehyde, which can oxidise to formic acid at very high humidities or if oxidising agents such as ozone are present (Hatchfield and Carpenter 1987, Thickett *et al* 1998, Raychaudhuri and Brimblecombe 2000). Copper and its alloys can also be disfigured by 'black spot' which was originally thought to be due to microbiological attack (Madsen and Hjelm-Hansen 1979). However, subsequent research has shown that 'black spot' is due to reaction of atmospheric sulphur compounds (Oddy

and Bradley 1989) often due to unsuitable display or storage materials. The copper alloys are converted into copper sulphides, such as brown digenite, $Cu_{1.8}S$, and black chalcocite, Cu_2S (Green 1992a). However, copper and its alloys tend to be less sensitive to sulphide attack than polished silver. Copper often possesses an oxide patina or a more extensive corrosion layer, which can be protective against atmospheric attack. If prolonged exposure to harmful gases has occurred, the patina/corrosion layer can itself be affected. Several occurrences of the black sulphide formation on copper carbonate patinas have been seen in museum collections (Oddy and Meeks 1982).

Pure lead is particularly vulnerable to atmospheric corrosion if stored inappropriately. Volatile organic acids such as acetic and formic acids, cause extensive disruptive corrosion, often producing hydrocerussite, basic lead carbonate (Rance and Cole 1958). Again there is evidence that formaldehyde can be oxidised in some environments to formic acid. In some instances, lead formate has also been identified as the major corrosion product on lead artefacts. This may be due to attack of formic acid or formaldehyde rather than acetic acid. One of the problems with lead objects in a collection is that they may be visually identified only as a 'white metal'; their true composition may often be discovered only when corrosion occurs. Alloys of lead with copper or tin are more resistant to corrosion than pure lead, but heavily leaded bronzes may contain large discrete particles of lead, which can corrode independently of the bronze matrix if stored in a corrosive environment.

When considering the effects of pollutant gases on metals, one generally focuses on silver, copper and lead, but these are not the only metals in museum collections. Ferrous metals are susceptible to attack by sulphur dioxide and nitrogen dioxide, and it has been reported that other pollutants, particularly acetic acid, are corrosive (Gilroy and Mayne 1965, Green and Bradley 1997). Zinc has been known for many centuries, for example in Bidriware from India. It will corrode in the presence of organic acids, formaldehyde, chlorides and sulphur dioxide. Zinc formate hydrate has been identified on zinc coins which have been stored in

Plate 1 Detail of a scroll by Matabei showing tarnishing of silver (JA 1946 02-09 032, Jap Ptg Add 194)

unsuitable wooden cabinets (Oddy and Bradley 1989, Oddy 1993). On a separate occasion, a number of corroding zinc coins were analysed and the presence of chloride was identified in some of the corrosion products (Green and Thickett 1991). This may have been due to their environment prior to acquisition, for example, they may have been recovered from the sea. Other sources of chlorides may have been from handling, or volatile chlorides from storage materials.

Artefacts made from modern metals such as aluminium and magnesium are now being collected by museums. Aluminium is generally stable due to the presence of a film of aluminium oxide. Formic acid, however, peptises this oxide film producing a gelatinous layer that is no longer protective. It is reported that organic chlorides and hydrogen chloride also disrupt the oxide layer. Alloys of aluminium with small concentrations of other metals, such as copper, have a reduced corrosion resistance. An examination of a number of aluminium objects housed in a variety of storage situations in the British Museum in 1991 revealed very little corrosion. Magnesium normally possesses a protective film of carbonates and sulphates but will corrode in the presence of organic acids (Green and Thickett 1991). Other modern metals such as nickel, cadmium and chromium are also generally corrosion resistant in normal atmospheres but with more of these metals being collected by museums the effects of pollutants need to be elucidated. Cadmium, for example, is corroded by organic acids (Rance and Cole 1958).

Non-metallic inorganic materials are also adversely affected by pollutants; certain glasses can deteriorate if exposed to high levels of formaldehyde or acetic or formic acid (Hatchfield and Carpenter 1987, Schmidt 1992). Soluble salts, for example in stone and ceramics, can react with volatile organic acids to form mixed salt compounds such as calclacite, $Ca(CH_3COO)Cl.5H_2O$ (West FitzHugh and Gettens 1971) of calcium chloride nitrate acetate , $Ca_3Cl(NO_3)2(CH_3COO)_3$ (Gibson et al 1997). Carbonate based materials, such as shells, also react with organic acids producing a crystalline alteration product, which has commonly been referred to as Byne's Disease, which was reported as early as 1899 (Byne 1899). Inorganic pigments can become discoloured, for example, lead white and red lead react with sulphide gases, resulting in black lead sulphide (Harley 1982, Daniels and Thickett 1990).

Organic materials suffer adverse effects when exposed to some pollutants. Cellulose based materials such as paper and some textiles may degrade due to acid or alkaline hydrolysis. This breaks the cellulose chains, thus lowering the strength of the material, which eventually becomes brittle and susceptible to damage by handling. Certain components of paper may cause it to be acidic, or become acidic on ageing. Paper may be sized with an acidic alum/rosin size, and papers made with a high proportion of groundwood pulp will contain lignin. Lignin has been reported to become acidic on ageing, and thus lignin-free papers are generally recommended for archival use. However, recent evidence has shown that the mechanical ageing properties of paper containing lignin are not significantly different to those of lignin-free papers. It has

been suggested that many of the papers used in previous trials contained alum/rosin size in addition to the lignin, and the increased acidity was due to the size and not the lignin (Priest and Stanley 1994). It was concluded that in a neutral or alkaline environment lignin will not degrade. However, papers containing lignin may discolour with time, and effects of atmospheric pollutants are not known. Low level concentrations of both sulphur dioxide and nitrogen oxides have been reported to affect cellulosic materials (Morris et al. 1964, Brysson et al. 1967, Lyth Hudson and Milner 1961, Langwell 1976). Acetic acid has been found to cause paper to degrade at high concentrations ($20,000\mu gm-3$ caused degradation of filter paper over 40 days, whilst 3000 did not, Dupont and Tereault 2000). Many museum environments can contain concentrations around $3000\mu gm^{-3}$, whilst only very rarely would $20,000\mu gm^{-3}$ be expected. Hence it is difficult to determine whether acetic acid poses a significant long term risk to paper with the knowledge presently available.

Textiles contain metal threads then these can be affected by pollutants as discussed earlier. Paper may also contain metallic inclusions. Reaction of these with sulphur containing pollutants can be one cause of the spots known as foxing (Daniels and Meeks 1992, 1995). Ozone does not pose a significant risk at ambient levels present in air, but at greater concentrations, such as could build up in a storage area it can increase the deterioration rate of cotton and rubber, and induce fading of dyes (Bogarty et al. 1952, Shashoua and Thomsen 1993, Shaver and Cass 1983). Synthetic fabrics and plastic materials are now being collected by museums. Nylon suffers accelerated degradation in the presence of low levels of sulphur dioxide (Zeronian et al. 1973). Polymethylmethacrylate and polystyrene are reported to be affected by acetic acid (Fenn 1995).

Sources of pollutants

Table I summarises the major sources and effects of common indoor pollutants.

In a museum situation a wide range of materials are used to construct and dress showcases, and in fitting out a store. Wood is one such material as it is versatile, comparatively inexpensive and easily worked. It also has the advantage of buffering changes in relative humidity (RH), an effect which may be beneficial to certain types of artefact. However all wood emits varying levels of organic acids and formaldehyde. As wood is a natural, non-homogeneous material, it is difficult to be specific about properties regarding outgassing of certain species or products, and lists of results from previous tests are of minimal use. General statements can however be made, for example oak and sweet chestnut emit higher levels of organic acids than beech or spruce (Arni et al. 1965, Blackshaw and Daniels 1978). Variations in emissions from the same species can be influenced by several factors including time of felling, whether the wood is heart or sapwood and treatment after felling; kiln drying has been found to produce higher levels of free organic acids in a sample of wood than air drying. The moisture content of wood and timber products also affects their corrosive nature. Certain woods have been

Table 1 Sources and effects of common museum pollutants

Pollutant	Main source		Affects
sulphur containing species, eg hydrogen sulphide H$_2$S, and carbonyl sulphide COS	wool	fabrics, eg felt	silver and copper
	rubber	adhesives	
organic acids, eg formic acid, CHOOH, and acetic acid, CH$_3$COOH	timber	all, especially oak	lead, copper, zinc, cadmium, magnesium, salt-laden stone and ceramic, shells, possibly paper
	timber composites	MDF*, plywood, blockboard, chipboard	
	paints	often oil based	
	adhesives, varnishes	polyvinyl acetate, some polyurethanes	
	sealants	some silicones	
	moth and rot proofing		
formaldehyde CH$_2$O	adhesives	urea and phenol formaldehyde	high levels can attack most metals and organic artefacts under suitable conditions
	timber	all	
	timber composites	MDF*, plywood, blockboard, chipboard	
	fabrics, paints		
chlorides	plastics	PVC†, PVDC‡	copper, aluminium, zinc and iron
	fire retardants	inorganic salts	
nitrogen oxides, NO$_x$	plastics	cellulose nitrate	copper and iron

Key
* medium density fibreboard
† poly vinyl chloride
‡ poly vinylidene chloride

found to be emitting significant levels of volatiles after twenty years (Grzywacs and Tennent 1994).

In addition to structural components, timber based products are often used for internal fittings of a showcase, ie baseboards and mounting boards. Plywood, chipboard, hardboard, blockboard and medium density fibreboard (MDF) are composite materials of timber and adhesive, the latter often formaldehyde based (Sparkes 1989). Products manufactured for internal use are generally bonded with urea formaldehyde resin, whereas those for external use utilise phenol formaldehyde resin. Urea formaldehyde adhesives emit more formaldehyde, due to hydrolysis; phenol formaldehyde resins are more stable, resulting in a lower release of formaldehyde (Pickrell et al. 1983). Therefore, phenol formaldehyde products are more desirable for use in a museum environment. Due to health and safety regulations in the furniture industry, there are limits to the maximum formaldehyde content of timber products such as MDF. MDF labelled 'E1' grade conforms to legislation for a lower formaldehyde content. Products which are manufactured using a formaldehyde free adhesive component are available, but have the inherent problem that it is not only the adhesive which gives off formaldehyde but also the wood particles. Therefore although a formaldehyde free adhesive can be used, this will not result in a completely formaldehyde free product. Also any wood product will emit acetic and formic acid and these are probably more damaging than the formaldehyde. Coatings for wood and

metals are discussed in chapter 3.

Fabrics are often used in a showcase display, and can also be a source of pollutants. Wool is known to be a source of sulphide gases, mainly carbonyl sulphide (Brimblecombe et al. 1992). However, although many other natural fibres may not be a major source of pollutants themselves, a fabric often has additions such as crease-resistant finishes or fire retardants, which may be a source of harmful substances such as formaldehyde or organic acids. Dyes can also be a source of pollutants

Since testing of display and storage materials was instigated in the British Museum in the early 1970s (Oddy 1973), examples of corrosion on display in its galleries have been minimised. However, on rare occasions, deterioration has been observed as illustrated by the three following case studies.

In a recent gallery project, large fragments of stucco were displayed, along with three small lead objects. Panels of medium density fibreboard were used to line the back of the large showcase (approximately 2 x 0.5 x 3.5 m). These panels were originally coated with a suitable decorative finish to blend with the colour scheme of the gallery. However, when placed in position, the colour of the board was found to be unacceptable, and due to pressures of time the untested gallery paint was used to recoat the board. After a few months white corrosion was noted on the lead pieces; this was identified as a mixture of basic lead carbonate and lead formate. Levels of acetic acid and formaldehyde inside the showcase were over 20 times higher than levels measured in the gallery. When the paint which had been used inside the showcase was tested, it was found to be a source of organic acids, and highly corrosive to lead. MDF board is also a known source of formaldehyde and organic acids. This highlights two potential problem areas; last minute decisions being taken without full consultation and the need for full testing of materials intended for use in an enclosed display case.

Where corrosion of objects due to pollutant gases does occur, it should be borne in mind that this may not always be due to inappropriate storage or display materials. It has been shown that human beings can 'outgas' producing sulphur-containing gases (Brimblecombe *et al.* 1992). Although human beings rarely form part of a display, they can be found in store rooms. Objects themselves may also outgas, and affect associated materials. A silver-copper alloy necklace was found to be corroding in the early 1980s, and after conservation, degraded again in storage within a few years, resulting in severe green copper nitrate corrosion as shown in **Plates 2 and 3**. Yellow beads on the same necklace had originally been catalogued as amber and copal, but analysis revealed they were in fact cellulose nitrate (Green and Bradley 1988). Due to loss of plasticiser, the cellulose

nitrate beads had become unstable, and degraded to produce nitric acid. This had attacked the silver-copper alloy components of the necklace to produce the copper nitrate corrosion product. Eventually the cellulose nitrate beads were isolated from the necklace to avoid further decay of the silver alloy, and also to minimise effects on other artefacts in the same storage area.

Low fired ceramics excavated from anaerobic sites have also been found to outgas, producing sulphide gases. This resulted in black deposits of copper sulphide forming on bronze objects in the same display case (Green 1992b). The ceramic vessels could have become impregnated with sulphur-rich or sulphide-producing materials during burial. Recently, it has been shown that iron artefacts from a similar site can also be a source of sulphides. This potential source of sulphide gases should be borne in mind when mixed media displays are planned.

Removal of harmful pollutant gases from museums with an air conditioning system is a costly approach, and not normally effective at reducing levels of gases generated inside enclosed showcases or storage units. In the first instance, it is more effective to ensure that materials used for the storage or display of artefacts are not a source of these pollutants. This is achieved by testing the materials.

Plate 2 Necklace from Somalia, with beads made of silver alloy and cellulose nitrate (Ethno 1933 11-14 82)

Plate 3 Detail of corrosion on silver alloy beads due to degradation of cellulose nitrate

2.
Test Methods

Introduction

In this section, detailed procedures for the tests used to assess the suitability of a storage or display material in the British Museum are given. Accelerated corrosion tests are used wherever possible to evaluate the effects of a material on metal artefacts. A modification of the standard accelerated corrosion test, known as the Oddy test, has now been introduced in the British Museum. This is the 3 in 1 test which is quicker and easier to set up. Accelerated corrosion tests take four weeks and therefore a range of shorter tests has also been developed. These shorter tests have some disadvantages which will be discussed before each test method is described. The tests have been found to cover the various types of material found within the collections at the British Museum. However, other applications may require different tests, for example the photographic activity test (ISO 10214 1991, Nishimura 1990). This particular method is not used at the British Museum as it necessitates a sample of the type of photographs being stored; this may be difficult to obtain. If the photographs are silver based, an accelerated corrosion test for silver can be undertaken, although this will not give any indication of a materials tendency to fade a photograph when in direct contact. Health and safety information is given at the end of each test method; names of suppliers of chemicals and equipment are provided at the end of the chapter. When carrying out these tests, relevant health and safety legislation should be adhered to.

The primary object of a test is to be able to know with confidence that a material will not cause any deterioration if used in either the same air space or in direct contact with artefacts. In the event of one of the tests giving the 'wrong' result, eg due to contamination of the test material or a species interfering with the test, it is important that it 'fails safe', ie that the test gives a positive result and the material is considered unsuitable for use. Although this may mean more materials need to be tested, it is far preferable to potentially corrosive materials passing a test.

Sampling

Before undertaking any tests it is important to obtain a representative sample of the intended display material, preferably from the batch of material being considered for use. Materials can vary from batch to batch and manufacturers may change their formulations without notification. Storage conditions can cause a material to become more or less corrosive with time. This is due to outgassing or absorption of gases from the storage environment.

Many materials are non-homogeneous and it is important that the sample tested contains all of the different components. For example, a patterned textile may contain threads treated with different dyes. Samples should always be presented to the tests in the form in which they are intended for use. For example, paints or lacquers should be tested as thin, dry films, which have been allowed to cure on glass or Melinex according to manufacturers' instructions. Such materials often emit corrosive gases as they cure. In some circumstances, a longer cure time can be allowed, to reflect that which will occur in practice when the material is used. Details of the time allowed for curing should be recorded with any test results.

Selection of tests

The flowcharts, **Figures 1 and 2**, provide a swift method to decide which tests need to be applied to a storage and display material proposed for use with specific groups of artefacts.

Two accelerated corrosion tests are included, the method as standardised and published in 1995 and a modification of that method designed to streamline the test production and reduce the amount of time required to set up the test. An alternative formaldehyde test has also been added to this edition, using less toxic materials than the chromotropic acid test.

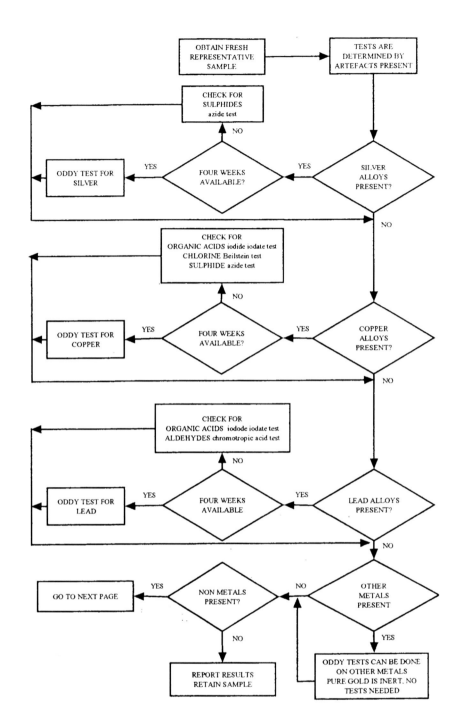

Figure 1 Flowchart to determine tests: metal artefacts

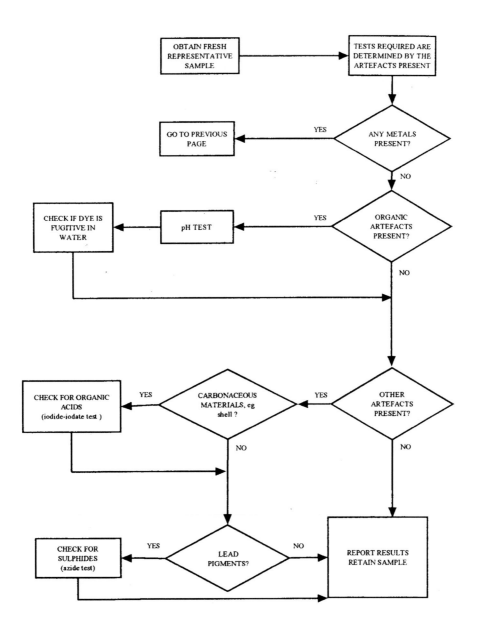

Figure 2 Flowchart to determine tests: non-metal artefacts

Tests for potential to emit harmful volatiles

Many materials emit gases which may cause deterioration of artefacts. Since the corrosive species are gases then a material does not need to be in contact with an artefact to cause deterioration, but only needs to be in the same airspace.

Accelerated corrosion tests

Introduction

The material under test is enclosed in a sealed glass boiling tube with a metal coupon. Corrosion of the metal is accelerated in a number of ways:

- the ratio of test material to airspace is much higher than would be encountered in a display case or storage area. Therefore the concentration of any volatile corrosive gases is higher;
- the metal coupon is abraded to expose a reactive metal surface;
- the relative humidity in the tube is raised to 100% which generally accelerates the corrosion;
- the temperature is elevated to 60°C which increases the rate of emission of any volatile degradation products from the material, and accelerates any corrosion reactions.

After 28 days the test is disassembled. The amount of corrosion on the metal coupon is used to classify the material as being:

- suitable for permanent use (no corrosion);
- suitable for temporary use – up to six months only (slight corrosion);
- or unsuitable for use (obvious corrosion).

Metal coupons are chosen to represent the composition of artefacts of concern. Copper, silver and lead have been found to be the most susceptible metals of those used in antiquity. Copper may be used to represent copper alloys (bronze, brass etc) although certain heavily leaded bronzes contain discrete lead particles and proposed storage or display materials should also be tested for their effects on lead. Such tests have been applied to magnesium, zinc and aluminium (Green and Thickett 1991), and also to iron (Green and Bradley 1997) with some success.

Although these accelerated corrosion tests were designed for use with metals, it is possible to deduce the effects of a display/storage material on non-metallic artefacts. As described in chapter 1, the pollutants which cause corrosion of certain metals are also known to be the cause of deterioration of various non-metal substrates. Therefore if a material passes an accelerated corrosion test, it is not producing the harmful species known to corrode the chosen metal coupon. For example, shells are attacked by organic acids; if a material passes the accelerated corrosion test with lead it cannot be a source of organic acids, and is therefore suitable for the display or storage of the shells.

The major advantage of accelerated corrosion tests are that they will detect the effects of ALL corrosive species emitted from the sample. Many of the species found to cause corrosion on display are in fact degradation products of display materials. As the tests accelerate the degradation of the test material it will detect if any of them are corrosive.

A drawback of accelerated corrosion tests are 28 days are required before the results are available. If the chosen material fails, ie the metal coupon corrodes, an alternative material needs to be found and tested, and the full testing period required can be extensive. The test methods need to be followed rigorously, as even small changes can lead to differing results (Green and Thickett 1993). The tests are designed to be as sensitive as possible and should indicate if a material has any potential to accelerate or cause corrosion of metals. This may lead to a small number of materials failing the test that under normal museum conditions may not cause corrosion. However, the many factors involved in a display case can be difficult to determine and can change with time and it is therefore important to have a sensitive test. Cleanliness of the apparatus is vitally important to avoid cross contamination between samples leading to erroneous results. It should be noted that such contamination would cause material to fail the test, which is far preferable to an unsuitable material passing the test. The coupon assessment stage has been found to be subjective (Green and Thickett 1993). Notes and reference photographs showing levels of corrosion from various tests are therefore supplied to help with assessing the metal coupons (see **Plates 4a–c**). These coupons are from tests with the newer method and are larger than those used in the older 'Oddy' test. To use these reference photographs for the 'Oddy' test, ignore the top 60% of the coupons shown.

General comments on sampling are given at the beginning of this chapter. Accelerated corrosion tests can accommodate any type of solid sample. The size is limited by the neck of the reaction vessel; 24mm diameter Quickfit glass tubes are used in the British Museum. Bulky materials, eg wood and plastics, will require cutting to size. Note that certain materials can swell in the 100% humidity atmosphere and this should be taken into account when sampling. Larger reaction vessels can be used with care, but the volume may affect the test results. It has been suggested to the authors that solid samples should be powdered to allow all corrosive vapours to escape. However the elevated temperature of the test will accelerate diffusion of gaseous degradation products from solids and it is unlikely that, given 28 days, such materials will remain trapped. It is therefore not thought necessary to prepare samples as powders.

The 'Oddy' test – an accelerated corrosion test for effects on metals (Green and Thickett 1995)

Note: This test was developed at the British Museum by Andrew Oddy and co-workers in the early 1970s and the method has been through several improvements in later years; it is now colloquially referred to as the 'Oddy' test.

Test method

The following recommended method should be followed exactly. Care should be taken to ensure all equipment is clean and that it does not become contaminated during preparation of the test. This can lead to erroneous results. The cleaning procedure previously used for the glassware at the British Museum involves cleaning in chromic acid, washing with hot detergent solution, rinsing with distilled water, drying and passing through a Bunsen flame. The chromic acid used is extremely toxic and may cause cancer, see safety notes at the end of this section.

1. AnalaR (99.5% pure or better) metal foils, 0.1mm thick, should be used: copper to assess the effects of the test material on copper-based artefacts, silver for silver-based artefacts and lead for lead-based artefacts. If artefacts are made of high lead bronze which can contain discrete particles of lead, then both copper and lead tests should be carried out. It is recommended that metal foils of the desired thickness are purchased, as processing of a thicker foil may introduce impurities and inconsistencies in the coupons, leading to irreproducible results.

2. A 10 x 15mm coupon is cut from the metal foil. Both faces of the coupon are lightly abraded using a glass bristle brush. Care should be taken to keep the coupons as flat as possible, as physical distortion can lead to problems at the assessment stage. A separate glass bristle brush should be reserved for each metal to avoid contamination.

3. A small hole is pierced in each coupon, close to one edge. It has been found that this can be done effectively by using the guide pin on a pair of dissecting tweezers.

4. Nylon monofilament (maximum diameter 0.053mm) is threaded through the hole in the coupon and tied in place.

5. The coupon is degreased in a glass dish of acetone for a few minutes with slight agitation. Using tweezers, the coupon is removed and allowed to dry between tissue paper. The coupon is subsequently handled using only tweezers and while wearing gloves.

6. Approximately 2g of the test material are added to a 50ml glass boiling tube with a ground glass seal, which is a convenient 'reaction vessel'. Bulky materials should be cut into pieces approximately 10 x 10 x 5mm. When it is impossible to fit 2g of certain materials in the tube eg expanded foams, as much test material as is reasonably practical should be used, ie without causing contact with the metal coupon.

7. A 0.5ml test tube is filled with distilled water, stoppered with a small plug of cotton wool and added to the boiling tube.

8. The nylon monofilament holding the cleaned coupon is trapped in the ground glass joint of the boiling tube. A collar of heat shrink tubing (type NMW360),

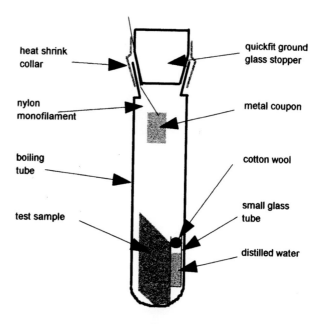

Figure 3 Diagrammatic representation of an Oddy test

Labels (clockwise): heat shrink collar; quickfit ground glass stopper; nylon monofilament; metal coupon; boiling tube; cotton wool; test sample; small glass tube; distilled water

approximately 15mm in length is shrunk onto the ground glass joint using gentle heat from a hot air blower.

9. A control is set up for each type of metal used, ie with a metal coupon and water but no test material.

10. The assembly is placed in an oven at 60°C. If possible, the boiling tube should be placed at a slight angle from the horizontal to avoid condensation settling on the metal coupon.

11. After 28 days the metal coupon is removed from the test and compared with the control coupon. In order to reduce reflections from silver and copper coupons it is recommended that a sheet of white paper is held at an angle of approximately 60° to the horizontal, over the coupons. The level of any corrosion is used to classify the test material as suitable for permanent use (P), temporary use (T) or unsuitable for use (U). See reference photographs and notes, **Plates 4a–c**. These photographs are of coupons from the '3 in 1' accelerated corrosion test and only the bottom 40% of the photograph should be taken into account when assessing coupons from the 'Oddy' test.

12. It is recommended that occasionally the tests are set up in duplicate, to act as a measure of reproducibility.

13. A manufacturer may change the processes by which a material is made, which may affect the suitability of that material for use with certain artefacts. Results on most materials are considered to be valid for up to four years, although this is an arbitrary value.

Health and safety information

The main risks associated with the chemicals and materials used in this test are listed below. Appropriate personal protective equipment should be worn to counter the risks in line with local legislation. For more information consult the suppliers' health and safety data sheets.

Chromic acid is very highly toxic, corrosive and a suspected carcinogen.

Assessment of metal coupons from accelerated corrosion tests

The reference photographs, **Plates 4a–c**, and associated notes are provided to help standardise the assessment stage of an Oddy test. The three categories on the photographs are P for permanent use, T for temporary use (up to 6 months) and U for unsuitable for use.

P   **T**   **U**

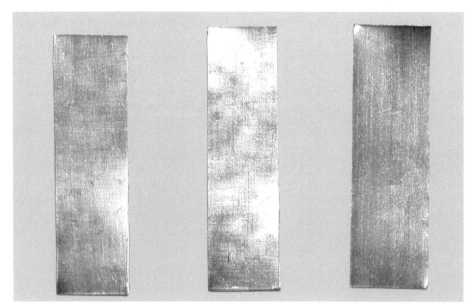

Plate 4a Reference photograph for silver coupons

Control: should show no change
P: no change compared with control. No discolouration of the coupon.
T: slight discolouration only, often seen along lower edge and sides. Alternatively a few localised small spots of tarnish.
U: clearly visible tarnish.

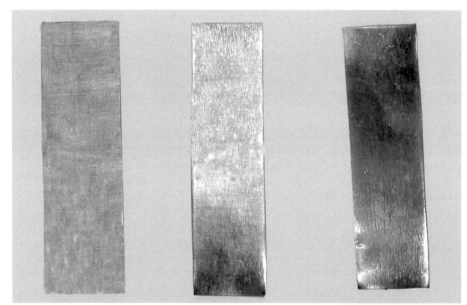

Plate 4b Reference photograph for copper coupons

Control: orange/red iridescence often appears, this is due to oxidation of the copper surface
P: no change compared with control. Coupon should not have lost polished surface.
T: slight discolouration of coupon compared with control. This may be black; coupons with only a few small specks of corrosion should also be classed as temporary.
U: clearly visible corrosion, often black or green, or loss of polish (see lower right coupon in this category), suggestive of a thin layer of corrosion over surface.

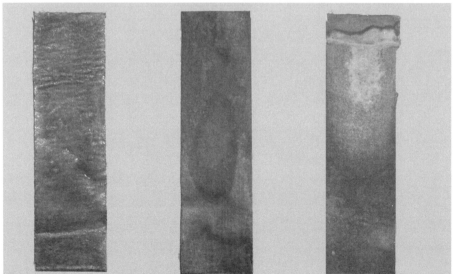

Plate 4c Reference photograph for lead coupons

Control: may acquire a purple hue, this is due to oxidation of the lead surface. Aqueous corrosion may occur on control coupon.
P: no change compared with control.
T: slight change in coupon, either slight overall corrosion or a few very localised spots.
U: severe corrosion – may be brown/yellow, red or white.

Lead is harmful if ingested. Gloves should be worn when handling this metal. The use of lead is regulated by the Lead at Work Regulations 1998 in the UK.

Acetone is extremely flammable; can cause serious damage on contact with the eyes and may cause dermatitis.

Silver dust is harmful if ingested.

Copper dust is harmful if ingested.

Glass bristle brushes produce many small fragments of glass fibre when used. Contact with the skin should be avoided to reduce risk of penetration into the skin.

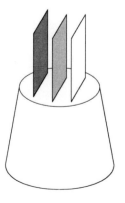

Figure 4 Metal coupons in silicone stopper, lead is in the middle

'3 in 1' accelerated corrosion test (Robinet and Thickett 2003)

Test method

The following recommended method should be followed exactly. Care should be taken to ensure all equipment is clean and that it does not become contaminated during preparation of the test. This can lead to erroneous results. The cleaning procedure used for the glassware at the British Museum involves cleaning in Decon 90 acid rinse overnight, chromic acid, washing with hot Centiclean detergent solution, drying and then passing through a Bunsen flame.

A prepared test is shown in **Figure 3**.

1. AnalaR (99.5% pure or better) metal foils, 0.1mm thick, should be used: copper to assess the effects of the test material on copper-based artefacts, silver for silver-based artefacts and lead for lead-based artefacts. If artefacts are made of high lead bronze which can contain discrete particles of lead, then both copper and lead tests should be carried out. It is recommended that metal foils of the desired thickness are purchased, as processing of a thicker foil may introduce impurities and inconsistencies in the coupons, leading to irreproducible results.

2. A 35 x 10mm coupon is cut from the metal foil. Both faces of the coupon are roughly abraded using a glass bristle brush to remove any oxide. Care should be taken to keep the coupons as flat as possible, as physical distortion can lead to problems at the assessment stage. A separate glass bristle brush should be reserved for each metal to avoid contamination.

3. The coupon is degreased in a glass dish of 'spectrosol' grade acetone for a few minutes with slight agitation. Using tweezers, the coupon is removed and allowed to dry between tissue paper. The coupon is subsequently handled using only tweezers and while wearing gloves. Many general purpose reagent or technical grade acetones leave residues after evaporation, such residues can make interpretation of the test difficult. Spectrosol acetone has been found to deposit much less residue after evaporation.

4. Three slots are cut in the bottom of the silicon stopper with the scalpel, about 5 mm depth and 10 mm across (see **Figure 4**). In order to avoid any contamination by absorption of harmful gases, such as acetic acid from wood, the stoppers should be stored in inert containers.

5. The three metal coupons are inserted into the slots, placing the lead coupon in the middle. (Ensure that coupons are not touching one another).

6. Approximately 2g of the test material are added to a 50ml glass boiling tube with a ground glass seal, which is a convenient 'reaction vessel'. Bulky materials should be cut into pieces approximately 10 x 10 x 5mm. When it is impossible to fit 2g of certain materials in the tube eg expanded foams, as much test material as is reasonably practical should be used, ie without causing contact with the metal coupon.

7. A 0.8ml test tube is filled with distilled water, stoppered with a small plug of cotton wool and added to the boiling tube.

8. The stopper is pushed into the end of the boiling tube, so that the metal coupons are inside the tube. Ensure that the stopper is firmly in place and that the metal coupons are not touching the glass of the tube.

9. A control is set up for each type of metal used, ie with a metal coupon and water but no test material.

10. The assembled tests is placed in an oven at 60°C for 28 days. The tubes should be kept upright, an aluminium incubator tray is suitable to achieve this with sets of up to eighty tests.

11. After 28 days the metal coupon is removed from the test and compared with the control coupon. In order to reduce reflections from silver and copper coupons it is recommended that a sheet of white paper is held at an angle of approximately 60° to the horizontal, over the coupons. The level of any corrosion is used to classify the test material as suitable for permanent use (P), temporary use (T) or unsuitable for use (U). See reference photographs and notes, **Plates 4a–c**. These photographs are of coupons from the new accelerated corrosion test. See above for notes on using the photographs with coupons from 'Oddy' tests. If the control tests show any corrosion, beyond the inevitable oxidation effects described in **Plates 4a–c**, then the whole set of tests should be repeated, with strict cleanliness of the apparatus

12. It is recommended that occasionally the tests are set up in duplicate, to act as a measure of reproducibility.

13. A manufacturer may change the processes by which a material is made, which may affect the suitability of that material for use with certain artefacts. Results on most materials are considered to be valid for up to four years, although this is an arbitrary value.

Health and safety information

The main risks associated with the chemicals and materials used in this test are listed below. Appropriate personal protective equipment should be worn to counter the risks in line with local legislation. For more information consult the suppliers' health and safety data sheets.

Lead is harmful if ingested. Gloves should be worn when handling this metal. The use of lead is regulated by the Lead at Work Regulations 1998 in the UK.

Acetone is extremely flammable; can cause serious damage on contact with the eyes and may cause dermatitis.

Silver dust is harmful if ingested.

Copper dust is harmful if ingested.

Glass bristle brushes produce many small fragments of glass fibre when used. Contact with the skin should be avoided to reduce risk of penetration into the skin.

The Azide test – for sulphur-containing materials
(Daniels and Ward 1982)

Introduction

Airborne species that contain sulphur, eg hydrogen sulphide and carbonyl sulphide, are a major cause of silver tarnish, and can also affect copper. The azide test detects sulphur in a material that can be reduced and hence become volatile; it is based on the catalytic action of such sulphur on a solution of sodium azide and iodine. This forms bubbles of nitrogen, which are viewed down a microscope.

$$2NaN_3 \text{ (solution)} + I_2 \text{ (solution)} \rightarrow 3N_2 \text{ (gas)} + 2NaI \text{ (solution)}$$

If no nitrogen bubbles are noted the material contains no harmful sulphur compounds and hence is suitable for use with silver. If bubbles are noted then the material is unsuitable for use with silver or copper.

The results from the azide test are available immediately and hence it has an advantage over accelerated corrosion tests. The test detects the presence of sulphur compounds in a material and hence there is no need to accelerate the material's degradation; if sulphide is there, the test will detect it. However, the azide test will ONLY detect harmful sulphur compounds. Other species are known to cause corrosion of silver and copper but this test will not detect them. At the British Museum the test has been carried out routinely on fibrous materials such as textiles or papers. The azide test has been of limited use for evaluating woods or adhesives, and certain textiles have been found to have coatings that make it impossible to separate the fibres sufficiently to be confident of the results. The glassware used for this test should be thoroughly cleaned as dust has been found to cause bubbling. The assessment of the degree of bubbling can be subjective and is especially difficult when only a few bubbles are produced. The test solution has a limited shelf life and requires frequent replacement.

General comments on sampling are given at the beginning of this chapter. Since the sample size for this test is small, it is essential to ensure all different fibre types present in the sample are tested. For most fabrics this will require testing the warp and the weft separately; and for velvets, the pile must also be tested.

Test method

1. 3g of sodium azide are dissolved in 100ml of Convol 0.05M iodine solution (supplied in solution form) and 3ml of industrial methylated spirits (IMS) are added. The reagent should be stored in a brown glass bottle and has a shelf life of 3 months.

2. A few fibres are separated from the test material with tweezers and placed on a clean microscope slide.

3. A clean cover-slip is placed over the fibres which are viewed under magnification of at least x20.

4. One drop of azide solution is placed on the microscope slide, away from the fibres and covered with a clean cover-slip. This is a control.

5. One drop of the azide solution is placed at the edge of the cover slip with the fibres. It will be drawn under the cover-slip and onto the fibres by capillary action.

6. The test should be observed under magnification for 2 minutes and the amount of bubbling assessed as follows:
    • no bubbles: suitable for permanent use;
    • several bubbles form gradually: suitable for temporary use only;
    • immediate and vigorous bubbling: unsuitable for use.
    Reference photographs for assessing results from the azide test are shown in **Plates 5a–c**.

Health and safety information

The main risks associated with the chemicals and materials used in this test are listed below. Appropriate personal protective equipment should be worn to counter the risks in line with local legislation. For more information consult the suppliers' health and safety data sheets.

Sodium azide is very toxic by ingestion or inhalation and is irritating to the skin and eyes and may explode if heated. It forms extremely explosive compounds if allowed to come into contact with acids.

Iodine solution is harmful if ingested and irritating to the skin and eyes.

Industrial methylated spirit is highly flammable, intoxicating if inhaled or ingested and irritating to the eyes.

Plate 5a Positive azide test – unsuitable for use (U) with silver or copper. Immediate and vigorous bubbling with nitrogen evolved from most of the sample

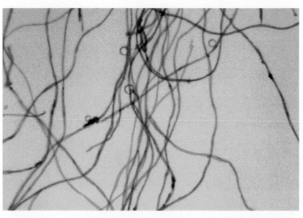

Plate 5b Slight positive azide test – suitable for temporary use (T, up to 6 months only) with silver and copper. A few bubbles gradually form

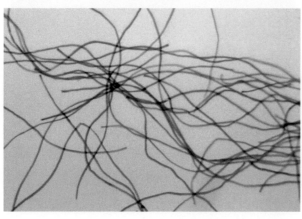

Plate 5c Negative azide test – suitable for permanent use (P) with silver and copper. No or very few bubbles

The Beilstein test – a flame test for the presence of chlorine (Vogel 1966)

This is a test for the presence of chlorine in a material. It relies on the reaction of chlorine ions with copper in a flame to give a green or blue colour. Chlorine-containing materials can degrade to produce hydrochloric acid which will cause deterioration of many types of artefacts. Chlorides can cause accelerated corrosion of copper, iron and silver.

The results from the Beilstein test are available immediately which gives it an advantage over accelerated corrosion tests. The test detects the presence of chlorine in a material and there is no need to accelerate the material's degradation; if chlorine is there, the test will detect it. However, the Beilstein test will ONLY detect chlorine. Other species are known to cause corrosion of copper, iron and silver and this test will not detect them. Certain other species will give a green flame colour with copper such as bromide and iodide ions. General comments on sampling are given at the beginning of this chapter.

Test method

1. A copper wire is cleaned by dipping in dilute nitric acid.
2. The wire is held in the hot region of Bunsen burner flame until red heat is attained.
3. A small sample of test fabric is held with tweezers and introduced into the Bunsen flame so that the products of combustion pass over the copper wire.
4. If a green colour is noted in the flame, the test material contains chlorine and is unsuitable for use with copper, silver or iron-based artefacts.

Health and safety information

The main risks associated with the chemicals and materials used in this test are listed below. Appropriate personal protective equipment should be worn to counter the risks in line with local legislation. For more information consult the suppliers' health and safety data sheets.

Nitric Acid is corrosive and may cause burns to eyes and skin.

The Iodide-iodate test – a colorimetric test for volatile acids (Zhang *et al.* 1994)

This is a test for volatile acids, normally acetic and formic, produced by display materials. A colourless test solution is suspended above the test material so that only airborne (volatile) acids are detected. The test solution contains iodide and iodate ions which react with the hydrogen ions of the volatile acid to produce elemental iodine.

$$5I^- + IO_3^- + 6H^+ \rightarrow 3H_2O + 3I_2$$

The iodine subsequently reacts with starch in the solution to produce a blue colour. The test is run at 60°C to volatilise any acids from the test material. The colour of the solution is noted after 30 minutes, if the solution remains colourless no volatile acids are present. If a blue colour is noted the test material has emitted volatile acids, and is unsuitable for use with metals such as lead.

The exact levels of organic acids that present a risk to artefacts are not known and the iodide-iodate test has been calibrated to agree with accelerated corrosion tests with lead. When testing a material for suitability for use with lead a test for formaldehyde (the purpald or chromotropic acid test, see next section) should also be carried out. The results from the iodide-iodate test are available immediately and hence it has an advantage over accelerated corrosion tests. However, the iodide-iodate test will ONLY detect volatile acids. Other species are known to cause corrosion of lead and copper and this test will not detect them. Many materials produce organic acids by degradation processes during use and it is possible that such species may not be present in a fresh sample of the material.

The iodide-iodate solution is essentially a very sensitive pH indicator and is therefore influenced by traces of acidic contamination. Over several hours the test solution will absorb enough carbon dioxide from the air to reach sufficiently acid conditions to produce a blue colour. If the same glassware is being used for the chromotropic acid test for formaldehyde, which requires a concentrated sulphuric acid test solution, thorough cleaning is required between tests.

General comments on sampling are given at the beginning of this chapter. Certain types of material will require cutting to size for the test. Although powdering a sample will present a very large surface area and may increase the rate of emission of gases, most materials, such as wood or plastics, would be present in a display case as sheets and cutting into small pieces is considered to be the most appropriate sample preparation for testing.

Test method

1. The following solutions are prepared using distilled water:
(a) potassium iodide, KI, 2%, weight to volume (w/v), shelf life six weeks in a brown glass bottle
(b) potassium iodate, KIO_3, 4% (w/v), shelf life eight weeks
(c) soluble starch, 0.1% (w/v), shelf life four weeks
2. Two drops of each of the solutions (a) (c) are placed into the reaction dish, shown in **Figure 5**.
3. 2g of the sample under test is added to the reaction flask, a 50ml Quickfit conical flask with a ground glass neck.
4. The stoppered flask is placed in an oven at 60°C.
5. The solution in the flask is examined after 30 minutes. If the solution shows any sign of blue, the sample is a source of volatile acids, and should not used with materials known to be susceptible to deterioration in the presence of such volatiles, for example lead.

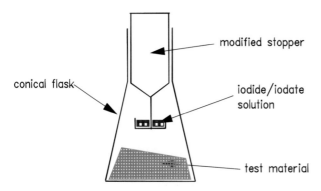

Figure 5 Diagrammatic representation of the iodide-iodate test for volatile acids

Health and safety information

The main risks associated with the chemicals and materials used in this test are listed below. Appropriate personal protective equipment should be worn to counter the risks in line with local legislation. For more information consult the suppliers' health and safety data sheets.

Potassium iodate may be harmful by ingestion; irritating to the eyes and irritating if inhaled as a dust.

Potassium iodide may be harmful by ingestion.

The Purpald® test – a colorimetric test for aldehydes
(Dickinson and Jacobsen. 1970)

This is a test for aldehydes in a material, of which formaldehyde is the most commonly encountered, and runs on a similar principle to the iodide-iodate test described in the previous section. The pale yellow test solution contains Purpald® (4-amino-3-hydrazino-5-mercapto-1,2,4-triazole) in concentrated sodium hydroxide, which reacts with aldehydes to produce a violet/blue colour. The solution is suspended above the test material so only airborne aldehydes are detected. The test is carried out at 60°C and the colour of the solution is noted after 5 minutes. If the solution remains yellow after this time the test material emits no aldehydes. If the solution has a blue colour, then aldehydes have been emitted from the material and it is unsuitable for use with lead. It is recommended that an iodide-iodate test is also run to determine the suitability of a material for use with lead. The exact level of aldehydes that present a risk has not been quantified. The chromotropic acid test (see following test) has been calibrated to agree with accelerated corrosion tests with lead and the Purpald® test has been calibrated to agree with the chromotropic acid test.

The results from the Purpald® acid test are available immediately and hence it has an advantage over accelerated corrosion tests. No species other than aldehydes are known to cause a violet colouration of the Purpald® solution, so there will be no interferences. However, the Purpald® test will ONLY detect aldehydes. Other species are known to cause corrosion of lead and copper and this test will not detect them. Many materials produce aldehydes by degradation processes during use and it is possible that such species may not be present in a fresh sample of the material. Although the Purpald® solution does not require to be heated to react; formaldehyde emission from materials can be strongly temperature dependant and it was thought prudent to control the temperature for the tests and allow sufficient time for the test material to come into thermal equilibrium in the oven. The temperature 60°C was selected as this temperature is used for several other tests.

General comments on sampling are given at the beginning of this chapter. Certain types of material will require cutting to size for the test. Although powdering a sample will present a very large surface area that may increase the rate of emission of gases, most materials, such as wood or plastics, would be present in a display case as sheets and cutting into small pieces is considered to be the most appropriate sample preparation.

Test method

1. A solution of Purpald® (7.5% w/v) is prepared in 0.1M sodium hydroxide. The solution should be stored in a tightly sealed, all glass container (plastics often emit formaldehyde), and used within 7 days.
2. Approximately 0.2ml (10 drops) from a Pasteur pipette of the Purpald® solution is placed into the reaction dish, shown in **Figure 6**.
3. 2g of the sample under test is added to the reaction flask, a 50ml Quickfit conical flask with a ground glass neck.
4. The stoppered flask is placed in an oven at 60°C.
5. The solution in the flask is examined after 5 minutes. If the solution shows any sign of blue, the sample under test is a source of aldehydes and is therefore not suitable for use with materials known to be susceptible to deterioration by aldehydes, such as lead.

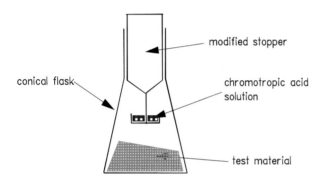

Figure 6 Diagrammatic representation of the Purpald® test for volatile aldehydes

Health and safety information

The main risks associated with the chemicals and materials used in this test are listed below. Appropriate personal protective equipment should be worn to counter the risks in line with local legislation. For more information consult the suppliers' health and safety data sheets.

Purpald ® is irritating to the eyes, skin and respiratory system.

Sodium hydroxide is corrosive and can cause burns to the eyes and skin.

The chromotropic acid test – a colorimetric test for aldehydes (Zhang *et al.* 1994)

This test is very similar to the Purpald test and also detects aldehydes. It has been superceded in the British Museum by the Purpald test which is less hazardous. The methods is as above, except the Purpald solution is replaced with chromotropic acid (4,5-dihydroxynaphthalene-2,7-disulphonic acid) in concentrated sulphuric acid. This also reacts with aldehydes to produce a violet/blue colour. The test is carried out at 60°C and the colour of the solution is noted after 30 minutes. Chromotropic acid requires heat to react with aldehydes.

Test method

1. A solution of chromotropic acid (1% w/v) is prepared in concentrated sulphuric acid (97%). The solution should be stored below 4°C, and used within 2 days.
2. Approximately 0.2ml (10 drops) from a Pasteur pipette of the chromotropic acid solution is placed into the reaction dish, shown in **Figure 6**.
3. 2g of the sample under test is added to the reaction flask, a 50ml Quickfit conical flask with a ground glass neck.
4. The stoppered flask is placed in an oven at 60°C.
5. The solution in the flask is examined after 30 minutes. If the solution shows any blue, the sample under test is a source of aldehydes and is therefore not suitable for use with materials known to be susceptible to deterioration by aldehydes, such as lead.

Health and safety information

The main risks associated with the chemicals and materials used in this test are listed below. Appropriate personal protective equipment should be worn to counter the risks in line with local legislation. For more information consult the suppliers' health and safety data sheets.

Sulphuric acid can cause severe burns to the eyes and skin.

Chromotropic acid is irritating to the eyes, skin and respiratory system. It can be absorbed through the skin. Full toxicological information for this chemical is not available.

.

Tests for materials to be used in direct contact with artefacts

Highly acidic or alkaline materials can cause deterioration when in direct contact with many kinds of artefacts particularly those made from organic materials. When a solution is acidic it contains an high concentration of hydrogen ions. If a material is alkaline it has a low concentration of hydrogen ions.

pH is defined as:

pH ' -log$_{10}$ (hydrogen ion concentration).

The pH of some solutions are shown in **Table 2**.

Table 2 Relationship between pH and hydrogen ion concentration

Hydrogen ion concentration (M)		pH	Description	Example
0.1	10^{-1}	1	very acidic	hydrochloric acid
0.001	10^{-3}	3	weakly acidic	acetic acid
0.0000001	10^{-7}	7	neutral	water
0.00000000000001	10^{-14}	14	alkaline	ammonia

The scale used in Table 2 is logarithmic so a small change in pH, say 1 pH unit, means a large change (of a factor of 10) in the hydrogen ion concentration.

Acidic or alkaline materials can cause rapid deterioration when in direct contact with organic artefacts through a number of mechanisms. Only materials with a pH close to neutral, 7.0 ± 1.5 (5.5-8.5) should be placed in direct contact with organic artefacts. pH is a relatively simple property to measure and several methods are available. It is possible to measure pH using litmus paper or universal indicator solution but these methods are not particularly accurate (± 1 pH unit) as they rely on the ability to judge colour. Electronic meters are readily and cheaply available but they require calibration before use. Two types of pH measurements are undertaken at the British Museum, aqueous extract and surface.

Aqueous extract pH (based on BS4971, 2002)

This method will measure the pH of the bulk sample. A known weight of sample is immersed in a known volume of freshly prepared water for a set period of time. The water is decanted, the pH electrode immersed in the water and the pH value read from the meter. The quality of the water used for aqueous extract is important; deionised or distilled water should be used and any carbon dioxide removed by boiling before use.

Test method

1. Distilled water is boiled for ten minutes to remove dissolved gases, covered with a watch glass and allowed to cool to room temperature. Water to 18.2MΩ quality can be used without boiling.
2. 1g of sample is weighed. If less than 1g is available, the volume of water should be scaled down accordingly.
3. The sample is cut into small pieces and soaked in 50ml of water for 1 hour.
4. The sample is removed from water. If any residual pieces/fibres are present, the solution should be filtered using a neutral filter paper such as Whatman's number 4 or syringe filter.
5. The pH meter is calibrated using suitable buffers (pH4 and pH7), according to manufacturer's instructions.

Note: Under normal experimental procedure, calibration values should lie on either side of the measured value, so if a pH reading greater than 7 is obtained the meter would normally be recalibrated using buffers of pH 7 and 10. However for this application it is only necessary to determine if the pH is greater than 8.5 and this is close enough to the pH 7 buffer value for any errors to be negligible.

6. The pH of the aqueous extract of the sample is measured using an immersion electrode.
7. If the pH is alkaline the reading may take up to 30 minutes to settle.
8. If the reading does not settle, the meter should be recalibrated using buffers, and the sample pH remeasured with ionic strength adjuster added. Some samples of materials such as plastic, contain very little water soluble ions. The measurement of pH from the such low ionic strength samples can differ from the real pH by as much as 0.5, if high ionic strength buffers were used to calibrate the meter. Unsteady readings can also be a sign of deterioration of the pH probe.
9. The pH of a material intended for direct contact with organic artefacts should lie in the range 5.5 to 8.5.
10. The colour of the aqueous extract should be noted. If the sample contains any water fugitive colours they will be transferred to the aqueous extract and the material should not be used in direct contact with artefacts susceptible to staining.

Surface pH (based on BS2924 1983)

A pH measurement of the surface may be more appropriate for materials with surface finishes or coatings as it is only the surface of the material which will be in contact with the artefacts. A special flat electrode is used for this purpose. A drop of water is placed on the surface of the sample and the electrode placed in contact with the wetted surface after a set time period. The pH value is read from the meter. This method requires at least five readings, which should be within 0.2 pH units of each other. The average of these five readings is used.

Test method

1. Distilled water is boiled for at least ten minutes to remove dissolved gases, covered and allowed to cool to room temperature. Water to $18.2M\Omega$ quality can be used without boiling.
2. A glass plate is cleaned with distilled water and dried.
3. The pH meter is calibrated using drops of buffers (pH7 and pH4) on a glass plate, according to manufacturer's instructions.
4. The sample is placed on a glass plate. A drop of boiled out distilled water is placed on the sample surface and left to stand for 1 minute. The surface electrode is placed onto the wetted surface, and the reading is allowed to settle. This step should be repeated at least 5 times on different areas of the sample, and the average pH calculated. All readings used to calculate the average should be within 0.2 pH units of each other. If the pH is alkaline the reading may take up to 30 minutes to settle.
5. The pH of a material intended for direct contact with organic artefacts should lie in the range 5.5 to 8.5.

The phloroglucinol test – a test for the presence of lignin (Barrow 1969, 12)

Papers and paper based boards are often used in the storage of artefacts. Papers produced from wood pulp can contain lignin. The presence of lignin in paper has often been associated with degradation, producing acidic species which may subsequently damage organic artefacts in contact with the paper. However, more recent evidence has shown that the acidity in such papers may be due to associated alum/rosin size (Priest and Stanley 1994). It is recommended that a test for alum is carried out in conjunction with the test for lignin (see next section). Although the mechanical properties of lignin-containing papers may be acceptable, the effects of atmospheric pollutants on the ageing properties of such papers have yet to be elucidated and therefore, it may be prudent to avoid lignin papers until further evidence is available.

The phloroglucinol test is a colorimetric spot test where a drop of the phloroglucinol solution is placed on the paper producing a purple colour in the presence of lignin. There has been debate in the literature as to the exact chemical reaction which occurs, and it has been suggested that, after certain chemical processes, a paper containing lignin may no longer react with the phloroglucinol (Doree 1947, Brauns 1952). A false positive test may occur if certain dyes are present in the paper, as these may become red in acidic conditions (Grant 1961). A colour change can be difficult to observe on darkly coloured papers. Where papers have been treated with a surface finish, the test solution cannot always penetrate into the paper and hence the test will not work. If the solution does not wet the paper then a negative test should be treated with some caution. If required further tests can be undertaken (Grant 1961)

Test method

1. 1g of phloroglucinol is dissolved in 50ml of 1M hydrochloric acid.
2. A drop of the reagent solution is placed on the paper being tested, which rests on a clean glass plate. If lignin is present, the solution spot will turn a deep purplish red, otherwise the solution will remain colourless, as shown in **Plate 6**.
3. The solution degrades with time and should be replaced when it becomes yellow.

NB: this test requires a discriminating eye and it is recommended that controls are run using papers known to contain lignin, eg newsprint, and conversely with papers known to be free of lignin.

Health and safety information

The main risks associated with the chemicals and materials used in this test are listed below. Appropriate personal protective equipment should be worn to counter the risks in line with local legislation. For more information consult the suppliers' health and safety data sheets.

Phloroglucinol is harmful if ingested in large quantities and irritating to the eyes.

Hydrochloric acid is irritating to the eyes and skin and may cause burns on prolonged contact.

The aluminon test – a test for the presence of alum
(Barrow 1969, 10-11)

Papers and paper based boards are often used in the storage of artefacts. Papermakers' alum, aluminium sulphate, is added to many papers. Alum decomposes and causes the paper to become acidic. The aluminon test is a method of detecting alum in paper. It is a colorimetric spot test where a drop of aluminon solution is placed on the paper and the development of an intense pink colour indicates the presence of aluminium, normally present as alum. The colour change can be very difficult to notice on darkly coloured papers. Where papers have been treated with a surface finish, the test solution cannot always penetrate into the paper and hence the test will not work. If the solution does not wet the paper then a negative test should be treated with some caution.

Test method
1. 1g of aluminon is dissolved in 1 litre of distilled water. This produces a pale pink solution.
2. A drop of the reagent solution is placed on the paper to be tested, while it is resting on a clean glass plate. It is allowed to dry.
3. If no aluminium (alum) is present then the reagent will remain pale pink in colour. If aluminium is present the reagent will turn a bright to deep pink colour, as shown in **Plate 6**.

NB: this test requires a discriminating eye and it is recommended that controls are run using papers known to contain alum, and papers known to be free of alum.

Health and safety Information
The main risks associated with the chemicals and materials used in this test are listed below. Appropriate personal protective equipment should be worn to counter the risks in line with local legislation. For more information consult the suppliers' health and safety data sheets.

Aluminon may be irritating to the eyes and skin. It is harmful by ingestion.

Plate 6 Reference photograph for the aluminon (alum) and phloroglucinol (lignin) tests

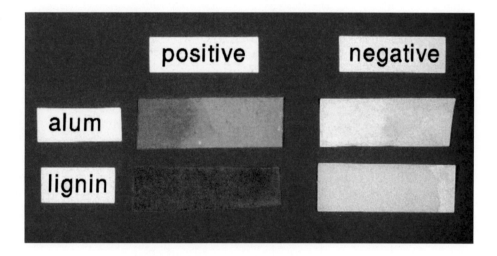

Suppliers of chemicals and apparatus

Accelerated corrosion tests

Quickfit glass tubes (50ml, size 24/29 joint); AnalaR lead foil; dissecting tweezers; small test tubes (Durham tube 0.5ml) for water; glass bristle brushes; Aluminium trays incubator, 50 universal bottles, cat. No 402/0683/00; Silicone rubber stopper No 21 (5), 21 mm x 24.5 mm i x 28 mm ref : 226/0100/21; Acetone (spectrosol)
VWR International Ltd
Hunter boulevard
Magna Park, Lutterworth
Leics LE17 4XN   Tel: 0800 223344

Copper and silver foil
Fisher Scientific Equipment
Bishop Meadow Road
Loughborough
Leicestershire
LE11 5RG   Tel: 01509 231166

Nylon monofilament (diameter 0.053mm)
Hook length (breaking strain 0.72lb)
made in Japan by: Toray Industries
distributed in the UK by Normark   Tel: 01626 832889
Available from angling suppliers.

Heat shrink tubing, NMW 360
Ness Heatshrink
Coal Products Ltd
Plas Ness
Harold Wilson Industrial Estate
Van Road
Caerphilly
Mid Glamorgan
CF8 3ED   Tel: 01222 851155

Centiclean Super Detergent
Century oils Ltd
P.O Box 2
New Century Street
Hanley
Stoke-on-Trent

Decon Acid rinse 5 l, ref : B 29021
Philip Harris
Novara HS
Excelsior rd
Ashby Park
Ashby de la Zouch
Leicestershire
LE65 ING

Silicone stopper (100), 21 mm x 27 mm i x 30 mm ref :
V263027 (alternative to VWR stopper)
Radleys
Shirehill
Saffron Walden
CB11 3AZ   Tel: 01799 513320

Azide test

Sodium azide, iodine solution (Convol), IMS, microscope slides and cover-slips
VWR (as above)

Beilstein test

Nitric acid
VWR (as above)

Iodide-iodate test

Potassium iodide, potassium iodate, soluble starch, Quickfit conical flasks (50ml, size 24/29 joint)
VWR (as above)

Modified stoppers (made to order)
Radleys
Laboratory Equipment and Scientific Glassblowing
Shire Hill
Saffron Walden
Essex
CB11 3AZ   Tel: 01799 513320

Purpald® test

Purpald®
Aldrich Chemical Company Ltd
The Old Brickyard
New Road
Gillingham
Dorset
SP8 4JL   Tel: 0800 717117

Sodium Hydroxide
VWR (as above)

Chromotropic acid test

Concentrated sulphuric acid, Quickfit conical flasks (50ml, size 24/29 joint), Pasteur pipette
VWR (as above)

Chromotropic acid
Aldrich (as above)

Modified stoppers (made to order)
Radleys (as above)

pH measurement

pH meters and buffers
VWR (as above)

Lignin and aluminon tests

Phloroglucinol
Aldrich (as above)

Hydrochloric acid and aluminon
VWR (as above)

3.
Practical Methods for Display and Storage

The purpose of this final chapter is to provide a practical approach to selection of materials for use in the storage or display of museum artefacts. Every material which is proposed for use with an object should first be tested to ensure that it is not a source of harmful gases.

Often, objects have been stored in what may be considered non-ideal areas for many years without any visible change. Conversely more sensitive objects may deteriorate within a few weeks in the wrong environment. Some of the initial research into effects of outgassing was undertaken due to deterioration of metal components in packing cases which occurred after transit to the tropics (Rance and Cole 1958). Although the components had been in the packing cases for a limited time only, the emissions from wood combined with exposure to high relative humidity and temperature resulted in corrosion. It is therefore essential to undertake a risk assessment process in order to identify the needs of different groups of artefacts and to prioritise necessary action regarding their environment, having consideration for the period of display or storage. A permanent display requires a more rigorous approach than, say, a three month temporary exhibition, but all materials should be tested. The temporary category was introduced into the results for those tests that produced a very slight effect. It is thought unlikely that such an effect would be very damaging over a few months at ambient conditions, when it was produced by 4 weeks at 100% RH and 60°C. However, it may be the precursor of more serious corrosion and the material should be excluded from long term use. The potential of a material to outgas within the airspace of a showcase is dependent on its surface area; for example a fabric used to line the baseboard of the case has a larger surface area exposed within the showcase and therefore the capacity to outgas more than an adhesive used to adhere labels where little, if any, surface area of the adhesive is exposed. An important exception to this, are the seals used for the doors and joints of showcases. Since most air ingress will pass over these seals any outgassing will be carried into the case and even the very small areas exposed can have catastrophic effects if unsuitable materials are used.

In most situations an open gallery will have sufficient natural ventilation to avoid the build up of any gases emitted from materials such as wall paints or carpets, and in such circumstances a more liberal approach may be taken when choosing materials used to furnish and decorate the gallery. However it is advisable to avoid a pure wool carpet, not only because it will emit sulphide gases but also for factors including durability and pest control. In a more enclosed situation, such as a store room or display case, choice of materials requires more rigorous selection. Floor coverings

in storage areas should be inert and easy to clean; suitable materials are quarry tiles or concrete sealed with a tested and approved epoxy coating.

It may be suggested that the ideal museum store or display case is made out of totally inert materials, ie glass and metal. However, metals for panels or cupboards are often coated, and care should be taken as some coatings may themselves emit gases. Stove-enamelled polyester or epoxy based coatings are generally considered to be inert, although, on occasions, problems have occurred due to insufficient curing of the coating during manufacture (Grzywacs and Tennent 1994). Oil based coatings have been shown to emit higher levels of acids after oven baking (Padfield 1982). It is also worth noting that many of the materials now described as stoved have not been heated to very high temperatures, and the term no longer necessarily implies the degree of inertness, that it once did. Another disadvantage of metal storage systems is that they may corrode if used in areas with elevated humidity.

Complete refurbishment of a gallery or store is not always an option but there are ways of avoiding some of the potential problems. If timber products have to be used for storage or display, or existing wooden fixtures are being reused, it is advisable to try and reduce concentrations of pollutant gases within the area holding the object. One method is to produce a positive pressure inside the case using a small pump, to ensure any pollutants inside the case were constantly being driven out. However, it may be easier to include ventilation holes to allow free movement of air and hence reduce the opportunity for build up of harmful gases. Ingress of particulates, which themselves can promote degradation, can be minimised by use of a suitable paper or fabric filter over the ventilation holes. If humidity control is required, ventilation in this manner will not be suitable.

Another option to reduce emissions is to seal the wood. However, it should be borne in mind that a coating does not eliminate volatiles but simply delays their egress from a source (Hatchfield and Carpenter 1987, Thickett 1998). The most efficient way to stop offgassing from wood product boards is wrap them in an inert and impermeable polymer film, such as Moistop or Marvelseal (aluminium/polythene laminates). The edges of the film need sealing and this is most effective when they are heat-sealed to form a bag around the board which can subsequently be covered with a suitable display fabric. A very fast way of achieving a reasonable edge seal is to place a sheet of Moistop or Marvelseal over each face of the board and use self adhesive aluminium tape such as 3M 425 on the edges. Such approachs work well for flat boards but are extremely difficult to apply to complex shapes. Both Marvelseal and Moistop also have the dissadvantage that many paints will not adhere to their surfaces. Liquid coatings are easier to apply to complex shapes and many will take paint finishes, however, those tested to date are not as efficient at reducing emmisions or the potential for corrosion from wood products (Thickett 1998). Trimite Selabond RJ119 is the best performing of the liquid coatings tested to date. Many coating products are sold for use as wood 'sealants', but this terminology often refers to preparation of a surface to receive further coatings, and is not particularly related to the ability of the 'sealant' to reduce emissions from the wood. Additionally, several types of paint and varnish will outgas, and could compound the problem (Sparkes 1989). For example, many polyurethane varnishes and oil based paints will emit organic acids. Consideration should be given to the properties of a coating which may change as it ages and through wear and tear during use. Therefore, it may become less effective with time. Manufacturers often quote lifetimes of a few years only for coatings and recommend regular reapplication.

Also, wood is an efficient material for buffering changes in relative humidity. A showcase containing wooden components can help stabilise the environment against changes in ambient RH which is important for artefacts that are susceptible to damage by fluctuating RH. Since the application of a coating is intended to reduce gaseous emissions from the wood by providing an impermeable barrier then it is probable that it will also provide a barrier to moisture movement into and out of the wood and hence reduce the buffering abilities of the wood (Miles 1986).

To facilitate display, objects may be pinned onto a board. At the British Museum, Sundeala K quality fibreboard is used for this purpose due to its physical properties; it accepts pins readily and holds them firmly in position. However, as Sundeala is a timber-based product it can cause corrosion of lead and it is therefore enclosed in a barrier film, to avoid harmful emissions into the showcase. The barrier film will be pierced if mounting pins are used, and the resulting holes have been found to reduce the effectiveness of the film. If used to enclose pinning boards, both Moistop and Marvelseal should be ironed onto the board at least in the area to be pinned as this will reduce this effect. Care should be taken to minimise perforations, caused by repositioning the pins. Inert foams have been considered as an alternative to Sundeala as a case insert, but trials with these have shown that minor adjustment of the position of pins cannot be undertaken, as a hole is eventually produced in the foam. In order to avoid scratching of the pinned artefact or galvanic corrosion occurring between a metal pin and metal objects, all pins should be covered with plastic tubing; polythene catheter tubing has been found suitable for this purpose.

Where the pH of a display or storage material falls outside the accepted range of 5.5-8.5, or it is shown to have the potential to transfer colour to an artefact, then a physical barrier may be used locally to isolate the artefact from the material. This can be effected by using Melinex or Perspex (polymethylmethacrylate) sheet cut to the profile of the base of the artefact, and placed between the artefact and the material of concern. Of course, such a barrier is completely ineffective if the display or storage material is a source of air borne species, as these can affect all objects within the same air space, not only those in direct contact.

In order to mitigate the effects of low levels of background pollution such as sulphur compounds, or when old cases containing unsuitable materials must be used, then an absorbent material can be included in the case. However, the use of sorbents should be additional to the correct choice of materials where possible, and not used as an alternative. The efficiency of a range of such materials, including molecular sieves and activated carbon, for removal of air pollution from showcases has been investigated (Grosjean and Parmar 1991).

Activated carbon is a broad range sorbent available as a powder or, more conveniently, as a fabric made of woven activated carbon fibres (for example 'Charcoal Cloth' and 'Kynol Activated Carbon Cloth'). The former has been used with some success to protect lead coins and medals which, although housed in an inert metal cabinet, were stored in a room containing a large amount of wooden furniture. Charcoal Cloth has also been used as a temporary measure beneath the display fabric in a showcase made from poor quality materials. Recently at the British Museum, it has been shown that Charcoal Cloth contains chlorides, and therefore direct contact with silver or copper based artefacts should be avoided. The white fabric coating available on some carbon cloths does not stop migration of the chloride and will not protect a susceptible object from direct contact with the cloth. Zinc oxide pellets (Puraspec 2040 and 5040 made by ICI Katalco) are made specifically for removal of hydrogen sulphide from natural gas. Preliminary trials with silver objects in showcases in the British Museum have shown a marked reduction in tarnishing when a tray of Puraspec pellets was placed adjacent to each object (Bradley 1989). A range of products which are designed to remove the pollutant gases from the environment have been evaluated to assess their effectiveness at preventing the tarnishing of silver. Apparatus has been specifically designed to provide background levels of gases naturally present in the ambient atmosphere, to measure the rate of tarnishing of silver coupons, each enclosed with one of the products being evaluated. In addition to the Charcoal Cloth and Puraspec materials, the products under examination include vapour phase inhibitors, impregnated cloths and papers. Results showed that Charcoal Cloth and zinc oxide pellets are the most effective materials, of those tested, in reducing the rate of tarnishing (Lee 1996). However, when placed in showcases the absorbents performed poorly. This has been ascribed to the difficulty of placing the absorbent between the silver and the incoming air (which will contain tarnishing gases even if the showcase materials are totally inert). The silver surface is extremely reactive and if the tarnishing gases pass over it, they will be absorbed and never reach the absorbent. This is a particular difficulty when using tall showcases, when gas ingress is often from the top and the most convenient place for the absorbents is the baseboard. Much better results were achieved by placing a bed of sorbent in a low pressure pump and introducing cleaned air into the showcases.

All exposed sorbent materials will eventually become exhausted and need to be renewed. The time for this to occur is difficult to project as it depends on variables such as rate of air change, pollutant concentration, relative humidity and temperature. Although the air can be sampled and analysed to assess the levels of specific pollutant gases, and thus assess the effectiveness of an enclosed sorbent material, this can be extremely costly. An alternative method of evaluating the environment is to monitor the corrosion of exposed metal coupons in a showcase or store, for example silver could be used to monitor sulphide gases and lead to monitor organic acids or formaldehyde. If the metal coupon has a freshly cleaned surface it will be more reactive than the artefacts and will show corrosion at an earlier stage. Trials in wooden storage drawers at the British Museum have shown that charcoal cloth was still reducing the acetic acid concentration to approximately half after five years of

exposure. Drawers with no cloth had acetic acid concentrations in the region of $3000\mu g/m3$ and measurements on the cloth showed it still had over 80% of its absorption capacity left. However, despite these reassuring figures lead was still found to corrode inside the drawers.

To conclude, materials which are intended for use in the storage or display of museum objects must be carefully chosen, to avoid any increased risk of damage to the objects. However, there is room for flexibility of approach in some circumstances, determined by the vulnerability of the particular object(s), site of intended use and period of exposure.

4
References

Arni, P.C., Cochrane, G.C. and Gray, J.D., 1965, The emission of corrosive vapours by wood II. The analysis of the vapours emitted by certain freshly felled hardwoods and softwoods by gas chromatography and spectrometry, *Journal of Applied Chemistry*, 15, 463-8

Barrow, W.J., 1969, *Permanence/Durability of the Book VI. Spot Testing for Unstable Book and Record Papers*, The Dietz Press Inc, Richmond, 9-18

Blackshaw, S.M., 1982, The testing of display materials, *Occasional Paper No. 1, The Care of Ethnographic Materials*, ed: D.L. Jones, The Area Museums Service for South Eastern England, 40-5

Blackshaw, S.M. and Daniels V.D., 1978, Selecting safe materials in the display and storage of antiquities, *ICOM Committee for Conservation, 5th Triennial Meeting*, Zagreb, 78/23/2-9

Blackshaw, S.M. and Daniels, V.D., 1979, The testing of materials for use in the storage and display in museums, *The Conservator*, 3, 16-19

Blackshaw, S.M., King, J. and Hughes, M., 1974, The testing and identification of new materials for conservation and display, British Museum Research Laboratory Report 1974/Con 2, unpublished

Bogarty, H., Campbell, K.S., and Appel, W.C., 1952, The oxidation of cellulose by ozone in small concentrations, *Textile Research Journal*, 22, 81

Bradley, S.M., 1989, Hydrogen sulphide scavengers for the prevention of silver tarnishing, in *Environmental Monitoring and Control*, SSCR, Dundee, 65-7

Brauns, F.E., 1952, *The Chemistry of Lignin*, Academic Press, New York, 24-38

Brimblecombe, P., 1990, The composition of museum atmospheres, *Atmospheric Environment*, 24B, (1), 1-8

Brimblecombe, P., Shooter, D. and Kaur, A., 1992, Wool and reduced sulphur gases in museum air, *Studies in Conservation*, 37, 53-60

Brysson, R.J., Trask, B.J., Upham, J.B. and Booras, S.G., 1967, The effects of air pollution on exposed cotton fabrics, *Journal of Air Pollution Control Association*, 17, 294 8

BS4971, 2002, *Repair and allied processes for the conservation of documents*, British Standards Institution, London

Byne, L., 1899, The corrosion of shells in cabinets, *Journal of Conchology*, 9, 172-178, 253-4

Daniels, V.D. and Meeks, N., 1992, An investigation into foxing phenomena with particular attention to the inorganic components, *Biodeterioration of Cultural Property 2*, 2nd International Conference, Yokohama, Japan, 292-305

Daniels, V.D. and Meeks, N., 1995, Foxing caused by copper alloy inclusions in paper, Symposium 88- *Conservation of Historic and Artistic Works on Paper*, Ottawa, eds: H.D. Burgess J. Krill, CCI, Canada, 229-33

Daniels, V.D. and Thickett, D., 1992, The reversion of blackened lead white on paper, *The Institute of Paper Conservation*, Manchester 1992, ed: S. Fairbrass, 109-15

Daniels, V.D. and Ward, S., 1982, A rapid test for the detection of substances which will tarnish silver, *Studies in Conservation*, 27, 58-60

Doree, C., 1947, *The Methods of Cellulose Chemistry*, Chapman and Hall, London, 339

Dupoint, A.L. and Tetrault, J., 2000, Cellulose degradation in an acetic acid environment, *Studies in Conservation*, 45, 201-210

Fenn, J., 1995, Secret sabotage: reassessing museum plastics in display and storage, preprints *Resins Ancient and Modern*, eds: M. Wright and J. Townsend, SSCR, Aberdeen, 38-41

Gibson, L.T., Cooksey, B.G., Littlejohn, D. and Tennent, N.H., 1997, Characterisation of an unusual crystalline efflorescence on an Egyptian limestone relief, *Analytica Chimica Acta*, 337, 151-164

Gilroy, D. and Mayne, J.E.O., 1965, The inhibition of the corrosion of iron in the pH range 6-9, *British Corrosion Journal*, 1, 107-9

Graedel, T.E. and McGill, R., 1986, Degradation of materials in the atmosphere, *Environmental Science Technology*, 20, (11), 1093-100

Grant, J., 1961, *Laboratory handbook of pulp and paper manufacture*, 2nd edition, Edward Arnold, London, 377

Green, L.R., 1992a, Investigation of black corrosion on bronze, British Museum Conservation Research Section Report 1992/8.

Green, L.R., 1992b, Low fired ceramics and H2S, *Museums Journal*, Nov, 36

Green, L.R. and Bradley, S.M., 1988, An investigation into the deterioration and stabilisation of cellulose nitrate in museum collections, *Modern Organic Materials*, eds: L. Eaton and C. Meredith, SSCR, Edinburgh, 81-96

Green, L.R., and Bradley, S.M., 1997, An Investigation of Strategies for the Long-Term Storage of Archaeological Iron, in *Metals 95*, eds: MacLeod, I.D., *et al.*, Proceedings of the International Conference on Metals Conservation, Semur en Auxois, September 1995, James and James, London.

Green, L.R. and Thickett, D., 1991, Modern metals in museum collections, *Saving the Twentieth Century- The Conservation of Modern Materials*, ed: D. Grattan, CCI, Ottawa, 261-9

Green, L.R. and Thickett, D., 1993, Interlaboratory comparison of the Oddy test, *Conservation Science in the UK*, ed: N. Tennent, James & James Science Publishers Ltd, 111-16

Green, L.R. and Thickett, D., 1995, Testing materials for the storage and display of artefacts- a revised methodology, *Studies in Conservation*, 40, (3), 145-52

Grosjean, D. and Parmar, S.S., 1991, Removal of air pollutant mixtures from museum display cases, *Studies in Conservation*, 36, 129-41

Grzywacs, C.M. and Tennent, N.H., 1994, Pollution monitoring in storage and display cabinets: carbonyl pollutant levels in relation to artefact deterioration, *Preventive Conservation: Practice, Theory and Research*, preprints Ottawa Congress, eds: A. Roy and P. Smith, IIC, London 164-70

Harley, J.D., 1982, *Artists pigments c.1600-1835*, 2nd edition, Butterworths Scientific, London, 171

Hatchfield, P. and Carpenter, J., 1987, *Formaldehyde: How great is the danger?*, Harvard University Art Museum, Cambridge, MA

ISO 10214, 1990, *Processed photographic materials-filing enclosures for storage*, International Organization for Standardization, Geneva.

Langwell, W.H.,1976, Measurement of the effects of air pollution on paper documents, *Journal of the Society of Archivists*, 5, 372 3

Lee, L.R., in press, Investigation of materials to prevent the tarnishing of silver, British Museum Conservation Research Group Report 1996/1

Lyth Hudson F. and Milner, W.D., 1961, Atmospheric sulphur and the durability of paper, *Journal of the Society of Archivists*, 2, 166 7

Madsen, H.B. and Hjelm-Hansen, N., 1979, Black spots on bronzes- a microbiological or chemical attack?, *The Conservation and Restoration of Metals*, SSCR, Edinburgh, 33-9

Miles, C.E., 1986, Wood coatings for display and storage cases, *Studies in Conservation*, 31, 114-24

Morris, M.A., Young, M.A. and Tove, A.M., 1964, The effects of air pollution on cotton, *Textile Research Journal*, 34, 563-4

Nicholls, J.R., 1934, Deterioration of shells when stored in oak cabinets, *Journal of the Society of Chemical Industry*, 1077-8

Nishimura, D.W., 1990, Improvements to the photographic activity test in ANSI IT9.2, *ICOM Committee for Conservation, Dresden*, ed: K. Grimstad, 1, 268-73

Oddy, W.A., 1973, An unsuspected danger in display, *Museums Journal*, 73, 27-8

Oddy, W.A., 1975, The corrosion of metals on display, *Conservation in*

Archaeology and the Applied Arts, IIC, London, 235-7.

Oddy, W.A., 1993, The conservation of coins- is it art, craft or science?, *Images for Posterity. The Conservation of Coins and Medals*, National Museums of Coins and Medals, Leiden, 29-45

Oddy, W.A. and Bradley, S.M., 1989, The corrosion of metal objects in storage and on display, *Current Problems in the Conservation of Metal Artefacts*, Thirteenth International Symposium on the Conservation and Restoration of Cultural Property, Tokyo, 225-44

Oddy, W.A. and Meeks, N., 1982, Unusual phenomena in the corrosion of ancient bronze, *Science and Technology in the Service of Conservation*, eds: N.S. Brommelle and G. Thomson, IIC, London, 119-24

Padfield, T., Erhardt, D. and Hopwood, W., 1982, Trouble in Store, *Science and Technology in the Service of Conservation*, eds: N.S. Brommelle and G. Thomson, IIC, London, 24-7

Pickrell, J.A., Mokler, B.V., Griffis, L.C. and Hobbs, C.H., 1983, Formaldehyde release rate from selected consumer products, *Environmental Science Technology*, 17, 753-7

Plenderleith, A.J., 1934, *The Preservation of Antiquities,* The Museums Association, London, 60

Priest, D.J. and Stanley, J., 1994, The ageing of paper containing chemithermomechanical pulp, *Environment et Conservation de l'écrit, de l'image et du son,* Association pour la Recherche Scientifique sur les Arts Graphiques, 154-6

Rackham, H., (translator), 1968, Pliny's *Natural History*, W. Heinemann, London, XXXIV, LV, 253

Rance, V.E. and Cole, H.G., 1958, *Corrosion of metals by vapours from organic materials. A survey,* HMSO, London

Rathgen, F., 1905, *The Preservation of Antiquities,* Cambridge University Press, London, 50-3

Rice, D.W., Cappell, R.J., Kinsolving, W. and Lawskowski, J.J., 1980, Indoor corrosion of metals, *Journal of the Electrochemical Society*, 27, (4), 891-901

Robinet L. and Thickett D., 2003, A new methodology for accelerated corrosion testing, *Studies in Conservation*, 48 no. 4

Schmidt, S. , 1992, The formation of sodium formate on glass surfaces: examination of historical objects, *Berliner Beiträge zur Archäometrie,* 11, 137-183

Scott, A., 1921, The cleaning and restoration of museum exhibits.

Report upon the investigations conducted at the British Museum, *Department of Scientific and Industrial Research, Bulletin 5*, HMSO, London

Scott, A., 1922, The restoration and preservation of objects at the British Museum, *Journal of the Royal Society of Arts*, LXX, (3), 327-38

Shashoua, Y. and Green, L., 1990, Analysis of corrosion on a silver bead, British Museum Conservation Research Section Report 1990/32

Shashoua, Y. and Thomsen, S., 1993, A field trial for the use of Ageless in the preservation of rubber in museum collections, Saving the twentieth Century- *The Conservation of Modern Materials*, ed: D. Grattan, CCI, Ottawa, 363-71.

Shaver, C.L. and Cass, G.R., 1983, Ozone and deterioration of works of art, *Environmental Science Technology*, 17, 748-52

Sparkes, T., 1989, The effect of surface coatings on formaldehyde emission, *Environmental monitoring and control*, SSCR, Dundee, 78-87

Thickett, D., 1998, Sealing MDF to Prevent Corrosive Emissions, *The Conservator*, 22, 49-56

Vogel, A.I., 1966, *Elementary Practical Organic Chemistry*, 2nd edition, Longmans, 96

Wayne, R.P., 1985, *Chemistry of Atmospheres*, Oxford Science Publications, Clarendon Press, Oxford, 195

Werner, A.E.A., 1972, Conservation and display: environmental control, *Museums Journal*, 72, (2), 58-60

Werner, G., 1986, Corrosion of metals caused by wood in closed spaces, *Recent Advances in the Conservation and Analysis of Artefacts*, ed: J. Black, Summer Schools Press, London, 185-7

West FitzHugh E. and Gettens, R.J., 1971, Calclacite and other efflorescent salts on objects stored in wooden museum cases, Science and Archaeology, R.H. Brill, MIT Press, 91-102

Weyde, E., 1972, A simple test to identify gases which destroy silver images, *Photographic Science and Engineering*, 16, (4), 283-6

Zeronian, S.H., Alger, K.W. and Omaye, S.T., 1973, Effects of sulphur dioxide on the chemical and physical properties of nylon 66, *Textile Research Journal,* 43, 222 37

Zhang, J., Thickett, D. and Green, L.R., 1994, Two tests for the detection of volatile organic acids and formaldehyde, *Journal of the American Institute of Conservation,* 33, 47-53